Sociology Basics

Sociology
Basics

Volume 2

Modernization and World-System
Theories—
Workplace Socialization

Consulting Editor
CARL L. BANKSTON III

SALEM PRESS, INC.
Pasadena, California
Hackensack, New Jersey

Essays originally appeared in *Survey of Social Science: Sociology*, 1994; new material has been added.

∞ The paper used in these volumes conforms to the American National Standard for Permanence of Paper for Printed Library Materials, Z39.48-1992 (R1997).

Library of Congress Cataloging-in-Publication Data

Sociology basics / consulting editor, Carl L. Bankston, III.

    p.   cm. — (Magill's choice)

Includes bibliographical references and index.

Selected articles previously published in: Survey of social science. Sociology series, 1994, in 5 vols.

Contents: v. 1. Anomie and deviance—microsociology—v.2. Modernization and world-system theories—workplace socialization.

ISBN 0-89356-205-X (set : alk. paper). — ISBN 0-89356-206-8 (v. 1 : alk. paper). — ISBN 0-89356-207-6 (v. 2 : alk. paper)

1. Sociology—Encyclopedias. I. Bankston, Carl L. II. Survey of social science. Sociology series. III. Series

HM425.S63   2000

301'.03—dc21   00-036775
                                                                                    CIP

First Printing

TABLE OF CONTENTS
Volume 2

Sociology
Basics

MODERNIZATION AND WORLD-SYSTEM THEORIES

Type of sociology: Social change
Field of study: Theories of social change

Modernization theory postulates that the United States and Western Europe are on the highest level of development and should be emulated by other societies, especially developing and Third World societies. World-system theory, however, argues that European capitalism expanded beyond its borders to establish an international division of labor within a world-economy. This world-economy inhibits developing countries from modernizing.

Principal terms

CORE: in world-system theory, Western European countries, the United States, and Japan, which have specialized in banking, finance, and highly skilled industrial production

DEPENDENCY THEORY: theory in which underdeveloped regions are considered "internal colonies" that are dependent on, or controlled by, modern industrial states

MODERN SOCIETY: society that emphasizes professionalism, rationality, planning, and progress; the meaning of this concept varies, but it generally connotes emulating Western European countries or the United States

MODERNIZATION THEORY: theory according to which the changes that occurred in non-Western societies under colonial rule were necessary to break down indigenous traditions so that higher levels of social development, or "modernity," could be achieved; to become "modern," new nations must emulate the patterns taken by the United States and Western Europe

PERIPHERY: in world-system theory, the exploited former colonies of the core, which supply the core with cheap food and raw materials

POLITICAL ECONOMY: framework linking material interests (economy) with the use of power (politics) to protect and enhance interests

SEMIPERIPHERY: in world-system theory, the intermediate societies between the core and the periphery

WORLD-SYSTEM THEORY: theory that European capitalism expanded beyond its borders, beginning in the late fifteenth and early sixteenth centuries, to establish an international division of labor within the framework of a world-economy

Overview

Modernization theory and world-system theory are frameworks within the field of political economy that deal with issues of development and underdevelopment in the Third World. Modernization theory, which prevailed in the 1950's and 1960's, explained the poverty of underdeveloped countries on the basis of either structural or psychological frameworks.

World-system theory became popular as an attack on modernization theory that used a global framework to explain the rise of the West and to analyze the problems of development and underdevelopment within the context of a global economy.

Modernization theory varies in meaning according to who is doing the planning. In general, it means becoming like the United States or a Western European country. The concept generally emphasizes professionalization, rationality, planning, and progress (as defined in the West).

Modernization theory has two frameworks: structural and psychological. Structurally, modernization theorists built on Talcott Parsons's *The Social System* (1951), which held that progressive differentiation was the key to modernizing. It was, however, economist W. W. Rostow, in *The Stages of Economic Growth: A Non-Communist Manifesto* (1960), who argued from an evolutionary position stating that all societies must pass through five fixed stages. All societies, according to Rostow, start as traditional societies in which methods of production are limited, the worldview is "pre-Newtonian," productive resources are largely devoted to agriculture, vertical social mobility is limited, and the value system is fatalistic. During the "period of preconditions," the idea of economic progress is perceived as possible and good, education broadens, enterprising individuals appear, and a suitable infrastructure, especially in the government, develops. In "take-off," the third stage, growth becomes a normal condition. Investment rate increases, one or more manufacturing sectors increase substantially, and a favorable political climate emerges. Finally, technological maturity follows, in which the society has the versatility to produce anything it chooses. Later, social scientists added a sixth stage, Daniel Bell's "post-industrial society" (1973), in which the society shifts from production to service and information processing. Rostow argued that underdeveloped societies have to follow the same process that developed nations have experienced. The problem with his approach was that not all societies pass through the same sequence in the same way.

The foundation of the psychological approach was laid by David McClelland, in *The Achieving Society* (1967), and by Everett Hagen, in *On the Theory of Social Change* (1962). Both argued, in different ways, that a society's development depended on the psychological makeup of its members. They completely neglected the function of social institutions. Alex Inkeles and David H. Smith, in *Becoming Modern: Individual Change in Six Developing Countries* (1974), argued that "modern" people were those who had contact with modern institutions. They did explain, however, why some countries had more modern institutions than others did.

World-system theory attacked modernization theory for its neglect of institutions, the ethnocentric concept that "modern" means being Western, and its erroneous stages of development and psychological postulates. World-system theorists argued that the power of strong manufacturing societies, such as England, resulted from their ability to redirect resources from weaker societies to serve their own ends.

A. G. Frank, in *Latin America: Under-development or Revolution* (1969), was influential in showing how resources were expropriated by the rich. It was Immanuel Wallerstein, however, who made the view prominent. Wallerstein argued that there were historical but not uniform stages of development. He showed that initially every society was a "minisystem"—a community that contained within itself a complete division of labor and cultural framework. Now, however, minisystems no longer exist or are extremely rare. Thus, anthropologists studying "traditional" society miss a major aspect—the community is not isolated.

Historically, what followed, according to Wallerstein, was a world-system in which a single division of labor system developed, cutting across multiple cultural systems. With the advent of capitalism in the 1500's, the state became less central. The state played a minor role in economic transactions, which resulted in the market's creation of incentives to increase productivity. Capitalism succeeded, according to Wallerstein, primarily because of two factors: transportation technology, which enabled long-distance markets to be maintained; and military power, which enabled terms to be enforced.

A world-economy developed that had a core, a semiperiphery, and a periphery. The "core" was made up of societies that developed in manufacturing and specialization but needed a surplus to expand. This they obtained from the "periphery," where resources and labor costs were kept low. The structure developed on both a national and an international level. A core, semiperiphery, and periphery can develop in a country and region as well as internationally.

Applications

World-system theory is important because it explains why some countries are underdeveloped and others are not. If world-system theory is correct in stating that the peripheries are poor and underdeveloped because resources are being siphoned off by the core, there are tremendous ramifications for aid and economic development policies. Unless the cause of the problem is addressed, peripheries will have little or no hope of breaking out of their situation.

World-system theory may not be popular in the United States outside the intellectual community, but it is part of the central thinking of other countries, especially those of the periphery. It is important to understand their perceptions of the world order. The world-system framework is also the result of a long history, and knowledge of what went before will make it possible to avoid needless repetitions in the debate concerning development.

There are many case studies that show how world-system theory works on both the global and the local level. On the global level, Sidney Mintz's classic 1985 study on sugar illustrates how a global system develops. He reveals that before the Crusades, which began in 1096, Europe was dominated by rural people who produced their own goods locally. As a result of the Crusades, Europeans sought to establish and extend trade routes. In 1271, Marco Polo opened trade with China, and by the early 1500's, Europeans were extracting materials from around the world.

Europeans, especially the English, became consumers of these resources, and by 1650, one very popular commodity that was desired by the English nobility was sugar. By 1750, even the poorest English farm laborers used sugar in their tea. The world demand was so great that whole regions adopted plantation and monocrop economy. Their need for labor led to the development of the slave trade and triangle trade systems. In the eighteenth century, the demand for raw cotton by the English led to rapid settlement in the southeastern United States, the development of a plantation and monocrop economy, and the use of slave labor.

As the demand for commodities such as cotton and sugar increased, international trade increased, which led to the rise of the capitalist world economy—a single world-system committed to production, sale, and exchange, with the goal of maximizing profits rather than satisfying local or domestic needs. The key attribute of capitalism is the economic orientation to the world market for profit.

What has developed is shown in Fernand Braudel's three-volume work, *Civilization and Capitalism: Fifteenth-Eighteenth Century* (1981-1984). Braudel demonstrates that the world is made up of a world-system with numerous subsystems, subsubsystems, and so on, which are all interrelated. Some societies are in the core and are served by those in the periphery. In the heyday of the British Empire, India was in the periphery and England was in the core. Currently, Malaysia is in the periphery and the United States is in the core. Even within the United States, however, there are core/periphery relationships; for example, Tennessee's Delta County supplies cheap labor so that products can be sold at a lower price to urbanites or communities in the North.

Malaysia has been colonized and has been on the periphery of the world-system for centuries, but it has now begun to industrialize. Initially, the world demand for Malaysian products resulted in the development of plantation economies and deforestation. By 1970, 10,000 people annually were being displaced from the land. To provide these people with jobs and to stem social discontent, Malaysia encouraged foreign companies to take advantage of Malaysia's cheap labor and build industry there. Western European, U.S., and Japanese companies complied and moved industry in to utilize cheap labor in Malaysia.

Malaysian villagers were hired, and these workers now live different lives. They work for bosses, whereas in the village they worked according to season and need. Schools were altered to teach children to be disciplined and to have values suitable for working in a factory. The work, such as assembling electronics components, is demanding and exhausting. Women are hired over men, and the financial rewards have not met expectations. After she works for a couple of years, the female worker's health typically deteriorates and she has to leave the job. One side effect has been an increase in mass hysteria. Some women see spirits in the factory; others become possessed by spirits. The reason for the rise of spirit possession is unclear; it may be a means of rebelling so that the women do not have to deal with authorities, or it may be a way of coping with inequality, something alien to the workers' world. Whatever the cause, however, the conditions are a result of the world-system and its influence on Malaysia.

Context

World-system theory has its origins in the seventeenth and eighteenth centuries. In 1817, David Ricardo formulated the classic modern theory of free trade. He argued that unrestricted trade between two countries was always advantageous if they produced mutually desirable goods at different degrees of efficiency. Friedrich List, in *National System of*

Political Economy (1841), challenged Ricardo, arguing that in the long term, it might be advantageous to protect or foster industries that cannot compete in the short term. The debate has continued, but world-system theory promoters generally conclude in one way or the other that Ricardo was wrong—they argue that free trade benefits the advanced industrial countries and slows development in the poor countries.

J. A. Hobson's *Imperialism: A Study* (1902) attacked imperialism. Hobson's ideas were built on by Vladimir Ilich Lenin's *Imperialism: The Highest Stage of Capitalism* (1939), which argued that imperialist exploitation prevented the final crisis of capitalism. Lenin neglected to examine the effect of imperialism on peasants in the colonies. Rosa Luxemburg, in *The Accumulation of Capital* (1913), filled that void by examining the spread of capitalism into Egypt and the way in which it deprived peasants of their land and drove them to ruin. Leon Trotsky, in *The Permanent Revolution* (1930), examined the place of semi-peripherals in prerevolutionary Russia. It was N. I. Bukharin, however, in *Imperialism and World Economy* (1929), who foreshadowed the work of Wallerstein and other world-system theorists. He wrote about the economic cleavage developing between town and country as well as between industrial and agrarian countries.

Right-wing intellectuals appealed to nationalism by using the world-system approach. Most notable was the Romanian Mihail Manoilescu, who, in *The Theory of Protection and International Trade* (1930), attacked Ricardo's concept of the comparative advantage.

It was in this intellectual climate that Paul Prebisch developed "dependency theory." Prebisch, an Argentinean, headed the United Nations' Economic Commission for Latin America (ECLA). Wallerstein credits him with introducing the concepts of core and periphery. The ECLA report *Relative Prices of Exports and Imports of Under-Developed Countries: A Study of Post-War Terms of Trade between Under-Developed and Industrialized Nations* (1949) showed that terms of trade favored industrial nations and worked against agricultural exporting countries. This report formed the basis of dependency theory, but the concept has since gone beyond economics to include sociological and political theories concerning development. The contribution of dependency theory is that it shows that economic growth has been accompanied by rising inequalities and that rapid urbanization and the spread of literacy have converged with the marginalization of the masses.

Dependency theorists have focused on the inability of Latin American countries to control their own finances. They have also studied the high correlation between repression and the application of capitalist efficiency criteria in Latin America, as well as the phenomena of "bureaucratic-authoritarian" regimes being favored for international finance, poorer countries not having access to current technology, and industrialization based on import substitution creating new forms of dependency.

World-system theory has influenced sociology and anthropology. Wallerstein's 1974 volume was published at a time when modernization theory was being discredited by the Vietnam War, social turmoil in the 1960's wakened social scientists to the inequalities within the United States, and young socialists desired a historical knowledge that was not presented in the functional positivist framework. Wallerstein's writings countered the antirevolutionary, anticommunist implications of modernization theory. They provided a coherent framework to explain local and international inequalities, and brought a historical perspective to the discipline.

Building on Wallerstein's core-periphery framework, Michael Hechter, in *Internal Colonialism: The Celtic Fringe in British National Development, 1536-1966* (1975), explains ongoing ethnic tensions in core societies. Frances V. Moulder, in *Japan, China, and the Modern World Economy: Toward a Reinterpretation of East Asian Development ca. 1600 to ca. 1918* (1977), shows that Japan developed largely because of its ability to resist economic colonialism.

Although Wallerstein's work was not quantitative, a school of quantitative world-system theorists has developed at Stanford University. It has become popular because it combines the ideological and political emphasis of Marxism and a statistical framework, which seems to bestow legitimacy.

In the field of anthropology, community studies have considered the international influences on behavior—Katherine Verdery's *Transylvanian Villagers: Three Centuries of Political, Economic, and Ethnic Change* (1983) is a good example of such work.

World-system theory is not without its critics and problems. Robert Brenner (1976) shows that Eastern Europe's backwardness caused its dependence, not the other way around. In addition, Wallerstein neglects cultural and social factors and the interplay between class structure and economic growth. Whether dependency is a cause or result still has not been determined. The world-system framework does not explain why different societies in similar context did or did not develop in a similar way. It also ignores the works of scholars such as Max Weber and Robert Merton, who have shown a relationship between religious rationality and the growth of science and development. It assumes that economic growth in the world is a zero-sum game, when in fact the quality of life in the whole world has improved over the last several decades. In spite of these problems, one cannot fault the new way of thinking and insight that Wallerstein and world-system theory have brought to the understanding of human behavior, especially because they have forced sociologists and anthropologists to consider behavior from a global perspective.

Bibliography

Bell, Daniel. *The Coming of the Post-Industrial Society: A Venture in Social Forecasting.* New York: Basic Books, 1973. Classic work that argues that modern industrial societies are entering a new phase in which production services and the processing of information are emphasized and in which white-collar jobs are most prominent.

Brenner, Robert. "Agrarian Class Structure and Economic Development in Pre-Industrial Europe." *Past and Present,* no. 70 (February, 1976): 30-75. Provides a counter-critique of world-system theory and the ideas of Wallerstein and some of his followers.

Chirot, Daniel, and Thomas D. Hall. "World-System Theory." *Annual Review of Sociology* 8 (1982): 81-106. An outstanding review of the concepts and criticisms of modernization theory and world-system theory.

King, Anthony D. *Urbanism, Colonialism, and the World Economy: Cultural and Spatial Foundations of the World Urban System.* New York: Routledge, 1990.

Mintz, Sidney W. *Sweetness and Power: The Place of Sugar in Modern History.* New York: Penguin Books, 1986. Demonstrates the place of sugar in developing core/periphery relationships in world-system theory.

Wallerstein, Immanuel. *The Capitalist World-Economy.* Cambridge, England: Cambridge University Press, 1979.

_____. *The Modern World-System: Capitalist Agriculture and the Origins of the European World-Economy in the Sixteenth Century.* New York: Academic Press, 1974.

Arthur W. Helweg

Cross-References

Industrial and Postindustrial Economies; Marxism; Technology and Social Change.

POLITICAL SOCIOLOGY

Type of sociology: Major social institutions
Field of study: Politics and the state

Political sociology is a subfield in the disciplines of political science and sociology which is primarily concerned with the social basis of power. Four competing perspectives—Marxist, neo-Marxist, pluralist, and elitist—have dominated the field since World War II.

Principal terms

ELITISTS: theorists who believe that in all societies, including industrial democracies, a small group (not the masses) rules

INSTRUMENTALISTS: those who believe that the state is an instrument in the hands of the ruling class

MARXISTS: followers of Marx and Engels, who believe that a capitalist state is an instrument for maintaining bourgeois domination of the working class

PLURALISTS: theorists who believe in multiple competing elites and a dispersion of power in a democracy

STRUCTURAL NEO-MARXISTS: theorists who believe in the relative autonomy of the capitalist state

Overview

Political sociology as a field of study overlaps the disciplines of political science and sociology. Political sociology has developed in its present form since World War II. It is primarily concerned with an understanding of the social basis of power and authority. Sociologist Marvin E. Olsen has defined political sociology as "the study of power relations between the political and social systems in nation-states that result in the creation and operation of sociopolitical organization."

Both sociologists—Talcott Parsons, Reinhard Bendix, Ralf Dahrendorf, C. Wright Mills, Seymour Martin Lipset, and G. William Domhoff, for example—and political scientists—such as Robert Dahl, Ralph Miliband, and Kenneth Prewitt—have contributed to the theoretical and empirical studies of political sociology. The writings of Karl Marx and Max Weber have substantially influenced the scholarship in this field. The followers of Marx and Weber take radically different views of a sociology of politics; the debate among political sociologists ·has often taken the form of a dialogue between and among the Marxists and the Weberians. Eclectic scholars, on the other hand, use the insights, concepts, and methodologies derived from the writings of both Marx and Weber in a selective and nondogmatic manner in order to clarify the dynamics of power and authority relationships in modern societies.

The question of where power resides and how it should be studied is at the core of the disagreement among the proponents of different approaches. In the vast literature on political sociology, four distinct approaches to power and authority can be identified: the

Marxist, the pluralist, the power elite, and the neo-Marxist. The Marxists take what has been called an "instrumentalist" view of political power. For Marx and Friedrich Engels, the state, which they considered to be in the realm of superstructure determined by the economic substructure of society, is an instrument in the hands of the ruling class, which dominates the state to further its own interest. In a capitalist society, according to Marx and Engels, the state acts as a "committee for managing the common affairs of the whole bourgeoisie."

According to Marx, class conflict is derived from economic factors or social relations generated by the mode of production. The capitalists' control of the means of production gives them direct (or strong indirect) control of the state. Marx, Engels, and later orthodox Marxists thus analyze the various ways in which the modern state is an instrument of class rule and is used for exploitation of the proletariat, or wage worker, by capital and for the maintenance of the political domination of the bourgeoisie.

Mainstream American political sociology is critical of a class-based theory of politics and generally rejects Marxist instrumentalism because it provides an economic determinist view of social stratification. By contrast, the pluralists—who take their intellectual inspiration from Weber's concepts of authority and rationality—have argued that modern societies consist of a variety of interest groups and that the government acts essentially as a broker to facilitate compromise among them. Power, in this view, is conceived to be widely dispersed among government officials, private individuals, organized interest groups, associations, and a variety of organizations; no one group holds all the power.

A commonly used pluralist definition of power is that of Robert Dahl: "[Person] A has power over [person] B to the extent that he can get B to do something that B would not otherwise do." In *Modern Political Analysis* (1984), Dahl suggests that power means getting others to comply "by creating the prospect of severe sanctions against noncompliance." Defined thus, power is a relational, rather than an abstract, concept: It exists in an interaction, not in a static state. Three types of power have been identified: authority, coercion, and manipulation. While authority is the exercise of legitimate power because it entails the voluntary submission of B to A's directives, coercion is accompanied by sanctions in the form of either rewards or punishments. Manipulation, on the other hand, is the use of power by A over B when A does not have legitimate power or authority over B and when B is unaware of A's intention.

In *The Theory of Social and Economic Organization* (1947), Weber distinguishes three ideal types of legitimacy upon which a power relationship may rest: "traditional," "legal-rational," and "charismatic" authority. Traditional authority rests on "an established belief in the sanctity of immemorial traditions," such as the authority of a king or tribal chief. Rational authority, by contrast, rests "on a belief in the 'legality' of patterns of normative rules," which means that the superior is "himself subject to an impersonal order, and orients his actions to it in his own dispositions and commands." An example is the exercise of authority in modern bureaucratic capitalist states in the West. Charismatic authority is mixed and transitional, and it rests on "devotion to the specific and exceptional sanctity, heroism or exemplary character of an individual person" and on "the normative patterns or order revealed or ordained by him." Authority of this kind has been exercised by such diverse religious and political leaders as Jesus Christ, Mahatma Gandhi, and Adolf Hitler.

Two divergent responses to the pluralist approach came in the 1960's and 1970's: the elitist and the neo-Marxist approaches. Elite theorists reject the pluralist notion that power in industrial democracies is dispersed among a number of competing groups. At the same time, they deny the Marxist claim that political power is a function of class location. Inspired by the works of C. Wright Mills and Italian political sociologists Vilfredo Pareto and Gaetano Mosca, the elite theorists believe that in all societies, including industrial democracies, only a minority—the elites—makes the major decisions and governs the masses. Unlike Marx's ruling class, elite membership changes over time. Social mobility allows non-elites to become elites through assimilation and cooperation; these elites share a consensus regarding certain basic values of the society and rules of the game, especially of the political system. Thus the elite theory posits that, in modern democracy, power is exercised by the elites over the masses.

The focus of a dominant neo-Marxist view is on political power and the imperative of capital accumulation and class conflict in capitalist societies. It is critical of instrumentalism as an adequate approach to a Marxist analysis of state and politics, because instrumentalism does not offer a coherent account of the distinctive properties and limits of state power. Nicos Poulantzas, Louis Althusser, Ernesto Laclau, and Claude Offe are among the leading structural neo-Marxists who reject economism and class reductionism. They agree with the position taken by structuralist writers such as Antonio Gramsci that state functions are determined by the structure of society, including its ideological and political practices, rather than by individuals in positions of state power.

In his most influential book, *Political Power and Social Classes* (1973), Poulantzas defines the state in terms of its necessary and objective function in the reproduction of social cohesion through its political and ideological apparatuses. He extends the concept of the "relative autonomy" of the capitalist state beyond any specific capitalists or the capitalist class and views the state as a crystallization of complex social relations. By doing this, Poulantzas "brought the state [which had been ignored in the pluralist literature] back in" to the center of political sociology in the 1970's. In *Class, Crisis, and the State* (1978), Erik Olin Wright examines the relationship between class and state and suggests ways to test the Marxist conception of class and state empirically.

Applications

The insights gained from the various theories, approaches, and concepts of political sociology have been applied by scholars in their empirical studies to locate the social basis of power and authority in industrial and industrializing societies. Since World War II, significant research has been done to analyze power in American society using pluralist and elitist perspectives.

Robert Dahl's *Who Governs? Democracy and Power in an American City* (1961) is the most important empirical study in the pluralist tradition and is one of the most widely cited books in the social sciences. In his study of community power structure in New Haven, Connecticut, Dahl employs decisional analysis and concentrates on analyzing power. He studies party nominations to public office, urban redevelopment, and public education and identifies the changing patterns of leadership and the politics of influence in New Haven. Dahl's findings refute the thesis of Floyd Hunter in *Community Power Structure: A Study of Decision Makers* (1953), in which Hunter found that local politics in Atlanta, Georgia, was largely controlled, directly or indirectly, by dominant economic interests. It also argues against the thesis of C. Wright Mills in *The Power Elite* (1956) that the United States is run by a combination of "the high military, the corporation executives, and the political directorate."

Through the use of sophisticated social science methodology combining middle-range empiricism with broad-range theory, Dahl showed that political power, which was once concentrated in a few hands, is widely dispersed among competing groups in New Haven. Based on the findings of the New Haven study, Dahl generalized that political power is widely dispersed among competing interest groups in a plural democracy. Following Dahl's classic study, pluralism emerged as the dominant approach in the field of political sociology in the 1960's, and scholars have since employed it to study power in the United States and other industrial democracies.

Dahl's thesis and the pluralist approach have, however, been challenged on empirical and theoretical grounds, notably by critics employing the elitist perspective such as G. William Domhoff, Thomas Dye, G. Lowell Field, John Higley, Kenneth Prewitt, and Alan Stone. Domhoff, a pioneer in research on the American ruling class who has advanced an analysis of American society based on the insights of power structure theory, has provided the most sustained critique of the pluralist view that power is lodged in a variety of interest groups and in the people as a whole through party politics and elections. Grounding his analysis in Mills's concept of the power elite and E. Digby Baltzell's American business aristocracy, Domhoff in *Who Rules America?* (1967) rejects Dahl's pluralist thesis and demonstrates that a small, socially identifiable group—a national upper class or power elite, whose members have well-established ways of training and perpetuating new members—is the governing class in the United States.

Domhoff elaborates his power-structure thesis in other studies. In *The Powers That Be* (1979), he shows that the upper class in the United States, a tiny segment of the population (0.5 percent), controls more than 25 percent of the country's private wealth and annual income. The economic power of the upper class, he argues, allows this class to subordinate the other social classes and dominate the government. Through contingency, reputational, and positional analysis, Domhoff demonstrates that the upper class is a cohesive ruling class in America. In *The Power Elite and the State* (1990), he elaborates his power structure thesis by applying Michael Mann's theory of social power to an analysis of several major policy initiatives at the national level in the twentieth century United States.

Thomas R. Dye's study *Who's Running America? Institutional Leadership in the United States* (1976) uses biographical data of more than five thousand members of government and business elites to demonstrate that power in the United States is concentrated in the hands of a small number of government and business elites. He shows that there is a corporate interlocking among a number of firms and a "revolving door" between governmental and business elites. Dye concludes that power is "concentrated in large institutions—

The most powerful fascist regime was that of Adolf Hitler's Nazi Party, which for a dozen years suppressed German democracy in the name of the national "will." *(Museum of Modern Art)*

corporations, banks, utilities, insurance companies, broadcasting networks, the White House, Congress and the Washington bureaucracy, the military establishment, the prestigious law firms, the foundations, and the universities."

The 1980's and early 1990's witnessed an effort by a few scholars, notably John Higley, Michael Burton, and G. Lowell Field, to develop a new elite framework for political analysis by synthesizing elements of elite and class theories. The new elite framework has been applied to the study of political stability and the emergence of democracy in the West. In "The Elite Variable in Democratic Transitions and Breakdowns," in *American Sociological Review* 54 (February, 1989), Higley and Burton analyze the relationships between types of national elites, elite transformations, and political stability in the Western nation-states since 1500. Their study shows that "a consensually unified national elite," as in Sweden, Britain, or the United States, "produces a stable regime that may evolve into modern democracy."

Context

The changing sociopolitical conditions in developed and developing societies since World War II have provided the context within which political sociologists have sought to answer important questions related to the central thrust of the field—the relationship between power and politics. Much of their scholarly attention has been focused on the study of the conditions that facilitate democracy. The Fascist and Nazi challenge to liberal democracy in the 1930's and 1940's and the communist challenge both before and after World War II gave impetus to a number of studies on democracy. In his classic study *Political Man: The Social Bases of Power* (1960), Seymour Lipset identified conditions that make democracy work in any society: an open class system, economic wealth, an egalitarian value system, a capitalist economy, literacy, and high participation in voluntary associations. A year later, Dahl offered the pluralist view of American democracy in his famous study of New Haven.

The political sociologists who were influenced by the radical antiestablishment movement of the 1960's, however, challenged the prevailing dominant pluralist approach. They applied Mills's power elite framework to the study of society and politics, which resulted in an intense debate between the pluralists and elitists in the 1960's. A new debate started in the 1970's when the neo-Marxists responded to the pluralist, elitist, and instrumental Marxist frameworks. The contribution of the structural neo-Marxists, who are inspired by the class analysis of Marx as interpreted by Althusser, Gramsci, and other structuralists, and who use the nation-state as a unit of analysis, has mostly been at an abstract theoretical level. In particular, they have interpreted the role of the capitalist state and its relationship to the capitalist class.

The neo-Marxist perspective was advanced at a time (the late 1960's and early 1970's) when the world was undergoing major changes. A détente was reached with the Soviet Union, a new diplomatic opening with China occurred, and the United States withdrew from Vietnam. The Watergate scandal focused attention on abuses of governmental power. Social scientists were searching for new frameworks to explain these changes. The 1970's witnessed a rich, lively, and often polemical debate between the neo-Marxists and the Marxists on the one hand and the elitists on the other. In a number of empirical studies, the neo-Marxists sought to verify their theory, especially the "relative autonomy of state." Their approach lost much of its appeal in the wake of the "Reagan Revolution" in the early 1980's, whereas scholarly interest in the elitist framework continued in the 1980's. Domhoff, Dye, and others refuted the pluralist perspective by producing new evidence in support of the thesis they had put forth in earlier studies. No such effort was made on behalf of the pluralist perspective. The elitist perspective was further enriched in the 1980's and early 1990's by the contributions of scholars who, by advancing an elite conflict theory and a new elite paradigm, sought to reestablish the classical elite theory.

In the 1980's, scholarly attention also went to the study of democracy, especially the breakdown of democratic regimes and the transitions from authoritarian to democratic governments. Through empirical studies on Mediterranean and Latin American states, political sociologists made an effort to discern a pattern and to identify the social, political, and economic conditions that allowed less industrialized and developing nations to become democratic. The collapse of communism in Eastern Europe and the former Soviet Union, accompanied by a global resurgence of democracy, provided further impetus to studies on democracy. Political sociologists in the early 1990's gave attention to the question of whether the democratic expansion of the 1980's and early 1990's will be stabilized, consolidated, and sustained in the environments of the new democratic states.

Bibliography

Dahl, Robert. *Who Governs? Democracy and Power in an American City*. New Haven, Conn.: Yale University Press, 1961. Examines the changing patterns of leadership and the distribution of political resources in New Haven, Connecticut.

Dahrendorf, Ralf. *Class and Class Conflict in Industrial Society*. Stanford, Calif.: Stanford University Press, 1959. Provides critique of various theories of class and class conflict and offers his own theory of the "coercion of social structure."

Domhoff, G. William. *Who Rules America? Power and Politics in the Year 2000*. 3d ed. Mountain View, Calif.: Mayfield, 1998. Using the perspective of the elite theory, especially that of E. Digby Baltzell, C. Wright Mills, and Paul Sweezy, Domhoff argues that a small, socially identifiable group—a national upper class or power elite—is the governing class in America.

Dye, Thomas R. *Who's Running America? Institutional Leadership in the United States*. 6th ed. Englewood Cliffs, N.J.: Prentice-Hall, 1995. Through the use of biographical data of five thousand members, Dye applies power structure theory to his analysis of the elites who, he holds, rule the United States.

Field, G. Lowell, and John Higley. *Elitism*. Boston: Routledge & Kegan Paul, 1980. Detailed survey of the literature on elite theory and restate the elitist paradigm focusing on elite unity and disunity.

Miliband, Ralph. *The State in Capitalist Society: An Analysis of the Western System of Power*. London: Weidenfeld & Nicolson, 1969. The leading British Marxist explains how class inequalities may be transformed into power differences within modern capitalist societies. His "instrumentalist" view came under serious criticism by structuralists such as Nicos Poulantzas.

Mills, C. Wright. *The Power Elite*. Afterword by Alan Wolfe. New York: Oxford University Press, 1999. Influential and controversial book, which initiated extensive discussion of power and the American social structure. Mills argues that the United States is run by a combination of "the high military, the corporation executives, and the political directorate."

Poulantzas, Nicos. *Political Power and Social Classes*. Translated by Timothy O'Hagan. London: NLB and Sheed and Ward, 1973. Deeply influenced by neo-Marxist structuralists such as Antonio Gramsci and Louis Althusser, Poulantzas presents a structural view of the state and classes. The most influential political sociology book of the early 1970's.

Prewitt, Kenneth, and Alan Stone. *The Ruling Elites: Elite Theory, Power, and American Democracy*. New York: Harper & Row, 1973. Excellent review of the various perspectives on elite theory and systematically test the propositions of the "power elite" versus pluralist theory using the data on American elites.

Sunil K. Sahu

Cross-References

Civil Religion and Politics; Democracy; Legitimacy and Authority; Power Elite.

POVERTY
Analysis and Overview

Type of sociology: Social stratification
Field of study: Poverty

Poverty refers to the status of individuals, families, or households whose income or consumption falls below a determined or fixed standard of need or within a stated fraction of a social average. Sociologists have devoted extensive study to determining the prevalence, causes, and effects of poverty.

Principal terms

ABSOLUTE POVERTY: conditions under which one's consumption or income falls below a fixed or objective standard of need, based on subsistence or minimum comfort levels

POVERTY AREAS: census tracts in metropolitan counties and minor civil divisions in non-metropolitan counties with a poverty rate of 20 percent or more

POVERTY THRESHOLDS: the dollar amounts that the U.S. Census Bureau uses to determine the poverty status of families and unrelated individuals; they are based on an average of a sample of families, applied to all families and unrelated individuals, and weighted accordingly by the presence or absence of children

RELATIVE POVERTY: a measure of poverty achieved by comparing one's condition to a social average—for example, one-half the average or median income of society at large

SUBJECTIVE POVERTY: measure of poverty achieved by comparing one's consumption or income level to social attitudes (gleaned, for example, through polling data) about what constitutes a decent standard of living

Overview

In the early 1990's, poverty resurfaced—after some years during which it received relatively little attention—as both a subject of scholarly inquiry and a matter of national concern. In *The Poverty Debate: Politics and the Poor in America* (1992), sociologist C. Emory Burton notes that poverty has become a major subject of academic study. The May, 1992, riots in Los Angeles focused attention on the role poverty played as an underlying factor of the disturbances. Several major issues dominate contemporary concern among scholars and policy makers about poverty; among them are the measurement and extent of poverty, the culture of poverty, the underclass, the homeless, welfare, and workfare.

Poverty is most often viewed in one of three ways. Absolute poverty refers to conditions in which individual, family, or household consumption or income falls below a fixed or objective standard of need, such as a standard based on subsistence or minimum comfort levels. In determining the extent of poverty in the United States, the U.S. Census Bureau relies on an absolute standard. Relative poverty compares an individual's or household's condition with a social average—for example one-half the average or median income of society at large. Measures of relative poverty range from fairly simple schemes (such as arbitrarily labeling the bottom 10 or 20 percent of the income distribution as "poor") to more complex schemes, such as examining each individual's consumption of a long list of commodities and social services and then calculating a "deprivation index" based on the number of areas in which the individual's consumption falls below social norms. Finally, subjective poverty compares individual or household consumption or income level to social attitudes about what constitutes a decent standard of living. Subjective definitions are based on surveys or polling data that use households' own assessments of the minimum or "just sufficient" amounts of income or consumption needed by people like them. Both the relative and subjective definitions of poverty are problematic in that they are "moving targets," varying beyond the point where programmatic responses to ameliorate poverty can be viably designed and implemented. Since the U.S. government uses an absolute definition, the remainder of this essay deals with that conceptualization of poverty.

In 1992, 36.9 million persons, 14.5 percent of the entire civilian noninstitutional population, fell below the official poverty level, an increase from the 35.7 million poor persons, or 14.2 percent of the population in 1991. The poverty rate for children under eighteen (21.9 percent) was slightly higher than the 21.6 percent in 1991 and was the highest since 1983. It was nearly as high as it was in 1964 (23 percent), when the Johnson administration declared its War on Poverty. Twenty-five percent of children under six fell below poverty thresholds. Nearly half of all black children under eighteen were poor.

The distribution of poverty varies along social and economic variables such as age, race, gender, education, the presence or absence of children under eighteen, and region of the country. In 1991, for example, 8.7 million (53.7 percent) of the 14.2 million poor children under eighteen lived in female-headed households with no male householder present. Nearly 4 million elderly, more than 12 percent of the population, were also poor in 1991. Of these elderly, 2.6 million lived in households as unrelated individuals, and the majority (by a 4:1 ratio) were women. Social scientists Eugene Smolensky, Sheldon Danziger, and Peter Gottschalk, in their essay "The Declining Significance of Age in the United States: Trends in the Well-Being of Children and the Elderly," in *The Vulnerable* (1988), edited by John L. Palmer, Timothy Smeeding, and Barbara Boyle Torrey, noted an inverse relationship between the poverty rates for the elderly and for children in the 1970's and 1980's. The poverty rate for all elderly persons fell substantially since 1939, but particularly since 1969, while the poverty rate for all children also fell substantially between 1939 and 1969, but rose since 1969. Beginning in 1974, the poverty rate among children exceeded that among the elderly.

Children and the elderly continue to be two of the country's most vulnerable groups with respect to poverty. In 1991, half the nation's poor were either children under eighteen years (40.2 percent) or elderly people (10.6 percent). A higher proportion of elderly than nonelderly were concentrated between 100 and 125 percent of their respective poverty thresholds. Consequently, 19.1 percent of the nation's 11.8 million "near poor" persons were elderly, compared with 10.6 percent of persons below the official poverty level.

The distribution of poverty in the United States also varies by race. In 1991, 17.7 million (9.4 percent) non-Hispanic whites fell below the official poverty level, contrasted with 10.2 million (32.7 percent) black, 6.3 million (28.7 percent) Hispanic, and 1 million (13.8 percent) Asian and Pacific Islander Americans. Despite the overall lower poverty rates for whites, the majority of poor persons in 1991 were white (66.5 percent). Blacks constituted 28.7 percent of all persons below the poverty level, a proportion that has remained fairly constant since the mid-1960's. In 1991, about 17.8 percent of the poor were persons of Hispanic origin, well above the 8.8 percent Hispanic representation in the population as a whole.

By region in 1991, the Northeast had the lowest poverty rate (12.2 percent). As has historically been the case, the poverty rate was highest in the South (16.0 percent). The South continued to have a disproportionately large share of the nation's poverty population; 38.6 percent of the poor lived in the South in 1991, compared with 33.5 percent of the U.S. population above the poverty level. The poverty rate in the West (14.3 percent) was higher than that in the Midwest (13.2 percent) in 1991. Based on a 3-year average (1989 to 1991), state poverty rates ranged from 5.8 percent in Connecticut to 23.8 percent in Mississippi. About 34.9 percent of the nation's poor in 1991 lived in areas of high poverty concentration or so-called poverty areas. Blacks living in cities, regardless of economic status, were more concentrated in poverty areas than whites or persons of Hispanic origin. About 52.9 percent of blacks living in central cities lived in poverty areas, and 64.3 percent of poor blacks living in cities were concentrated in poverty areas. Only 16.6 percent of all central city whites lived in poverty areas, while 37.9 percent of poor whites did; 43.4 percent of central city persons of Hispanic origin lived in poverty areas, while 57.7 percent of the poor did.

Applications

There has been much debate about the nature and causes of poverty in contemporary America. Political scientist Lawrence M. Mead, in *The New Politics of Poverty: The Nonworking Poor in America* (1992), for example, asserts that poverty is attributable to a lack of the work ethic—that the poor have voluntarily chosen to shun work. For the most part, Mead attributes poverty less to structural factors (such as the proliferation of low-wage jobs and the loss of high-paying manufacturing inner-city jobs) that limit opportunity and more to personal failures and cultural shortcomings that reflect a sense of internalized helplessness. The structural versus cultural polemic is most profound in the research and debate about what has been termed the "underclass." *Fortune* magazine editorial board member Myron Magnet furthers the cultural view of poverty in *The Dream and the Nightmare: The Sixties' Legacy to the Underclass* (1993). Magnet notes the self-defeating behavior of the underclass. Like Mead, Magnet saw the 1980's as boom years creating millions of jobs and offering a way out of poverty to almost any poor person with the willingness and discipline to work.

On the other side of the issue, sociologists Herbert J. Gans, William J. Wilson, and Christopher Jencks and historians Michael Katz and Mark Stern, among many others, attribute the preponderance of poverty more to structural than cultural factors. They view with alarm the moral overtones that pervade Mead's, Magnet's, and others' analyses of poverty and diatribes against the underclass. For them, erosion of the work ethic is not the relevant poverty-related issue. Instead, they link poverty to the erosion of jobs and lack of public will to fund the types of programs and policies that might more adequately deal with the issue. For example, in an article entitled "Making Jobs," in *The Nation* (September 20, 1993), Gans iterates the need for the government to start deliberately creating new jobs, despite the successful Senate filibuster against the Clinton administration's proposed economic stimulus package. There is sufficient evidence to support challenging the "erosion of the work ethic" arguments.

Although some scholars have argued that poverty is caused by lack of a work ethic, some poor people—such as the head of this Los Angeles family—hold multiple jobs to meet their families' needs. *(Library of Congress)*

In 1991, according to the U.S. Bureau of the Census, 39.8 percent of poor persons fifteen years old and older worked, and 9.0 percent worked year-round, full-time. As expected, the percentages were much higher for nonpoor persons: 72.0 percent worked and 45.0 percent worked year-round, full-time in 1991. Nevertheless, despite some slight variations, the proportions of poor adults who worked and who worked year round, full time in 1991 were not statistically different from those in any year since 1978. There was no great diminution of labor force participation on the part of poor persons throughout the 1980's "boom."

In addition to the underclass debate, there is much contemporary discussion about the relations between poverty and the changes in the structure of the American family. Although children and the elderly are often cast as the two most vulnerable segments of American society, many scholars, public policy analysts, political figures, and others have expressed concern about increases in the numbers of out-of-wedlock childbirths and of female-headed poor households. Gertrude Schaffner Goldberg, in her chapter entitled "The United States: Feminization of Poverty Amidst Plenty," in *The Feminization of Poverty* (1990), which she coauthored with Eleanor Kremen, summarizes the factors and forces contributing to what she and others call the feminization of poverty. Goldberg notes the paradox that at the very time when women have been "emancipating themselves from unpaid domestic work," female-headed households with no husband present have become preponderant among the poor. Earlier, policy analyst Irwin Garfinkle and sociologist Sara S. McLanahan characterized female-headed family poverty as a new American dilemma in *Single Mothers and Their Children* (1986). Social science research studies such as Garfinkle and McLanahan's have linked single-headed family households with higher rates of poverty, school dropouts, and delinquency. The issue about the consequences of changes in family structure remains hotly contested terrain in academic, political, and popular literature.

Finally, no other poverty-related issue generated as much concern throughout the 1980's and early 1990's as the problem of homelessness. Two works highlight the salient issues. From the left of the political spectrum, policy analyst Joel Blau in *The Visible Poor: Homelessness in the United States* (1992) views contemporary homelessness as a product of a transformed U.S. economy. From the right, former antipoverty planner in President Lyndon Johnson's Office of Economic Opportunity Richard White in *Rude Awakenings: What the Homeless Crisis Tells Us* (1992) argues that there are far greater numbers of mentally ill people and drug addicts among the homeless than appear in official reports. Although White views the homeless as more personally responsible for their plight than does Blau, both maintain that the changes in the American economy are part of the story. As with poverty in general, homelessness has multiple causes that defy either/or categorization of fault and that demand societal responses that address structural as well as personal factors.

Context

Throughout the twentieth century, if not most of its history, the United States has grappled with the problem of poverty. Richard K. Caputo notes that concern with identifying poor persons and groups of poor people goes back as far as the mid-nineteenth century. For the most part, those who described poverty prior to the 1960's took what might be called snapshots of the poor population rather than making detailed studies. Robert Hunter's 1904 classic *Poverty*, for example, estimated that 10 million Americans (about 12 percent of the population) were poor and that 20 percent lived in northern industrial areas, while 10 percent lived in the South. Such estimations, however, failed to distinguish the short-term from the long-term poor and therefore underestimated the poverty problem. In the 1960's, such writers as Michael Harrington conveyed the idea that most early twentieth century poverty resulted from economic weaknesses endemic to the development of industrial capitalism. By the 1960's and afterward, however, the United States' "new" poor comprised deprived minorities who were immune to the country's economic progress. Abandoned and hopeless, they lived in what has been called a "culture of poverty." Historian James T. Patterson chronicles this development in *America's Struggle Against Poverty, 1900-1985* (1986).

Modern technology and more sophisticated statistical tools have enabled researchers to conduct longitudinal studies of the poor, and these have challenged some of the snapshot views about the nature and extent of poverty. Greg J. Duncan's *Years of Poverty, Years of Plenty* (1984) reports findings from a "truly unique" social study, the Panel Study of Income Dynamics, originally funded by the Office of Economic Opportunity in 1968 and undertaken by the Survey Research Center of the University of Michigan. According to the study, by and large, many more Americans become poor during the course of a given year than had been previously assumed, but the durations of poverty for most tend to be short-term. About 2.6 percent of the population can be viewed as persistently poor—that is, as having an income below the poverty line in eight of ten consecutive years. Economist David T. Ellwood captured the diversity of the poverty population in *Poor Support: Poverty in the American Family* (1988). Ellwood distinguishes two-parent from single-parent poverty and further differentiates these from ghetto poverty. He suggests different legislative, social, and economic policies for each.

Bibliography

Boger, John Charles, and Judith Welch Wegner, eds. *Race, Poverty, and American Cities.* Chapel Hill: University of North Carolina Press, 1996.

Burton, C. Emory. *The Poverty Debate: Politics and the Poor in America.* Westport, Conn.: Praeger, 1992. Includes chapters on the measurement and extent of poverty, the culture of poverty, the underclass, the homeless, welfare, welfare dependency, workfare, solutions to poverty, and political implications, in addition to a theory for reform. In addition, 1990 poverty data are presented in an appendix.

Gans, Herbert J. *People, Plans, and Policies: Essays on Poverty, Racism, and Other National Urban Problems.* New York: Columbia University Press, 1991. Two of this book's five parts contains essays on poverty-related matters. Its focus is on how to think about national problems and contains chapters on the uses of poverty, the role of education in the escape from poverty, the black family, and the dangers of the underclass.

Magnet, Myron. *The Dream and the Nightmare: The Sixties' Legacy to the Underclass.* New York: William Morrow, 1993. Traces cultural straitjacket endemic to poverty in the 1980's and 1990's to the liberal and counterculture ideas spawned in the 1960's.

Mead, Lawrence M. *The New Politics of Poverty: The Nonworking Poor in America.* New York: Basic Books, 1992. Focuses on extent to which segments of the poor population have become dependent on governmental sources of income and other benefits as well as the extent to which these government programs discourage or diminish the work ethic and thereby exacerbate the problems they are meant to ameliorate.

Patterson, James T. *America's Struggle Against Poverty, 1900-1985.* Cambridge, Mass.: Harvard University Press, 1986. Explores how and why Americans, especially authorities on poverty and welfare, have altered their fundamental assumptions about the good society during the industrial and postindustrial age. Notes that major shifts in social philosophy occurred in 1930, 1960, and 1965.

Rodgers, Harrell R., Jr. *Poor Women, Poor Children: American Poverty in the 1990's.* 3d ed. Armonk, N.Y.: M. E. Sharpe, 1996. Highlights the plight of America's poor single-parent female households and includes chapters on the feminization of poverty, the social welfare response to female-headed family poverty, and ideas for reforming the American welfare system.

Richard K. Caputo

Cross-References

Culture of Poverty; Gender Inequality: Analysis and Overview; Industrial and Postindustrial Economies; Racial and Ethnic Stratification.

POWER ELITE

Type of sociology: Social stratification
Fields of study: Dimensions of inequality; Politics and the state

In 1956 C. Wright Mills introduced the notion of the power elite—the interconnected leaders of political, economic, and military institutions in American society. This analysis offers insightful explanations for many realities of life in the modern world, including the formation of opinion and the structure of class relations in the contemporary United States.

Principal terms

COERCION: removal of resistance through the exertion of power

CONTROL: power used against the relatively powerless in such a way that the exertion of power removes any possibility of choice from those affected

CO-OPTATION: the power elite's acceptance of credentials of power groups from other parts of society (for example, former military officers may be accepted on corporate boards)

INFLUENCE: power that affects others with probable but not determinable outcome, as seen in forms of persuasion and propaganda

POWER: ability on the part of a person or group to affect human thought, action, and disposition despite resistance

POWER ELITE: group of persons in power who control parallel social institutions and lead them as connected interests

Overview

The concept of a "power elite" in modern American society involves the idea that the leaders of a combination of economic, political, and military institutions together wield tremendous power and control over society. Each of the separate institutions within these areas of society possesses its own ruling class. Formal groups of Pentagon officials, including generals, admirals, and appointed officials, govern the military hierarchy. Likewise, boards of directors provide both leadership and control for the large corporations that dominate the economic sphere, along with institutions such as the securities markets, the Federal Reserve Board, the banking system, major pension funds, and other large sources of capital. Within politics, elected officials join with career bureaucrats and other appointees to direct the national government. Each of these institutions creates its own elite group of leaders, and each of these elite groups exercises considerable power and influence over a variety of affairs within American society.

Sociologists have identified a high degree of overlap among these distinct elite groups, and C. Wright Mills, in his influential book *The Power Elite* (1956), coined the term that has been widely used to describe them. The power elite concept points to several characteristics of the overlapping elite groups. The members of the power elite tend to share many life experiences, such as education and class notions of responsibility. Many of them know one another, even across institutional lines. For example, politicians and corporate executives not only create policies that affect one another's institutions but also socialize together, share loyalties to the same schools, join the same clubs, attend the same functions, and contribute to the same causes. Also, members of the power elite possess extensive personal resources in addition to their control over larger societal resources.

As the power elite in the United States has grown in influence, traditional institutions such as family, education, and religion have assumed lesser roles in determining values and orientations. In the case of education, advanced degrees do not confer or limit membership in the power elite. Even when certain affiliations arise between graduates of certain universities (especially Ivy League law schools), more importance may well be attached to membership in certain campus clubs reserved for elites than to factors such as academic performance and degrees earned. Likewise, regional concerns diminish in comparison with the national (and international) perspectives of the elites, who tend to be urban (or suburban) rather than rural in their perspectives.

The presence of a power elite correlates with the creation of celebrity. Some persons attain high celebrity and name recognition through their personal wealth, their corporate leadership, their political position, or their military prominence. Again, this celebrity is related not to any sort of objectively measured "success" but rather to power and influence. The corporate chief executive officer (CEO) who turns the highest profit ratios is not necessarily a member of the power elite, but the chairs of the largest corporations probably are. Similarly, politicians do not receive celebrity for high efficiency or great service, but instead for their ability to persuade and influence others with power. Celebrities become well known throughout the culture, both inside and outside their particular group of institutions. For example, many Americans do not know the names of their own senators or congressional representative, but most could name several prominent politicians from other states who have attained the celebrity accorded those members of the power elite who seek it.

The American power elite forms an entrenched class of leaders. Though celebrity attaches itself to many of them, most work behind the scenes, attaining celebrity for only brief periods of time if at all. Examples include a corporate lawyer who wields extensive power over decades but gains fame only during a cabinet appointment late in life. Even though partly enshrouded, the power elite controls most sectors of social existence. The interlocking nature of the power elite allows for interchange between different sorts of institutions, maintaining and strengthening the power of each. This co-optation of elites from one field to another furthers the connections between different sectors of power.

In theory, the United States government contains a series of checks and balances. The typical understanding of government that emphasizes checks and balances between different branches of the federal government, however, fails to recognize the interlocking nature of political, economic, and military power throughout the society. The same economic entities that exert direct financial influence on the lives of many citizens not only participate in the military-industrial complex but also donate sizable funding to the political campaigns of congressional and presidential candidates. This reduces the effectiveness of any true balances within the political system itself. At the same time, the power elite fractures the nonpowerful classes into dispersed minority interests. This appearance of pluralism obscures the power of the elite, who often exercise their power subtly through the creation of a mythical "common interest" of the majority, against which the minority interests are doomed to fail. Such a common interest often does not reflect the wishes of any true majority but instead serves as an expression of the power of the dominant group. The mass media, controlled by the same interlocking forces of the power elite, play an increasingly significant role in the creation of such "majority" opinion. They become lenses that control public perceptions of reality and create public desires. This in turn creates "public opinion."

Applications

Since the Civil War, the United States has provided the clearest example of a power elite. As Alexis de Tocqueville had noted in 1835, early American society was highly mobile, functioning on the basis of loose affiliations rather than strict class systems. While this was true for the first century of the United States' existence as a nation, the late nineteenth century saw a variety of changes. The earliest American middle class consisted of small business owners who worked for themselves as independent proprietors. Throughout the second half of the nineteenth century, the middle class shifted. Corporations grew, and economic monopolies arose to take control of vast market segments. With the growth of corporations came the existence of numerous white-collar jobs that paid enough to maintain middle-class incomes but denied mobility into the upper class. Instead, the new middle class became dependent upon corporations for its continuation. Concurrent with this change, organized labor gained in influence. The unions allowed a more significant political and economic role for groups of the lower class and lower middle class, offering a new voice for those segments of society with inadequate resources to form their own businesses. The dependent middle class and the influence of organized labor tended to cancel each other out, allowing room for the enhanced growth of the power elite at the expense of both.

In the 1930's, President Franklin Delano Roosevelt's New Deal expanded the welfare state, increasing government involvement in all economic aspects of American society. This replaced traditional laissez-faire economics with a financial situation more closely controlled by the power elite. Thus, these governmental changes combined the economic and political institutions of power. Shortly thereafter, the war economy of the World War II years produced a political and economic dependence on military production. Once the military expanded its power into the economic and political arenas, the power elite became thoroughly entrenched. Whereas President Dwight David Eisenhower decried the "military-industrial complex" that had taken over the economy and the society, C. Wright Mills emphasized the problem of the military-economic interests allying themselves with the political status quo in Washington, D.C.

A further example of the influence of the power elite can be seen in twentieth century American educational systems. The power elite combines political, economic, and military interests, making other social institutions subservient. Thus, education serves the interests of the power elite as well. Private schooling provides a place for members of the upper class to meet while they are children and adolescents, forming the basis for permanent alliances of power and for strategic marriages and other affiliations. Public education claims to increase the values of common citizenship, but too often such education emphasizes acceptance of the reality of life, increasing the power of the status quo and the present power elite. Throughout the history of the United States' public educational system, there has been no increase in the sophistication or participation of the electorate in public debate. Instead, the growth of a "conservative mood" (Mills's phrase in *The Power Elite*) has marked the acceptance of society's status quo. Such a conservative mood holds that tradition is sacred and upholds the position of the power elite. It provides ideological undergirding for the society as it stands. Education as the transmission of tradition thus enhances the values of the power elite and their influence over society.

In addition to these forms of socialization that ease the propagation of the power elite's assumed rule, the cross-pollination of the elite institutions tends to enhance the insulation of the power elite. As elite groups co-opt elites from other societal sectors, the leaders appear more and more alike, increasing the dependency on a small number of elites. Thus, corporation boards become interlocking directorates in which individuals may belong to a number of executive bodies, each doing favors for others and tending to keep the same people in power. Likewise, political leaders tend to favor graduates of certain schools; the institutions then gain influence and provide power to their graduates. For example, President John F. Kennedy had strong ties with the governmental policy programs of Harvard University. Similarly, President Bill Clinton, upon election, immediately employed large numbers of Rhodes scholars. Mutual experience becomes an important commonality forming the power elite through personal affiliation and shared loyalties to the alma mater, but this process also increases the power of elite educational institutions.

Context

C. Wright Mills's development of the concept of the power elite followed earlier notions of power systems within American society and reacted against them. Alexis de Tocqueville had provided an early statement on American power; he emphasized the affiliational elements and the possibility of social mobility. Despite the great degree of accuracy in his description of the postrevolutionary United States, de Tocqueville's analysis had grown seriously out of date as power became more entrenched in the hands of a few and as social mobility declined. During the early twentieth century, other notions of power had become prevalent. Conservative theorists often devised conspiracy theories that rooted power in devious groups of hidden actors working for personal gain. Mills, however, argued that the United States is ruled by a class or group of power elites with interlocking but not synonymous goals. At the same time, liberal theories of power emphasized the importance of common people and thus the impotence of power groups to affect public opinion. Mills asserted the naïveté of such positions and demonstrated that these views obscured and justified the true nature of power in American society.

The notion of the power elite also drew on other social concepts. Against many eighteenth century social theories, the power elite model assumes the irrationality of social actors, seeing them as influenced more by power than by thought. This incorporates essentially

Freudian ideas about human behavior into a larger model of social action and organization. Likewise, the power elite model assumes that ideas about reality are socially conditioned. Because members of the power elite occupy social positions of influence, they can affect people's assumptions about reality and thus enhance their own capacity for power.

Power elite models maintain a certain popularity within sociology, and they are evolving as studies continue. These models will need to give greater attention to the processes by which power elites reorganize themselves internally and to the related processes by which the power elite brings about (and reacts to) social change. The power elite joins disparate groups from different social institutions such as politics, the economy, and the military; not all elites are equals. Not all elites experience the same opportunities for upward mobility or horizontal mobility into other social institutions. Thus, the internal organization of the elites needs further study. At the same time, some power elite models tend toward static functionalism, overemphasizing the ability of elite groups to maintain their systems of privilege. This overstatement can limit understanding of how elites not only cause change but also must react to changes in the social situation.

Studies of power have produced more recent concepts of power than Mills's, and power elite models still need full integration of these views. For example, many theorists now assert that power is interactive and relational; this view challenges the idea of a separate, autonomous power elite. The specific relationships between the elites and their constituencies need further study, with special attention paid to the means by which the populace participates in the relationships of power. Refinement of power elite models must explore further the distinction between the elites' use of power and their potential for power, since these are not equivalent phenomena. Furthermore, sociology should investigate the role of ideology in producing, maintaining, and changing the power elite. Ideological issues are especially important in understanding the role of the media in forming public opinion and in influencing the opinions and attitudes of the elites themselves.

Bibliography

Giddens, Anthony. *The Constitution of Society: Outline of the Theory of Structuration.* Berkeley: Calif.: University of California Press, 1984. One of the major theorists of the late twentieth century, Giddens connects power with the larger theory of structuration, which is the process by which social structures develop. This roots power and the existence of a power elite within a larger context of social change and development. Provides an important neofunctionalist interpretation of social structures such as the power elite.

Lenski, Gerhard E. *Power and Privilege: A Theory of Social Stratification.* New York: McGraw-Hill, 1966. Perhaps the most influential study of power of the 1960's, arguing that position and private property are the only two sources of power. Shows the roots of the power elite.

Lukes, Steven, ed. *Power.* New York: New York University Press, 1986. Essays providing easy access to many of the key writings in contemporary discussion of power and thus offers a good introduction to the issues in the current evaluation of power elite models.

_____. *Power: A Radical View*. London: Macmillan, 1974. Essential discussion of the connections between power and conflict, interpreting instances of power as disclosures of latent conflict. He also analyzes power as an interpretation placed upon certain events, since the attribution of power depends on the unprovable counterfactual assumption that something else would have happened had power not been exercised.

Mills, C. Wright. *The Power Elite*. Afterword by Alan Wolfe. New York: Oxford University Press, 1999. Most important study on the power elite, a concept that Mills was first to articulate. Provides strong analysis of the different segments of elites within the power elite and gives excellent descriptions of the process of the power elite's historical development in American society.

Olsen, Marvin E., and Martin N. Marger, eds. *Power in Modern Societies*. Boulder, Colo.: Westview Press, 1993. Mix of both contemporary and historical theoretical articles and case studies within American society and other worldwide examples. It provides an excellent first resource for understanding the power elite and the wider context of theoretical approaches to social power.

Prewitt, Kenneth, and Alan Stone. *The Ruling Elites: Elite Theory, Power, and American Democracy*. New York: Harper & Row, 1973. Updates Mills's classic work through a number of methodological refinements, including a better integration of Marxist theory and a strong critique of democratic notions. They emphasize political and ideological dimensions, perhaps to the detriment of economic issues.

Tocqueville, Alexis de. *Democracy in America*. Translated by Henry Reeve. New York: Schocken Books, 1961. First published in 1835, classic study of social structure, power relationships, and the high degree of social mobility in the postrevolutionary United States. The author, a French observer of American society, offered many first-hand anecdotes to support his assertions of high mobility and voluntary associations within the culture.

Zweigenhaft, Richard L., and G. William Domhoff. *Diversity in the Power Elite: Have Women and Minorities Reached the Top?* London: Yale University Press, 1999.

Jon L. Berquist

Cross-References

Capitalism; Conflict Theory; Legitimacy and Authority; Political Sociology; Social Stratification: Analysis and Overview.

PREJUDICE AND DISCRIMINATION
Merton's Paradigm

Type of sociology: Racial and ethnic relations
Field of study: Theories of prejudice and discrimination

Prejudice refers to an unfavorable attitude toward certain individuals or people by virtue of their being members of a particular racial or ethnic group. In contrast, discrimination refers to an overt action, such as the denial of opportunities and equal rights to the members of that particular racial or ethnic group. Merton's paradigm shows that prejudice does not always lead to discrimination and suggests that discrimination is not always directly caused by prejudice.

Principal terms

ETHNIC GROUP: group distinguished by its common ancestry and cultural heritage

ETHNOCENTRISM: tendency to judge other people's behavior and values on the basis of one's own culture, which is usually considered superior

IN-GROUP: group to which an individual belongs and feels loyalty

INSTITUTIONAL DISCRIMINATION: denial of opportunities and equal rights to individuals or groups, resulting from the normal day-to-day functioning of a society

MINORITY GROUP: subordinate group whose members receive unequal treatment and have unequal access to society's resources

OUT-GROUP: group composed of people who are not members of one's in-group and are considered outsiders

SOCIAL DISTANCE SCALE: a technique for measuring the degree of one's tolerance for different people according to how close to or far from one's own group they are

STEREOTYPE: oversimplified or exaggerated and shared negative belief concerning the characteristics of members of a group (such as an ethnic, racial, or religious group)

Overview

"Prejudice" and "discrimination" are crucial terms in the study of race and ethnic relations. In general discourse, they are often used as if they were interchangeable, but they actually denote distinct phenomena. Prejudice involves attitudes, thoughts, and beliefs about members of different groups (such as ethnic, racial, religious, or political groups). Discrimination, on the other hand, is action, either overt or subtle, that treats members of different groups differently. Prejudice may be expressed in various ways, as through negative terms, slurs, or jokes that denigrate members of ethnic or racial groups. Prejudice may also be expressed in discriminatory actions—hence the popular linkage between the terms. Discrimination may take overt forms, as in an employer's refusal to hire an Italian American or African American because the employer thinks that all people of Italian or African descent are incompetent, basing this perception on stereotypes rather than on an objective appraisal of the applicant's qualifications. Discrimination also appears in the form of institutional discrimination or racism, which is a denial by society's institutions of opportunities and equal rights to individuals or groups; this type of discrimination may be unintentional. A crucial point, and one that was long unrealized, is that individual prejudice does not necessarily express itself in discrimination; moreover, discrimination may result from causes other than prejudice.

Sociologist Robert K. Merton proposed a typology or paradigm in 1949 regarding the relationship between prejudice and discrimination. Merton's work was influential in clarifying these distinctions and in expanding the definition of discrimination to include institutional and unintentional discrimination. This paradigm appeared in an article entitled "Discrimination and the American Creed." Merton attempted to show that, although prejudice and discrimination are related, one does not necessarily cause the other. Merton identified four categories of people according to how they rate on a scale of prejudicial attitudes and discriminatory behavior.

The "unprejudiced nondiscriminators," or "all-weather liberals," are low in both prejudice and discrimination. People in this category usually believe firmly in the equality of all people, and they try to practice this belief. Yet committed as they are to equality, they often do have some shortcomings, according to Merton. For one thing, the all-weather liberals tend to be removed from reality, in the sense that they do not experience face-to-face competition from members of minority groups for limited resources.

The second category consists of "unprejudiced discriminators," whom Merton also calls "fair-weather liberals." Fair-weather liberals are low in prejudice, but they tend to discriminate against other people when it is expedient, as when it is profitable to do so. In Merton's words, this person's expediency

> may take the form of holding his silence and thus implicitly acquiescing in expressions of ethnic prejudice by others or in the practice of discrimination by others. This is the expediency of the timid: the liberal who hesitates to speak up against discrimination for fear he might lose status or be otherwise punished by his prejudiced associates.

In South Africa, for example, under the rigid racial caste system of apartheid that existed until 1994, many whites who themselves were not prejudiced remained silent about the injustices of apartheid, under which the white minority maintained privileges and absolute control over society. The fair-weather liberals did not condemn the system simply because they were benefiting from it.

The third category of Merton's paradigm involves people who do not believe in equality. These are "prejudiced nondiscriminators," whom Merton identified as "fair-weather illiberals" and called "timid bigots." They discriminate if there is no sanction against it; their discriminatory practices are situational. In the early 1930's, social scientist Richard LaPiere conducted a study in which he traveled in the United States with a Chinese couple to see how much discrimination they would encounter; prejudice against Asians was still quite strong at that time. LaPiere and his companions received warm treatment at nearly all motels, hotels, and restaurants they visited; only once were they refused service. Six months later, LaPiere sent a questionnaire to all the establishments, asking whether they would accept Chinese people as guests or customers. To his surprise, more than 90 percent of the responses revealed prejudiced attitudes and said that they would refuse service to them. This is a clear example of how prejudice does not necessarily translate into discrimination. A similar test was conducted in the 1950's with a black couple, and similar results were obtained. People seem to be able to adjust their actions and attitudes according to what sociologist W. I. Thomas called the "definition of the situation."

The final category in Merton's paradigm is the "prejudiced discriminators," also called "active bigots." These people are high in both prejudice and discrimination. They openly express their beliefs and do not hesitate to discriminate publicly. Sociologist Thomas F. Gossett presented a good example of such people, noting that in 1932 a white Southern Baptist refused to sit at a banquet table at a meeting because a black person was present. Since court decisions and civil rights legislation in the 1950's and 1960's outlawed discrimination, active bigots in American society have found it more difficult to practice individual discrimination. Hate groups such as the Ku Klux Klan, for example, continue to espouse their prejudiced views, even on national television, but when evidence of discriminatory actions is uncovered, legal cases are filed against the perpetrators. According to the social distance scale, active bigots tend to show a high degree of intolerance for, and unwillingness to accept, members of out-groups such as racial and ethnic minorities.

Applications

The use of Merton's paradigm has enabled the development of many insights into the complexity of the problems of prejudice and discrimination. It has, for example, pointed to the possibility that many unprejudiced people are struggling with the issue of discrimination, particularly if they are surrounded by, and influenced by, prejudiced people. Particularly since the late 1950's, discrimination has been confronted in a number of arenas. With the major focus that has been applied to prejudice and discrimination, both in sociology and in intense debates over public policy, many people have become more aware of their own prejudices. Many nongovernmental institutions, including church organizations, have explored various means of confronting prejudice. Since the 1980's, the focus has expanded beyond the issues of black and white prejudice to include the diverse spectrum of racial and ethnic groups in the United States in efforts to promote understanding and reduce prejudice. Workshops on diversity and the educational emphasis on multiculturalism are representative of this trend.

The application of Merton's paradigm to discussions of how different types of people act or react with regard to discrimination has shed light on a number of behaviors. For example, it has been revealed that some people choose to minimize their social contact with members of society's out-groups even though they consider themselves to be unprejudiced nondiscriminators. Sociologist Vincent Parrillo has called this "social discrimination," which also refers to the creation of "social distance" between the individual and minority group members. This type of social discrimination is applied not only to racial and ethnic groups but also to a number of other groups, including the elderly, poor people, and people with acquired immune deficiency syndrome (AIDS). The observation of such behavior being applied to such disparate groups has made it apparent to some experts that there is probably no single approach that can deal effectively with prejudice or discrimination. A combination of approaches is necessary; among the approaches that have been used are legal methods (including affirmative action).

Legal approaches to combating discrimination are sometimes opposed by people who argue that laws cannot effectively regulate morality or control personal habits and attitudes. Although there is much truth in this argument, there is also truth in the argument that many changes which have occurred in the United States, particularly in the education system, have occurred because of legal action. The 1954 Supreme Court decision in *Brown v. Board of Education*, which ended segregation in public schools, is a prime example. Because of the policy of segregated schools, seven-year-old African American student Linda Brown had to walk about two miles to an all-black school even though there was a white school only five blocks from her house in Topeka, Kansas. When the case reached the Supreme Court, it ruled that segregated schools were inherently unequal, thus overturning the 1896 decision that "separate but equal" facilities were acceptable. This decision wrought profound changes in American education—and in American life in general—as it gave a new force to the growing Civil Rights movement. It should be noted, however, that although segregation is illegal, many schools are still unofficially segregated because of residential patterns, a condition referred to as de facto segregation (segregation "in fact" rather than sanctioned by law).

Since the 1980's, many organizations and companies have been encouraging their members or employees to take diversity workshops or undergo sensitivity training in an attempt to counter prejudicial attitudes and discriminatory behavior. Many examples can be found of ways that prejudices affect perceptions. A television news crew in Minnesota, for example, conducted a four-month study of the security personnel who monitor stores to observe shoplifters. They found that many of the security personnel, because of their own prejudices and stereotypes, targeted African Americans for observation. As a result, records from these stores showed that African Americans were overrepresented among shoplifters. When store officials were confronted with this information by the observers from the news team, some immediately dismissed the security people who were watching only African Americans. The store officials believed that the security personnel had violated company policy. Some of the store owners and officials noted that the situation indicated a need for sensitivity training. This study suggests ways that discrimination can occur and ways that it can be attacked.

Context

Sociologists and other scientists have been interested in the study of race and race relations since the 1920's. Racism and ethnocentrism have been among the central issues studied. Sociologist William Sumner is credited with coining the term "ethnocentrism" to describe the tendency for people to view their own group as the best. In-groups tend to view the race, ethnicity, and culture of out-groups as being inferior to those of the in-groups. Sociologists in the first half of the twentieth century saw a link between ethnocentrism and prejudice. For example, members of an in-group may express their dislike of an out-group by using stereotypes to rationalize their views: "I don't like black people because they are lazy," for example, or "I don't like Jews because they are stingy." Columnist Walter Lippmann described stereotypes in 1922 as "pictures in our heads" that have no scientific evidence to support them. The study of stereotypes has helped in the redirection and refinement of efforts to overcome discrimination.

Between the 1920's and the 1960's, two of the prominent subjects in studies of race relations were immigration and assimilation. Debates on these issues were highly charged. Prejudicial overtones often crept into the discussion. Prejudiced attitudes were expressed in discriminatory practices such as campaigns to restrict immigration because certain immigrants were seen as lacking the desirable characteristics of the in-group. Restrictive immigration policies targeted certain racial and ethnic groups, such as Asians, Africans, Hispanics, and people from certain parts of Europe. It was not until the mid-1960's that restrictionist sentiments in the law were reduced. The Immigration and Nationality Act of 1965 eliminated the system of quotas based on national origin, which discriminated against certain nationalities. The 1965 law did not eliminate discriminatory practices, but it did attempt to confront some of the prejudice of the past which had been codified into law.

The assumption of many people before the 1940's that prejudice was the single cause of discrimination was challenged when Merton introduced his paradigm in 1949. Since the 1950's, both social scientists and civil rights activists have made marked progress in confronting discrimination. Instead of focusing only on prejudice as the cause of discrimination, many scholars and activists have broadened their perspectives. Prejudice and discrimination have been viewed in various lights and attacked in various ways. Activist Paula Rothenberg, in her work *Race, Class, and Gender in the United States: An Integrated Study* (1992), brings to light various facets of prejudice and discrimination. She also calls attention to the use and internalization of words that subtly perpetuate prejudice, such as "culturally deprived" and "underdeveloped," which tend to be misleading as well as reflective of the attitude that only the dominant culture is acceptable and others are inferior. Awareness of how language can perpetuate prejudice and discrimination is another way of confronting the problem of racism. A broad analysis of the ways prejudice and discrimination actually exist in society, as in the case of Merton's paradigm, shifts the focus from blatant and intentional expressions of racism to all forms of discrimination—some unintentional, some incorporated into the institutions of society—in the day-to-day functioning of society.

Bibliography
Doob, Christopher Bates. *Racism: An American Cauldron*. 3d ed. New York: Longman, 1999. Concise examination of racism in American history. Useful for both college and general audiences, providing insights into racism and how it influences individuals' behaviors and attitudes without their being aware of it.

Feagin, Joe R., and Clairece Booher Feagin. *Racial and Ethnic Relations*. 6th ed. Upper Saddle River, N.J.: Prentice-Hall, 1999. Introductory text on important basic concepts and theories as well as various social and ethnic groups. It also provides research current at the time of publication on various topics, including prejudice and discrimination.

Gossett, Thomas. *Race: The History of an Idea in America*. New York: Oxford University Press, 1997. First published in 1963, rich in historical background on the American racist ideology and its influence in all social institutions.

McLemore, S. Dale. *Racial and Ethnic Relations in America*. 3d ed. Boston: Allyn & Bacon, 1991. Introductory work on minority groups; well-documented and footnoted summaries of research studies.

Marden, Charles F., Gladys Meyer, and Madeline H. Engel. *Minorities in American Society*. 6th ed. New York: HarperCollins, 1992. Valuable text on minorities and the prejudice and discrimination they face in American society.

Marger, Martin N. *Race and Ethnic Relations: American and Global Perspectives*. 2d ed. Belmont, Calif.: Wadsworth, 1991. Introductory text taking broad and comparative approach. Themes of prejudice and discrimination are especially well presented throughout as they apply to various social and ethnic groups.

Merton, Robert K. "Discrimination and the American Creed." In *Majority and Minority: The Dynamics of Race and Ethnicity in American Life*. Edited by Norman R. Yetman. 4th ed. Boston: Allyn & Bacon, 1985. Collection of essays on issues pertaining to racial and ethnic relations. Merton's own essay introduces his paradigm, demonstrating that discriminatory behaviors are not always directly related to individuals' negative attitudes or prejudices.

Rothenberg, Paula S. *Race, Class, and Gender in the United States: An Integrated Study*. 2d ed. New York: St. Martin's Press, 1992. Well-written book on the consequences of racial, class, and gender prejudice and discrimination. One of the best integrated texts on racism, sexism, and classism. The author presents many examples of direct and indirect individual and institutional discrimination and sexism.

Schaefer, Richard T. *Racial and Ethnic Groups*. New York: HarperCollins, 1992. One of the best introductory texts on racial and ethnic minorities. The author presents the research evidence of consequences of inequality resulting from prejudice and discrimination against minority groups. The discussion of theories and basic concepts is very good.

Rejoice D. Sithole

Cross-References

Cultural and Structural Assimilation; Gender Inequality: Analysis and Overview; Protestant Ethic and Capitalism; Race Relations: The Race-Class Debate; Racial and Ethnic Stratification.

PREJUDICE AND STEREOTYPING

Type of sociology: Racial and ethnic relations
Fields of study: Basic concepts of social stratification; Theories of prejudice and discrimination

Prejudice consists of negative attitudes toward certain groups and members of groups based on classifications such as gender, race, and religion. Stereotyping is rigidly believing that individuals have certain traits simply because they belong to a particular group. Discrimination, often fueled by prejudice and stereotypical thinking, is behavior that leads to the denial of basic rights and opportunities.

Principal terms

DISCRIMINATION: denial of basic rights and/or opportunities for economic, personal, or social advancement based on variables such as race, gender, age, and disability

HATE CRIMES: crimes of violence toward or degradation of others prompted by extreme prejudice against them, because of their race, gender, sexual orientation, or religion

IN-GROUP/OUT-GROUP DISTINCTIONS: tendency to look favorably on actions of people like oneself and to attribute negative motives to the same actions by people outside one's group

MULTICULTURAL EDUCATION: educational approach that strives for inclusivity and fairness regarding the contributions of all cultures and races, and both genders, to society; it sometimes challenges the dominant culture's views

PREJUDICE: belief (a "prejudgment") about people, often entailing dislike of all members of a particular group, such as an ethnic or religious group

STEREOTYPE: inflexible, generalized belief about the attributes of all members of a particular group

Overview

Prejudice, stereotyping, and discrimination are three closely related but distinct phenomena. Prejudice is literally a "prejudgment"—a belief about something or someone that is based on assumptions rather than on actual experiences. Strictly speaking, a prejudice may be either for or against something, but in common usage it refers to a dislike of all the members of a particular group, such as a racial, ethnic, religious, gender, or age group. Sociologist Gordon Allport defined prejudice as "an antipathy based upon a faulty and inflexible generalization." A crucial point is that a prejudice is an attitude, not a behavior.

A stereotype might simply be defined as one of the "inflexible generalizations" to which Allport referred. Stereotyping is the attributing of certain characteristics to people simply on the basis of their membership in a group. Stereotypes are oversimplified and rigid mental images; they may contain a "kernel of truth," but that kernel is overwhelmed by the false generalization that has grown around it. One of the interesting things about stereotypes is that people tend to continue to believe them even when they are presented with evidence that refutes them. People often discount their own observations, shrugging them off as "exceptions to the rule." Stereotypes therefore can be extremely persistent.

Discrimination, in contrast to prejudice, refers to behavior: the denial of basic rights and/or opportunities to members of certain groups based on such surface variables as race, age, gender, religion, or disability. An interesting finding of a number of studies of prejudice and discrimination—and one that surprised the researchers who first noted it—has been that prejudicial attitudes do not necessarily result in discriminatory behavior. Many people who state their dislike of a particular ethnic group, for example, in practice treat them with equality and civility. Moreover, discrimination can have causes other than prejudice; institutional discrimination may be unwittingly practiced by people working for institutions who are unaware that their policies and actions are discriminatory. Nevertheless, prejudice and the stereotyping that helps reinforce it can lead to discriminatory behavior as well as to the commission of hate crimes and other harmful, violent, and even fatal acts.

Prejudice and stereotyping have led to the sociological phenomena of exclusion and, in some cases, elimination of certain groups from "mainstream" society. In the United States, for example, a combination of prejudice and economic greed led to the near extinction of the American Indian population, the previous mainstream culture of the Americas, between the seventeenth and twentieth centuries. Other groups, such as women, African Americans, Hispanics, and Asians, have also felt the brunt of prejudice at various times in the history of the United States. The effects of prejudice, such as the discrimination that it can produce, are destructive both to the individuals who suffer violence or psychological harm as a result of discrimination and to the integrity of society as a whole.

A number of sociological theories have speculated about the causes of prejudice. Socialization—the process of teaching people (particularly as children) the knowledge and attitudes of a group or society—has been implicated as a cause of prejudice. Adults in society pass their prejudicial beliefs on to impressionable children. Thus, prejudicial attitudes are learned. Another theory on the cause of prejudice involves the principle of relative deprivation; relative deprivation is the gap between people's expectations and their actual condition or situation. When people see themselves as relatively deprived, they experience frustration and may look for scapegoats on which to blame their situation (a situation that is usually a result of a number of interrelated, complex causes). Historically, minority groups such as women or ethnic minorities have been "scapegoated," or blamed for someone else's economic or social misfortunes. A number of sociologists have also observed that competition increases prejudice, stereotyping, and discrimination. Muzafer Sherif, a sociologist, conducted studies showing how boys at a boys' camp could learn prejudice very quickly. The boys became biased and hostile when they were divided into groups and intergroup competition was introduced into their activities.

Social conformity is another concept that has been used to explain the cause of prejudice. Social norms—the expectations for behavior in a culture—define what kinds of behaviors or attitudes are acceptable. Thomas Pettigrew demonstrated this idea in the 1950's when he found that people from the South became less prejudiced toward African Americans when they were in the army. The army had norms that accepted blacks, so prejudice and discrimination were reduced in that social context. Robert A. Baron, a social psychologist, has written about theories that hypothesize conditions in which prejudice may occur. Baron (as well as many others) believes that periods of economic hardship and scarce resources can contribute to the occurrence and intensity of various types of prejudice. In the field of social psychology, this premise forms a part of what is known as "realistic conflict theory."

A growing body of research illustrates that class status has a profound effect on both influencing and buffering prejudicial beliefs and expectations. The interdisciplinary text *Race, Class, and Gender: An Anthology* (1992), by Margaret Andersen and Patricia H. Collins, contains a variety of articles that illustrate the intricate interplay of race, class, and gender in human experience. The text notes, for example, that racial and ethnic bias has been found to exist even among mental health professionals, a group of professionals who should, by definition, be objective and neutral in their work.

A critique of the various theories concerning the causes of prejudice suggests that there is no one single cause for the perpetuation of prejudice. Rather, sociologists believe that prejudice and stereotyping are socially determined and that multiple methods of transmission are involved. Prejudice may be said to be "multidetermined."

Applications

Research has provided a number of classic studies demonstrating the effects of prejudice. Kenneth Clark and Marie Clark, for example, conducted a study on preschool children's color preference regarding dolls. This study, published in 1947, showed that even very young African American children preferred "white" dolls to those with their own skin color. This study was among those cited in a "friend of the court" brief that was consulted by the Supreme Court in 1954 when it decided, in *Brown v. Board of Education*, that segregated schools could no longer be allowed.

In the 1970's, Jane Elliot conducted an experiment with elementary schoolchildren in which she instructed the brown-eyed children to sit in the back of the room and told them they could not use the drinking fountain. Blue-eyed children were given special privileges such as extra recess time and extra lunch helpings. The two groups of children were told not to interact with each other. Elliot belittled and berated the brown-eyed children, and their academic performance faltered. The favored blue-eyed group soon became even more belittling to the brown-eyed children than the teacher was. After several days, roles were reversed, and the negative effects of prejudice were repeated. Eventually all the children disliked one another, demonstrating the destructive effects of status inequalities.

Prejudicial attitudes regarding people with disabilities (a category including more than 36 million Americans in 1986) have been found to be an insidious form of misunderstanding. In American society, those with emotional or learning disabilities (the "invisible disabilities") often face misunderstanding and discrimination because of ignorance, perpetuation of myths, and social ostracism. People without disabilities have demonstrated lack of empathy, avoidance of social interaction, lack of eye contact, and lack of respect for those with disabilities. In reality, most people with physical disabilities have been found to have strong self-concepts and good social interaction skills and have often been more able to provide support to others than the other way around.

An aspect of stereotyping that has concerned many observers through the years and has outraged a number of groups (particularly since the Civil Rights movement of the 1960's and the women's movement of the 1970's) has been the stereotypical portrayals of minorities in the mass media. Motion pictures and television, particularly, have a tremendous effect on helping shape people's perceptions and attitudes. In the early years of film, it was tacitly assumed that the audience was primarily composed of white Americans, and members of minorities were nearly always depicted in stereotypical roles—such as a meek, timid "Chinaman" or, in the words of communication theorist Douglas Kellner, "eye-rolling, foot-shuffling, drawling" African Americans, "usually in the role of servant or clown." This pattern repeated itself half a decade later when television began. Particularly in visual media, pulling on old stereotypes was handy for writers or performers because they involve a sort of shorthand—comically depicting a hard-drinking, fighting Irishman, a shrewish housewife, or a foot-shuffling black person called up a host of associations and permitted a writer or performer to get laughs easily. A number of advocacy groups have adamantly protested such stereotyping, and blatant negative stereotypes in the media have been reduced significantly. Yet new stereotypes arise nearly as soon as old ones fade.

An interesting and surprising study on the media and ethnic images was done by S. Robert Lichter and Linda Lichter, codirectors of the Center for Media and Public Affairs in Washington, D.C., in 1988. They found that youth in the Howard Beach area of New York, even after the considerable turmoil there that had surrounded what was thought to be a racially motivated murder of a black youth by whites, felt positively about ethnic characters in the media. They also found that some (about one-third) of their sample of 1,200 high school students of various ethnic backgrounds said that there were negative stereotypical images of ethnic groups on television, but the students believed that these images were largely countered by positive role models also appearing on television.

A combination of factors, including the health care crisis of the 1990's and a fear of the disease itself led to prejudice and discriminatory actions toward victims of the acquired immune deficiency syndrome (AIDS) epidemic. The fact that the early rise of the disorder was associated with homosexual behavior and intravenous drug use also biased people against members of those populations. Even though, by 1993, a higher percentage of new AIDS cases was reported in teens, women (especially minority women), and their infected infants, the original prejudices proved difficult to correct. An advocacy group for people with AIDS called AIDS Coalition to Unleash Power (ACT-UP) was formed in 1987 to take more dramatic measures in order to call national attention to the serious epidemic of AIDS.

In the educational arena, efforts have taken the form of the development of prejudice-reduction programs, disability awareness programs, and workshops and intensive efforts directed at developing a multicultural curriculum at all levels of education. The book *Teaching a Psychology of People: Resources for Gender and Sociocultural Awareness*

(1988), edited by Phyllis A. Bronstein and Kathryn Quina, discusses the refinement and inclusion of a multicultural approach to psychology. Another important text is *Issues in Diversity: Voices of the Silenced* (1990), edited by sociologist Mary Stuck.

A wide variety of social supports, both formal and informal, have been created to combat prejudice and stereotyping. Some cities have established programs that celebrate diversity, and they hold festivals and ethnic heritage events that are open and inclusive to all people. Colleges have held "Rainbow Months" in their dormitories in celebration of cultural and ethnic diversity and have presented seminars and workshops on prejudice and issues such as sexual harassment. Corporations also hold antibias workshops and some have begun to set a tone that even subtle discrimination or harassment based on gender or ethnicity will not be tolerated.

New Jersey's Ethnic Festival in Jersey City, is an example of a communal program to celebrate ethnic and cultural diversity. *(Chimera Photos)*

Context

It is widely thought that persecuting others is not innate but rather is a learned behavior; nevertheless, the effects of prejudice and stereotyping have been observed since time began. In medieval Europe, and later in the United States, many women fell victim to religious persecution and were executed for being witches. Those scapegoated included some who were homeless, some who only had a "sharp tongue," and some who were probably mentally ill. All told, this period of religious persecution, led by religious male patriarchs of the time (representatives of the church), resulted in thousands being tortured and put to death. A key thesis underlying this massive persecution and application of prejudice was that the Roman Catholic Church feared women's sexuality. This prejudice was so strong that everything from bad crops to miscarriages was blamed on certain women.

In the nineteenth and twentieth centuries, prejudice against women and various racial and ethnic groups has both persisted in large segments of the population and been opposed by groups fighting for their rights. The fight to gain legal rights and social equality for women, for example, has been ongoing. Prejudicial and stereotypical beliefs about women, including the beliefs that they were possessions of men and that their proper sphere was shaping the moral climate of the home, were quite strong. They were thought of as not being capable of pursuing higher education. Women began to fight for their rights, however, winning the right to vote in 1920. Many of the gains women have made since the 1960's in terms of educational achievement and economic pay equity have their origins in the women's movement's fight against stereotypes and prejudice.

Social psychologist Gordon Allport wrote *The Nature of Prejudice* (1954), considered a classic book on prejudice. It elaborates Allport's approach to prejudice, an approach consistent with contemporary perspectives because of the emphasis on cognitive factors such as categorization and cognitive bias. According to Allport, there are two forms of prejudice, personal prejudice and group prejudice. Allport's model involves in-group and out-group distinctions. In an extension of Allport's theory, Thomas Pettigrew proposed the "ultimate attribution error" in an article he published in 1979. Pettigrew suggests that people tend to look favorably on the actions of people in their in-group (those whom they perceive to be like them) and attribute negative motives to the same actions by out-group members. If an in-group member observes a negative act by an out-group member, the in-group member is likely to attribute the action to genetic causes or some other concrete factor. If, on the other hand, an in-group member observes a *positive* act by an out-group member, he or she may attribute it to luck, being an exception to the rule, high motivation and effort, or the particular situational context in which the behavior occurred.

In the areas of health, mental health, and people with disabilities, several relevant advances have occurred since the early 1980's. In the late 1980's, educational information about the AIDS epidemic was sent to every household in the United States in the form of a brochure to inform the public about the ways the virus is transmitted. This concerted effort was necessary because of the number of myths and biases that people held about the disease and its transmission, including a belief that only homosexual behavior would expose someone to the disease. Social stigmatization and negative stereotypes can have far-reaching consequences. Fewer than one-third of the children in American society who have a diagnosable mental illness receive psychological or psychiatric treatment, perhaps in part because of a fear of negative stereotyping or labeling.

Bibliography

Allport, Gordon W. *The Nature of Prejudice*. Cambridge, Mass.: Addison-Wesley, 1954.
Classic social psychological book on prejudice, with an emphasis on cognitive factors such as categorization and normal cognitive bias.

Andersen, Margaret, and Patricia H. Collins, comps. *Race, Class, and Gender: An Anthology.* 3d ed. Belmont, Calif.: Wadsworth, 1998. Interdisciplinary collection that integrates race, class, and gender into the overall framework of prejudice, oppression, and discrimination. Excellent for its first-person accounts.

Baron, Robert A. *Social Psychology: Understanding Human Interaction.* 7th ed. Boston: Allyn & Bacon, 1994. Popular undergraduate social psychology text with excellent chapter on prejudice and discrimination. Explores social categorization, intergroup conflict, cognitive sources of bias, and stereotypes.

Freeman, Howard E., and Norman R. Kurtz, eds. *America's Troubles: A Casebook on Social Conflict.* Englewood Cliffs, N.J.: Prentice-Hall, 1969. Well-written study of issues of prejudice in American society with many first-person accounts that bring home the significant impact of bias on individuals, groups, and society.

Lips, Hilary M. *Sex and Gender: An Introduction.* 3d ed. Mountain View, Calif.: Mayfield, 1997. Thorough review of myths, theories, and research regarding sex and gender. Also explores behavior and experiences of males and females, comparing similarities and differences. Sex and gender are examined in social relationships, political life, and the workplace.

Stuck, Mary, ed. *Issues in Diversity: Voices of the Silenced.* Acton, Mass.: Copley, 1990. Carefully chosen articles that review historical and sociological phenomena related to the problem of oppressed groups in American society.

Thomas, Gail E. *U.S. Race Relations in the 1980's and 1990's.* New York: Hemisphere, 1990. Explores issues involving racial stratification and education, occupational mobility, economics, and cultural pluralism; special attention is paid to the neglect of the problems of the American Indian population.

Karen M. Wolford

Cross-References

Cultural and Structural Assimilation; Gender Inequality: Biological Determinist Views; Prejudice and Discrimination: Merton's Paradigm; Racial and Ethnic Stratification.

PROTESTANT ETHIC AND CAPITALISM

Type of sociology: Major social institutions
Fields of study: The economy; Religion

Sociologist Max Weber described the "Protestant ethic" as a religious perspective which advocates hard work, sobriety, financial prudence, and deferred gratification. He concluded that this religious perspective helped the capitalist economic system to develop in Western societies such as England and the United States.

Principal terms

ASCETICISM: characteristic of the Protestant ethic that stresses the self-denial of worldly pleasures in favor of religious principles

BREAKTHROUGH: Weber's term for historical periods in which circumstances push a group either toward a new way of action or toward a reaffirmation of traditional ways

INSTITUTION: stable social arrangement, including values, norms, statuses, and roles, that develops around a basic need of a society

LEGITIMATION: set of beliefs, values, and attitudes (often religious) that attempts to explain and justify existing social conditions and inequalities

PREDESTINATION: John Calvin's Protestant doctrine which stated that all individuals are born into (and must forever remain in) one of two groups, the Elect or the Damned

THEODICY: religious explanation that provides believers with a meaningful interpretation of everyday events, including traumatic events such as personal suffering and death

Overview

The sociological study of religion focuses on the measurable social consequences of religious beliefs and institutions for individuals and for society as a whole. German sociologist Max Weber's interest in the sociology of religion was extremely wide ranging. He studied both Eastern and Western religions, including Judaism, Christianity, Islam, Hinduism, and Confucianism. His most widely known work in this area, however, involves his theory that the tenets of Protestantism helped enable the growth of capitalism.

In relating religious ideas to the growth of capitalism, it should be noted that although industrial capitalism in England and the United States during the nineteenth century is usually regarded as the model for laissez-faire capitalism, some features of capitalism existed much earlier in the commercial activities of the preindustrial European economy. Weber writes about the emergence of capitalism at a time when commerce was conducted by many small firms owned by individuals or families rather than by large corporate organizations.

In his writings, Weber reacted strongly against the analysis of religion in capitalist societies suggested by another influential theorist of his time, Karl Marx. Weber's unique perspective can be better understood by noting that to Marx, religion was simply an ideology, a set of beliefs and values that attempts to legitimate (explain and justify) the economic exploitation of the majority of workers by the capitalist class. Using religion as an ideological tool, the capitalist class is able to convince the majority of workers that their lack of power, prestige, and wealth in society is somehow divinely sanctioned. Marx concludes that, like a drug, religion distracts and pacifies the masses with its promises of a better life in the hereafter. In this way, the capitalists maintain their control over society and the social class system.

In his work entitled *Die Protestantische Ethik und der Geist des Kapitalismus* (1904; *The Protestant Ethic and the Spirit of Capitalism*, 1930), Max Weber disagreed with the viewpoint that religion is only an ideology, although he acknowledged that religion can certainly be used as such by those in power. Instead, Weber argued that religious ideas themselves may change society rather than merely reflecting the way in which society is already structured economically and politically. Weber referred to historical periods in which this occurs as periods of "breakthrough." To demonstrate his theory, Weber found a historical example in the rise of Protestant Christianity and its effects on economic conditions in England and the United States.

A comprehensive, wide-ranging theory such as Weber's naturally engendered criticism and debate. For example, some have argued that secular developments in the areas of finance, commerce, and industry were also important in the rise of capitalism. Others have suggested that, contrary to Weber's analysis, ideas congenial to capitalism could be found among Roman Catholics of the time as well as among Protestants. To the first criticism, Weber is careful not to deny the existence of secular economic factors that contributed to the development of capitalism. Rather, his focus is upon the religiously grounded ideas which produced the intellectual and ethical "spirit" of capitalism. Regarding the second criticism, Weber does not insist that the human desire for economic gain began with capitalism. Instead, it took on new, more rationalized and systematic forms particularly among, but not exclusively among, Calvinist Protestants.

First, Weber studied occupational statistics in Europe and found that business owners and managers as well as the highly skilled workers in business enterprises were overwhelmingly Protestant. Through such research he discovered an important connection between religious beliefs and economic activities. How was it possible for religious ideas originating in the sixteenth century Protestant Reformation to help capitalist economics develop? There was no deliberate effort or plan involved; rather, a long, slow evolution of popular religious ideas among the general public took place over many years. Specifically, the ideas of two influential Protestant reformers came together in an unplanned, unanticipated manner.

One of these reformers, Martin Luther, opposed the Roman Catholic Church's insistence that only certain occupations (those directly associated with the Roman Catholic religion) could be considered legitimate in the sight of God. Luther proclaimed that honest, hard work in any occupation constituted one's "calling" by God and was therefore legitimate in the sight of God. This included secular occupations not related to any religion. According to this concept, performing work in one's calling was considered an inescapable moral obligation.

The Protestant reformer John Calvin proposed another radical idea: that all individuals are born into one of two groups, the Elect or the Damned. This doctrine, which was most powerful among the English and American Puritans, stated that an individual's fate in this world and in the afterlife (heaven or hell) was determined at birth. The Elect could be identified by their pious living and resultant material success while on Earth, and they were guaranteed salvation in an eternal heavenly afterlife. The Damned received none of these divinely determined benefits and could be identified by their lack of morality and their material poverty (because of which they deserved eternal damnation in the afterlife). Moreover, there was nothing an individual could do to change his or her eternal membership in one of these groups. Even doing a multitude of good works made no difference to the Calvinists. This idea became known as "predestination."

Weber notes that one significant economic effect of Calvinism in areas where it was dominant was that it reduced charity for those who begged or did not work—such individuals were seen as members of the Damned, and their poverty was assumed to be divinely ordained. For example, social welfare programs among the English Puritans were designed not so much to reduce human suffering as to discourage the allegedly slothful.

The cumulative effect of these two doctrines as they became widespread in the population in the decades and centuries following the Protestant Reformation was to create a deep sense of anxiety and uncertainty. Obviously, no one wanted to be one of the eternally damned, and how to determine one's own membership in the Elect or the Damned was unclear. According to Weber, what emerged from this psychologically distressing situation was the "Protestant ethic." Over many decades, these ideas about one's calling and predestination converged, and individuals came to believe that hard work and attaining material success in one's calling were moral obligations; moreover, having material prosperity was a sure sign that one was a member of the Elect. Put differently, material affluence and success in the secular world were viewed as divine rewards for hard work in one's calling (occupation) and as proof that one would be rewarded in the afterlife as well.

Weber also discussed the strong sense of self-denial (asceticism) and deferred gratification found in the Protestant ethic. Well illustrated by the English Puritans in the latter half of the seventeenth century, it meant that leisure, spontaneity, socializing, luxurious living, and even excessive sleep were considered sinful. Only hard, continuous physical or mental labor was considered a worthy activity in the sight of God. If one did accumulate personal wealth, it should not be flaunted or spent on frivolous personal pleasures or self-aggrandizement. As a result, wealth was typically saved and reinvested in the businesses owned by individuals, thus concentrating wealth and strengthening such businesses. When practiced on a large scale in society, this reinvestment of wealth (capital) encouraged capitalism to grow and flourish in Western societies.

Applications

Weber's conclusions have many implications for American society. For many Americans, the Protestant ethic (sometimes simply called the "work ethic") provides a strong motivation for honest, hard labor in one's chosen occupation. Weber's theory also enables one to identify the Protestant ethic at work in everyday events, as well as its use by political leaders and its impact on attitudes toward poverty and the poor.

The modern "work ethic" in American society has lost much of its originally religious meaning and become a common secular concept; this development was also predicted by Max Weber. In showing how the ideas in Protestantism contributed indirectly to the rise of modern capitalism in Western societies, he acknowledged that advanced capitalist societies would become self-sustaining and would no longer require such religious justifications. In other words, once capitalistic practices become widespread, standardized, and institutional-ized in the economy, they become self-perpetuating regardless of their original source.

Even so, both mainstream and Fundamentalist Protestant churches still emphasize the virtues of hard work and tend to assume that material success is a sign of God's reward for such work. Popular television evangelists often go so far as to interpret their acquisition of material wealth publicly in this manner. In addition, the notion of finding or accepting one's calling in life is commonly expressed in religious circles and is frequently used as an explanation for everyday behavior and activities among believers.

The influence of the Protestant ethic is not confined to religious groups and individuals. It also plays a role in American politics. Sociologist Robert Bellah has described the often blurry line between church and state in the United States as a case of "civil religion." Civil religion includes religious beliefs regarding the past, present, and future of the United States as a nation. It generally expresses a nondenominational conviction that Americans are a God-fearing people and that God favors their country. In everyday life, civil religion includes religious statements found on U.S. currency, in oaths of office, at political party conventions, in courtroom procedures, and at nearly all formal public ceremonies. Civil religion has a strong Protestant ethic component. For example, religion is typically used by political administrations and political candidates as a way of legitimating American society and the capitalist economic system. Conservative political leaders who are critical of government assistance to the poor often appeal to the work ethic as a justification for cutting social services for those who are not working.

Another important effect of the Protestant ethic has been its impact on prevailing societal attitudes toward wealth and poverty. For example, once hard work and obtaining material prosperity are defined as moral obligations, those who do not or cannot succeed in the economic system are often stigmatized as being sinful as well as poor. This viewpoint is often found among those who advocate abolishing welfare and other social services for the poor. This attitude represents an ironic historical reversal, in that Christianity originated among the poor and was hostile toward the worldly pursuit of wealth and power. In those earlier times, the pursuit of wealth was morally suspect and was often regarded as a threat to the soul. In modern capitalist societies, the poor are doubly stigmatized in that they may be seen as morally inferior to the wealthy.

In analyzing the relationship between religion and economics, Weber used the concept of theodicy—a religious interpretation of life events that provides believers with an emotion-ally satisfying, meaningful explanation. Theodicies provide a sense of meaning or purpose for otherwise chaotic and distressing life events by placing them in a larger religious context and suggesting that, in the long run, things are as they should be. According to Weber, theodicies vary according to the socioeconomic status of the groups that subscribe to them. For example, a theodicy of dominance is often found among elites or rulers. This type of theodicy tends to explain and justify their possession of power, prestige, and wealth in society. It might, for example, claim that the present leaders have a "divine right" to govern. A theodicy of mobility is often found among middle-class members of society. It may state in some fashion that hard work and piety will lead to worldly success and great rewards in the afterlife. Finally, a theodicy of escape is common among the poor, oppressed, and outcast. In such theodicies, those with wealth and power are often viewed as sinful or corrupt, and emphasis is placed not on achieving worldly success in the present but on personal salvation and eventual rewards in the afterlife.

By using the concept of theodicy, Weber linked the individual with the larger society and with concrete, identifiable social conditions. He concluded that religion serves to legitimate both the powerful and the powerless, both the wealthy and the poor in society.

Context

Max Weber, Karl Marx, and Émile Durkheim are often regarded as the three founders of the discipline of sociology. All three theorists lived between 1818 and 1920, and all wrote extensively about the nature and effects of religion in society. Although each came to different conclusions, their theoretical perspectives continue to influence contemporary sociologists, including those who specialize in the sociology of religion.

The historical period in which Weber wrote was filled with political turmoil and conflicting theories about human behavior and the nature of society. Like other scholars, Weber studied the prevailing ideas of his time and reacted to these conflicting ideas, especially to the ideas of Karl Marx.

Of the three classical sociological perspectives on religion that emerged during this time, the theories of Durkheim and Marx were quite different from that of Max Weber. For example, as the most conservative of the three, Durkheim's theory argued that religion holds society together by morally unifying its members and increasing their sense of community. All other social institutions, including the economic system, depend on the common acceptance of religious beliefs and values. On the other hand, Marx insisted that the opposite was true regarding the economic system. He argued that religion as it existed at his time was an outgrowth of the capitalist economic system, an ideological institution that attempted to explain and justify the economic exploitation of the majority of people in society.

To these two contrasting theories, Weber added a third alternative for understanding the impact of religion in society. Weber argued that religion is not always an ideology of society's rulers and that religious ideas themselves may change society. In this way, Weber changed the course of the sociological study of religion forever. His interests included not only religion but also other sociological concerns such as the nature of authority, social stratification, and bureaucracy. In all of his writings, Weber identified a trend in modern societies that he called "rationalism." In the case of economics, this meant that economic activities are based not on custom or tradition but on deliberate, calculated efforts to achieve profits. In the case of religion, it meant that the practice of magic has been replaced by religious organizations with standardized rituals and formal doctrines.

Bibliography

Allport, Gordon. *The Individual and His Religion*. New York: Macmillan, 1970. Classic, nontechnical study of individual religiosity and its associated personality characteristics. Includes the important distinction between intrinsic and extrinsic religion. Allport suggests that for many individuals, religion is used to further secular self-interests.

Berger, Peter. *The Sacred Canopy: Elements of a Sociological Theory of Religion*. Garden City, N.Y.: Doubleday, 1967. Short but incisive analysis of religion as a socially constructed reality. Discusses vital concepts such as theodicy, alienation, legitimation, and the secularization of the modern world. Best suited to college readers.

Campbell, Joseph. *The Power of Myth*. New York: Doubleday, 1988. General, interview-style book captures the lifelong insights of a philosophy professor as he discusses the importance of myths and religion in all cultures. He argues that even modern capitalist societies such as the United States need nonempirical explanations of human nature and the universe.

McGuire, Meredith. *Religion: The Social Context*. 4th ed. Belmont, Calif.: Wadsworth, 1997. Introductory college-level text providing overview of major concepts, theories, and perspectives in the sociology of religion. Includes sections on Weber, Marx, Durkheim, and modern theorists.

Weber, Max. *The Protestant Ethic and the Spirit of Capitalism*. Translated by Talcott Parsons, with a foreword by R. H. Tawney. New York: Charles Scribner's Sons, 1958. Definitive statement of the Protestant ethic by Max Weber, first published in 1904. Provides Weber's alternative to the Marxian view of religion and its place in modern society. Parsons adds summaries of Weber's major ideas and extensive chapter notes.

_____. *The Sociology of Religion*. Reprint. Boston: Beacon Press, 1972. Best suited to the college level, this book goes beyond the Protestant ethic to include Weber's complete perspective on world religions, such as his theory on the origins of religion and concepts of supernatural beings, types of religious prophets, and the concept of theodicy and its relationship to different social classes.

Mark W. Weigand

Cross-References

Capitalism; Civil Religion and Politics; Industrial and Postindustrial Economies; Industrial Sociology; Religion; Religion: Functionalist Analyses; Religion: Marxist and Conflict Theory Views; Socialization: Religion.

QUALITATIVE RESEARCH

Type of sociology: Sociological research
Field of study: Basic concepts

Qualitative research involves research techniques that allow investigators to study the special and unique aspects of human interaction. These techniques, while they do not allow for generalizations to other settings, allow scientists to uncover more detailed nuances of the behavior under study than is possible when using quantitative research methods such as surveys.

Principal terms

CASE STUDY: detailed study of a particular individual, group, or situation; a combination of research techniques may be used to describe the "case"

DATA: information collected or observed that is relevant to the research question under study

ETHICS: rules and guidelines that guide the research and work of professionals; ethics in the social sciences are primarily concerned with protecting the rights of the human subjects being studied

NORMS: learned rules and expectations that influence human interaction and individual behavior

RESEARCH DESIGN: plan followed by a researcher to structure data collection and analysis

SAMPLE: smaller group taken from a population for research purposes; the goal of sampling is to make generalized statements about the larger group (population)

SOCIAL SCIENCES: behavioral sciences, including sociology, anthropology, political science, psychology, and economics; these sciences are differentiated from the "natural" or "physical" sciences in that their subject of study is the group or individual behavior of human beings

Overview

As a research science, sociology relies on both qualitative and quantitative techniques of observation. The essence of the discipline implies a precise investigation of the environmental factors that influence how (and why) humans interact in patterned ways. Qualitative researchers employ specific techniques including participant observation, case study, content analysis, ethnography, and in-depth interviewing. Qualitative research is distinguished from "quantitative" research in that quantified (numerically based) research involves hypotheses testing, data collection, data analysis, statistics, and generalizations from samples to populations. Qualitative research, on the other hand, allows description of the unique. Case study analysis, for example, allows examination of the many complicated elements of a particular group or situation; qualitative research permits an understanding of human interaction. The lack of formal hypotheses in qualitative research does not negate the scientific contribution, significance, or value of such research.

One poignant example of qualitative research is the book *Savage Inequalities: Children in America's Schools* (1992), written by Jonathan Kozol, a former teacher in Boston and other urban and suburban school systems. The text was a series of case studies of schools in the affluent and diverse United States of the early 1990's. Kozol pinpointed and described some of the severe problems associated with the demise of urban public education in the last half of the twentieth century. He delineates race-based funding disparities, deteriorating resources, teacher and administrative apathy, white flight, and instances of political corruption in the face of increasing school failure.

According to the *Oxford American Dictionary*, a "quality" is "something that is special in a person or thing." Qualitative research is designed to unravel social events or situations in order to reveal the particular and the idiosyncratic. On the most basic level, qualitative investigation involves observation of situations that interest one personally; in this sense, most people have engaged in qualitative social research all their lives. Targets of observation in the social sciences include deviance, gangs, riots, religious movements, and the mass media. Some of the techniques sociologists utilize in their qualitative research have been borrowed from the field of anthropology. The most common form of observation is "participant observation," which forces the "objective" researcher, much like an anthropologist studying a foreign culture, to become subjectively and physically engaged in the phenomenon of scientific interest.

The level of involvement in a participant observation study varies widely. Sociologist Laud Humphreys, in a study published in 1970 as Tearoom Trade: Impersonal Sex in Public Places, studied casual and transient sexual encounters among male homosexuals in sites called "tearooms." He was able to learn much about the social characteristics and lifestyles of male homosexuals by becoming marginally involved in their activities. (Humphreys volunteered to serve as the lookout in the public restroom used as a tearoom.) His study was widely criticized because of its second phase: He actually identified and contacted the households of the research subjects. He was accused of being unethical, because he obtained the license plate numbers of the cars by which some of the males left the scene. By tracking the identity of the participants through the police and by surveying households, he found that most of the males lived as heterosexuals. Some were married and lived with their wives and children. In that he located the names and addresses of the men, Humphreys violated their individual rights (and the ethics of social science) by subjecting them to possible prosecution, blackmail, divorce, or embarrassment. Even though he took special precautions to protect the privacy of the men, he nevertheless placed them at risk. Another danger of participant observation is that of "going native"; the observer may become obsessed with the research context and become fully engaged in the activity, forgetting about the research goals. Passive observation is similar to participant observation except that this method constrains the researcher to remain detached (by distance, one-way mirrors, or other approaches) from the research setting, thus avoiding some of the pitfalls of participant observation, such as loss of scientific objectivity, possible physical danger, and changes in the research setting because of the presence of an outsider.

From the perspective of sociologists, qualitative research methods such as participant observation allow one to ascertain cause and effect or to describe some behavior or phenomena. The qualitative description of what transpires between and among members of society provides the details necessary to an understanding of social behavior and therefore of society. Other forms of social research (such as large statistical or survey research) tend to neglect or miss some of the details which form the "social fabric" of norms and values that help to regulate human interaction.

In a study first published in 1943, sociologist William Foote Whyte compiled a fascinating case study of an Italian slum neighborhood near New York City. He demonstrated that such working-class, urban neighborhoods maintained a social structure that influenced behavior. This study helped sociologists to recognize the fact that poor neighborhoods were not simply "disorganized" but were alienated from the mainstream in ways that helped to maintain high rates of poverty and deviance.

Content analysis is a research method that provides a vehicle for measuring "the amount of something" within various mass media productions. The method is appropriate for studies of television programming, recordings, books, letters, speeches, radio talk shows, news articles, and works of art. The "something" measured may embrace the themes presented in the work, the numbers of persons with certain characteristics, the words, expressions, stereotypes, or points of view expressed. The type of analysis performed varies from a mere enumeration (quantification) of the occurrences of a word or concept to a subjective thematic analysis and interpretation of various works.

Semistructured interviews are less specific or standardized than the types of interviews used in quantitative research; they provide sociologists with the flexibility to ask research subjects follow-up questions that they might not have anticipated prior to the interview. "Probes" may be used to induce discussion. New topics can be discussed; these might take the research project in a new and different direction. Serendipitous findings such as these sometimes create breakthroughs in knowledge not possible when the researcher's preconceived ideas are used to formulate research and interview questions.

A form of qualitative research which may involve either passive or participant observation is ethnography. According to James Spradley's *Participant Observation* (1980), "Ethnography is the work of describing a culture. The central aim of ethnography is to understand another way of life from the native point of view." This technique, which originated in anthropology, may also be used to study diverse groups within a given society.

This combination of research techniques adds another dimension to the quantitative work of sociologists. Many social problems and issues require research grounded in the cultural subtleties of human behavior and social interaction. While quantitative research maintains its importance in the discipline, qualitative methods complement statistics, experiments, and surveys in many important ways, thus providing sociologists with insights they would have missed if they had confined themselves solely to quantitative research methods.

Applications

Sociologists and other social scientists use qualitative research to look beneath the veneer of acceptable behavior in society. The complexities of human interaction are usually difficult to interpret unless one is familiar with the cultural rules and sociological contexts that constrain the persons involved. Zora Neale Hurston, an anthropologist, novelist, and writer, conducted qualitative research on African American and African Caribbean cultures (folklore and belief systems) during the 1930's and 1940's. She was one of the first researchers able to document specific folklore and religious practices of African Americans; many of these practices had "survived" the trek from Africa to North America and the Caribbean. One such study, *Tell My Horse* (1938), was an ethnographic investigation of African survivals and adaptations in Jamaica and Haiti. A similar Hurston study, *Mules and Men* (1935), was published as a collection of tales and essays on African Americans living in the southeastern United States.

Erving Goffman, an eminent sociologist, performed a content analysis study of advertisements involving men and women that was published as *Gender Advertisements* (1979). The ads indicated not only the mindset of the producers and directors of commercial advertising but also the attitudes and images the public maintains about gender groups and gender relationships. Goffman treats the ads as ritual displays of societal attitudes toward men and women. The "ideal representation" of women (and other minorities) presents them as limited, in need of support, emotional, vulnerable, and subordinate. These displays both reflect and influence societal attitudes and behaviors associated with relationships between the sexes. One common ritual found in advertising is the "mock assault." This pretend attack is said to convey not only an image of playfulness but also of the implied threat of what could happen if the male exhibiting the behavior were actually to assault the "victim." Another ritual display is the head or body "cant" (bend or tilt) that projects an image of persons (usually women) as dependent, less than serious, and nonthreatening as a result of their nonvertical posturing.

Context

The historical context of qualitative research methods stems from classical sociology and the discipline of anthropology. Émile Durkheim (1858-1917) was a French sociologist who helped to take sociological investigation from a philosophical endeavor to one grounded in science. Much of his research and writing addressed the issue of how society (social forces such as rules, laws, or traditions) controls the individual. He helped to establish a perspective in sociology that concentrated on the consequences or "functions" of social phenomena. This concentration was employed by anthropology and contributed heavily to the field of sociology. Ethnography and participant observation began as research methods in anthropology and were later adopted by sociologists such as Whyte and Humphreys.

A pioneer of the case study method in sociology was W. E. B. Du Bois. His *The Philadelphia Negro: A Social Study* (1899) was one of the first empirical or scientific studies published in sociology. Du Bois's manuscript was an advance which demonstrated the importance of the case study (including census data) as a way of unraveling and interpreting social behavior and social problems. Content analysis was used by John Naisbitt in the book *Megatrends: Ten New Directions Transforming Our Lives* (1982). After monitoring several thousand local newspapers, Naisbitt was able to describe some of the major trends in American society.

Given the vast importance of culture in today's globally interdependent and diverse world, qualitative research methods are becoming increasingly necessary. These techniques will allow human groups (within and between societies) to understand each other and to interact in less violent ways than in the past. Such techniques will also help to provide solutions to social problems that are more relevant and more effective than some of the solutions of the past.

Bibliography

Berger, Arthur Asa. *Media Analysis Techniques.* 2d ed. Thousand Oaks, Calif.: Sage Publications, 1998. Handbook on research techniques geared to mass media. Readable and contains specific techniques on how to use each research method.

Coser, Lewis A. *Masters of Sociological Thought: Ideas in Historical and Social Context.* New York: Harcourt Brace Jovanovich, 1977. Study of classical sociologists from Auguste Comte through Florian Znaniecki. Provides insights and details on their personal lives, intellectual influences, theories, and social contexts of each major theorist in the classical era of the discipline.

Du Bois, W. E. B. *The Philadelphia Negro: A Social Study.* Philadelphia: University of Pennsylvania Press, 1899. A case study of life among working-class African Americans based on participant observation and survey research in Philadelphia circa 1895. One of the first empirical studies completed and published in sociology.

Goffman, Erving. *Gender Advertisements.* New York: Harper & Row, 1979. Analytical study of how gender is portrayed in advertisements. Goffman, as one of the major proponents of the sociological paradigm called "symbolic interactionism," used his insight to describe how gestures and other symbols are used to portray and interpret how women and men feel about each other.

Humphreys, Laud. *Tearoom Trade: Impersonal Sex in Public Places.* Chicago: Aldine, 1970. Case study of male homosexual encounters in a public restroom ("tearoom"). The study involved participant observation, tracking the identities of the males observed, and survey research to describe their lifestyles..

Hurston, Zora Neale. *Mules and Men.* Reprint. Bloomington: Indiana University Press, 1978. Collection of African American folklore and religious practices which was the initial publication of such material. The data were collected through informal interviews and participant observation. First published in 1935.

Kozol, Jonathan. *Savage Inequalities: Children in America's Schools.* New York: Harper-Perennial, 1992. Highly readable and insightful series of case studies of urban and suburban schools in American cities. Written by a former teacher, the book provides useful data on the decay of public education in America, fueled by racism, corruption, political neglect, and changes in the American economy.

Moore, Joan W. *Going Down to the Barrio: Homeboys and Homegirls in Change.* Philadelphia: Temple University Press, 1991. Ethnographic study of two Chicano street gangs in East Los Angeles. Uses a sociological framework to contextualize the behavior of two particular gangs. Even though random sampling survey techniques were part of the research design, qualitative methods were used to derive the sample. Gang cliques were located as part of a collaborative study of gangs undertaken by former gang members and social scientists.

Spradley, James P. *Participant Observation*. New York: Holt, Rinehart and Winston, 1980. Textbook on participant observation methodology, techniques, and issues. Includes several well-written articles on the different phases and problems associated with this technique of data collection.

Whyte, William Foote. *Street Corner Society: The Social Structure of an Italian Slum*. 4th ed. Chicago: University of Chicago Press, 1993. Investigation of life in an Italian, working-class neighborhood. With the assistance of a local guide, Whyte investigated the complicated behavior and social structure of the neighborhood.

Bruce H. Wade

Cross-References

Ethnography; Quantitative Research; Samples and Sampling Techniques; Sociology Defined; Surveys.

QUANTITATIVE RESEARCH

Type of sociology: Sociological research
Field of study: Basic concepts

Quantitative research attempts to categorize and summarize observations through the assignment of numbers. The numbers generated from this kind of study are frequently presented using descriptive statistics.

Principal terms

CONTENT VALIDITY: type of experimental validity determined by whether an experiment measures a property that it is intending to measure

DESCRIPTIVE STATISTIC: type of statistic used to summarize and describe existing data; calculations of the median and the mode represent descriptive statistics

EMPIRICISM: method for acquiring knowledge about the world through direct observation and experience

EXTERNAL VALIDITY: quality that enables the generalizing of results from a limited sample of subjects to a larger population

INFERENTIAL STATISTICS: statistics used to apply data obtained from a small (sample) population to a larger population

OPERATIONAL DEFINITION: specific description of a variable that will enable it to be measured; it outlines the precise steps or operations for other researchers to use in assessing the variable

RELIABILITY: ability of an instrument to measure a variable or construct consistently over repeated measurements

RESEARCH HYPOTHESIS: specifically worded statement or prediction that can be verified or falsified through the collection of data; a tentative answer to a research question

SCIENTIFIC METHOD: method for acquiring knowledge that is characterized by systematic observation, experimentation, experimental control, and the ability to repeat the study

Overview

The discipline of sociology has evolved into a well-defined body of knowledge that is composed of both factual information regarding specific areas of content and theories that attempt to organize and systematize what is currently known. In order for sociology to grow and evolve as a discipline, it must be continuously infused with new ideas. Not only is new information important for the development of sociology, but there must be a refinement of the methods and tools that are used to acquire new knowledge. One method used by social scientists that contributes to this discovery process is called quantitative research.

Quantitative research, in its most basic form, is a research strategy that attempts to assign numbers to characteristics in order to quantify specific observations that have been made. It is an epistemological approach that is closely aligned with empiricism and the scientific method. This relationship can be seen from the emphasis that quantitative research places on studying phenomena that can be directly observed. Similar to the scientific method, quantitative research strives for objectivity, systematic observation, and the analysis of quantifiable information.

Quantitative research is an approach to studying behavior that entails a series of steps. This process begins with the formulation of a statement or prediction called a research hypothesis. The research hypothesis is a special kind of statement which must meet two criteria. First, it must be verifiable. That is, once data have been collected, the data can be found to either support or falsify the research hypothesis. Second, it must be specific. It needs to clearly delineate what results would, in fact, support the hypothesis; otherwise it would not be possible to draw conclusions from the data.

Another step in conducting quantitative research concerns the emphasis placed on the measurement of variables. This step implies that a variable chosen to be studied has been adequately defined. For example, take the variable "altruism." Altruism can be defined in a number of different ways. One definition might be "concern for the welfare of others." Someone conducting quantitative research would ask the question, "How can we measure a person's concern for the welfare of others?" A specific type of behavior must be chosen that the researcher believes would adequately demonstrate an individual's concern for another person. The process of conducting quantitative research requires that altruism be operationally defined. That is, it must be defined in a way that makes it publicly observable; moreover, it must consist of a behavior or sequence of behaviors that can be both seen and recorded. The recording of an operationally defined variable most typically involves the assignment of numbers. In this case, different numbers would be assigned on the basis of differing degrees of altruistic behavior observed. Altruism could be operationally defined as the degree to which people offer assistance to a person standing on a highway next to a disabled car. A researcher could use a three-point rating system in which a score of 0 indicates that someone offered no assistance, a score of 1 indicates that someone stops and offers to call for help when arriving at his or her destination, and a score of 2 indicates that a subject offers to take the stranded person to the nearest telephone. Although this example is simplistic and by no means covers all possibilities, it demonstrates an attempt to quantify an abstract concept.

Quantitative research is characterized by the attention it gives to the topic of validity. When a researcher is conducting a study, it is important that the behaviors chosen to be observed and recorded do in fact measure the trait (or sociological attribute) that they are intending to measure. The ability of an operationally defined behavior to measure adequately what it is supposed to measure gets at the heart of content validity. Content validity is a necessary prerequisite for conducting good quantitative research. Another aspect of validity concerns the degree to which a study can obtain results from a sample of subjects and then generalize the results to a larger population. For example, if the results of a study conducted on five hundred college students from a single school can be generalized to students from nearby colleges, the study possesses external validity.

Reliability is equally important. Reliability refers to the ability of a study to measure accurately a variable over different time periods. For example, a researcher might want to study the concept "authoritarianism" using a pencil and paper test that is administered on more than one occasion. A subject might take the test and receive a score of 80 on a scale from 1 to 100. One week later, the same subject might take the test again and receive a score of 79. This test would be considered a reliable test (assuming that there had been no change in the actual level of authoritarianism in the person for that week), since it produced consistent scores over repeated testings. If, on the other hand, the second test had produced a score of 60, the discrepancy between the two scores would probably indicate that the instrument lacked reliability.

Quantitative research is also characterized by data analysis. Once the data collection is finished, the numerical information is summarized through the use of descriptive statistics. There are a number of ways to summarize data by using descriptive statistics. One such procedure involves calculating a measure of central tendency such as the arithmetic mean (average score)—one adds together all the scores and divides by the total number of scores. Another procedure would be finding the mode (the most frequently occurring score). It is also helpful to calculate a measure of variability that lets the researcher know how similar or dissimilar the scores are.

Another characteristic of quantitative research is that it uses probability theory to determine whether a research hypothesis is supported or unsupported. Basically, hypothesis testing leads to a probabilistic confirmation. To test a hypothesis, a researcher must determine how the variables expressed in the hypothesis will be measured, must make the necessary observations, must collect the data (usually in the form of numbers), and then must subject the data to quantitative analysis. Quantitative analysis attempts to summarize the vast array of numbers; it also attempts to determine whether the same results obtained in the study could also be obtained through random chance. This is accomplished through determining the probability of obtaining the results randomly. Therefore, quantitative analysis usually results in a probability statement in which the following rule applies: If the probability of obtaining the results of the study through random chance is extremely low, then the results are thought very likely to be attributable to the variables of the study. Either confirmation or falsification of the hypothesis would be presented in terms of a probabilistic statement.

Applications

A study by Robert V. Levine can be used to explore how quantitative research is implemented and how it can contribute to scientific knowledge. In his article "The Pace of Life," published in *American Scientist* (1990), Levine attempted to understand how different cultures perceive time. He suspected that attitudes toward time could impact the pace of life for a society and ultimately could lead to health problems in the form of hypertension and stress for its members. Levine was interested in testing the following research hypothesis: Cultures differ in terms of their general pace of life. This hypothesis was an outgrowth of Levine's consideration of the commonly held notion that some cultures move at different paces from that of the United States. American visitors to Japan, for example, frequently say they are overwhelmed by a faster pace of life than that in the United States

Levine chose to collect data from the largest city of six different countries: Japan, Taiwan, Indonesia, Italy, England, and the United States. To gauge the general pace of life of each country, he chose to study three unique objective indicators: the accuracy of outdoor clocks, the average time it took pedestrians to walk a distance of 100 feet, and the time needed for a postal clerk to complete a transaction that entailed selling stamps and returning some change. Notice that none of these measures relies on the subjective evaluations of pace of life by the person collecting the data. These indicators serve as multiple operational definitions for the construct "pace of life." In addition, the indicators are measures that can be easily assigned a number—another characteristic of quantitative research. Uninhibited walking speed and the amount of time it takes to complete a transaction at the post office both provide measures of how quickly people go about their business. The rationale behind measuring the accuracy of town clocks was somewhat different. Levine believed that the more a culture is driven by an adherence to time, the more accurate the public clocks in the culture will be. More time consciousness should translate into more accurate clocks.

These measures for pace of life fall on a scale of measurement known as a ratio scale. A ratio scale, such as time, is a scale that not only has equal intervals between different points on the scale (the amount of time between one and two seconds is the same as between nine and ten seconds) but also has an absolute zero point. Quantitative research assigns numbers to specific observations that fall on the ratio scale, interval scale (in which there are equal intervals between points, but there is no absolute zero point), or the ordinal scale (in which values can be ranked from highest to lowest). Levine preferred these particular "objective" measures to a survey approach, which might have required subjects to respond to how they "feel" about the pace of life. Thus, he was strongly concerned about the validity of the data he was collecting.

Standardized techniques were employed while collecting the data to ensure that the pace of life indicators would be measured fairly. For example, walking speed would not be measured if it was raining outside. Levine chose a covert approach to collecting data, since he did not want subjects to be aware that they were in a study. Levine thereby eliminated any bias that could be attributable to the subject's knowledge that he or she was in an experiment.

The data were collected primarily by Levine's students, who visited the countries during their summer recess from school. The data were analyzed using basic descriptive statistical procedures. Average scores for the accuracy of public clocks, the time it took people to walk 100 feet, and the completion of a postal transaction were calculated and compared across the different countries. Using probabilistic confirmation, Levine found that Japan had the fastest pace of life of all six countries; it scored the highest on all three measures. The United States came in with the second fastest pace, followed by England. Indonesia was last, having the slowest walkers and the most inaccurate clocks.

Levine extended this research by looking at associations between pace of life and both psychological and physical health. He found that the tempo of a society is significantly related to the prevalence of heart disease. In fact, the time-related variables often turn out to be better predictors of heart disease than psychological measures used to identify high-energy behaviors in individuals. He concluded that a person who chooses to live in a fast-paced city should take precautions to keep from becoming a time-urgent person. Living in a busy and stressful city, for example, can lead to unhealthy behaviors such as smoking and poor eating habits. It should be noted that, because Levine undertook a new approach in his study, a repetition of the study by other researchers would increase its credibility within the scientific community.

Context

From the beginning of humankind, people have tried to increase their understanding of the world they live in. Two approaches to acquiring knowledge that preceded the modern era were authority and rationalism. In the former, people simply accepted the words of an authority figure presumed to have inside knowledge of the topic at hand. The person could have been a priest or other societal leader. Rationalism was an approach to coming to an understanding of something through using individual reasoning skills in order to arrive at knowledge of the world. Both methods are still in evidence today in certain situations. In the scientific world, however, the scientific method has replaced such methods. This method is characterized by systematic observation, experimentation, and experimental control. Quantitative research grew out of the scientific method.

Quantitative research attempts to systematize and categorize data in order to provide as much objectivity to the data collection process as possible. The methods associated with conducting quantitative research emphasize objective data-gathering techniques and discourage casual or informal data gathering. Collecting data via informal methods can bring about a number of biases and errors. In his book *How We Know What Isn't So: The Fallibility of Human Reason in Everyday Life* (1991), Thomas Gilovich points out a number of cognitive, motivational, and social determinants that influence how people gather data and interpret the world. Informal methods can cause humans to misinterpret incomplete data. In addition, informal observers can be biased so that they see only the data they want to see. For these reasons, there has been a gradual move toward the use of more "objective" techniques, such as standardized rating scales, behavioral checklists, and structured surveys. These methods were created in order to quantify social science observations more accurately, thereby increasing the truthfulness of data. Once behaviors could be quantified, specific behaviors could be assigned numbers. They could be statistically analyzed to find real, rather than apparent, differences. This approach to data collection played a significant role in improving research practices in the social and behavioral sciences.

Bibliography

Baker, Therese L. *Doing Social Research*. New York: McGraw-Hill, 1988. General introduction to quantitative research, observational studies, data collection methods, survey research, and sampling techniques, as well as other topics that will help the reader discern good research from poor research.

Gilovich, Thomas. *How We Know What Isn't So: The Fallibility of Human Reason in*

Everyday Life. New York: Free Press, 1991. Marvelous book that educates the reader about how the human mind distorts information.

Judd, Charles M., Eliot R. Smith, and Louise Kidder. *Research Methods in Social Relations*. 6th ed. Fort Worth, Tex.: Harcourt Brace Jovanovich College Publishers, 1991. Broad overview of quantitative statistics. Chapters of particular importance include those on measurement, scaling, and laboratory research.

Katzer, Jeffrey, Kenneth Cook, and Wayne Crouch. *Evaluating Information: A Guide for Users of Social Science Research*. 3d ed. New York: McGraw-Hill, 1991. Excellent source on good quantitative research, as opposed to bad research. Written with a general audience in mind, it attempts to teach the important questions that need to be asked about research in order to assess its quality.

Levine, Robert V. "The Pace of Life." *American Scientist* 78 (September, 1990): 450-459. Levine describes his research on cross-cultural perspectives of time. The article provides a good example of quantitative research. It describes research done internationally and within different regions of the United States.

Pagano, Robert R. *Understanding Statistics in the Behavioral Sciences*. 5th ed. Pacific Grove, Calif.: Brooks/Cole, 1998. Excellent introduction to learning descriptive and inferential statistics. Only a limited mathematical background is necessary to read and comprehend most of the information in this text.

Singleton, Royce, Jr., Bruce Straits, Margaret Straits, and Ronald McAllister. *Approaches to Social Research*. New York: Oxford University Press, 1988. Well-written text on aspects of quantitative research such as selecting a research setting, gathering information, scales of measurement, and differences between quantitative and qualitative research.

Bryan C. Auday

Cross-References

Causal Relationships; Qualitative Research; Samples and Sampling Techniques; Sociology Defined; Validity and Reliability in Measurement.

RACE AND RACIAL GROUPS

Type of sociology: Racial and ethnic relations
Field of study: Basic concepts

Arguments have been advanced to support both biological and social concepts of race, but most scientists believe that race is a social concept rather than a biological reality. Subjective elements in the definition and categorization of races have helped allow such problems as racism and discrimination to continue.

Principal terms

AFFIRMATIVE ACTION: policy designed to redress past discrimination against minority groups by targeting them for recruitment into jobs and educational institutions

DISCRIMINATION: situation in which individuals are treated differently because they belong to a particular group

ETHNIC GROUP: group that is defined by cultural characteristics that are held in common, such as religion and language

RACISM: belief system that views groups of people (identified by various physical characteristics) hierarchically in terms of superiority and inferiority

SPECIES: naturally occurring population of organisms that is characterized by sexual cross-fertilization and outside which fertile offspring cannot be reproduced

SUBSPECIES: population within a species that exhibits variations from the larger species because of geographic and social isolation

Overview

Controversy and confusion surround the term "race" for a number of reasons. One central problem is that it has multiple meanings; another is that the term itself has become emotionally loaded, leading some experts to suggest abandoning it altogether. In the nineteenth and twentieth centuries, race has been viewed both biologically and socially. That is, some have argued that there are biologically distinct races with unique, identifiable characteristics. Others, however, have argued that the idea of race is not defensible scientifically and that the "racial" characteristics of humans exist in a continuum rather than as discrete groups. The taking of one or the other of these views leads to very different implications. Most scientists today favor a view of race as essentially a social construct.

Anthropologist M. G. Smith offers the following biological definition of race in his 1989 article "Pluralism, Race, and Ethnicity in Selected African Countries": "Races are biological divisions of mankind differentiated by gross phenotypical features which are hereditary, polygenic, highly resistant to environmental influences, distinctive and of doubtful adaptive value." Some scholars prefer such biological definitions of race because they view them as being objective. In this view, races are seen as naturally occurring groupings of humans who exhibit obvious physical differences from one another.

Anthropologist Ashley Montagu (one of those who dislike the use of the term "race") has stated that these differences result from isolation (geographic and social), the selection of mates with particular physical features, internal chemical changes in cells (genetic mutation), and the ability of mutants to adapt better to the environment (natural selection). Because all biological races belong to the same species, *Homo sapiens*, the racial groups that result from these forces can interbreed with one another. Thus, as biologist Theodosius Dobzhansky has stated, biological races are best regarded as subspecies, or variations on a common theme. (It should be noted, however, that many scientists classify modern humans as *Homo sapiens sapiens*, indicating that all modern humans belong to the same species and the same subspecies.)

Many scientists, however, view this conception of race as extremely problematic. First, there is the problem of deciding which criteria are to be used in distinguishing one race from another. The difficulty is that no single criterion (or even combinations of criteria) can conclusively separate humans into different races. The criteria that have most often been used to classify races are skin color, the shape and size of heads, noses and lips, hair color and type, and blood group. All of these criteria have failed as boundary markers for racial groups because exceptions can always be found. For example, skin color—the single most widely used criterion—seems at first to classify adequately the native population of Africa south of the Sahara as a distinct racial group, usually called Negroid. Populations in other parts of the world, however, have skin as dark, if not darker, than some Africans. Examples include the inhabitants of the southern part of the subcontinent of India and the Aborigines of Australia, yet neither of these groups is considered Negroid.

The African example raises another problem, that of how many races exist. A survey of the literature shows that no agreement on this number exists. For example, many people view Africans south of the Sahara simply as Negroids. Anthropologist C. G. Seligman has noted, however, that according to some definitions at least five distinct races can be found in this region. Another problem with the biological view of race is that even if it could be shown beyond any doubt that racial groups differ fundamentally with respect to their physical characteristics, there would still be the need to discover what significance, if any, such differences really have. Do these physical differences enable racial groups to cope better with their environment? Do they correlate with such factors as culture and a group's standing in society? Most authorities do not accept the idea that such correlations exist beyond the ones created by society itself.

Because of these problems, many authorities view race as a social, rather than a biological, phenomenon, and some, including Montagu, believe that the term should be dropped altogether. In his book *Racism* (1989), sociologist Robert Miles argues that, socially speaking, a race is a collectivity that is defined using biological criteria that a society views as significant. The important point is that these biological criteria are given meaning by a particular society; they have little intrinsic meaning apart from their social context. Moreover, because societies differ from one another in their views, it is possible that the same biological characteristics will be assigned different meanings in other societies. For example, sociologist F. James Davis has shown in his book *Who Is Black? One Nation's*

Definition (1991) that in the United States, regardless of how an individual looks, having one sub-Saharan African ancestor is enough to define an individual as "black." That same individual, however, might be viewed as "white" in regions such as Brazil and the West Indies that have different criteria for defining whiteness and blackness.

Thus, the social view of race sees race as a relative concept. Essentially, it says that a racial group exists because a society defines it as such. Miles describes the process of racial formation within society as racialization. In this process, societies arbitrarily select seemingly important biological criteria (for example, skin color) and impute to the groups thus created additional nonbiological characteristics. For example, some races may come to be viewed as cultured, while others are viewed as uncivilized. When these additional evaluations assume a negative slant, and when the negative evaluations are used to justify the subjugation of particular races, racialization turns into racism.

Applications

A number of applications flow from the distinction between biological and social concepts of race. First, most social scientists agree that confusion surrounds the concept of race. Specifically, they argue that a wide gap exists between everyday beliefs about race and scientific fact. Ashley Montagu believes that making careful distinctions between the social and biological conceptions of race helps dispel this confusion by raising important questions in people's minds. Confronting erroneous "commonsense" beliefs about race with scientific fact challenges their ready acceptance. This counters the belief system known as racism and its active corollary, discrimination.

With respect to this, another important related concept must be taken into account: ethnicity. This concept is similar to socially defined race, and consequently the two are often confused. Ethnic groups, however, are defined using cultural rather than biological criteria. Thus, Hispanics and Jews are ethnic groups, while African Americans may be considered both a racial and an ethnic group. As Montagu points out, making these fine distinctions helps to show that much racism rests on weak foundations and may cause individuals expressing racist views to reexamine their assumptions about other groups. Furthermore, awareness of the idea that races are socially defined leads one to question the widespread assumption that races are groups with fixed characteristics and that all individuals who are seen as belonging to these races must necessarily exhibit these characteristics. Anthropologist Richard Jenkins criticizes this assumption in his article "Social Anthropological Models of Inter-ethnic Relations," noting that from the point of view of the social construction of race, races are categories that are imposed by powerful groups on the less powerful. This implies that the powerful groups gloss over differences among the individuals who are being defined in order to accentuate the differences between groups.

In practical terms, problems arise because individuals who are being racialized attempt to assert their own individuality or the uniqueness of the particular group to which they belong. This identity is often expressed in ethnic terms. Any group's sense of identity is complex and should never be oversimplified or taken for granted. Groups that are defined by society as being primarily racial might, in fact, view themselves in ethnic terms. An example is black immigrants to the United States from the Caribbean, many of whom view themselves as separate from African Americans even though the larger society views the two groups as belonging to the same race. Similarly, the term "Asian" is often used in the United States to describe people of Far Eastern descent. This racial term lumps together a number of sometimes antagonistic groups that have unique cultures. Thus, while Asians are viewed by some Americans as a single racial group, individuals who are so categorized may strongly prefer to define themselves in terms of their particular culture.

The reduction of racism and discrimination has been an active goal of many agencies. The passing of legislation to curb discrimination, for example, was the primary goal of the groups (such as the National Association for the Advancement of Colored People and the Congress on Racial Equality) involved in the Civil Rights movement of the 1960's. Many ethnic groups have founded organizations seeking to illuminate and end ethnic slurs and discrimination against them; one well-known such group is the Anti-Defamation League, founded by American Jews in 1913. These efforts remain important because the United States is an attractive destination for immigrants of all races and ethnicities, but immigration often brings conflict with native groups as well as between immigrant groups themselves. Thus, finding ways to urge groups to be tolerant of one another is extremely important, and the dissemination, throughout society, of adequate definitions of concepts such as "race" and "ethnicity" helps to achieve this goal.

Having precise definitions of these concepts is also important in the administration of affirmative action programs. These programs are predicated on the assumption that histori-cally disadvantaged groups can be clearly identified. Any group must be identified and defined before any program can be effectively targeted at it, but this task is not always easy. The *Jane Doe v. the State of Louisiana* case of 1983, though not an affirmative action case, illustrates some of the problems involved in determining an individual's race. In that case, a Louisiana woman (Susie Phipps) who was only three thirty-seconds black was denied a passport because she checked "white" on her application form. Even though Phipps thought of herself as white (and had twice married white men), three courts held that she was legally black. This case illustrates the dilemma faced by individuals with ancestors considered to be from different races, and it underscores the importance of the concept of race as a social one.

Knowledge of this concept also facilitates smoother relationships for those individuals and organizations that deal regularly with other societies that have different conceptions of race. Cross-cultural communications can be hampered if people assume that their ideas on race are similar to those of other societies. For example, Japanese people are viewed as Asians in the United States, but in white-ruled South Africa they were categorized as "honorary whites." Similarly, in the United States, individuals such as Susie Phipps are black, but in South Africa they are accorded a separate, distinct status, "colored." A third example is that Asian Indians, though generally regarded by anthropologists as "Cauca-sians," are often regarded as black when they migrate to Britain. Since an individual's racial status often determines how the person is treated, knowledge of how such statuses vary cross-culturally is essential for multinational corporations and political organizations such as the United Nations.

Context

Historical analysis of the concept of race shows that ideas of race are different at different periods in history. Historian Thomas Gossett, in *Race: The History of an Idea in America* (1963), notes that race thinking stretches as far back as the ancient Egyptians (1350 B.C.E.). Ancient peoples, however, while conscious of color differences, did not systematically discriminate against one another on this basis.

European world dominance following the age of exploration in the fifteenth and sixteenth centuries caused modern discussions of racial issues to be centered on Eurocentric models. European expansionism brought Europeans into closer contact with unfamiliar peoples in Africa, North and South America, Australia, and the Pacific, and this contact challenged established old assumptions about race. Theories had to be constructed to account for the evident differences between Europeans and the new peoples with whom they came into contact. From the sixteenth century to the middle of the nineteenth century, debate focused on the question of whether humankind had had a single origin and had differentiated into contrasting races or whether the various races had originated separately. The first school was known as the monogenic school of thought and the latter, the polygenic school.

This debate proved inconclusive because of the lack of firm scientific evidence. Charles Darwin's work in the middle of the nineteenth century, however, through its emphasis on natural selection (which provided a plausible mechanism for the process of evolution), seemed to lend scientific support to monogenic theories of race. The idea soon arose that the different races represent different stages on the ladder of evolution. Gossett shows that in the climate of nineteenth century European imperialism, whites widely assumed that they—especially the Nordics and the British—were the most advanced of all the races. Both biological and nonbiological ideas were adduced to support the notion of a hierarchy of races. Discussions of race began to incorporate the idea known as social Darwinism (although Darwin himself never espoused this viewpoint). Social Darwinism applied the mechanism of evolution to human social groups, arguing that human groups (particularly racial and ethnic groups) are in a conflict that results in the "survival of the fittest" and that various groups "deserve" what they get. For example, supporters viewed European culture as being far superior to all others; on the other end of the spectrum, the enslavement of Africans, they argued, "proved" the inferiority of that group.

A turning point occurred early in the twentieth century with the work of anthropologist Franz Boas, who questioned the racist assumptions of the age. It was the Nazism of the 1930's and 1940's and the genocide that it engendered, however, that decisively turned the tide away from biological notions of race. The world was horrified at the attempts of the Nazis to exterminate the "Jewish race" (as well as Gypsies and others), and world leaders vowed that it must never happen again. After World War II, scientists increasingly relied on social factors to explain human behavior. Two United Nations statements on race (on July 18, 1950, and July 15, 1952) reflected this change in underlying assumptions. These statements cast doubt on the notion of superior and inferior races and recognized the notion of socially constructed races. The hope was that revealing the complexity of the issue of race would hinder the development of destructive racist ideologies such as Nazism.

Bibliography

Cashmore, E. Ellis. *Dictionary of Race and Ethnic Relations.* 4th ed. New York: Routledge, 1996. Very sharp and comprehensive discussions of topics on race. Covers many fundamental concepts in depth and has a strong cross-cultural perspective.

Davis, F. James. *Who Is Black? One Nation's Definition.* University Park: Pennsylvania State University Press, 1991. Required reading for those interested in how racial groups are defined. He argues that since historical and social forces shape these definitions, they change over time. Throughout, Davis compares the United States with other societies to show the uniqueness of its definition of who is black.

Downs, James F., and Hermann K. Bleibtreu. *Human Variation.* Rev. ed. Beverly Hills, Calif.: Glencoe Press, 1972. Introductory textbook with clear and simple discussions of complex issues relating to race.

Gossett, Thomas. *Race: The History of an Idea in America.* New York: Oxford University Press, 1997. Gossett's influential book, first published in 1963, is required reading for those interested in the history of the concept of race. It discusses in detail the various historical strands that interwove to create current American ideas on race. Although long, the book is absorbing and the writing style clear.

Miles, Robert. *Racism.* London: Routledge, 1989. Valuable because of its carefully argued and detailed treatment of many issues relating to race. He treats these issues historically and, significantly, relates them to the concept of social class.

Montagu, Ashley. *Race, Science, and Humanity.* Princeton, N.J.: Van Nostrand, 1963. Small but useful collection of essays on issues relating to race. Shows why the concept of race, as employed in the everyday world, is problematic. He argues for the abandonment of the term because of its embodiment of false stereotypes.

Seligman, C. G. *Races of Africa.* 4th ed. London: Oxford University Press, 1966. Small but detailed book needs to be read with a map to be truly appreciated, since it assumes familiarity with African tribes and regions. Discussions of the varieties of groups present in Africa illustrate the problems involved in classifying groups into races.

Smith, M. G. "Pluralism, Race, and Ethnicity in Selected African Countries." In *Theories of Race and Ethnic Relations*, edited by John Rex and David Mason. Cambridge: Cambridge University Press, 1986. Argues strongly against the idea that race is a socially constructed concept. Instead, Smith views races as objective, genetically based phenomena.

Milton D. Vickerman

Cross-References

Ethnicity and Ethnic Groups; Immigration and Emigration; Prejudice and Discrimination: Merton's Paradigm; Race Relations: The Race-Class Debate; Racial and Ethnic Stratification.

RACE RELATIONS: THE RACE-CLASS DEBATE

Type of sociology: Racial and ethnic relations
Field of study: Policy issues and debates

The race-class debate refers to the scholarly argument concerning whether racial group membership or socioeconomic status is more significant in determining an individual's life chances. At its heart, this debate also concerns whether race is a fundamental organizing feature of American society or whether economic stratification is of central importance.

Principal terms

RACE: socially defined group for which membership is based on a combination of cultural heritage, historical circumstance, and/or the presence of distinguishable physical features such as skin color

RACIAL DISCRIMINATION: behavior, practices, or policies that result in harm, intended or not, to individuals on the basis of their racial group membership

SOCIAL CLASS: category of group membership generally based on economic resources, income, occupational prestige, and educational attainment

SOCIAL STRATIFICATION: hierarchical ranking system with differences in access to social resources; individuals at the top ranks have more access, while those at the bottom lack social resources

UNDERCLASS: refers to a social class at the bottom of the social strata; the poorest of the poor, among whom poverty is an ongoing feature from generation to generation

Overview

In the sociological field of race relations, great attention has been given to the ongoing subordinate status of racial minority groups. This subordinate status is manifest in many areas of social life. According to political scientist Andrew Hacker (1992) in *Two Nations: Black and White, Separate, Hostile, Unequal*, "a black woman . . . can expect to live five fewer years than [her] white counterpart. Among men, the gap is seven years." Besides lowered life expectancy, Hacker states that racial minorities are more likely than whites to experience poverty, with the result that, "among black and Hispanic single mothers, somewhat over half are on welfare, while for white women the proportion is about 34 percent." While Hacker states that the racial gap in income narrowed considerably between 1940 and 1990, there is still a significant difference between the races. White families of all types earn more income than their black counterparts. Even when blacks have the same levels of educational attainment as whites, they are likely to earn less income, though the gap between women of both races is considerably smaller than that between men.

One of the major debates to arise in the field of race relations is referred to as the "race-class debate." It centers on the issue of whether it is the treatment based on the racial group membership of minorities which explains their failure to achieve social mobility, or whether it is only poor racial minorities who face roadblocks in social mobility. Some sociologists think that racism and racial minority status are more important in determining one's life chances than is social class; racial organization, some say, is an independent and fundamental facet of American society. Others view the economic arrangement under capitalism and one's social class to be more significant than race. They view racism as an outgrowth of capitalism and the economic exploitation which, they claim, is an ongoing feature of capitalist society.

Scholars who place significance on racial organization often cite black sociologist and political activist W. E. B. Du Bois, who proclaimed in his 1903 publication, *The Souls of Black Folk*, that "the problem of the twentieth century is the problem of the colorline." This implies that racial categorization is fundamental in American society; hence, issues of poverty and social mobility, along with persistent race discrimination can be traced to the issue of a "colorline" in American society. A major race relations theory supporting such a view is internal colonialism, articulated by Robert Blauner in his *Racial Oppression in America* (1972). Internal colonist theorists view contemporary race relations as growing out of a distinct process of colonialism, which describes the manner in which people of color were incorporated into American society. In this view, the low status of racial group members results from their nations being attacked and conquered, and then from them being defined as inferior, placed in the lowest positions of the society as labor or commodities, and excluded from the means for social mobility (such as education and political participation). In contemporary society, this subordinate status is maintained by the political, economic, and social practices of a powerful white majority that continues to exclude racial minorities from positions of power and privilege and to define them as comparatively inferior.

Another sociological perspective mirroring internal colonial theory's contention that race is central to social organization in American society is articulated in the 1986 book *Racial Formation in the United States*, authored by Michael Omi and Howard Winant. Omi and Winant, following the Du Bois thesis, argue that "[f]rom the very inception of the Republic to the present moment, race has been a profound determinant of one's political rights, one's location in the labor market, and indeed one's sense of 'identity.' " Their "racial formation" argues that class-based theories and colonial or nation-based theories subsume race under other social categories (class or nation). Furthermore, they argue that both mainstream (assimilationist) theories and radical (class and colonial) theories have underestimated the tremendous significance of race in American society.

On the other side of the debate, class-based theories view economic forces as most significant in both determining and understanding race relations. For example, the Marxist sociologist Oliver C. Cox, in his 1970 work *Caste, Class, and Race: A Study in Social Dynamics*, argues that racism is a product of capitalism, which maintains the power of the ruling class by dividing workers from one another on the basis of race. Furthermore, racist ideology justifies the economic exploitation of people of color. Similarly, in the 1981 publication *Racial Inequality: A Political-Economic Analysis*, sociologist Michael Reich argues that workers who allow themselves to be divided by race are victims of "false consciousness" because they would benefit more from uniting and organizing as an economic class (against capitalists). In both views, racism flows from economic exploitation, and it is economic exploitation, not racism, which is the fundamental problem.

Another class-based sociological theory is that of William J. Wilson, presented in his 1978 work, *The Declining Significance of Race*. Wilson argues that, historically, race was more significant in determining where blacks would fall in the United States' stratified society. He says that in contemporary society, however, Americans have achieved racial equality through changes brought about by civil rights legislation, which, he argues, resulted in social mobility for those blacks who are now in the middle and upper classes. According to Wilson, those blacks who remain subordinated in society are in that position primarily because of their membership in the lower class, not because of their race. Wilson, then, stresses class differences among blacks, rather than racial solidarity, as being of greater significance. He bases this conclusion on changes brought about through massive protest and the protective legislation that ensued; he believes that these changes resulted in the broader inclusion of some blacks, who were able to advance economically, and thereby to distance themselves from the ghetto. To Wilson, their poor counterparts, unable to take advantage of those gains because of their low class position, have remained stuck in the inner cities which have only continued to deteriorate.

Applications

The race-class debate has tremendous consequences for public policy, with widely divergent strategies resulting from taking either of these theoretical orientations. Generally, if the race thesis is more influential, policy makers respond by continuing to investigate the extent and manifestations of racism. They also create policies designed to minimize the social differences between racial groups and to break down barriers created by racism. If policy makers are influenced by arguments that economic deprivation, not racism, is responsible for the problems of racial minorities, then racially directed policies (such as affirmative action) lose their mandate for achieving parity between racial groups.

If racism is viewed as the critical issue, the distance between whites and people of color is the focus. Solutions revolve around protective measures to shield racial minorities from white racism. Labor experts and civil rights activists argue that when people have similar levels of educational attainment and work in similar occupations, any remaining inequality (such as Hacker documents) may be the product of race discrimination. This remains a powerful argument for both the maintenance and strengthening of civil rights legislation against race discrimination and for protective hiring practices such as affirmative action. The Civil Rights Act, Voting Rights Act, and Fair Housing Act, all enacted in the 1960's, are examples of legislation designed to promote equal opportunity and end racial discrimination. Furthermore, special educational programs in higher education, such as "remedial" courses, mentoring programs, and the like are designed to target racial minorities, who appear far more likely than their white counterparts to drop out of college.

Despite civil rights legislation, racial minority group members who believe their lives are shaped more by race than by social class may not expect the white majority-dominated government to provide relief against racial barriers. This may lead to the generation of grass-roots efforts to redress grievances and to the organization of political protest among fellow racial group members, regardless of their socioeconomic status.

On the other hand, policy makers who are convinced that the major problems confronting racial minorities afflict only the poor among them may seek one or both of two routes: They may seek to abandon any and all racially designed policies such as affirmative action or school integration; and they may create policies and programs specifically targeted for poor racial minorities. For example, scholars with remarkably differing views, such as William J. Wilson and neoconservative economist Thomas Sowell, have argued that affirmative action programs benefited only middle-class blacks and that group no longer faces racial discrimination. Moreover, Wilson highlights the differences between affluent and poor people of color, focusing upon African Americans, to say that class conflict has been heightened among group members and that middle-class African Americans inhabit a vastly different social universe than that of the poor, inner-city African American underclass with which he is primarily concerned.

Wilson advocates government intervention for poor people of color, particularly in the devastated inner cities, to assist them in education, job training, and financial assistance. He claims that they suffer from economic dislocation caused by societal changes in the economy. Meanwhile, Sowell argues that inner-city dwellers lack the kind of "human capital," such as motivation, values, skills, and training, that employers are seeking. Sowell also finds that affirmative action policies constitute "reverse discrimination" against whites. This kind of argument formed the rationale for the well-known Bakke case (*Regents of the University of California v. Bakke*, 1978), in which the Supreme Court held that a white man, Allan Bakke, had been unfairly blocked from admission to medical school because of his race. Generally, adoption of the class-based thesis results in the advocation of policies that are color-neutral, or racially blind. Policies and programs such as the Equal Opportunity Program in higher education are generally color-blind, targeting all economically disadvantaged students for special advising, mentoring, and tutoring to overcome deficiencies in their secondary education and ensure their successful completion of college.

Context

The sociological study of race and ethnic relations has had three major variants: the assimilationist perspective, which argues that all racial and ethnic groups will ultimately be integrated into one group within the larger society; the colonialist/internal colonialist model, which characterizes American society as a dual society divided by race; and the class-based models, which propose that those problems facing racial minorities are the result of their economic exploitation as members of the lower classes. The "racial formation" thesis advanced by Omi and Winant suggests that race be considered a distinct social category in American society and that economic and cultural considerations alone cannot adequately explain the dynamics of race relations.

The race-class debate has been an ongoing feature in American sociology; however, it was heightened in the late 1970's with the publication of Wilson's *The Declining Signifi-cance of Race* and its descriptions of what he calls the African American underclass. The debate that ensued returned scholarly attention to the question of whether Du Bois was correct in his 1903 assertion that race is a fundamental problem in American society. The race thesis represents a break with traditional sociological race relations theory, which is assimilationist. It also represents a break with what Blauner refers to as the "Eurocentric" bias in both assimilationist and class-based theories. According to Blauner, this bias resulted in a tendency among scholars to give greater priority to issues of industrial society and class stratification. He claims that race is not given priority because of the assumption by assimilationist and class-based theories that race and ethnicity are social categories that lose importance in industrial capitalist society. In such a formulation, racial group identity is expected to erode in significance, both for racial minority group members and in terms of their treatment by majority group members.

Not all theorists put themselves in an either/or situation of advocating the class thesis or the race thesis. Milton Gordon was first to advocate the concept of the "ethclass," holding that both ethnicity and class are important dimensions for social organization and identity. In his 1978 book *Racial Stratification in America*, James Geschwender elaborates on Gordon's ethclass concept, arguing that both the class thesis and the colonial thesis offer valuable insight into the situation of racial minorities. Yet his concept of a colonial-class model, which combines the two, still fails to address the criticisms of Omi and Winant, who argue that race cannot be explained by class or nation models.

Generally, the race-class debate has stimulated sociological researchers to use compara-tive analyses of various race and class groupings in order to assess and distinguish the effects of racial minority group membership and social class. Sociologists continue to diverge, however, on whether the fates of racial minorities are bound together in the quest for racial equality or whether middle-class racial minorities have more in common with their white counterparts than with the abjectly poor members of their own race. More significantly, shifts in sociological theories of race relations have had profound effects on American race policies. Perhaps the most famous example is the case of Daniel Patrick Moynihan's publication, *The Negro Family: A Case for Social Action* (1965), known as the Moynihan Report, which presented policy makers with an opportunity to "blame the victim," if they were so inclined, by claiming that blacks' cultural mores were at odds with those of others, resulting in their low socioeconomic status. Generally, when policy makers shift away from the mandates of the race thesis, civil rights legislation is weakened, as it was under the Reagan and Bush administrations. The claims of unequal treatment by racial minority group members go unheeded in favor of "race-neutral" policy. If the race-based theories are correct in assessing the persistence of racism and race distinction at all levels of the United States' stratified society, such policies bode ill for the possibility of achieving racial parity.

Bibliography

Barnes, Annie S. *Say It Loud: Middle-Class Blacks Talk About Racism and What to Do About It*. Cleveland, Ohio: Pilgrim Press, 1999.

Blauner, Robert. *Racial Oppression in America*. New York: Harper & Row, 1972. Criticizes trends in the sociology of race and ethnic relations for not giving racism and race relations priority in theorizing and research. He analyses racism using a colonial model, positing that American society remains divided by race and that the division is by design.

Geschwender, James. *Racial Stratification in America*. Dubuque, Iowa: Wm. C. Brown, 1978. Discusses racial stratification in the work of major sociological theorists and surveys major models in race relations, including assimilationist, colonial, and class models. After discussing the historical experience of blacks, with particular attention to slavery and labor force characteristics, he concludes by proposing a colonial-class model.

Hacker, Andrew. *Two Nations: Black and White, Separate, Hostile, Unequal*. Expanded and updated ed. New York: Ballantine Books, 1995. Clearly written exposition of thesis that race remains critical to the maintenance of the United States as a dual society in which African Americans are subordinated to their white counterparts at every level of society.

Omi, Michael, and Howard Winant. *Racial Formation in the United States*. New York: Routledge & Kegan Paul, 1986. Critical assessment of the major race relations theories. The authors then propose that race be addressed as an independent force in American society. They apply this thesis to an analysis of the role the state plays and to an analysis of political contention among divergent racial groups.

Wilson, William J. *The Declining Significance of Race*. 2d ed. Chicago: University of Chicago Press, 1980. Surveys major epochs of race relations in American society, detailing the influence of race historically and the contemporary emergence of class stratification among blacks and of an entrenched underclass.

Sharon Elise

Cross-References

Class Consciousness and Class Conflict; Ethnicity and Ethnic Groups; Immigration and Emigration; Prejudice and Discrimination: Merton's Paradigm; Race and Racial Groups; Racial and Ethnic Stratification.

RACIAL AND ETHNIC STRATIFICATION

Type of sociology: Racial and ethnic relations
Fields of study: Basic concepts of social stratification; Theoretical perspectives on stratification

Racial and ethnic stratification refers to a persisting ranking system in which rewards, privileges, and power meted out to racial and ethnic groups are unequal and supported by social structures and institutions. This concept helps to explain how stratification can emerge as a result of the contact between racial and ethnic groups.

Principal terms

ASCRIBED STATUS: status obtained at birth, such as sex, race, or family background

DIFFERENTIAL POWER: a situation in which the majority group and minority groups have unequal access to power; it results in the dominance of the majority group and subordination of minority groups

ETHNOCENTRISM: attitude that one's own culture is superior and should be used as the basis on which to judge other cultures

EXTERNAL EXPLANATION: belief that the lower social positions minorities occupy primarily result from the unequal opportunity structure that restricts minorities

INTERNAL EXPLANATION: belief that the lower social positions minorities occupy are attributable to their deficient cultures

MAJORITY GROUP: ethnic group that enjoys the social, political, and economic advantages of a society

MOBILITY: movement in people's position in a system of social stratification

SEMICASTE STRUCTURE: class stratification within racial and ethnic groups that are also stratified

Overview

Strictly speaking, race and ethnicity are two different concepts. Race is socially defined on the basis of physical characteristics, whereas ethnicity is socially defined on the basis of cultural characteristics. Because these two concepts overlap to a certain extent, the terms are sometimes used loosely, even interchangeably. In the broadest sense, racial and ethnic stratification can be understood as the inequality between different ethnic groups in social, economic, and political areas.

It is necessary, however, to point out that stratification means more than inequality. Stratification is a hierarchical ordering of social categories supported by social institutions. In other words, stratification is characterized not by individual differences but by structured patterns. Moreover, inequality in a social stratification system is intergenerationally transmitted; that is, inequality is perpetuated from generation to generation.

As a type of social stratification, racial and ethnic stratification is a system of structured social inequality. Those who are situated at the top of the stratification system form the majority group, while those who are located at the bottom become minority groups. "Majority" and "minority," in a sociological sense, do not depend on actual numbers. Regardless of the groups' sizes, the politically, economically, and socially superior group becomes the majority group, while those that are subordinate constitute minority groups.

All social stratification systems are based on one of two stratifying criteria: ascribed status or achieved status. Ascribed status refers to the status one obtains at birth, such as skin color, sex, or belonging to a wealthy or poor family. Achieved status is the status one manages to achieve after making substantial efforts. Lawyer, physician, and teacher are all examples of achieved status. Racial and ethnic stratification is a system that ranks people according to cultural or physical characteristics of social groups. Hence, it is a type of stratification based on ascribed status. In such a stratification system, rewards and resources such as power, privilege, social status, and wealth are meted out to majority and minority groups in a systematic and disproportional way.

Under what kind of situation is racial and ethnic stratification likely to emerge? Sociologist Donald L. Noel identified three elements in his influential 1968 article "A Theory of the Origin of Ethnic Stratification": ethnocentrism, competition, and differential power. Ethnocentrism refers to an attitude that one's own culture is superior to all other cultures and should therefore be used to judge other cultures. Noel contends that ethnocentrism, competition, and differential power are essential for the emergence of ethnic stratification:

> Without ethnocentrism the groups would quickly merge and competition would not be structured along ethnic lines. Without competition there would be no motivation or rationale for instituting stratification along ethnic lines. Without differential power it would simply be impossible for one group to achieve dominance and impose subordination to its will and ideals upon the other(s).

Of the three, differential power is essential not only for the emergence of racial and ethnic stratification but also for the maintenance of a stratification system. Sociologist Marvin Olsen notes that "the twin themes that link together stratification and race relations are inequality and conflict, both of which are direct outcomes of power exertion." In a racial and ethnic stratification system, the majority group is at the top of the ethnic hierarchy. Its access to the society's resources, including power resources, is disproportionately large in comparison to that of minority groups. Hence, it is able to employ power resources to make decisions in its own favor. This is not to say, however, that all the majority group members enjoy equal power advantages. Rather, it means that the majority group, as a social category, possesses disproportionately large amounts of resources. Placed at an advantaged position, it is able to use its resources to perpetuate its advantages.

Similarly, although minority groups are situated at a disadvantaged position as a whole, it does not mean that all members of minority groups find themselves in the lower strata of the society. In fact, class stratification has emerged within minority groups in the United

States. Despite the barriers they have faced as minority group members, some minority group members have managed to achieve certain degrees of social mobility. That is, they have risen on the social ladder by obtaining better social, economic, and political positions. Such a hierarchical ordering of social class within ethnic and racial categories that are also hierarchically ordered is called a semicaste structure. Sociologist William Julius Wilson suggests that class structure for African Americans, for example, has become more differentiated and that the meaning of race is declining in the economic sector of American society. Upper-class African Americans, however, are not as upper class as upper-class whites, and the lowest positions in the social class hierarchy still belong to nonwhites without exception.

Applications

Racial and ethnic stratification is a hierarchical system that ranks categories of people rather than individuals. The full significance of racial and ethnic stratification is thus best seen by comparing the majority and minority groups in social, economic, and political terms.

In a multiethnic society such as the United States, racial and ethnic lines can be drawn according to country of origin, nationality, religion, skin color, language, and so on. When sociologists examine racial and ethnic stratification, they tend to view whites, especially the so-called WASPs (white Anglo-Saxon Protestants), as the majority group and nonwhites as minority groups. Hence, African Americans, American Indians, and Asian Americans are all minority groups. Hispanics are also considered a minority group (Hispanic people may be of any race).

While the combined population of African Americans, Hispanics, American Indians, and Asians constituted around 20 percent of the American population in the 1980's, a study by Richard D. Alba and Gwen Moore in 1982 revealed that members of minorities held only 3.9 percent of elite positions in social, economic, and political institutions. WASPs alone held 43 percent of all elite positions. Business and mass media were the two fields entirely dominated by whites; in them, minorities found no representatives among the elite at all. The percentages of minorities who were members of Congress or who held elite political positions also were low—3.4 and 3.0, respectively, compared to 53.4 and 39.4 for WASPs. Obviously, whites, especially WASPs, not only were overrepresented in most sectors of the elite but also were numerically dominant.

The economic position of the majority and minority groups is one of the most important dimensions of racial and ethnic stratification. A comparison of the majority group and minority groups in this regard also displays some structured patterns. A central indicator of economic position is the median household income. In 1990, whites had a median household income of $31,231, while African Americans had a median of $18,676. Translated into a percentage, household income for African Americans was 59.7 percent of that for whites. Median household income for Hispanics also was low. In 1990 the figure was $22,330, or 71.5 percent of what whites were making. Asian Americans seemed to be an exception; their median household income was $38,450 in that year.

Since the economic position for a particular racial and ethnic group is closely related to the unemployed proportion of that group, it is necessary also to examine this percentage for whites and nonwhites. The picture remains consistent. In 1992 only 4 percent of the white population age sixteen and over was unemployed. The unemployed proportions for African Americans, Hispanics, and American Indians were all high, with 8 percent for African Americans, and 7 percent each for Hispanics and American Indians. Asian Americans provided another exception, with 3 percent unemployment.

Although education is not a central indicator of political and economic position, it is the major means by which minorities can overcome racial and ethnic barriers and achieve upward mobility. As a whole, minorities seem to have made some progress in this area. The 1992 census indicates that among those who were between the ages of twenty-five and forty-four, the percentage that had received some college education did not differ much across racial and ethnic groups. The percentage for whites was 27, compared to 26 for African Americans, 20 for Hispanics, and 30 for American Indians. When the college graduation percentage is examined, however, minorities still lagged significantly behind. Twenty-eight percent of whites in the age range of twenty-five to forty-four had been graduated from college, while only 14 percent of African Americans, 10 percent of Hispanics, and 11 percent of American Indians had done the same. The educational attainment for Asian Americans was exceptional: Forty-seven percent had been graduated from colleges or universities.

These examples reveal only a part of the picture, but the whole picture looks exactly as this part has suggested. In terms of wealth, occupational prestige, poverty rate, and living standard, a systematic and consistent pattern is constantly found. When a person from a certain ethnic group suffers from lower income, receives little education, or is unemployed, this is an individual phenomenon. When a particular racial and ethnic group suffers from such disadvantages, this becomes a social phenomenon. When a number of minority groups suffer from such disadvantages, this is definite evidence of racial and ethnic stratification.

Because Asian Americans have moved far ahead of the other minority groups and even surpassed the majority group in certain areas, some people believe that they have climbed to the top of racial and ethnic stratification. Asian Americans have been proclaimed the "model minority." Sociologist Ronald Takaki points out that the so-called model minority is only a myth. The higher median family incomes can be explained by Asian Americans' locations in large cities, where income is generally higher; their incomes, in any case, are not comparable with their higher educational achievements. Moreover, many Asian Americans are located in the labor market's secondary sector, where wages are low and promotional prospects minimal. When Asian Americans are viewed in this light, the relationship between the majority and minority holds.

Since the Civil Rights movement of the 1960's, the practice of affirmative action and the widening of opportunities for minorities to obtain higher education have helped improve the disadvantaged position occupied by minority groups. Yet these advancements have contributed more to the establishment of class stratification within minorities than to the eradication of racial and ethnic stratification. To the extent that social, economic, and political rewards for minorities are systematically disproportional to those enjoyed by the majority group, racial and ethnic stratification persists.

Context

The study of racial and ethnic stratification in the United States did not really start until the 1920's. The two important themes that run through such studies are the specific ways in which ethnic groups come into contact and the different ways in which ethnic groups fare in American society.

Sociologist Stanley Lieberson distinguished two types of contact situations: migrant superordination and indigenous superordination. Migrant superordination refers to the situation in which a powerful migrant group subdues the native population, while indigenous superordination means that migrant groups are made subordinate to a resident group.

A brief review of American history reveals that the conquest of American Indians is a good example of migrant superordination, whereas the immigration of Asian and Hispanic Americans serves as an example of indigenous superordination. The situation with African Americans is different; originally brought to the Americas as slaves, they immigrated in an entirely involuntary way. No matter the type of contact situation, a racial and ethnic stratification structure with whites as the majority group soon was established following contact.

Although initially situated at the lower stratum of the racial and ethnic stratification structure, Asian Americans have managed to move up socially and economically, if not politically, while African Americans as a whole are still occupying the bottom position in the stratification system. This raises a question as to the perpetuating and changing forces behind this racial and ethnic stratification structure.

One approach has been called the "internal explanation," which suggests that an ethnic group's achievement is primarily the result of the traits, qualities, and characteristics of the ethnic group. According to this approach, groups that possess cultural traits that foster success in American society—such as achievement motivation, future orientation, and reverence for scholarship—will succeed in the society, while groups lacking these traits are doomed to failure. Studies have found Asian Americans to possess these qualities. It follows that they are able to change their position in the stratification system. Characteristic of African Americans, however, according to studies, are unstable family structures, high dropout rates at school, and a value of living for the moment. According to this approach, African Americans' low positions in the racial and ethnic hierarchy are attributable to such characteristics.

The other approach is in sharp contrast with the internal explanation. Referred to as "external explanation," this approach focuses on the opportunity structure of American society. It emphasizes the external constraints, limitations, and barriers to which minorities are subjected and ascribes the low achievement of minority groups to such structural obstacles. Moreover, the distinctive cultural traits of disadvantaged minorities are regarded as responses to the externally imposed conditions. Sociologist John U. Ogbu argues that the absence of high educational aspirations, high achievement motivation, and a future orientation on the part of African Americans is a response to the realistic perception that their opportunities in the society are extremely restricted.

The external, or structural, explanation is a view more prevalent among sociologists. If

379

external barriers are decisive in affecting group outcomes, it follows that the breakdown of racial and ethnic stratification is dependent on change in the social structure over all else.

Bibliography

Hacker, Andrew. *Two Nations: Black and White, Separate, Hostile, Unequal.* New York: Charles Scribner's Sons, 1992. Analysis of white and African Americans. Part 2 is especially important because it discusses the dimensions of racial and ethnic stratification: income, employment, education, political power, and so on. Contains tables comparing whites and blacks in many regards.

Noel, Donald L. "A Theory of the Origin of Ethnic Stratification." In *Majority and Minority*, edited by Norman R. Yetman. 5th ed. Boston: Allyn & Bacon, 1991. Influential article on racial and ethnic stratification. Advances a theory and applies it to the experiences of African Americans. Recommended for college readers.

Parrillo, Vincent N. *Strangers to These Shores: Race and Ethnic Relations in the United States.* 2d ed. New York: John Wiley & Sons, 1985. Popular introductory text divided into four major parts: the sociological framework of race and ethnicity, European Americans, racial minorities and other minorities, and an analysis of the status of minority groups. Highly readable.

Smedley, Audrey. *Race in North America: Origin and Evolution of a Worldview.* 2d ed. Boulder, Colo.: Westview Press, 1999. Discusses the concept of race both historically and comparatively and delineates the historical and cultural context in which racial and ethnic stratification starts and persists. For general readers.

Willie, Charles Vert. *Race, Ethnicity, and Socioeconomic Status: A Theoretical Analysis of Their Interrelationship.* Bayside, N.Y.: General Hall, 1983. Despite its title, not primarily a work of theoretical analysis. The author's study of social problems such as disease, mortality, delinquency, poverty, and residential stratification as well as the research on family, school, and community will enhance the reader's understanding of ethnic stratification in American society.

Shengming Tang

Cross-References

Conflict Theory; Cultural and Structural Assimilation; Ethnicity and Ethnic Groups; Prejudice and Discrimination: Merton's Paradigm; Race Relations: The Race-Class Debate; Social Stratification: Analysis and Overview.

RELIGION

Type of sociology: Major social institutions
Field of study: Religion

The sociology of religion examines sacred ideologies and associated social practices from an objective and empirical perspective. In contrast with theology, which grapples with the claims of truth made by various religions, sociological analysis considers the social behavioral implications of religious activity, with particular emphasis on its effects on social integration and social change.

Principal terms

ASCETICISM: practice of self-denial of pleasure so as to achieve greater spiritual purity

FUNCTION: sociological concept that designates how a particular social element serves (either openly or in a hidden manner) to enhance the larger social whole

IDEOLOGY: set of ideas, beliefs, and attitudes that provides legitimation for particular patterns of social behavior

INTEGRATION: binding or holding together of various parts of a social whole, a process frequently viewed by sociologists as "problematic" rather than automatic

LEGITIMATION: social belief that serves to justify a particular social pattern of behavior by rendering it meaningful

PHENOMENOLOGY: study of everyday social life in terms of the central role played by human consciousness in social interaction and the "social construction of reality"

RELIGION: unified system of sacred beliefs and corresponding social practices

SACRED: social classification of phenomena that includes extraordinary and awe-inspiring events and processes distinct from the everyday, mundane aspects of social life

THEODICY: religious belief that provides a meaningful explanation to an otherwise inexplicable trauma or undesirable event, thereby strengthening the established legitimations of a given social order

Overview

The sociology of religion is a major subfield within the discipline of sociology. Classical sociological theorists considered religion to be a crucially important area of social investigation. Émile Durkheim, for example, defined religion as a system of sacred beliefs and practices shared by a community of followers such as a church. In contrast to the established tendency to see religious practice in personal and individualistic terms, Durkheim wished to stress the social reality of religion. He believed that even the most profoundly personal religious experiences obtain their human meaning through socially shared symbols that are based in a particular cultural context.

The sociology of religion has carried the basic issues of sociological inquiry into the sphere of sacred belief systems. The question "How is social order possible?" is of paramount concern to sociology. Durkheim ultimately answered this question, in part, through his pathbreaking work in the sociology of religion, in which he asserted that religious behavior serves the socially necessary function of enhancing social cohesion. Through the ritual practices associated with sacred beliefs, social communities are strengthened or "integrated" to a degree that would otherwise be difficult to achieve.

Other functions of religion implied in Durkheim's work include its ascetic character, which encourages self-discipline and self-sacrifice in favor of meaningful and orderly moral conduct. Religion further tends to instill euphoria into the otherwise mundane circumstances of everyday life, providing positive and desirable feelings that are otherwise not reliably present. This in turn revitalizes existing social institutions, enhancing the eagerness of social participants to maintain existing social patterns and promulgate them to their children through socialization.

Having identified the various social functions that religion serves, Durkheim concluded that religion could ultimately be seen as a process whereby "society worships itself." Sacred beliefs essentially embody the moral binding of socially ordered, human collectivities. This conjecture led to Durkheim's concern that the breakdown of sacred beliefs in the context of rapid social change and increasing specialization in the division of labor could create major problems for social stability. Durkheim believed that only by the formation of new sacred belief structures could society continue to maintain harmony and continual growth.

Durkheim's work initiated the functionalist approach to the sociological study of religion. Karl Marx is responsible for consolidating the critical perspective on sacred ideologies and practices. Through forming his own critique of Hegelian philosophy, Marx accepted much of Ludwig Feuerbach's materialist critique of religion. According to Feuerbach, religion is essentially a human projection in which people create and then worship supernatural entities that are in reality based firmly in their collective imagination. Feuerbach believed that the immense power that humans attribute to supernatural entities is actually a mystical and indirect reflection of the vast creative potential rooted in the human species itself. Feuerbach concluded that once this "secret" is discovered, atheism becomes the ultimately desirable human condition because it signifies a sober look at the human potential to pursue higher forms of social life.

Marx was greatly influenced by Feuerbach's materialist critique of religion and synthesized it into his critical view of exploitation in class societies. From Marx's perspective, religion is an "opiate of the masses" because it tends to mystify and obfuscate people's awareness of unjust social structures and preach acceptance of the status quo rather than its revolutionary transformation. Marx greatly influenced the sociology of religion by emphasizing the need to consider critically the social implications of religious practice and the intimate relationship between religion and social change.

Max Weber further explored the relationship of religion and social change by his critical engagement with Marxism. Weber helped to show that religion helps to legitimate social orders. In doing so, however, Weber showed that religion can also become an autonomous force for social change. By researching in tremendous detail the dynamics of change within religious ideologies, Weber hypothesized that changing beliefs in history converge upon human actors in a way that can bring about collective social change. Ultimately, Weber attempted to illustrate this process by arguing that the Protestant ethic (the "work ethic") as an ideological upsurge within Christianity, decisively helped to bring about the rise of capitalism.

The work of Weber, Marx, and Durkheim helped to set the theoretical parameters for the sociology of religion. Modern sociologists of religion, operating almost entirely within the theoretical permutations established by classical sociological theory, have set about the task of systematizing the subfield. Much work has been dedicated to understanding the organizational dynamics of religious communities, the institutional characteristics of religion, and religion's relationship with other human institutions. Sociologists have also developed more methodologically rigorous means of elaborating and verifying sociological theories of religion. The worldwide resurgence of religious movements that began during the 1970's led to a renewed interest in the sociology of religion. Contemporary theorists have been forced to grapple with the reality that religion can both contribute to social harmony and stability and promote destabilization and change.

Applications

The sociology of religion has produced various seminal studies that have attempted to create a general paradigm for the subfield. Peter L. Berger's *The Sacred Canopy: Elements of a Sociological Theory of Religion* (1967) is one of the most widely cited works that attempt to synthesize classical sociological theories into a working framework for scientifically approaching religion. Despite its many strengths, however, Berger's work displayed substantial weaknesses.

Berger's framework was developed from an earlier work he coauthored with Thomas Luckmann (*The Social Construction of Reality: A Treatise in the Sociology of Knowledge*, 1966), in which they attempted to demonstrate the importance of using phenomenological sociology as the basis for a general "sociology of knowledge" which in turn could serve as the central paradigm for all sociological analysis. Although Berger and Luckmann's work was initially received with great acclaim, numerous critics subsequently argued that their phenomenological approach placed too much emphasis upon subjective meanings in explaining social interaction while failing to account adequately for such objective aspects of social reality as power relations. Its shortcomings notwithstanding, Berger and Luckmann's perspective is useful in "knowledge-intensive" areas of everyday life such as religion.

Berger, a strong religious believer, asserts that the sociology of religion must rigidly "bracket" any questions concerning the ultimate "truth" or validity of religious activity. By remaining "disinterested" in theological questions, the analyst is free to consider the ways in which religion forms part of the process of "world building." This detached approach is essential to the sociology of religion and echoes the tradition of Max Weber's "value-free" approach as well as that of Alfred Schutz, the founder of phenomenological sociology.

From Berger's perspective, the social reality of everyday life is "socially constructed" through patterns of symbolic meanings which became shared in social interaction. According to Berger, all social orders are precarious because they are essentially arbitrary historical creations that are subject to modification and change. The stability of social orders therefore requires a distinctive set of reinforcing symbols that, once collectively shared, can provide ongoing support for a social status quo. Such meanings constitute a special form of humanly constructed knowledge known as legitimations, which specifically seek to explain and justify other existing sets of meanings associated with an established social order.

Berger points out that legitimations have both a normative and a cognitive character. Their cognitive character deals with "what is"—with explaining how it is that the world exists. Their normative character, in contrast, refers to a belief in "what ought to be"—an explanation of how things should properly be done. By exhibiting both of these traits, legitimations help to maintain the socially constructed world. When legitimations are woven together into a complex system of beliefs, they provide a "higher reality" in which the everyday real world can be placed into a meaningful context, a sacred and cosmic frame of reference. In this, religion ultimately constitutes the highest expression of shared social legitimations.

Because legitimations are themselves precarious and subject to breakdown, they require constant reenactment through ritual practice. Perhaps the greatest threat to legitimating beliefs, and therefore to social orders themselves, is chaotic or traumatic events such as death and natural catastrophes, which by their inexplicable nature can lead to serious challenges to the established set of legitimated social meanings. A specialized set of legitimations known as theodicies are frequently employed to defend the social order from such challenges.

A theodicy specifically seeks to explain an apparently inexplicable event by placing it into a meaningful context. This helps to alleviate the strain being placed on the established system of legitimation, thereby protecting the social status quo. In animistic religions, for example, a prolonged drought can be explained by the human collectivity's fall from favor with the nature god. A series of remedial rituals is employed as a practical theodicy which allows social participants to reharmonize themselves with nature, thus addressing what is believed to be the source of the problem.

Berger shows how monotheistic Christianity employs a particularly sophisticated kind of theodicy that seeks to address challenges that emerge in times of severe adversity. Rather than attempting to answer the trauma-induced question directly, Christianity employs a strategic theodicy that challenges the very right of the traumatized questioner to pose the question. Thus, the question "How could God allow such a thing to happen?" becomes addressed by a theodicy which asks in turn, "Who are you to question the motives of the all-knowing Creator?"

While Berger's framework amply illustrates many of the key concepts within the contemporary sociology of religion (such as legitimation and theodicy), it has nevertheless been subjected to numerous critiques. His inability to conceptualize the dynamics of social power adequately leaves issues such as class-based, race-based, and gender-based oppression unaddressed at best and trivialized at worst. More recent studies have attempted to rectify these weaknesses by exploring the contributions that neo-Marxist and feminist perspectives can make to the field. In addition, considerable cross-fertilization from liberation theology has generated excitement within the discipline.

Context

The sociology of religion dates back to the concern which the earliest sociologists displayed for understanding the key role played by sacred belief systems. Auguste Comte, the French founder of sociology, saw within religion a developing intellectual sensibility that contained the seeds for what he predicted would eventually lead to a rational pursuit of enlightened morality. Comte's "social dynamics," or theory of social change in stages, postulated evolutionary relationships between religious beliefs, morality, and social order. Ultimately, Comte attempted to form a scientifically based "church of positivism" in which he was the "high priest." His work is generally regarded to be most important for its influence on other key French thinkers, such as Émile Durkheim.

Durkheim was extremely influential in establishing the academic jurisdiction of sociology. He gleaned from Comte an understanding of religion's role in sustaining the social order and went on to postulate the indispensable role that religion plays in maintaining social "integration" or harmony. In his last major work, entitled *Les Formes élémentaires de la vie religieuse: Le Système totémique en Australie* (1912; *The Elementary Forms of the Religious Life: A Study in Religious Sociology*, 1915), Durkheim attempted to show how collective social processes in primitive societies require the binding effects that religion provides. Rather than becoming less important in modern societies, Durkheim argues that the increasing specialization of modern societies requires religious beliefs in order to maintain social integration. The functionalist approach that Durkheim pioneered has remained prominent ever since, influencing contemporary sociological theorists such as Talcott Parsons and Robert K. Merton.

Max Weber's *Die Protestantische Ethik und der Geist des Kapitalismus* (1904; *The Protestant Ethic and the Spirit of Capitalism*, 1930) has likewise been extremely influential in the sociology of religion. Weber, a German sociologist, sought to show that ideas, as part of a "superstructure," could have dramatic effects upon society's "infrastructure," or material base, in the course of history. This argument opposed Marx's view that the superstructure generally reflected changes in the infrastructure. Weber's work had a great impact upon Alfred Schutz, his German contemporary, who integrated Weberian concerns into the phenomenological philosophy pioneered by Edmund Husserl. Schutz's phenomenological interpretation of Weber was the principal inspiration for Peter L. Berger's attempt to reintegrate the sociology of religion more squarely into the mainstream of sociology.

Marx's critical conception of religion spawned generations of neo-Marxist theorists who in general viewed religion as a "false consciousness" or an obfuscatory ideology in the context of exploitive social orders. Marx's sociology of religion began with his "Economic and Philosophic Manuscripts of 1844," which forms a part of Marx's collected works, published in 1932. Like other aspects of his work, it has profoundly affected social life itself. Beginning in the 1960's, theologians in Latin America, and later in Africa and Asia, were influenced by Marxist concepts. The infusion of Marxist concepts into the lexicon of the spiritual leaders of popular grassroots political movements helped spur the development of the movement known as liberation theology. This upsurge of religious activism has been instrumental in galvanizing revolutionary movements in Latin America and elsewhere.

Ironically, this has forced many neo-Marxists to revise Marx's nineteenth century assertion that religion serves only as the "opiate of the masses."

Bibliography

Beckford, James A. *Religion and Advanced Industrial Society*. London: Unwin Hyman, 1989. Interesting theoretical analysis arguing that the sociology of religion has been relegated to the periphery of sociology. Contends that the theoretical imagery of classical sociology showed ample interest in religion but remained immersed in assumptions concerning the rise of industrial societies in a way that rendered the study of religion in advanced industrial societies problematic.

Berger, Peter L. *The Sacred Canopy: Elements of a Sociological Theory of Religion*. Garden City, N.Y.: Doubleday, 1967. Attempt to outline a general model for the sociology of religion. Because of its phenomenological approach, however, it has been widely criticized for its inability to provide a critical view of religion, particularly in terms of an analysis of social power relationships.

Berryman, Phillip. *Liberation Theology: Essential Facts About the Revolutionary Religious Movement in Latin America and Beyond*. New York: Pantheon Books, 1987. Case study of liberation theology written from a critical sociological perspective. Strongly sympathetic to the movement, the author seeks to introduce readers to the wide-reaching social implications of radicalized religious currents that challenge the established orders of Latin America.

Hargrove, Barbara. *The Sociology of Religion: Classical and Contemporary Approaches*. 2d ed. Arlington Heights, Ill.: Harlan Davidson, 1989. Accessible introduction to the sociology of religion that examines the nature and function of religion, its cultural basis, the relationship between institutionalized religion and other key social institutions, and the dynamics of religious change.

Homan, Roger. *The Sociology of Religion: A Bibliographical Survey*. New York: Greenwood Press, 1986. Excellent resource for those seeking to do research in the sociology of religion.

McGuire, Meredith B. *Religion: The Social Context*. 4th ed. Belmont, Calif.: Wadsworth, 1997. Survey of the sociology of religion that examines all major areas within the field, including consideration of the role that religion plays in promoting social stability and social change. Brief appendix gives tips on doing a literature search in the sociology of religion.

Turner, Bryan S. *Religion and Social Theory*. 2d ed. London: Sage Publications, 1991. Theoretical treatise for advanced students focusing on the challenges that feminist and postmodern theories pose for the sociology of religion. Explores problematic concepts such as theodicy and secularization, positing that a "sociology of the body" that builds upon the "philosophical anthropology" advanced by Peter L. Berger and others may be a fruitful means of advancing the field.

Yinger, J. Milton. *The Scientific Study of Religion*. New York: Macmillan, 1970. Comprehensive and interdisciplinary approach to religion, stressing the interconnections between the sociology, psychology, and anthropology of religion. This book provides an excellent beginner's guide for the serious student of religion and includes chapters on the organizational, political, and economic factors that interrelate with religious institutions.

Richard A. Dello Buono

Cross-References

Civil Religion and Politics; Protestant Ethic and Capitalism; Religion: Functionalist Analyses; Religion: Marxist and Conflict Theory Views; Socialization: Religion.

RELIGION
Functionalist Analyses

Type of sociology: Major social institutions
Field of study: Religion

Functional analyses of religion examine the role of religion according to the "functions" it performs in a society. An understanding of the basic functions of religion helps to explain the historical trends and current makeup of the American religious landscape.

Principal terms

ANOMIE: state in which the norms of society are weakened to the point that they no longer affect the behavior of individuals

FUNCTIONAL ANALYSIS: method of studying social institutions and patterns and how they contribute to stability in society by examining their functions

LIBERAL MAINLINE RELIGIOUS GROUPS: often referred to as "liberal Protestant," the three major religious groups defined as liberal mainline are the Episcopalian church, Presbyterian church, and United Church of Christ (Congregationalist church)

RELIGION: system of beliefs and practices regarding sacred things that unites people into a religious group, community, or congregation

SECTARIAN RELIGIOUS GROUP: religious group that is usually conservative in theology and that maintains strong tension between its values and those of the rest of society; examples of sectarian religious groups are conservative Baptists, the Church of Christ, and the Assemblies of God

Overview

Interest in examining the role of religion in society is as old as sociology itself. Many of the early social theorists, such as Karl Marx, Max Weber, and Émile Durkheim, were interested enough in the role of religion in society to write major works on the subject. One reason for this interest is that virtually all societies, no matter how simple or complex, have some form of religion.

Historically, many sociologists have assumed that religion was a dying institution because of the rationality brought on by scientific advances and industrialization. Many studies, however, have found this not to be the case. In reality, American society has not been turning away from religion. According to sociologist Jeffrey Hadden, church membership, attendance, individual devotional life, and financial contributions were all remarkably stable between 1950 and 1990. It appears that this pattern is not simply a short-lived modern trend. Religion has most likely increased in its importance since the American Revolution. In their book *The Churching of America, 1776-1990: Winners and Losers in Our Religious Economy* (1992), sociologists Roger Finke and Rodney Stark found that in 1776 roughly 17 percent of people in the colonies were church members. This figure had risen to approximately 56 percent of the United States population by the late 1980's and early 1990's.

Why does religion remain so strong in American society? Functional analysis addresses this question by examining what religion accomplishes that makes it an indispensable part of the society. Functional analysis views society as a system of interrelated parts. Like the human body, each part serves a function that benefits the whole system. Each of the various parts of society must fulfill its function if the entire social system is to run smoothly. If one part ceases performing its function, it must be replaced with something else that provides the same function if society is to continue normally. This perspective can be used to analyze the persistence of religion in society by examining its functions. While there are numerous levels at which religion may be functional (such as global, societal, and individual), this discussion will focus on the functions that religious groups perform in the lives of individuals who participate in religion.

There have been many functions attributed to religion, but the two most lasting and important are the provision of meaning and the creation of a sense of belonging for members of society. Religion provides meaning in the lives of individuals by promoting sacred explanations for worldly events. In his book *Why Conservative Churches Are Growing* (1986), sociologist Dean Kelley calls the provision of meaning the "indispensable function of religion." He asserts that meaning is the one function over which religion has a true monopoly. No other social institutions attempt to explain worldly events through sacred means, so people are drawn to religion to obtain this commodity. Religion continues to exist because human beings have an insatiable appetite for "explaining the meaning of life in ultimate terms," and they cannot obtain it elsewhere in society.

In his book *The Sacred Canopy: Elements of a Sociological Theory of Religion* (1967), sociologist Peter L. Berger discusses the important role of religion in creating and maintaining a sacred world that provides ultimate explanations for events and meaning for those who live in that world. Berger states that every human society engages in a similar activity, called "world-building." Unlike animals, which are programmed with natural instincts, human beings are "underspecialized." Stated simply, humans have few instincts to define their world for them. Neither do they have a program regarding how to relate to others with whom they share the world. In order for human beings to survive, human societies must create their own culture, including norms, values, and beliefs to help them make sense of their world. According to Berger, religion contributes in a crucial way in providing the beliefs that create meaning for people.

The belief system that provides meaning also serves as a remarkable social control mechanism. According to Berger, religion in a society is necessary to create and maintain sacred legitimation of the norms and values of that society. If religion ceases to provide sacred meaning associated with society's norms, those norms tend to lose their power to control people's behavior. Berger asserts that sacred meanings are most powerful when they are followed without being questioned. These sacred meaning systems become humankind's protection from anomie. Anomie refers to a state in which the norms of a society have little meaning and are not rooted in any transcendent values. When this occurs, people have no sense of moral guidance. In Berger's estimation, this is society's "hell on earth." Without the sense of ultimate (sacred) meaning provided by religion, the existing social order would eventually break down. Avoiding this state of anomie is the prime importance of the "meaning" function of religion. Religion helps society to avoid anomie by maintaining belief in a system of sacred rewards and punishments (such as the belief in heaven and hell), which goes beyond that offered in the secular realm.

An additional and related function of religion is to provide a sense of belonging. People feel the greatest sense of belonging among those with similar values, beliefs, and social characteristics as themselves. They also tend to make friendship and marriage choices based on similarity of values, beliefs, and social characteristics. In fast-paced industrial society, it is often difficult for individuals to find opportunities for personal relationships with others who hold similar beliefs and live similar lifestyles. People often turn to religion for the sense of "fellowship" they feel when interacting with others holding beliefs like their own. In a study of Pentecostals published in 1980, sociologist Douglas McGaw found that belonging was as important as meaning for many people who were members of Pentecostal churches. Religious groups accomplish this function by binding people together in social relationship within an integrated community with similar beliefs and lifestyles. Obviously, people cannot interact with "society" as a whole, but they can develop social relationships with members of the social institutions to which they belong. The important role of religious groups in providing friendship opportunities is clear when one notes that church members often draw most of their closest friends from within their congregation. Religious groups give people the opportunity to engage in religious practice and to interact socially with people they would choose as close friends. These relationships not only provide social support but also reinforce the religious beliefs that people already hold. According to Berger, religious meaning systems remain plausible as long as people are engaged in this type of social interaction with others who share their beliefs. When these beliefs are not reinforced through regular social interaction, the meaning they provide is eroded.

Applications

Functional analysis can be used to explain the development of the religious landscape in the United States. Using the functions of meaning and belonging, one can gain insight into why some religious groups are increasing while others are declining. Many sectarian religious groups have been increasing their share of the religious "market," while liberal groups have declined.

Among liberal Protestant denominations, the Episcopal church, Presbyterian church, and United Church of Christ all declined in membership between 1965 and the early 1990's. In that same time period, sectarian religious groups such as the Southern Baptist Convention, Assemblies of God, Church of Jesus Christ of Latter-day Saints, Seventh-day Adventists, and Church of the Nazarene increased the size of their memberships.

Although liberal denominations began their numerical decline in the 1960's, Finke and Stark found that the liberal decline actually began as early as 1776. In 1776, the Episcopalians had 15.7 percent of the religious marketplace, while the Presbyterians and Congregationalists (now the United Church of Christ) had 19.0 percent and 20.4 percent respectively. By 1850, the share of adherents (church members) held by the Episcopalian church had declined to 3.5 percent. The Presbyterian share declined to 11.6 percent and the Congregationalist share declined to 4.0 percent of all church members. During this time period, the Baptists increased from 16.9 percent of all religious adherents to 20.5 percent, while the Methodists increased from 2.5 percent to 34.2 percent.

Why have many sectarian religious groups prospered while liberal groups continue to decline? Some insight can be gained through an examination of which groups are more successful at providing a sense of meaning and belonging. Sectarian religious groups provide meaning and belonging for their members in very distinct ways. First, they claim to possess ultimate truth. At times, these beliefs appear to others as dogmatic and intolerant, but this unwavering commitment to one set of beliefs and rejection of all others prevents relativism from becoming a threat to established beliefs. When relativism and diverse beliefs are allowed to exist within a social group, no particular set of beliefs can be totally accepted as truth without alienating other members of the group. Because sectarian religious groups tend to maintain very homogeneous belief systems, those beliefs are not severely questioned and they provide a strong sense of meaning.

In contrast, liberal mainline denominations tend to value ecumenism, maintaining working relationships with many other denominations of various faiths. While this teamwork approach to religion has many advantages, it also tends to foster a relativist view toward other faiths outside the belief system of the group.

Growing religious groups also tend to maintain a morality that is distinct from other churches and the surrounding culture. This anti-ecumenical approach is called "boundary maintenance" and emphasizes differences between group members and outsiders. Among sectarian religious groups, this distinctive morality is stressed as an all-encompassing worldview that extends into all other spheres of life. Members of these groups have the advantage of a set of beliefs and values that give religious significance to all of life's events.

The importance of belonging is also easy to see by examining the American religious scene. Members of growing denominations (usually conservative) tend to view their church as a large family, while members of liberal mainline denominations are more likely to view their congregation as a loose association of individuals. Churches that are drawing many new members also tend to have members who draw more of their closest friends from church than members of declining denominations. In a study published in 1989, sociologist Daniel V. A. Olson found that conservative churches tend to be very successful in providing a strong sense of belonging (often referred to as "fellowship"). Members of conservative religious groups place considerable emphasis on friendship with fellow church members. Olson states:

> Persons with many church friends appear bound by their friendship ties; they are less likely to leave when dissatisfied with other areas of church life. . . . Such ties renew the relevance of attenders' beliefs and become social plausibility structures that counter the privatizing effects of life in a pluralistic society.

In a pluralistic society such as the United States, people are forced to interact with others holding a variety of beliefs and values. This may create a sense of normlessness, because one's own beliefs are called into question by the various beliefs of others with whom one interacts. In this type of society, religious groups function as subcultures to re-create a social world in which others support one's own beliefs. This makes each individual's religious worldview more plausible because it is supported by the consensus within the group. Communal ties reinforce the sacred worldview constructed by the group, maintaining a sense of social solidarity even in a highly differentiated and pluralistic society.

The Roman Catholic experience is also a good example of the importance of a distinctive, nonaccommodating morality. Prior to the Second Vatican Council (1962-1965), the Roman Catholic Church was unwilling to recognize any other religious group or lifestyle as legitimate. Since Vatican II, Catholics have been allowed to marry non-Catholics, individual confession has been replaced by nonobligatory counseling (resembling that of many Protestant denominations), and Catholics have been allowed to eat meat on Fridays. Soon after this accommodation, the Roman Catholic Church experienced its first numerical decline in the twentieth century.

Thus, the strength of religious groups lies in their ability to provide the two crucial functions of religion. These two functions, meaning and belonging, are related. Because of this, it is difficult for a religious group to provide one and ignore the other. Strong religious beliefs are constructed and maintained through regular social interaction among people with strong emotional ties. On the other hand, those strong social ties are much more likely to exist among people with similar beliefs.

Context

Religion is among the oldest concerns in sociology. The classical sociological theorists (such as Karl Marx, Émile Durkheim, and Max Weber) devoted great attention to explaining the relationship between religion and the rest of society. In the broadest sense, all the classical attempts to explain religion incorporated functionalist elements in them even though they were not functionalist theories. Karl Marx, when he called religion the "opiate of the masses," implied that religion functioned to help maintain the status quo by directing the attention of oppressed people away from the inequalities of the present life and toward the promises of the afterlife. In his book *Die Protestantische Ethik und der Geist des Kapitalismus* (1904; *The Protestant Ethic and the Spirit of Capitalism*, 1930), German theorist Max Weber discussed how religion functioned to create sacred legitimation of a capitalist lifestyle. Despite these superficial similarities, however, it was from French sociologist Durkheim that the functionalist perspective originated. In his book *Les Formes élémentaires de la vie religieuse: Le Système totémique en Australie* (1912; *The Elementary Forms of the Religious Life: A Study in Religious Sociology*, 1915), Durkheim discussed how religion creates a sacred reality that helps people to organize and find meaning even in the mundane experiences of everyday life.

Religion remained of primary interest to sociologists until the end of World War I and the death of Max Weber in 1920. Interest in the sociological importance of religion was more or less dormant from that time until after World War II. The 1950's saw a renewed interest in religion among the American population. The percentage of the American population who attended church on an average Sunday rose from about 39 percent in 1950 to approximately

50 percent in 1955. Along with the renewed interest in religion on the part of the population came renewed academic interest in trying to explain the phenomenon.

During the 1940's and 1950's, Talcott Parsons was proposing the sociological perspective called "functionalism," which studied social institutions based on the "functions" they perform for society. Since that time, other approaches to the study of religion have become popular, but the basic functions of religion have remained an important topic of discussion in the sociology of religion. Sociologists have continued to make great contributions in explaining the role of religion in society through the use of functional analysis.

Bibliography

Berger, Peter L. *The Sacred Canopy: Elements of a Sociological Theory of Religion*. Garden City, N.Y.: Doubleday, 1967. Classic work in the sociology of religion. Berger proposes that religion creates and maintains a social world that allows people to survive in their environment. Easily understood.

Finke, Roger, and Rodney Stark. *The Churching of America, 1776-1990: Winners and Losers in Our Religious Economy*. New Brunswick, N.J.: Rutgers University Press, 1992. Major contribution in the discussion of the social history of American religion. Challenges conventional wisdom and examines data that explain how many sectarian religious groups prospered while mainline groups declined. Well written and easily understood.

Hatch, Nathan O. *The Democratization of American Christianity*. New Haven, Conn.: Yale University Press, 1989. Beautifully written historical analysis explaining how sectarian religion came from a marginal status to dominance on the American religious landscape.

Kelley, Dean. *Why Conservative Churches Are Growing*. Macon, Ga.: Mercer University Press, 1986. Originally published in 1972, but still a valuable study of the growth of sectarian religion in the United States. Data are somewhat dated, but the patterns persist and have been supported by subsequent research.

McGuire, Meredith B. *Religion: The Social Context*. 4th ed. Belmont, Calif.: Wadsworth, 1997.

Roberts, Keith. *Religion in Sociological Perspective*. 3d ed. Belmont, Calif.: Wadsworth, 1995. Perhaps the best overview of the sociology of religion available. Includes a detailed discussion of the various theoretical approaches to religion including functional, conflict, and social psychological theories.

Roof, Wade Clark, and William McKinney. *American Mainline Religion: Its Changing Shape and Future*. New Brunswick, N.J.: Rutgers University Press, 1987. Fine work on trends associated with liberal mainline religion. Explains social factors that have affected the liberal mainline in the past and will probably have a profound influence on its future.

David P. Caddell

Cross-References

Churches, Denominations, and Sects; Cultural Norms and Sanctions; Functionalism; Religion; Religion: Marxist and Conflict Theory Views; Secularization in Western Society; Socialization: Religion; Values and Value Systems.

RELIGION
Marxist and Conflict Theory Views

Type of sociology: Major social institutions
Field of study: Religion

Karl Marx's description of religion as the "opiate of the masses" pointed to religion's possible use as a weapon in battles within societies, by means of which one class induces docility in another.

Principal terms

CONFLICT THEORY: framework for sociological interpretations that assumes competition among human individuals and groups for limited resources

CRITICAL THEORY: framework for understanding culture that began in 1930's Germany and integrates conflict theory, Marxism, and other strains of social thought

FALSE CONSCIOUSNESS: in Marxist theory, a notion believed to be true by one sector of the populace that is misleading in ways that are beneficial to a more powerful group

IDEOLOGY: collection of human thoughts about the assumed nature of reality, as shared by a group and used as a basis for thinking about the world

MARXIST THEORY: framework for sociological interpretations that is based upon Karl Marx's assertion that the mode of production determines social organization

PRODUCTION: in Marxist theory, the creation of material goods and resources that occurs when human labor interacts with the environment

RELIGION: system of human thoughts and beliefs about the assumed nature of reality which involves some supernatural or transcendent nonhuman deity or principle

REPRODUCTION: in Marxist theory, society's ongoing attempt to continue itself through new members who hold old values, orientations, and behaviors

Overview

Though sociologists have not produced a commonly accepted definition of religion, there have been many attempts to do so. Common to most definitions is the recognition that religion remains a powerful motivating factor for human behavior. In the supposedly "secularized" societies of the modern Western world, it may be fashionable to downplay religion's importance, but its ability to influence action is readily apparent.

Karl Marx developed a thoroughgoing theory of society's organization and interaction. Marx held that the primary determining factor in human social existence was the means of production—that is, the way that capital is used to harness labor and turn the environment into produced resources. One's position within this society-wide process of production determined one's class, and one's class shaped one's consciousness. This shaping process included the broad spectrum of notions called "ideology"—all those basic assumptions about reality on the basis of which humans see alternatives, evaluate options, and make decisions. From the dictum that "class creates consciousness" comes the conclusion that the economic reality shapes the ways in which people think about things and the very basis of what is held to be real.

Within different ideologies lie different assumptions, and these assumptions move people to act in different ways. Marx tied these actions to the groups who would benefit from them the most, noticing the inevitable connections between ideology and interest. For example, a national ideology that included the idea of the king's divine right to rule served the king's interest. By making it more difficult to question publicly the king's judgment, the society would shift more of its resources toward the king, and the presence of surplus capital would support the continuation of the ideology of the king's blessed nature. Marxist theory identifies some set of interests with every class and every ideology.

Religion, then, is a special case of ideology, according to Marxist theory. Since religion roots the rationale for social organization in the divine, where it holds sway all classes tend to accept the status quo. In the specific case of European religion in Marx's time, Marx interpreted the dominant forms of Christianity as supporting a hierarchicalized worldview that supported the elite group that possessed the society's capital. The wealthy benefited from a religion that emphasized hard work in this world (the so-called "Protestant work ethic") in exchange for benefits in the afterlife, since that religion enabled the wealthy to gain more from the labor of the working poor. The ideology served the interests of the wealthy. This was perhaps Marx's chief contribution to the society of religion: He held that the sociologist must analyze religion by determining who materially benefits from it and noticing the ways in which religion functions as an ideology to protect the interests of those who receive that benefit.

Religion's ideological function was, however, even deeper than that. Ideologies can alter the perceptions of reality by changing the ways in which people categorize their experience. Not only did Western European religion reinforce the presumed "right" of the materially powerful to keep their power and encourage the working class to remain in their oppression, but it also limited the population's ability to conceive of nonhierarchical ways of organizing society. The religion so strongly answered the question "Who should be rich and powerful?" that the people never thought to ask, "Should wealth and power exist at all?" In this context, Marx referred metaphorically to religion as the opiate of the people. In that day, an opiate was a mild analgesic or palliative; Marx was saying that the religion kept the people from feeling their own pain and thus from perceiving their own reality. Religion was thus a false consciousness; it was a way of perceiving reality that removed people from the material base of their reality and subjugated them to the desires of an oppressive upper class.

Many of the conflict theories of religion share the same orientations as Marxist theory; at times, the terms are used interchangeably. In general, however, conflict theories are less interested in the material basis for the ideology than in the contests of power between different ideological groups. Whereas Marxist (and other materialist) theories of religion remain rooted in concrete economic concerns, conflict theory makes it possible to analyze other struggles within cultures around the issue of religion. For example, wealth is not the only form of power. In recent political campaigns for the presidency of the United States of America, power has been the key issue, even though the president does not directly receive money in proportion to the power of the office. Still, conflict theorists would correctly note the use of religious themes and images in presidential campaigns, in attempts to establish support for a particular candidate. Religion is a powerful motivating force, and it can certainly swing votes. When candidates use religious images to produce a popular ideology that is in the candidate's own interest, conflict theory can be used to analyze the use of the power that is embodied in those religious symbols.

Marxist theory tends to look for the economic bases of power, but conflict theory asserts the importance of power in and of itself. Similarly, whereas Marxist theory locates interests (and thus the origins of corresponding ideologies, including religion) in classes (defined in the economic terms of the mode of production), conflict theory opens up new possibilities. Interest groups can define themselves in many different ways. Most of the larger American Protestant denominations, for example, have experienced deep conflict, at times leading to divisions into competing churches. Each faction forms its own "interest group," and the intensity of the political fighting may be completely disproportionate to the amount of capital that is involved. At the same time, the sociologist should not be blind to the examination of who benefits materially as well as in terms of power and influence.

Applications

During the 1950's and 1960's, the United States (especially in its southeastern regions) experienced great upheaval in racial relations. As it had in the conflicts over slavery three-fourths of a century earlier, Protestant Christianity occupied vocal and active positions on both sides of the issue. Marxist and conflict approaches can help to illuminate the role of religion in this time of social movement around the issue of civil rights.

The Marxist theoretical perspective offers a strategy that begins with the question of material benefit. To the extent that the continued prosperity of European Americans was dependent upon the continued existence of an African American underclass, the elites' interest resided in the suppression of the Civil Rights movement. The presence of "second-class citizens" meant that European Americans would have higher rates of employment and lower rates of poverty than they would have had if such misfortune were shared equally throughout the community. Thus, many European American churches proclaimed that African Americans were not deserving of God-given (and constitutionally guaranteed) rights. The continued exclusion of persons of color from the buildings of the church (and thus symbolically from the presence of God) paralleled the exclusion of those same persons from full economic participation. Certainly, the long-persuasive teaching of the dominant churches that African Americans needed European Americans to guide them in the way of Christian faith served to anesthetize many people from the pain of segregated life; religion operated then (as it often has) as a system for the denial of oppression. It allowed both rich and poor to declare themselves the same before God, joint recipients of a heaven set aside for them. This encouraged both sides to remain within the status quo.

Some historians of the period have noticed that the European American churches that were most willing to accept African Americans were those of "mainline" Protestantism, whose adherents constituted one of the wealthy segments of the society. Since these people had less to lose than the more marginal members of their class did, they may have seen integration as less of a potential loss. Perhaps they even thought of racial integration as a means of reaching new markets. Regardless of conscious motivation, the African Americans with the most material advantage to gain were the first to make religious arguments for equality, followed much later by those European Americans who were least likely to suffer material loss. The middle class embraced integration and its theological warrants only afterward, in most cases.

Marxist analysis of religion becomes more problematic in other situations, such as those that exist throughout much of contemporary Central America. In many Central American countries, the church (usually the Roman Catholic Church) has been involved in both sides of the civil unrest. Often, the church owns sizable amounts of land and other capital; therefore, some of the official religious rhetoric encourages workers to strive in this life for the rewards of the next, thereby benefiting the totalitarian leaders of the Central American government. Many local priests, however, have embraced the doctrines of liberation theology, a religious system that affirms the right of the poor to overthrow their oppressors and begin a new life for themselves.

The competing ideologies match well with the conflicting interests in many cases, but the role of the priests is distinctive. Many priests have taken vows of poverty in exchange for guaranteed employment within the church, and thus they have no direct opportunity for material gain. (The presence of the central church's large resources, however, should make one hesitant to rule out economic motives and results.) Conflict theory, however, allows a more thorough analysis of the priests' participation. Through their immersion in the culture of the indigenous populations, the local priests have taken on many of the values of their parishioners. They identify themselves with the interest groups of the locals, rather than with the hierarchy of their own institution. This shift in loyalty is represented both in ideology and in interest. In other words they have not only cast their cultural lot with the oppressed but also have adopted the theological positions that reflect that social position in life. Such notions may include ideas of God's valuation of the poor and love for the oppressed, or God's vengeance against those who hoard resources. The theology may also provide norms for a new way of life, such as equality and respect. These theological resources are in no way to be minimized, and they may produce long-term economic benefits for the priests as well, but the more immediate concern is the conflict between different ideological groups. Even within the upper echelons of ecclesiastical bureaucracy and in the rarefied air of academic theology, careers are made and lost over the battles between conflicting religious ideologies.

Context

Émile Durkheim understood religion as the personification and deification of society's understanding of itself, providing a way for society to justify and enforce its own values and norms. Karl Marx's interpretation of religion is not much different, except that Marx perceives society as being fragmented into classes. Religion, then, is not the reification of society for itself, but the justification of one class's way of life as opposed to another class's interests. If the elites have sufficient power, they may be able to construct ideologies that the lower classes will accept and use as reasons to maintain the situation of domination.

Conflict theory has allowed the sociology of religion (as well as the sociology of ideology) to include nonmaterial factors more readily in its analysis. Power becomes a resource with value in and of itself, rather than merely as a corollary of capital and wealth. Religions are contentious by nature; that is, it is the nature of a religion to contend its truth, and thus to seek its defense and its expansion in the context of other systems of belief.

The so-called Frankfurt School has developed a form of "critical theory" that builds upon many of these insights about culture and ideology, especially in the work of scholars such as Hans-Georg Gadamer, Jürgen Habermas, Max Horkheimer, Herbert Marcuse, and others. By constructing theories about the interest-ideology connection in the light of postmodernist understandings of language and society, this group has pushed the frontiers of Marxist sociology of religion. This new field has not yet, however, produced much interaction with the traditional descriptive study of the sociology of religion, and that integration needs to take place in order to complete the development of critical theory.

There is a need for theories that more directly connect values and the material aspects of religion. In many cases, the self-interest and class-consciousness of religious belief is apparent, but there are also many other cases in which religion promotes the abandonment of self-interest. These cases are still poorly understood in sociological terms, and in most cases they receive treatment only as individual psychological deviations from the sociological expectation.

In a related area, sociologists need to examine the interplay between materialist perspectives (which stress external observation) and subjective interpretations of religion (which emphasize the actor's self-perception). How do believers feel when they undertake acts that have material ramifications? What do they think they are doing?

Finally, sociologists of religion are becoming increasingly interested (and should become even more so) in conflicts within religious groups. What are the processes for choosing leadership within a group with a shared belief system? Furthermore, to what extent is any belief system "shared" by a group? Many opportunities for study exist, including clergy-parishioner relationships and the presence of power issues in them, the infighting among clerics of one or more denominations, and the degree of diversity that is allowed within a single church. In the same way that Marx expanded the field of sociology by examining competing interests within one society, the sociology of religion should examine the interaction of religious beliefs on the microsociological level in order to understand its importance for the larger scale of religious activity.

Bibliography

Brown, Michael E. *The Production of Society: A Marxian Foundation for Social Theory.* Totowa, N.J.: Rowman & Littlefield, 1986. Attempt to integrate Marxist theory into several other theoretical movements, from psychoanalysis to postmodernism. Contains stimulating chapter on ideology and culture that shows the connections that neo-Marxist studies make between all forms of ideology and the means of production.

Elster, Jon. *An Introduction to Karl Marx.* Cambridge, England: Cambridge University Press, 1986. Excellent short introduction to Marx's thought. One might wish for more detail on Marx's sociology of religion, but the book gives a solid overview of Marx's original concepts, emphasizing the thought of Marx rather than that of his later interpreters.

Kellner, Douglas. *Critical Theory, Marxism, and Modernity.* Baltimore: Johns Hopkins University Press, 1989. Thorough retracing of the historical steps between early twentieth century European Marxist and materialist thought and the rise of the so-called Frankfurt school of critical theory. Though it provides very little material on religion, the book offers clues to the future of at least some neo-Marxist interpretations of religion.

Kinloch, Graham C. *Sociological Theory: Its Development and Major Paradigms.* New York: McGraw-Hill, 1977. Ideas of Karl Marx and other conflict sociologists are presented here in brief form for easy comparison with other sociological perspectives. Kinloch's typological arrangement of sociological methods betrays a functionalist predisposition, but there is still much good information here to help place Marx's sociology of religion within the larger context of sociological theories.

McGuire, Meredith B. *Religion: The Social Context.* 4th ed. Belmont, Calif.: Wadsworth, 1997. Excellent introductory text for the entire field of religion's social dimensions. Particularly useful is a chapter on religion's role in both cohesion and conflict, which offers a very balanced view with a strong emphasis on conflict among civil religions.

McLellan, David. *Marxism and Religion: A Description and Assessment of the Marxist Critique of Christianity.* New York: Harper & Row, 1987. Helpful for disentangling Marx's sociology from the many forms of Marxism present today and throughout the past century. The clear historical presentation demonstrates the ways in which Marxist thought has changed in its evaluation of religion's protection of bourgeois power, and it also indicates some of the major responses to the Marxist critique.

Wuthnow, Robert. *Meaning and Moral Order: Explorations in Cultural Analysis.* Berkeley: University of California Press, 1987. Integrates issues of religion into an investigation of how humans produce meaning. Though the core of the book does not reflect particular Marxist strands, there are good chapters on the connections of religion and state order, as well as the role of technological change in affecting ideology.

Jon L. Berquist

Cross-References

Civil Religion and Politics; Conflict Theory; Marxism; Religion: Functionalist Analyses; Socialization: Religion; Values and Value Systems.

ROLE CONFLICT AND ROLE STRAIN

Type of sociology: Social structure
Field of study: Components of social structure

Role conflict is theorized to develop when an individual experiences competition within or among his or her social positions and their corresponding expectations. Role strain is the general stress experienced when the demands of one or more roles are inappropriate, unfair, or unrealistic. Stress and conflict within social groups and personal relationships may be explained in terms of role conflict or role strain.

Principal terms

BURNOUT: emotional exhaustion, depersonalization, and a reduced sense of accomplishment caused by role strain of human services work

DEPERSONALIZATION: loss of emotional commitment to work and people as a result of role strain

INTERROLE CONFLICT: conflict between the demands of two or more roles occupied by one person

INTRAROLE CONFLICT: stress caused by different views of a role

NORM: accepted and expected guideline for social behavior

PERSON-ROLE CONFLICT: mismatch between an individual's abilities and the demands of a role

ROLE: set of norms attached to a particular social position

ROLE CONFLICT: stress created when roles are ambiguous, unrealistic, or inappropriate

ROLE REVERSAL: stress reduction strategy in which parties assume each other's perspectives to establish understanding

ROLE STRAIN: stress created by role conflict, role change, mismanagement, or misunderstanding

Overview

A role is a set of norms (obligations or expectations) attached to an individual's social position, occupation, or relationship status. People are motivated to adhere to norms and perform roles in order to win approval, avoid social penalties, and develop self-esteem. Role conflict is the psychological stress created when persons do not fit their roles (person-role conflict), when relevant others disagree with the individual about his or her role (intrarole conflict), or when several different roles make mutually exclusive demands on an individual (interrole conflict).

Role strain is a collective term including different kinds of role conflict as well as the general stress experienced when roles are changed, misunderstood, or mismanaged. For example, because roles are composed of norms, and norms undergo social change, people may find that during the time they are filling a given role, social expectations of the role have altered. For example, a man whose boyhood models of masculinity emphasized strength and independence will experience role strain in adulthood, when he discovers that such macho ideals are outmoded and no longer optimally valued in the workplace or the family.

In addition to role conflict, sources of role strain include overload and misallocation. Overload occurs when one person has too many roles to perform adequately or when demands placed on a group exceed the group's resources. The problem of overload is particularly difficult in understaffed environments, where there are more roles than there are people to fill them. Misallocation occurs when people disagree about who should perform which roles in a relationship. For example, the chairperson of a problem-solving group may believe that it is her duty to dictate group values, whereas members may think she should refrain from unduly influencing group deliberations. Their disagreements about how responsibilities have been allocated will be a source of role strain for all in the group. Misallocation can also plague personal relationships, as when husbands and wives disagree on the division of household labor and decision-making power.

Research on marital satisfaction frequently implicates role misallocation as a source of distress. Particularly challenging are the changes and innovations associated with nontraditional household arrangements. For example, if one spouse carries a disproportionate share of household chore assignments, yet both work outside the home, this inequality (unfairness) will contribute to marital role strain. Some critics argue that a return to traditional household roles—husband as breadwinner, wife as homemaker—would simplify labor and reduce stress for all concerned. While this may be true in a limited sense, multiple roles are inevitable now that women as well as men seek the benefits of education and careers. Additionally, economic conditions make it advantageous, and often necessary, for both spouses to work.

Do multiple roles—each partner performing roles related to work as well as the home—necessarily create relationship distress? In *Intimate Relationships* (1992), social psychologist Sharon S. Brehm describes the contrasting predictions of two hypotheses about multiple roles. According to the scarcity hypothesis, more social roles invariably lead to more stress, since an individual's limited resources are spread to meet more demands. According to the enhancement hypothesis, however, defining oneself through more roles means less stress, since disappointments in one role can be compensated for by success in others. According to Brehm, research evidence favors the enhancement hypothesis: "Having multiple roles is usually associated with increased well-being." Whether multiple roles increase or reduce stress may depend on such factors as the quality of one's job, one's commitment to working, and the social support provided by partners and other members of one's social network.

Two sources of role strain with clear applications to work performance are depersonalization and burnout. Depersonalization occurs when an individual's work requires him or her to occupy an emotionally detached or dehumanizing role. By consistently withholding involvement and intimacy from other people, people in depersonalization roles learn to "blame the victim": to hold needy persons responsible for their own plight. Professional caregivers may lose their ability to care, and educators may lose the desire to teach. When detachment is combined with overload, human service workers are at risk for burnout, described by Christina Maslach as "a syndrome of emotional exhaustion, depersonalization, and reduced personal accomplishment" (*Burnout: The Cost of Caring*, 1982). Victims of burnout experience "compassion fatigue," an inability to connect emotionally with their clients. They begin to intellectualize or trivialize others' suffering and seek to escape or minimize their contact with those who seek their help. Finally, burnout victims find that their work is no longer satisfying. They feel helpless, inadequate, and joyless. They may also develop physical and behavioral symptoms of stress, such as sleeplessness, psychosomatic illness, depression, anger, and inflexible thinking. Research has identified several strategies to solve the problems of role strain, conflict, and burnout.

Applications

If a group member's talents do not fit an assigned role, he or she experiences person-role conflict. For example, most work groups involve two sets of duties: task-oriented roles and relations-oriented roles. A task-oriented person who is assigned to perform a relations-oriented role, such as improving group morale, may find such activity uncomfortable and difficult. Many person-role conflicts stem from individuals' uncertainty about what is expected of them or how they should achieve it. Thus some role conflicts are based in role ambiguity. Person-role conflict may also result from temporary stresses. For example, an individual with serious personal problems may be unable to act as the good listener his friends have come to expect, so that at least temporarily he experiences person-role conflict in his relationships with others.

Perhaps the most common form of role conflict is interrole conflict, the stress experienced when one person attempts to fulfill two or more competing roles. For example, an employee who is also a student may find that, as an employee, he is expected to work additional hours on occasion, but as a student, he should not let changes in his work schedule disrupt his class attendance. In order to perform one role well, he must disappoint expectations in the other. Interrole conflict can also cause problems in personal relationships. For example, a woman trying to care for her ailing mother may be unable to spend enough time with her own children because of the interrole conflict between her duties as daughter and mother.

A subtler but no less stressful problem is created by intrarole conflict, experienced when one's role is perceived differently by different groups or individuals. For example, a newly elected employee representative will experience role conflict on learning that her coworkers expect her to represent their interests to management, while her supervisors expect her to represent management's point of view to her fellow employees. In order to meet one group's expectations, she must disappoint the other group, and vice versa. The individual is caught between different, even contradictory, interpretations of the same role.

Intrarole conflict can challenge personal relationships as well. For example, if a man thinks that he can fulfill the role of "good husband" merely by financially supporting his family, his self-perception is challenged when his wife argues that, in her view, a "good husband" must also meet the family members' social and emotional needs.

General role strain, in addition to specific forms of role conflict, includes changes in role expectations as a result of time or experience. Some roles, such as jobs, are rigidly defined and resist change over time. Other roles, however, especially those in the interpersonal domain, are sensitive to subtle social changes, personal experience, and interpersonal redefinition. For example, as a result of financial pressures and personal frustrations, a married couple may reexamine their assumptions that the husband should be the breadwinner for the family. The family may decide that it will be best for all members if the wife earns the income by working outside the home while the husband works in the home, caring for the house and children. Their decision is not unique, but their arrangement is not normative—it is not typical of other households like theirs—so they lack external models or guidelines for their new roles. The wife may find that she has difficulty redefining herself as a "good wife" if she is not doing most of the cooking and cleaning; her husband may have difficulty feeling like a "good husband" now that he no longer brings home a paycheck. Even if the arrangement works well for the family, it will probably strain their self-concepts and their sense of community acceptance. Role strain in this example is pervasive: Prior to rearranging household duties, both spouses experienced role strain because their work was unsatisfying; after establishing the new arrangement, both are still under stress—this time because of their lack of standards or experience.

Because people who work in human services professions must meet many demands in relationships with their clients, researchers have closely examined the causes and consequences of job-related role strain. This work has led to the development of stress-reduction recommendations for coping with role conflict and burnout.

One strategy recommended for alleviating role conflict is the technique of role reversal. Because roles often come in pairs—teacher and student, parent and child, employer and employee, physician and patient—each party to a conflict can benefit from briefly adopting the other's perspective. Role reversal may be effective either as a mental exercise (imagining each other's perceptions) or as a spoken dialogue in which each person attempts to articulate the other's position to the other's satisfaction. Role reversal may be effective because it reestablishes empathy and cooperation after polarizing circumstances.

Because burnout is a complex and gradual process, it is difficult to remedy. Social psychologist Christina Maslach has recommended several strategies for coping with burnout. Among her suggestions are to set realistic goals, perform the same tasks in different ways, take intermittent breaks or rest periods, resist the tendency to take things personally, concentrate on successes rather than failures, pay attention to one's own needs and feelings, and get adequate rest and relaxation. She advises engaging in "decompression" exercises to resolve work-related problems before going home and developing satisfying nonwork interests and activities. If all else fails, she concludes, change to a job with less risk of role strain.

Context

A role organizes several norms—guidelines and standards that govern one's behaviors, especially in social situations. Norms are seldom transmitted formally, in the form of rules, doctrines, or obvious standards. Instead, people tend to infer norms and roles on the basis of personal experience and social observation. For example, the role of student at one institution may involve many precise customs, including expectations for attendance, class participation, interacting with instructors, and following dress codes, whereas at another school the minimum standards for accepted student behavior might be less clear and more flexible. Through a process of social comparison— observing others' actions—an individual learns how to behave acceptably in a particular social context.

Most people conform to norms and roles in order to reap the benefits of social acceptance and approval and to escape being judged as deviant or a failure. The severity of sanctions varies for different kinds of roles. For example, in most cultures the penalties are harsher for being a "bad mother" than for being a "bad student," or even a "bad father." During childhood socialization, individuals learn to base their self-concept to some extent on role adherence. For this reason a person who fails to fulfill role expectations may suffer not only social punishments such as disapproval and ostracism but also self-punishments such as personal embarrassment, self-recrimination, and reduced self-esteem.

Originally, role theorists characterized roles in terms of group structure and function. Within any problem-solving or social group, different individuals take on different activities and perform different functions, such as providing leadership, conflict resolution, or moral support. One form of role conflict, person-role conflict, develops when an individual's personality or abilities are mismatched with his or her role. In the context of group function, interrole conflict can also develop when an individual who belongs to two or more different groups finds that a role in one group competes with that of another. Intrarole conflict involves several different perceptions of a single group role. Eventually, the concept of role was expanded to include the context of larger "groups" such as institutions, culture, and gender. The concepts of role strain and role conflict in this broader sense have also been expanded.

As studies of roles within social groups have been extended to include dyads (two-person groups such as married couples) as well as families and friendship networks, the concept of role conflict has been applied to interpersonal relationships as well as to groups and institutions. Because roles vary with culture, it is obvious that much, if not all, of a role's specifics are acquired through learning. The flexibility of a role may depend on whether it is achieved or ascribed. The components of achieved roles, roles adopted through personal effort or training, may be learned through schooling or experience. For example, the role of supervisor is achieved: An employee who begins in a lower-status position can advance through effort and education. In contrast, the components of an ascribed role are determined by one's relationships to other persons. For example, a man who fathers a child acquires the ascribed role of father, regardless of whether he has earned or prepared for that role. He cannot be dismissed as one could from an achieved role. Yet the expectations and standards for an ascribed role may be more ambiguous and susceptible to social change.

Because roles and role expectations are learned, through both formal education and socialization, role strain in general and role conflict in particular can be mediated by new information and experience. By learning about common sources of role strain, people can anticipate stressors, recognize the symptoms of inequity or burnout, and take action to reduce the damage. Ultimately roles are useful in assembling and transmitting the norms of one's culture and aspirations. Despite social change and role ambiguity, people can learn to meet the challenges of changing expectations and social structure, to meet their own and their society's goals.

Bibliography

Baron, Robert A., and Jerald Greenberg. *Behavior in Organizations: Understanding and Managing the Human Side of Work.* 7th ed. Englewood Cliffs, N.J.: Prentice-Hall, 1999. Management text exploring ways in which workers are assigned to roles in group contexts and the various agendas that groups must learn to address.

Brehm, Sharon S. "Conflict and Dissolution." In *Intimate Relationships.* 2d ed. New York: McGraw-Hill, 1992. Contains chapter on personal relationships that puts the concept of role strain in the context of other sources and causes of relationship breakdown. Ideal for a college audience.

Hochschild, Arlie. *The Second Shift.* New York: Viking, 1989. Hochschild interviewed couples about their job arrangements, household labor, child care, and leisure in this study of how working people spend their time.

Maslach, Christina. *Burnout: The Cost of Caring.* Englewood Cliffs, N.J.: Prentice-Hall, 1982. Relatively short book by the acknowledged expert in the field of burnout. Full of case studies, practical suggestions, and sound advice. Appropriate for college-level readers and human service professionals seeking to understand and address their own needs and experiences.

Ann L. Weber

Cross-References

Cultural Norms and Sanctions; Dramaturgy; Social Groups; Socialization: The Family; Statuses and Roles.

SAMPLES AND SAMPLING TECHNIQUES

Type of sociology: Sociological research
Field of study: Basic concepts

A sample is a portion of a population. Based on scientific sampling techniques, a sample is an accurate representation of the larger population, and study findings in the sample can be extended to the population.

Principal terms

BIAS: deviation of the expected value of a statistical estimate from the true value for some measured quantity

ELEMENT: basic unit of a population, such as an individual, household, segment, or social organization, for which information is sought

MUTUALLY EXCLUSIVE: situation in which, if outcomes 1 and 2 are mutually exclusive, and 1 occurs, then 2 logically cannot occur

POPULATION: entire collection of elements of a specific type defined over a given space and time

SAMPLE: portion of all the elements in a population that is used to obtain information about the entire population

SAMPLE SIZE: number of population elements contained in a sample

SAMPLING: process of selecting a sample from an existing population

SAMPLING FRAME: actual list of sampling units from which the sample, or some stage of the sample, is selected

SAMPLING UNIT: element or a set of elements considered for selection in some stage of sampling

TARGET POPULATION AND SAMPLE POPULATION: former is the population about which information is desired, while the latter is the population to be sampled

Overview

Sampling is the process of selecting a representative group from a larger population for the purpose of providing statistical information on the nature of the larger population. Sampling is employed in almost every area of research in social science and business.

Sampling has several advantages over collecting information on every member of a population, a process called a census or complete enumeration. First, a sample can provide useful information at a much lower cost than a complete enumeration. Second, therefore, data from a sample are usually more up to date than data obtained from a complete enumeration. Third, sampling can allow resources to be directed to hire personnel better qualified, give intensive training to interviewers, improve supervision of both the field, work and data management processes. Consequently, the sample may provide more accurate data than complete enumeration. Finally, by virtue of its flexibility and adaptability, sampling has greater scope regarding the variety of information accessible.

Moreover, sampling is the only option in some situations. Because investigation of product quality, such as the strength of construction materials, often requires the destruction of the product itself, only a sample can be tested. Measuring air pollution is an extreme example of a situation in which complete enumeration is unattainable, because of the target population's infinite size.

Approaches to sampling, or selecting elements from a population, fall into two broad categories: nonprobability (nonrandom) sampling and probability (random) sampling. With nonprobability sampling, the chance of being selected is unknown. Methods for nonprobability sampling include convenience sampling, judgment sampling, and quota sampling. All nonprobability samples are potentially biased by nonrepresentative selection. With probability or random sampling, each element has a known chance of being selected from the population. Probability sampling avoids selection bias and permits effective statistical generalization from sample to population. In this article, probability sampling methods are emphasized.

In probability sampling, a sample is selected from a sampling frame, or list of sampling units. Basic probability sampling techniques include simple random, systematic, stratified, and cluster sampling. Simple random sampling is the most basic probability sampling method. In this method, each element of the population has an equal chance of being selected, much as a coin has equal probability of landing on heads or tails. Systematic sampling selects elements at even intervals, such as every fifth house on a street, often beginning with a randomly selected element. Stratified sampling divides a population into mutually exclusive groups, or strata, each of which is relatively homogeneous, and then a simple random sample is selected from each stratum. Finally, the separate simple random samples are combined. Cluster sampling divides a population into clusters, such as dividing a city into neighborhoods. A smaller number of clusters is then selected at random, with all members of a selected cluster included in the sample.

An important variation of clustering is called two-stage sampling. In many situations, particularly when the target population is very large, such as the population of a nation, a list of clusters is the only available sampling frame. Even if the list of every element of a population were available, it would be very expensive to conduct a single-stage random sample. In order to concentrate location of selected population elements, and thereby reduce the travel expenses of conducting interviews, a multistage sampling plan is often preferred. Clusters are selected in the initial stage of sampling, followed by random selection of elements from within each selected cluster. The clusters selected at the initial stage are commonly termed primary sampling units (PSUs).

If multiple stages of sampling are required, sampling frames are needed at different stages. Elements of the target population are randomly selected at the final stage of the multistage sampling from the list of sampling units selected in the prior stage. Multistage sampling is often employed in population research. Census tracts, residential blocks, segments, and dwellings are defined as clusters at different stages. When dwellings are finally drawn from the selected segments, households are selected from each sampled dwelling. Finally, individuals are selected from the sampled households.

No matter how good a sample is, it always carries some error; this fact must be explicitly considered for effective sampling design. Error is usually composed of three parts: nonsampling bias, sampling bias, and sampling error. Nonsampling bias is error that can arise when the target population is not properly defined, questions are poorly constructed or poorly presented, respondents do not respond or furnish inaccurate information, and mistakes occur in recording information. Sampling bias occurs when sampling frame is inaccurate or when nonprobability sampling is applied. Nonsampling and sampling bias cannot be reduced by simply increasing sample size. It can be reduced or eliminated only if the above problems are carefully handled.

Sampling error results from the sampling process itself. Different samples, drawn from the same population at the same time using the same procedures, should produce similar, though not identical, results. The average value of many such samples is considered to be an unbiased estimate of the population value. The variability among these samples is called sampling error. With probability sampling, sampling error can be estimated from a single sample itself.

Sampling error or sampling variability does not cause bias or systematic differences between the population and the sample. If the sampling error is large, however, the precision of the sample is said to be low. Sampling error or sample precision is affected by sampling techniques used and sample size. Usually clustering increases, and stratification reduces, sampling error. When sample size is sufficiently large, sampling error is very low with probability sampling.

Applications

In most cases, sampling is the most affordable method for collecting demographic and socioeconomic data. Since 1940, sampling has been used by the U.S. Bureau of the Census along with the census itself to obtain additional information about occupation, income, education, reproduction, migration, and so on, as well as to speed publication of results. In addition, a great majority of Bureau of the Census activities have been devoted to a series of sample surveys, providing up-to-date demographic and economic data between decennial census surveys. As statistician William G. Cochran said of the 1960 and 1970 censuses, "except for certain basic information required from every person for constitutional or legal reasons, the whole census was shifted to a sample basis."

Another familiar application of sampling is the opinion poll. Polls, undertaken to determine the opinions and attitudes of the public on issues of interest, are usually carried out on only a small fraction of the total population, yet they can provide accurate information about people's opinions. For example, in the final weekend of the 1992 presidential campaign, five polls with different sample sizes, conducted by different agents, had striking agreement. They showed that Bill Clinton's support was about 44 percent, George Bush's was about 36 percent, and Ross Perot's was about 16 percent. The poll predictions were very close to actual election results. The predictions were all based on small samples relative to the voting population, ranging from the *Washington Post* sample of 722 to *The New York Times*/CBS sample of 2,248 likely voters.

At one time, polls relied on the notion that the larger the sample size, the more representative the sample. This is not true. A classic example is the *Literary Digest* opinion poll that was taken before the 1936 presidential election. About 10 million sample ballots were mailed to *Literary Digest* subscribers, people selected from telephone directories, and automobile owners. About 2.3 million ballots were returned, showing Alfred Landon to be the winner over Franklin Roosevelt by 57 percent to 43 percent. Yet Roosevelt won the election by the huge margin of 62.5 percent to 36.5 percent. The large error was attributable to nonresponse and selection bias: Only about 23 percent of the ballots were returned, and the people selected by the magazine were likely to have higher-than-average incomes.

The World Fertility Survey (WFS), the largest social survey in history, is a good example of applying the multistage probability area sampling method for data collection. The world population has experienced tremendous growth since World War II. The WFS was designed to document the pace and regional distribution of population growth. A "world census" is clearly impossible. Instead, the International Statistics Institute (ISI), the United States Agency for International Development (USAID), and the United Nations Fund for Population Activities (UNFPA) sponsored the worldwide survey during the period between 1974 and 1982. A total of 330,000 women between the ages of fifteen and forty-nine were interviewed in sixty-two countries, countries that made up 40 percent of the world's population. Three-stage probability area sampling was applied. Large-area, primary sampling units (PSUs), were identified, and some were then randomly selected. Each selected PSU was divided into subareas, called second stage units (SSUs), and some SSUs were randomly selected from each PSU. Ultimate area units (UAU) were then randomly selected within each of the selected SSUs. Finally, a systematic sample of households was selected from each selected UAU, and all eligible women in the selected households were interviewed.

Sampling is used extensively and has far-ranging applications in many areas of contemporary society. Sampling has been adopted by manufacturing and business for quality control of goods and services. When the quantity of goods produced is large, a complete investigation is costly and, in fact, unnecessary. When an investigation requires the destruction of products, such as testing the life of electric bulbs, one can only investigate a sample. Small samples of products are frequently drawn, and appropriate quality measures are plotted on a chart. If the values shown on the chart are not randomly scattered around the expected average value, it is a warning that some part of the manufacturing process may be defective.

Sampling is the only means of estimating population size in the study of wildlife populations. A frequently used method is to select a random sample of a wildlife population of interest with a size of n_1. Each animal is tagged and released. Sometime later another sample is taken from the same population with a size of n_2. The estimated wildlife population size is approximately n_1/p, where p is the proportion of animals with a tag in the second sample.

Context

Sampling has a relatively short history. At the beginning of the twentieth century, the demand for social and economic data in Europe increased. This social need stimulated the development and application of sampling techniques. After vigorous debate among statisticians on the validity of sampling, the International Statistical Institute (ISI) accepted the principles of sampling techniques in 1903. Since then, a range of sampling techniques for survey samples has been developed.

The contemporary development of survey sampling is largely attributed to American researchers. The Statistical Research Division of the Bureau of the Census made substantial contributions to the development of sampling methods for use by the bureau in the late 1930's and 1940's. Commercial polling firms, such as those organized by George Gallup, Elmo Roper, and Louis Harris also generated significant support for the development and use of sample survey methods, particularly in the areas of marketing and opinion polling. In addition, the U.S. Department of Agriculture played an important role in the development of sampling methods. To meet the need of predicting crop yields, the U.S. Department of Agriculture developed a comprehensive probability sampling procedure to sample land areas. This sampling method was successfully extended to social surveys by social scientists in the 1940's. This method has evolved in both theory and practice, and since the 1940's it has become the most highly regarded population sampling method.

Methods of sampling have become increasingly useful, sophisticated, and extensively applied. Besides area probability sampling, the most notable advance probably has been the development of telephone sampling techniques. Since the 1970's, more than 90 percent of American households have used telephones. As a result, telephone sampling methods have undergone a rapid development in response to the sharp increase in the costs of conducting face-to-face household surveys. Telephone samples based on new sampling techniques are much more representative than ever before. Besides the advantages of cost-effectiveness and fast data collection, telephone sampling permits supervisors to monitor the process of ongoing interviews, thereby increasing data quality.

With improvements in sampling techniques and successful applications, increased use of sampling has become an international trend. Most data now used in government statistics, business, social, and policy sciences are collected from samples. In return, the achievements of sampling stimulated the growth of empirical research in those fields in the late twentieth century. The role of sampling will become even more important with the advent of widespread computerization.

Bibliography

Cochran, William G. _Sampling Techniques_. 3d ed. New York: John Wiley & Sons, 1977. Widely recommended textbook that provides a comprehensive account of sampling theory. Familiarity with advanced algebra and probability is recommended.

Fowler, Floyd J. _Survey Research Methods_. Rev. ed. Beverly Hills, Calif.: Sage Publications, 1988. Describes the standards and practical procedures for drawing a representative sample. Fowler melds the three components (sampling, questionnaire design, and interviewing methodologies) of survey together and shows how each of the components affects the quality of a sample.

Govindarajulu, Z. *Elements of Sampling Theory and Methods.* Upper Saddle River, N.J.: Prentice-Hall, 1999.

Henry, Gary T. *Practical Sampling.* Newbury Park, Calif.: Sage Publications, 1990. Oriented toward the researcher who needs to apply sampling as a research tool. It addresses fundamental concepts of sampling and includes detailed examples of practical alternatives of sampling.

Hess, Irene. *Sampling for Social Research Surveys: 1947-1980.* Ann Arbor: University of Michigan Press, 1985. Rich source of practical survey sampling for social research. Provides extensive information for sampling design based on the sampling experience of the Survey Research Center of the University of Michigan.

Kalton, Graham. *Introduction to Survey Sampling.* Beverly Hills, Calif.: Sage Publications, 1983. Valuable text for those with limited knowledge of mathematics and statistics. It provides readers with a broad overview of survey sampling and a firm understanding of the major components of survey sampling design; also discusses practical considerations.

Kish, Leslie. *Survey Sampling.* New York: John Wiley & Sons, 1965. Probably the best specialized textbook on sampling methods and application. It has been nicknamed the "green bible" of survey sampling because of its color and utility. Indeed, many solutions can be found in this book concerning difficulties with sampling design.

Lavrakas, Paul J. *Telephone Survey Methods: Sampling, Selection, and Supervision.* 2d ed. Newbury Park, Calif.: Sage Publications, 1993. Designed to assist persons who do not consider themselves experts in planning and executing telephone surveys. It discusses how to conduct a telephone survey and how to control and monitor the data collection process.

Trapper, Richard. *The Interpretation of Data: An Introduction to Statistics for the Behavioral Sciences.* Pacific Grove, Calif.: Brooks/Cole, 1998.

Jichuan Wang

James H. Fisher

Jiajian Chen

Cross-References

Qualitative Research; Quantitative Research; Surveys; Validity and Reliability in Measurement.

SECULARIZATION IN WESTERN SOCIETY

Type of sociology: Major social institutions
Field of study: Religion

Secularization is the process by which cultural and social institutions become independent of religious domination and relatively autonomous in relation to each other. Simultaneously, individuals gain more freedom in choosing their religions and meaning systems but also experience higher levels of doubt in relation to their chosen beliefs.

Principal terms

ANOMIE: situation characterized by perceptions of meaninglessness and a lack of moral order, resulting in personal frustration and social disorganization

BUREAUCRACIES: impersonal forms of administration that govern by means of rationally constructed rules that are applied uniformly to all

DISENCHANTMENT: human mode of perception in which the world loses its spiritual significance and is viewed in terms of material utility

INSTITUTIONAL DIFFERENTIATION: process in which social functions are delegated to specialized institutions, each performing a particular activity and filling a social role (for example, political or educational)

LEGITIMATION: process in which accepted structures of knowledge and beliefs explain and justify the social order and its policies to its members

PLURALISM: situation characterized by the existence of a variety of religions and worldviews, none of which is fully dominant

PRIVATIZATION: loss of public significance of certain institutions and their relegation to the realm of individual preference and meaning (for example, religion, family, and the arts)

RATIONALIZATION: organization and evaluation of human activity according to measurable, logical criteria related to immediate, empirical ends and with a stress on efficiency

Overview

In the past, people lived in societies and cultures dominated by religion. Religious stories, rituals, and rules prescribed every activity and provided legitimation for the social order. Political leaders were viewed as deities or else as descended from or appointed by them. Laws, such as those contained in the Ten Commandments, were understood as having come directly from the divine. Economic activity was governed by religious ritual, and rites were performed to facilitate hunting, planting, and harvesting. The whole of life had religious significance, and people were careful not to offend the spiritual world.

Modern societies are radically different. They are distinguished by high levels of institutional differentiation, with distinct functions and rules pertaining to each institution. Economic institutions are governed by rules of efficiency and probability. Education has standards of excellence that are expected to be unrelated to religious or political ideology. Consequently, institutions are no longer legitimated by reference to religious authority but by how well they perform their appointed roles. Nevertheless, while all modern secular societies have separate standards, another characteristic of such societies is that all the individual standards are related to the process of rationalization. These standards are set through the use of human reason as it attempts to discover universal, empirical standards of evaluation. The physical sciences (biology, chemistry, physics) attempt to find laws that explain physical processes. Psychology searches for laws with which to explain the human mind and personality. Similarly, the other social sciences, political science, sociology, and economics, search for laws that explain social life, societal interaction, and change. Even in the realm of morality, the work of the German philosopher Immanuel Kant (1724-1804) initiated an ongoing process to find universal, rational moral laws that can be used to regulate the behaviors of all people in all societies. The final goal of the rationalization of all spheres of life is to bring all spheres of existence under human control, thus freeing people from fear of the random and the arbitrary.

Additionally, secularization focuses on the changed relationship between believers and their religious beliefs. In traditional cultures, persons are immersed in uniformity of religious belief and practice. Religion permeates all of existence, which makes it seem real and objective. Doubt is not a serious possibility in such settings. In the modern world, however, the public world is divorced from the religious. The performance of economic, political, and public tasks is not informed by religious belief. Modern societies are also marked by religious pluralism as well as open, avowed atheism. The individual is thus forced consciously to choose to continue or affirm a religious tradition. The very act of being forced to choose makes religious beliefs seem less certain and more arbitrary; therefore, doubt becomes an inescapable part of religious belief. Religion is reduced to the realm of individual meaning and thus becomes privatized.

Secularization appears to be a product of Western (Christian) civilization but has spread globally in the twentieth century with the spread of Western colonialism. Although it became highly visible in the nineteenth century with the rise of industrial capitalism, secularization is, in fact, a long historical process. The disenchantment of the world begins with the Jewish concept of monotheism and its doctrine of creation, in which God creates the world and stands apart from it. The world becomes a material creation and is no longer populated by gods and spirits. Similarly, Greek culture, in the work of its philosophers, especially Plato and Aristotle, begins the process of rationalization, using the human mind to analyze all phenomena and all human experience. While Christianity accelerated the process by synthesizing elements from both traditions, it was not until the sixteenth century Renaissance and Protestant Reformation that the logical implications of these earlier claims began to be developed. This period marks the beginnings of modern science, philosophy, and the social sciences. It also marks the beginnings, as Max Weber demonstrates in his famous work *Die Protestantische Ethik und der Geist des Kapitalismus* (1904; *The Protestant Ethic and the Spirit of Capitalism*, 1930), of modern capitalism.

While the economic sector became the primary force in driving the process of secularization, that process was further encouraged by several centuries of religious warfare and a growing awareness of religious pluralism. In response to both, an attempt was made to find beliefs and a morality that transcended particular religious claims. Modern societies are thus marked by patterns of religious tolerance, and people are expected to commit themselves to forms of government and law based on rational rather than religious principles. In sum, secularization freed human inquiry and activity from the constraints of religion and tradition, giving birth to concepts of individual freedom and liberty; the development of modern science; a new political system, democracy; and an explosive, wealth-generating economic system, capitalism. In exchange, religious belief was reduced to a matter of personal preference, leading to increased levels of doubt and anxiety regarding the issue of the ultimate meaning, if any, of human existence.

Applications

The concept of secularization has been used as a broad analytical tool to study and suggest policy in a wide range of areas related to societal and cultural change. Political scientists and economists who are concerned about development and modernization have used it to analyze various Third World countries to discover impediments to development. They focus on elements of tradition, religion, and superstition that they believe prevent societies from adopting rationalized modes of economic production, and political and legal systems based on merit, equality, and constitutional rather than on religious or informal law. Special emphasis is given to transforming education and relegating religious influence to the private realm.

Many sociologists, following the lead of French sociologist Émile Durkheim, have focused on the issue of political legitimation and political instability in modern societies. These scholars focus on the ability of modern pluralistic societies to generate a set of morals and beliefs that will be accepted by the vast majority of the populace. Similarly, they are concerned about the ability of secular societies to elicit the loyalty required if people are to accept the sacrifices of taxation, legal restrictions, and military service that are necessary for the smooth functioning of government. In response, theorists such as sociologist Robert Bellah have argued that modern societies generate a universally shared, cohesive "civil religion" that functions as traditional religions once did. A civil religion has symbols such as flags and national heroes, rites and celebrations in the form of national holidays, and a set of shared beliefs and values that are often identified in the nation's founding documents. Such functional religion can be found in self-proclaimed secular states such as the People's Republic of China and the former Soviet Union as well as in nations such as the United States and the European nations, which are supportive of religion but practice separation of church and state. Theorists attempt to identify the components of the civil religions of various nation states as a way of gaining greater cross-cultural understanding and therefore improving international communication.

Other theorists are more pessimistic about the possibilities of finding a source of political legitimation once religion is banished to the realm of the personal. The sociologist Peter

Berger is part of a group that uses the concept of secularization to explain current social instability and the rise of social problems. According to these scholars, as people lose their sense of shared commitments and values, society becomes increasingly conflictive. People refuse to make sacrifices for the common good, and society becomes more litigious. These observations have been used by religious fundamentalists to attack secular society and to support the claim that the loss of religious values is causing social collapse. Although religious fundamentalists have called for a return to traditional religion and the dominance of society by a single religious tradition, social scientists have been less certain about how to counteract the disintegrative effects of secularization in pluralist societies.

Yet another approach is to explain the change in the individual's relationship to religion and the change in religious structures. While traditional religions have lost much of their social power, their structures have also changed. Like other modern organizations, they have become bureaucratically structured and governed by technically trained specialists. This has led to a separation between the clergy and laity by virtue of which the religious concerns and policies of the two groups are often at odds. This has led to both a decline in membership in some traditional religious bodies and the emergence of popularly based religious movements, both conservative and liberal (as found in certain forms of liberation theologies). Similarly, since individuals are free to choose a religion and shape it to their personal wants and needs, modern religious institutions have become less concerned about preserving the essentials of their traditions and more concerned about packaging a message that will attract adherents. In the process, religious traditions have been minimizing uncomfortable moral requirements and emphasizing and creating alleged benefits of the religion to its subscribers. So, for example, the popularized Christianity of televangelism promises healing of physical and emotional traumas, economic enrichment, and eternal salvation, but seldom encourages listeners to love their enemies or sell all they have and give it to the poor, which are moral tenets of the Christian faith.

Finally, the theory has been used to analyze the fundamental discontent that seems to be inherent in modern cultures. Economic prosperity was expected to bring happiness and contentment. The end of religious ideology was expected to usher in an age of unprecedented peace. Neither has come to pass. Sociologists such as Andrew Greeley and Thomas O'Dea question whether people can be content without some sense of ultimate meaning and purpose. Yet secularized societies provide no such meaning and purpose; they focus only on immediate political, societal, and economic tasks. In such societies, people live with an inescapably high degree of anxiety and anomie. A related question is whether people are innately religious or religion is a holdover from the childish, superstitious past. Bellah and others see religion as being part of human consciousness and therefore hold that the reemergence of religious fundamentalisms and the emergence of new religious movements, including forms of feminist and ecological spirituality, provide evidence of religion's natural persistence. Bellah's theory of religious evolution argues that social instability is a transitional phase in a process in which religion is being transformed into symbols and structures that are more suited to the modern era.

Context

The emerging independence of culture and society from religious control was evident as early as the sixteenth century in the Church's struggle against Copernicus to suppress modern science and in the struggles of the European monarchs to free themselves from papal influence. The full significance of the shift was first clearly articulated by Auguste Comte, the nineteenth century French philosopher. He described the shift as freeing the human mind from bondage to a superstitious, prerational past. He mirrored the optimism of the early rationalists, who saw the change as ushering in a new age of prosperity, peace, achievement, and happiness.

Responding to the conditions generated by the early Industrial Revolution, a group of late nineteenth and early twentieth century sociologists, including Max Weber and Émile Durkheim, began to articulate more clearly the nature of the changes that were occurring. They highlighted the appearance of institutional differentiation and specialization, the emergence of forms of bureaucratic rationalization, and the focus on efficiency that are defining characteristics of modern societies. While still guardedly optimistic, all began to notice the negative underside of modern culture, with its dehumanizing bureaucracies, destruction of natural communities, suppression of emotion, and amoral character. In *The Protestant Ethic and the Spirit of Capitalism*, Weber worried that the society of the future may feel like an "iron cage" to its inhabitants.

The concept of secularization, however, did not receive full definition and elaboration until the 1960's. In response to growing societal unrest and rapid social change, especially in the area of public morality, a group of sociologists began to focus on the interaction of religion, society, and culture. Of particular interest were the individual's need for a system of ultimate meaning and society's need for a final source of legitimation for its laws and policies. According to Peter Berger, both are secure only if they reside in a sacred, unquestioned realm, a "sacred canopy." It is this very canopy that secularization is dismantling. Consequently, persons are being left without meaning and societies are becoming unstable, lacking legitimation. Other theorists, such as Bellah, argued that secularization created instability as new systems of meaning emerged to replace the old, but also held a new order was emerging. Still others, such as Thomas O'Dea, view secularization as an ambiguous process that frees individuals and societies from captivity to traditions and therefore offers new freedoms and creativity. Inevitably, the same process threatens social stability and human meaning. Debate surrounding the theory of secularization continues to center on the evaluation of modern social systems, their promises, and their limitations.

The recent global revival of religion in all its forms, including fundamentalism, liberation theology, and new religions, raises questions about both the extent and the reversibility of secularization. Is this religious revival simply the "last gasp" of religion before it is swallowed by a totally secular future? Alternatively, have the discontents generated by modern societies become so great that religion, in some form, will return to a position of cultural and social preeminence?

Bibliography

Bellah, Robert N. *Beyond Belief: Essays on Religion in a Post-Traditional World.* New York: Harper & Row, 1970. Important collection of essays that includes essays on civil religion and religious evolution. It provides cross-cultural examples on the influence of religion in modern societies.

Berger, Peter L. *The Sacred Canopy: Elements of a Sociological Theory of Religion.* Garden City, N.Y.: Doubleday, 1967. Traces the process of secularization in Western culture. The primary analytical focus is on the problem of legitimacy and the shift in religious institutions and beliefs.

Durkheim, Émile. *The Elementary Forms of the Religious Life.* Translated by Joseph Ward Swain. New York: Free Press, 1965. Classic text, first published in 1915, presents religion as primarily a set of social symbols and rites. As such, religion is seen as the basis of social cohesion. This work is the foundation for contemporary theories of civil religion.

Greeley, Andrew. *Unsecular Man: The Persistence of Religion.* New York: Schocken Books, 1972. Presents evidence of the persistently religious nature of human beings. He argues that both people and society are much less secular than theorists indicate.

Hammond, Phillip E., ed. *The Sacred in a Secular Age.* Berkeley: University of California Press, 1985. Essays exploring the changing nature of religion and its influence in modern societies. Collection covers ongoing debate on secularization thesis.

Luckmann, Thomas. *The Invisible Religion: The Problem of Religion in Modern Society.* New York: Macmillan, 1967. Classic study in the privatization of religion in modern culture. Traces the decline of traditional religious institutions as individuals construct their own individualized systems of meaning.

McGuire, Meredith B. *Religion: The Social Context.* 4th ed. Belmont, Calif.: Wadsworth, 1997. General textbook on sociology of religion. Provides overview of the social function of religion. Two chapters summarize the secularization debate and a good discussion of religion and social change.

Martin, David. *A General Theory of Secularization.* New York: Harper & Row, 1978. Traces the secularization of Western culture but argues that it may take a variety of forms. The author then traces some of these patterns by reference to Western societies.

O'Dea, Thomas F. *The Sociology of Religion.* 2d ed. Englewood Cliffs, N.J.: Prentice-Hall, 1983. Brief, readable introduction to the sociology of religion. Focuses particularly on the role of religion in modern society and the social and religious effects of secularization.

Weber, Max. *The Protestant Ethic and the Spirit of Capitalism.* Translated by Talcott Parsons, with a foreword by R. H. Tawney. New York: Charles Scribner's Sons, 1958. First published in 1904, this influential work traces the contributions of Protestantism to the development of modern capitalism. Weber highlights the components of modern societies, including rationalization and institutional differentiation.

Charles L. Kammer III

Cross-References

Bureaucracies; Churches, Denominations, and Sects; Civil Religion and Politics; Religion; Religion: Functionalist Analyses; Religion: Marxist and Conflict Theory Views; Socialization: Religion; Values and Value Systems.

SIGNIFICANT AND GENERALIZED OTHERS

Type of sociology: Socialization and social interaction
Field of study: Interactionist approach to social interaction

The American philosopher George Herbert Mead developed the theory of significant and generalized others as an integral element of his theory of self. According to Mead, it is only through interaction with significant others and the development of a generalized other that people are able to develop a sense of who they are.

Principal terms

LOOKING-GLASS SELF: sense of personal identity that is the image reflected by the "mirror" of other people; it includes both identity and self-esteem

NORM: rule or expectation about appropriate behavior for a particular person in a particular situation

PEER GROUP: people who are the same age and are roughly equal in authority

REFERENCE GROUP: group or category that people use to evaluate themselves and their behavior

ROLE-PLAYING: acting out the script that is usually clarified in role-definition

ROLE-TAKING: seeing the world from the perspective of other individuals and groups, and directing one's own actions accordingly

ROLES: behaviors that are expected of a person who occupies a social position; counterparts to social norms

SELF: person's representation of himself or herself as an object in the world of experience

SOCIALIZATION: process by which people learn the culture of a society and become full participants in that society

SYMBOLIC INTERACTIONISM: theoretical perspective according to which mind and self are not innate parts of the human body but are created by communicating with other people

Overview

The philosopher George Herbert Mead is widely acknowledged as the founder of the largest and most influential field in modern American sociology: symbolic interactionism. Symbolic interactionism is a theoretical perspective that, among other things, holds that people create their own meanings and reality through communication with one another. One of the most important elements of symbolic interactionism is the concept of self. In referring to the human being as having a self, Mead meant that an individual acts socially toward himself or herself just as he or she acts toward others. People may blame, praise, or encourage themselves; they may become disgusted with themselves and seek to reward or punish themselves. Thus, individuals may become the objects of their own actions.

The self is absent at birth. It develops only in the process of social experience through taking the role of the other, through using the attitudes and evaluations of others as a basis for attitudes and evaluations about oneself. The self is reflexive; it has the ability to be subject and object to itself at the same time. Symbolic interactionists believe that the self is formed in the same way that other subjects are—through the definitions made by other people. Mead placed these definitions into two categories: those made by significant others and those made by generalized others.

Significant others are those who have had or still have an important influence on a person's thoughts about self and the world. For a child, the most obvious significant others are parents, but they can also be other relatives, television heroes, and friends. As a person grows older, the potential number of significant others increases greatly, and can include such individuals as Socrates, Jesus, a parent, a spouse, a child, a boss, the president of the United States, a minister, a movie star, or a rock musician. A significant other does not have to be physically present and can be living or dead. Although significant others are directly responsible for the internalization of norms in an individual, the character of one's emotional ties with them may differ. It is possible to love, like, or respect some significant others and to dislike or hate other significant others. There is no limit to the number of significant others one has, but they usually change according to one's stage in life. For example, as people grow older, their peers may become more important as significant others than their parents or other family members.

While significant other refers to a specific person, Mead viewed the generalized other as consisting of the general expectations and standards of the community in which the individual lives. These expectations and standards may include specific customs and normative patterns or highly abstract ideals and values in terms of which people define their overall orientations and life goals. The generalized other appears as the attitude of the community in direct or indirect manifestation, as an instrument of the social control of the self, and as the abstract formulation of the ethos of a community or society. A generalized other is a set of rules which develops in interactions and which individuals use to control themselves in interactions. Although Mead does not always make it clear whether the individual has one generalized other or several, other sociologists who have elaborated on his theory say that what begins as one generalized other increasingly becomes several. Because most people interact with many different groups, they most likely will develop more than one generalized other.

Mead used the term "generalized other" to describe the shared culture of a group—its religious systems, philosophies, legal systems and ideologies, mythology, literature, and art. The development of a generalized other by a person is the internalization of society as the individual has come to know it, and once a person has developed a generalized other, he or she can act in an organized, consistent manner and can view himself or herself from a consistent standpoint. The individual can transcend the local and present expectations and definitions with which he or she comes into contact.

According to Mead, it is in the form of the generalized other that the community exercises control over the conduct of its individual members. In abstract thought, the individual takes the attitude of the generalized other toward himself or herself, without reference to its expression in any particular other individual. In concrete thought, the individual takes that attitude as it is expressed in the attitudes toward his or her behavior of the other people with whom he or she is involved in a given social situation.

Although Mead was careful to point out that the generalized other does not necessarily correspond to any particular individual but is a composite, he nevertheless conceived of the relationship as an interactional one: The person takes the attitude of the generalized other toward itself, interprets it, understands it, and then incorporates it into his or her own self-conceptions.

Applications

The concepts of significant and generalized others are essential in the development of self, which is an important part of socialization. Mead described self-development as consisting of three stages: the preparatory stage; the play stage, in which the role of significant other is crucial; and the game stage, in which the role of the generalized other is necessary.

The preparatory stage is one of meaningless imitation by the infant, such as "reading" the paper, "feeding" the doll, or "cooking" the dinner. The child does certain things that others around him do without any understanding of what he or she is doing. Mead did not specifically name this stage, but he described it and said that it was necessary because the imitation implies that the child is incipiently taking on the roles of those around him or her and is on the verge of actual role taking.

The play stage occurs once the child has begun to acquire a vocabulary by means of which people and objects can be designated. The child plays at various roles made evident by others, including their use of language. The child plays at being mother, police officer, grocery clerk, or teacher. What is of central importance in such playacting is that it places the child in a position from which it is able to act back toward itself in these roles. At this point, the individual becomes a social object to himself or herself. During the play stage, the child assumes the perspective of his or her significant others as a boy, for example, learns how the significant others label him: John, good boy, handsome, smart, bad, slow, funny, and so on.

Mead called this second stage the play stage because the child assumes the perspective of only one significant other at a time. The child segregates the significant others, and the view of self is a segmented one. Play refers to the fact that group rules are unnecessary because the child takes the role of one significant other—mother, father, Superman—and acts in the world as if he or she were that individual. Therefore, play is an individual affair, subject to the rules of single persons. It is in this stage that the child first begins to form a self by taking on the roles of others. This is indicated by the use of the third person instead of the first person in referring to himself or herself; for example, "Mary is a bad girl" or "Mary can run fast." Because the child takes the role of only one significant other at a time, however, he or she has no unitary standpoint from which to view himself or herself; therefore, he or she has no unified self-conception.

The third stage of self-development is the game stage. According to Mead, this stage completes the development of self by creating a self that incorporates all of one's significant others into one generalized other. Mead called this stage the game stage because he believed that the organized game epitomized what must be done in taking the role of the generalized other. Using the example of baseball, he said that playing catcher, unlike playing mother or Superman, requires the child to take the perspective of the team as a whole toward himself or herself as a particular player. To view oneself as a catcher, one must have a composite, simultaneous idea of a baseball team, the various positions that are involved, the object of the game, and the relationship of the catcher's position to the activity as a whole. Beyond this, the participants in a baseball game are also oriented toward the general rules that define the game of baseball, and they control their own actions in terms of these impersonal rules. In this situation (playing baseball), the child must take the roles of groups of individuals instead of a specific role. The child is able to do this by abstracting a composite role out of the concrete roles of specific people. By doing this, the child builds up a generalized other, a generalized role or standpoint from which he or she views himself or herself and his or her behavior. According to Mead, it is this generalized other in the child's experience which provides him or her with a self.

The concepts of significant and generalized others are also important in understanding how people develop self-esteem. What people think and feel about themselves, like all else about the self, results from interaction; self-judgment is a result, to a high degree, of judgment by others. A person's very first important self-judgments come from significant others. As people develop their senses of self and progress past the game stage, the judgments of their community as embodied in their generalized other become increasingly important. The relationship between self-esteem and significant and generalized others is not, however, as simple as it appears. It is not the judgments of others per se that are important; it is how a person defines his or her views that matters. A person selects from whatever others think; he or she ignores, exaggerates, or alters whatever fits his or her self-image. As people get older, they sometimes select their significant others in order to enhance their self-judgments. This is usually not possible when a person is younger (in the play stage) and the self is developing. When that situation exists, a person is usually dependent upon significant others—usually parents, other family members, and teachers—to guide his or her self-judgments. If the information that the child receives from these significant others is negative, the child's self-esteem also will be negative. The negative feelings about self that emerge from such encounters affect subsequent actions. Low self-esteem leads to anxiety and may make it difficult for the person to be an accurate role-taker or to feel well-disposed toward others, which in turn will result in negative judgments being given, and so on. Significant others have a very large impact on a child's actual and potential interactions with others.

Context

The existence of significant and generalized others is what makes it possible for people to develop a sense of self that enables them to view themselves as social objects. This ability to create a sense of self is one of the central tenets of symbolic interactionism; therefore, significant and generalized others are essential to the theoretical perspective of symbolic interactionism. It was in the early part of the twentieth century that the concept of symbolic interaction emerged as one of the most important developments in American sociology, but its roots can be found as far back as the eighteenth century. For example, the concepts of the generalized other and role-taking, which is essential to the idea of the significant other, were heavily influenced by a school of philosophers called the Scottish moralists. These philosophers—David Hume, John Millar, Thomas Reid, Adam Ferguson, and Adam Smith—introduced the concepts of sympathy and the impartial spectator, which laid the groundwork for Mead's theory of significant and generalized others.

The concepts of significant others and generalized others are important because they explain how individuals receive the information they need to form the self. Since, according to Mead, the self is not present at birth, but develops in a three-stage process, people must use the judgments of others to form their own selves. It would be impossible to explain symbolic interactionism without the existence of significant and generalized others.

In addition to being an integral part of symbolic interactionism, the concepts of significant and generalized others have led to the development of several other important concepts in sociology, such as role theory, reference-group theory, and self theory. Mead's concept of the self as developed by significant and generalized others explains how the development or socialization of the human being both enmeshes the individual in society (through the use of the generalized other as a regulatory tool) and frees him or her from society (by allowing the self to choose different significant and generalized others). These ideas are important not only for symbolic interactionism but also for other areas of sociology, such as child and adult socialization, culture, deviance, and social control.

In the 1980's and 1990's, there was growing concern among parents, teachers, and politicians regarding the influence exerted by some television characters and rock musicians on young people who considered them to be significant others. An even greater concern was the increasingly large number of adolescents who were joining gangs. Gang members exchange the more traditional generalized other of society as a whole for the generalized other of the gang. These concerns illustrate the continuing importance of significant and generalized others in modern society.

Bibliography

Aboulafia, Mitchell, ed. *Philosophy, Social Theory, and the Thought of George Herbert Mead*. 8th ed. Boston: Allyn & Bacon, 2000. This book provides a thorough analysis of Mead's theories and their development.

Hewitt, John. *Self and Society: A Symbolic Interactionist Social Psychology*. 5th ed. Boston: Allyn & Bacon, 1991. Defines and discusses Mead's conceptualization of the significant and generalized others in great detail. His discussion of the generalized other in a complex situation is an especially interesting extension of Mead's original theory.

Manis, Jerome, and Bernard Meltzer, comps. *Symbolic Interaction: A Reader in Social Psychology*. 3d ed. Boston: Allyn & Bacon, 1978. Excellent introduction to Mead's theory of significant and generalized others; it is also very readable and interesting.

Mead, George Herbert. *Mind, Self, and Society from the Standpoint of a Social Behaviorist.* Edited by Charles W. Morris. Chicago: University of Chicago Press, 1934. Compilation of student notes on Mead's lectures. Presents Mead's theories in a clear and readable form. Includes chronologically arranged bibliography of Mead's writings.

_____. *The Social Psychology of George Herbert Mead.* Edited by Anselm Strauss. Chicago: University of Chicago Press, 1956. Discusses the role of self, the generalized other, significant others, and society in great detail. Very readable and suitable for a college audience.

Meltzer, Bernard. *The Social Psychology of George Herbert Mead.* Kalamazoo: Western Michigan University Center for Sociological Research, 1964. Concise yet thorough discussion of the roles of the significant and generalized others in the genesis and formation of the self.

Meltzer, Bernard, John Petras, and Larry Reynolds. *Symbolic Interactionism: Genesis, Varieties, and Criticism.* London: Routledge & Kegan Paul, 1975. Explains Mead's theory of the development of self, and they put his theory in context with the theories of those who influenced him.

Stone, Gregory, and Harvey Farberman. *Social Psychology Through Symbolic Interaction.* 2d ed. New York: John Wiley & Sons, 1981. Detailed discussion of the role of "play" and "game" in the development of self, and the roles played by significant and generalized others.

Karen Anding Fontenot

Cross-References

Dramaturgy; Looking-Glass Self; Socialization: The Family; Symbolic Interaction.

SOCIAL CHANGE
Sources of Change

Type of sociology: Social change
Fields of study: Sources of social change; Theories of social change

The two major approaches to viewing social change are the evolutionary perspective and the revolutionary perspective; in other words, change can be viewed as gradual or as sudden and disruptive. Technological, environmental, and demographic factors have all been identified as sources of social change.

Principal terms

ADAPTATION: way in which social systems of any kind respond to their environment

ALIENATION: individual's feelings of estrangement from a situation, group, or culture

CONFLICT: overt struggle between individuals or groups within a society or between nation-states

CULTURE: socially shared symbolic system composed of values, meanings, beliefs, and knowledge

DEMOGRAPHY: study of the size, structure, and change of human populations

ENVIRONMENT: surroundings or context within which humans, animals, or objects exist or act

EVOLUTIONARY: view of change that emphasizes continuities or analogies between biological evolution and sociocultural evolution

INTEGRATION: extent to which the activities or functions of different institutions or subsystems within a society complement rather than contradict one another

MODERN: pattern of social organization and social life that is linked to industrialization

REVOLUTIONARY: form of social movement that arises from strong dissatisfaction with the existing society and seeks radical change

SOCIAL PROCESSES: ways in which social systems or units influence and respond to one another when a society changes

TECHNOLOGICAL DEVELOPMENT: application of scientific or other forms of knowledge to the solution of practical problems

WORLD SYSTEMS: relationship between the developed and less developed countries in the context of economic, geographical, historical, and political factors

Overview

The attempt to understand or determine sources of social change has coalesced into two broad theoretical perspectives: evolutionary and revolutionary. The evolutionary approach focuses on long-term and large-scale change. Influenced by Charles Darwin's model of biological evolution, proponents of social evolution assume a commonality of social pro-

al laws" of human behavior; they assume also that societies progress. Thus,
s such as Lewis Henry Morgan and Edward Burnett Tylor, following the
mou.   ogists studying evolution, sought to determine stages of social and cultural
progression and to observe the regularities that all societies follow in that developmental
process. Later, because of the apparent conflicts between the works of Leslie White and
Julian Steward, Marshall D. Sahlins and Elman R. Service in *Evolution and Culture* (1960),
distinguished between two types of evolution: "general evolution," which dealt with humankind as a whole and was the focus of White, and "specific evolution" or "multilinear
evolution," which deals with the specific ecological adaptation and the development of
different levels of sociopolitical complexity in specific societies. (This was the focus of
Steward's work.) Specific or multilinear evolution tends to deal with the revolutionary
perspective of social change.

Building on the works of Auguste Comte, Herbert Spencer, and Émile Durkheim,
functionalist analysis of social change perceives change as an adaptation of a social system
to its environment by the process of mental differentiation and increasing social complexity.
Proponents of modernization theory also accept these tenets, as they assume a uniform and
linear progression by which all societies advance to modernity.

The revolutionary framework is less ambitious in that its goal is to hypothesize about the
general causes of social change within a society. Instead of looking for historical development and a general evolutionary law, it connects social change with specific causative
factors: adaptation, conflict, environment, demography, idealism, integration, conflict, and
technology. The revolutionary perspective has the advantage that detailed social histories
can be compared and general conclusions and uniformities can be determined.

Environmental and demographic factors, along with technological changes, have been
and continue to be the most important and general causes of social change. Among the three,
technology is often considered the most important. The technological revolution enabled
humankind to shift from hunting and gathering to sedentary agriculture and later to develop
civilizations. Technological revolution enabled societies to industrialize, urbanize, specialize, bureaucratize, and take on other characteristics that are considered central aspects of a
modern society. The development of industrial technology is also crucial in Karl Marx's
analysis of how alienation became a prominent part of the human condition in Western
societies. According to general evolutionists, the development of technology enabled humankind to extract energy from the environment more efficiently, thus facilitating sociocultural evolution.

Environmental factors include the sum of outside influences on society. These may
include the social reaction to ecological aspects of the physical environment and social
response to an action of a state on the other side of the world. This global perspective is
prevalent in world-system theory, under which all such aspects are considered part of a
society's environment, whether the influence is direct or indirect. The point, however, is that
the society must adapt to the influences impinging on it.

Culture consists of socially shared mental concepts that define relationships between and
among people. These ideas change through three processes: innovation, the creation of new

ideas; discoveries, the gaining of empirical knowledge; and diffusion, borrowing from others. Diffusion is the most prominent source of change. As the culture changes, the society responds because it is from the culture that rules, goals, and acceptable means are defined to guide social behavior. If the response is not proper, the units are malintegrated and must adjust to one another until integration is achieved.

Migration, a changing birthrate, wars, and disease are all factors that influence the demographic composition of a group. This composition is continually changing, and societies continually respond. Sometimes these changes can lead to internal conflict, in which groups within the society fight with one another. Conflict results in change, but the conflict does not have to be destructive. As Lewis Coser shows in *The Functions of Social Conflict* (1956), dissension within a society can have integrative and adaptive functions. As the causative agents of social change are examined, it must be kept in mind that there is generally no single cause of change; almost all aspects of social life, at one time or another, singly or in combination, can produce change.

Applications

The applications of evolutionary and revolutionary schemata to social change are many and varied. In the evolutionary framework, some concepts deal with the development of institutions such as the family, while others deal with whole civilizations or even with humankind in general. The formulations of Lewis Henry Morgan can be used to illustrate this idea. Concerning social institutions, Morgan set forth five successive family forms: "consanguine," based on group marriage; "punaluan," group marriage in which brothers cannot marry sisters; "syndyasmian" (or pairing), a transition between group marriage and monogamy; "patriarchical," in which supreme authority rests in the male head of the family; and "monogamian," which features female equality and monogamy. An example dealing with humankind as a whole is Morgan's postulation that history has three major "ethical periods": savagery, barbarism, and civilization. In both frameworks, according to Morgan and others, civilizations and institutions follow similar linear paths of progression. The concept of linear stages of evolution was highly criticized and fell into disrepute until Leslie White redefined general evolution in terms of efficient energy use rather than levels of complexity. Under this definition, Western civilizations may be viewed as being on a higher level of evolution because they capture more energy from the environment.

Within the revolutionary framework, an example of the ramifications of environmental change can be seen in the Fang people of Central Africa. After being colonized, they had to respond to the policies and practices of French society and government that originated thousands of miles away. Being Christianized and colonized by the French, the Fang had to face three challenges to their worldview: The "far away," represented by the colonizers, challenged "the near" and familiar; the traditional protective powers of "the below" were challenged by the missionaries' message of divinity "from above"; and the pluralism of colonial life was challenged by the stratification and double standard of the colonized being treated differently from the colonizers. They responded to the far away challenging the near by using *ebago*, a drug which enabled the Fang to go out to the far and convert it to the near.

Concerning the Christian God above and their own deities below, they incorporated both of them into the Bwiti religious pantheon, establishing a creative tension between the two. To deal with the double standard of colonial life, they promoted rituals that developed a "one-heartedness" among themselves.

The adaptation of the Fang included a cultural—more specifically a religious—change that enabled them to cope with social dislocation and exploitation. Some old metaphors (such as the forest and the body social, or kinship system) were reanimated. Additionally, new metaphors (such as red and white uniforms, a path of birth and death, and the world as a globe or ball) were created. The old and new fitted together. The Fang have closed themselves off from the wider society, and Bwiti, their religion, is a kind of escape from the pressures of the outside world.

Max Weber, in *Economy and Society* (1922), concluded that it was only in Western Europe that there was a singular drive toward orderly, predictable, and rational explanations of social life and the natural universe. The ecological and political setting of Europe in the Middle Ages favored the development of independent towns run by merchants and artisans, who were generally considered more rational and calculating than peasants. Kings used economic strength and administrative expertise to overpower feudal lords and control the church, which also provided administrative talent. By the fourteenth century, towns, nobles, and the church had compromised to support strong states.

Thus, it was no accident that with Protestantism flourishing where weak royal power and strong towns existed, Protestantism became associated with economic and scientific progress. Nor is it surprising that the Industrial Revolution first appeared in the late eighteenth century in Northwestern Europe, where all the right historical circumstances (the commercial and scientific progress of the seventeenth century) were present.

Context

In essence, the field of sociology is a result of the study of social change because it emerged as a discipline when theorists attempted to understand the dramatic social, economic, and political upheavals associated with the Industrial Revolution of the eighteenth and nineteenth centuries. Émile Durkheim, Karl Marx, and Max Weber were the key figures in developing the foundation of the revolutionary perspective on social change. Durkheim, following in the positivist tradition of Claude-Henri de Rouvroy (comte de Saint-Simon), argued that social phenomena exist in the objective realm and are external to individuals. In other words, societies operate according to their own principles, which are different from the sum of the behavior of individual members. Thus, for Durkheim, social phenomena are not explained in terms of the motivation of individuals; rather, individuals are seen as molded and constrained by society.

One goal of this perspective is to understand social systems in terms of their function—that is, their contribution to the maintenance of the whole society. This approach gave rise to the school of functionalism. Modern functionalism, deeply indebted to the work of Talcott Parsons, views society as a social system of interrelated and interdependent parts. This system seeks equilibrium or balance. Therefore, when this stability is disturbed or society is malintegrated, change occurs. In other words, to Durkheim and the functionalist school, change results from a causative agent that causes malintegration; social institutions then seek integration to adapt or assimilate to the new circumstances. The precepts of functionalism and Durkheim's thinking are prevalent in modernization theory.

Karl Marx, on the other hand, saw technology and the economy as the major causative factors, a perspective known as conflict theory. Marx argued that in industrial and capitalistic societies, social classes develop from a group's relationships to the means of production. As one class exploits another, tensions arise. The reconciliation of these tensions results in something new—social change. Marx's ideas provided a basis for world-system theory. Marx also developed the concept of alienation, according to which, because of industrialization, workers are estranged from their products; because of other results of industrialization, they also become estranged from their world, their fellow creatures, and themselves. Basically, Marx postulated a "materialist" explanation for social change; that is, economic and technological systems are the primary determinants of social and cultural systems as well as the prime source of social change (ideological and social relationships do have an impact, but to a much lesser degree). This materialistic perspective, along with his analysis of capitalism, arguably made Marx the most influential figure in twentieth century political, economic, and social thought.

Max Weber argued that orientations to certain religious, political, and social values created ideas and structures that inhibited progress in some cases and facilitated it in others. In the case of western Europe, he postulated in *The Protestant Ethic and the Spirit of Capitalism* (1930), that the Calvinists and their concept of predestination helped facilitate the rise of capitalism. Weber did not negate economic or technological factors, but he believed that beliefs and values were not being given sufficient emphasis in explaining social change.

These three major figures studied social change by focusing on industrial and capitalist societies; other theorists, ranging from Auguste Comte to Edward Tylor, focused on the evolutionary framework, within which society was analyzed on grandiose terms, with history and development interpreted in terms of progressive stages. Many of the problems of evolutionary theory were addressed in the works of its adherents. Karl Popper, however, in *The Poverty of Historicism* (1957), examined change from a philosophical perspective and argued that social development is inherently unpredictable because it is affected by the growth of knowledge, which is unpredictable. Thus, processes can be described but not in terms of a universal law. Ernest Gellner added to the criticism of evolutionary approaches by noting that the ordering of stages is superfluous if the mechanism, sources, or causes of change are not identified or are insufficient; simply placing something in a sequence does not explain it.

Charles Tilly, in *As Sociology Meets History* (1981), has shown that a society can be partially understood through the study of its origins. He classifies two major types of change that have occurred during the last four centuries and are continuing today: the increasing power of the state and the proletarianization of labor. Studying these changes helps clarify changes in family organization, political structure, types of protest, work habits, and many other areas. Barrington Moore, in *Social Origins of Dictatorship and Democracy* (1966), explains why the modernization process can produce different outcomes—democracy, fascism, and communism. His proposition is that development under a state-noble alliance results in fascism. When the state's power is curbed by a noble-bourgeois alliance, democracy results. Failed state-noble alliances, which allow successful peasant revolutions, result in communism. Theda Skocpol, Moore's student, in *States and Social Revolutions* (1979), shows that the failure of states to keep up with foreign competitors and intrusions has been the cause of most revolutions.

A number of key issues remain for future research to explore. Will poor parts of the world be able to achieve rapid economic growth, or will the world social system have to be altered to spread modernity more equitably? As states strengthen, will scientific and technological progress decrease? Third, will the proletarianization of labor and the strengthening of the state result in a drastic reduction of freedom for individuals? Finally, will ecological changes brought on by technology create problems for future generations?

Bibliography

Chirot, Daniel. "Social Change." In *The Social Science Encyclopedia*, edited by Adam Kuper and Jessica Kuper. 2d ed. London: Routledge & Kegan Paul, 1996. Excellent review and analytical article concerning social change and the relevance and place of various causative factors concerning social change.

Durkheim, Émile. *The Rules of the Sociological Method*. Edited by George Catlin. Translated by Sarah A. Solovay and John H. Mueller. 8th ed. New York: Free Press, 1938. First published in 1895, sets forth the foundation of functionalism. It is not Durkheim's most popular work, but it presents his basic premises concerning the means for understanding social behavior.

Fernandez, James W. *Bwiti: An Ethnography of the Religious Imagination in Africa*. Princeton, N.J.: Princeton University Press, 1982. Good ethnography of social change in which revolutionary change is examined. In this case, the response is to environmental and political changes resulting from colonialism.

Marx, Karl. *The Communist Manifesto*. Edited by Friedrich Engels. Translated by Samuel Moore. New York: New York Labor News, 1948. Short but representative work presenting Marx's analysis of capitalism and the Industrial Revolution; first published in 1848.

Steward, Julian H. *Theory of Culture Change: The Methodology of Multilinear Evolution*. Urbana: University of Illinois Press, 1955. Classic account setting forth the specific or multilinear evolutionary perspective on social change.

Vago, Steven. *Social Change*. 4th ed. Upper Saddle River, N.J.: Prentice-Hall, 1999.

Weber, Max. *The Methodology of the Social Sciences*. Translated and edited by Edward A. Shils and Henry A. Finch. New York: Free Press, 1949. Sets forth Weber's concepts of understanding social behavior; first published in 1903.

White, Leslie. *The Evolution of Culture*. New York: McGraw-Hill, 1959. Classic account setting forth the general evolutionary perspective on social change.

Arthur W. Helweg

Cross-References

Demographic Factors and Social Change; Marxism; Modernization and World-System Theories; Technology and Social Change.

Social Groups

Type of sociology: Social structure
Field of study: Key social structures

Social groups are ubiquitous, and they have profound effects on human behavior and interaction. Sociologists often categorize certain types of groups as primary, complex (or secondary), and reference groups. Primary groups, small groups such as family and friendship groups, generally have the strongest influence on people's lives.

Principal terms

COMMUNITY: subgroup of a society that contains all or most of the features of a society

COMPLEX GROUP (secondary group): large group that typically exists to achieve a single goal; its members have more distant and indirect relationships than those among members of primary groups

PRIMARY GROUP: small social group whose members interact frequently with one another on a face-to-face basis, have intimate knowledge of one another, and share emotional ties

REFERENCE GROUP: set of individuals or a social group that provides a standard of comparison for an individual who is evaluating his or her own accomplishments or opinions

SOCIAL GROUP: set of individuals who interact with one another in patterned ways, share elements of a culture, and identify with one another

SOCIAL INSTITUTION: set of beliefs and practices that emerge in response to a need or interest of those in a society; examples include the family, education, the economy, and religion

SOCIETY: social group whose members reside within a fixed geographical area and that contains all of the major social institutions

Overview

Sociology has several related definitions, one of which is that it is the study of social groups. A social group is a set of individuals who interact with one another in patterned ways, who share a culture that contains beliefs about the group and rules of conduct that shape behavior, and who identify with one another.

The identification of individuals with the group and with one another results in two statuses: member and nonmember. Identification creates a wall or boundary separating members from nonmembers. Identification may result from sharing a surname or living in the same household (as in the case of the family), feeling a special bond with someone else (as in the case of a clique), or from satisfying explicit conditions of membership (as in the case of a club or an organization).

Saying that interaction is organized or patterned means that members have ways of interacting with one another that are different from the interactions that they have with nonmembers. For example, the group may have designated certain times when members are to meet. At those meetings, individuals may occupy statuses, in addition to that of member, such as president, vice president, department head, treasurer, and so on.

When members meet as a group, their behavior follows certain routines; there are various group customs by which members abide. Further, what happens at one time is similar to what happens at another time. For example, two members' way of interacting in a meeting, when all or large numbers of members are present, is similar, though not necessarily identical, to the ways they interact when only the two of them meet. Finally, group members share a culture that contains beliefs about the group and explicit or implicit rules of conduct (or role expectations) that prescribe and proscribe how members should act. This culture sustains the customs and patterned behaviors in which members engage.

Examples of various groups are families, cliques, schools, factories, businesses, sports teams, clubs, fraternities, hospitals, churches, legislative bodies, professional associations, neighborhoods, and communities. Each of these shows the three features that distinguish groups from nongroups.

In the classification of groups, one major distinction is between primary groups and complex (or secondary) groups. The differences lie in size (or number of members), reason for existence, and, because of these first two, nature of interaction. Primary groups are small, consisting of a few members who interact with one another on a face-to-face basis. Examples are the family and friendship groups. These groups exist primarily to meet the psychic needs of members and, in the case of the family, to meet the important function of replenishing members of the larger society and socializing the young to the customs and beliefs of the larger society. Because there are few members, each can gain intimate knowledge about the others. Because primary groups exist to meet psychic needs, their members typically have emotional ties to one another.

Another type of group is known as either a secondary group or complex group. Secondary group is the older term; it is still used, but many sociologists now prefer the designation complex group. This type of group is large. Its many members cannot all have direct face-to-face contact with one another; hence their relations are typically distant and indirect. Further, such groups exist to meet specified goals—often a single goal: to produce and sell a product, to educate students, to enforce laws, to care for the sick, and so on. Because there are many members, the rules of conduct must become codified in constitutions, bylaws, or operating procedures. This is in contrast to the primary group, in which the rules of conduct are "carried around in peoples' heads." The ties among members of a complex group are instrumental (they exist to carry out the group's goals) rather than expressive (existing to provide emotional gratification). In the complex group there may be an elaborate division of labor and a highly articulated hierarchy, with the hierarchy dictating relations of authority and communication.

Other kinds of social groups are the community and society. A society is a social group whose members reside physically or symbolically within some geographic area and among whom are found all of the major social institutions. Social institutions are those practices and sustaining beliefs that emerge to meet a need or interest of the members of society. The major social institutions are family, economy, government, religion, and education. Some writers would also include the military, entertainment, and recreation, as these also reflect interests of most members of society. Though some communities and societies are large, these are distinguished from complex groups not by size but by the activities that occur in the groups. Some complex groups are larger (have more members) than some communities, such as small rural towns.

Another type of group, the reference group, is not, strictly speaking, a social group, but it is of interest to sociologists studying social groups. One of the things that a person in a modern, other-directed society frequently does is to ask himself or herself questions such as "How am I doing?" or "How should I think about *x* or *y*?" In attempting to answer questions such as these, the individual seeks standards of comparison. These standards frequently are the views of other people. Individuals compare their situations with those of others, who then constitute a reference group. A reference group may be a loose collection of individuals or a social group (one's family or work group). It might also be the set of all individuals of one's own age or members of a group (such as a certain profession) whom one does not know but uses as a model.

Applications

Perhaps the most frequent and useful application of the concept of the social group is in studies of the effects that group membership has on individual behavior. One example of this is found in studies of social control. Social control refers to the mechanisms that are used by group members to convince or force one another to conform to the rules of conduct of the group.

To explain delinquent behavior, for example, sociologist Travis Hirschi developed a control theory that contains four interrelated elements: attachment of the individual to the group, which means that the individual is sensitive and responsive to the opinions of group members; commitment, by which Hirschi means the rational decision not to deviate because deviant behavior would exact a cost to the individual; involvement, or the participation of the individual in conventional activities, which makes it more difficult to deviate; and belief—the individual's belief in the rightness of the rules. Hirschi provided evidence from a large-scale study (a survey of more than four thousand youths matched with police records) to support his theory.

In 1964, Bernard Berelson and Gary A. Steiner examined a large number of studies and essays, from which they compiled a set of propositions on behavior. They listed seventeen major propositions and a number of corollaries on relations in small groups. For example, the effects of the group on individual behavior are greater if members interact frequently (rather than infrequently), if group members all tend to be social equals (rather than relating in a hierarchical fashion), and if members like one another (as opposed to being indifferent or being divided into cliques). In addition, they listed eleven propositions and a number of corollaries on organizations (complex groups), which also contain some propositions about the effects of group membership. For example, the stronger a member's commitment to group values, the more likely he or she is to move up in the hierarchy. Additionally, the more decentralized the organization is, the stronger its members' identification with the organization will be.

Over the years there have been a number of other studies of social groups and their effects. In a study of 652 voters, reported in *Public Opinion Quarterly* in 1991, Paul Allen Beck arrayed evidence on the influence of group membership on people's political knowledge and thinking. While television and the print media had some effect, an individual's family and work friends had substantially greater effects. Further, individuals talked most frequently with those who shared their beliefs.

An example from political science occurs in one explanation of the so-called paradox of voting. This paradox holds that the benefits of voting are very low (it is quite unlikely that one's single vote will change the course of the election and therefore influence policies to be more favorable to oneself); the costs, when compared with the benefits, are relatively high—one must take the time to vote (perhaps leaving work early) and travel to a designated location. Therefore, if people are seen as attempting to maximize expected utility, they should refrain from voting; yet people vote anyway. One explanation for this behavior has been supplied by incorporating the influence of social groups into a model of voting behavior. Voters are seen as being influenced to vote by the groups to which they belong; the utility of voting then has to do with one's standing and membership in groups and with the effect the election may have on the groups.

Another body of thinking and research relevant to groups was initiated by Mark Granovetter's article "The Strength of Weak Ties," in the *American Journal of Sociology* 78 (May, 1973); he noted the effects of "weak ties" between individuals. In the "Overview" section, it was noted that one defining characteristic of a group is that group members have ties with one another. Granovetter noted that the ties between pairs of individuals can have varying strengths (they are quantitative rather than simply being present or absent), which depends on the frequency of interaction between individuals, the "services" they provide one another, the amount of personal information that is transmitted, and the feelings they have for one another. He argued that if such ties are weak, they can nevertheless have effects on diverse social phenomena, such as the diffusion of innovations. Research by others has sustained some of Granovetter's conclusions.

One of the many issues in the study of social groups concerns the stability of groups: What factors determine which groups survive? Much work has discussed this problem. Illustrating work at one extreme, Kathleen Carley's paper "A Theory of Group Stability," in the *American Sociology Review* 56 (June, 1991), developed a theoretical model of competing organizations in a society; the central elements in her theory were the number of groups, the size of the population of the society, and a culture consisting of facts to be known. Carley used a technique known as Monte Carlo simulations—in which a computer runs a number of probabilities randomly—to evaluate how these elements affect group stability.

An illustration at the other extreme is found in Martin Jankowski's participant-observation study of gangs, reported in his 1991 book *Islands in the Street*. He found that gang persistence is a complex phenomenon that depends on the internal structure of the gang, the gang's changing environment, and the tenuous relation between the gang and its environment.

Context

The notion of social groups has existed since sociological writing began, though the concept was not explicitly analyzed for many years. Herbert Spencer's early *Principles of Sociology* (1876) makes no reference to social groups as such. Though he discussed several types of organizations (ecclesiastical, ceremonial, and industrial), his main concern was to describe society as a whole. Franklin Giddings, influenced by Spencer as well as a number of others, used the notion of the group, but he did not explicitly define or analyze social groups; he primarily makes references to groups in explicating Spencer's sociological ideas. Albion Small, in his text *General Sociology* (1905), also invoked the notion of the group, but as the unit in which individual interests become organized and expressed. Many would probably trace the explicit and focused entry of the notion of the social group into sociological thinking with Charles Horton Cooley's book *Social Organization* (1909). Here Cooley introduced and defined the notion of the primary group and distinguished it from the secondary group (this latter term having subsequently lost favor in sociological thinking). This distinction parallels the one made by Ferdinand Tönnies in *Gemeinschaft und Gesellschaft* (1887; *Community and Society*, 1957).

Robert K. Merton's *Social Theory and Social Structure* (1949) provided a clear definition of the social group; his book also provided one of the best discussions of reference groups in the sociological literature. Apart from this, discussions of social groups have tended to focus on theorists or theoretical orientations. This suggests that the social group is one of those ideas that has become so incorporated into sociological thinking that it is taken for granted; explicit analyses of the concept itself are no longer thought necessary.

Bibliography

Berelson, Bernard, and Gary A. Steiner. *Human Behavior*. New York: Harcourt, Brace & World, 1964. Compilation of findings from studies and essays presenting several propositions, some of which are supported by more evidence than others. The propositions are classified into sections dealing with major sociological areas of concern (culture, institutions) as well as a few of psychological concern, such as perceiving and motivation.

Hirschi, Travis. *Causes of Delinquency*. Berkeley: University of California Press, 1969. Using a unique conception of social control, this is a classic and widely read analysis of the causes of delinquency. Beautifully written and free of jargon.

Homans, George C. *The Human Group*. New York: Harcourt, Brace, 1950. Using research from well-known studies, a classic and influential theoretical essay on small groups.

Kephart, William M., and William W. Zellner. *Extraordinary Groups: An Examination of Unconventional Life-Styles*. 4th ed. New York: St. Martin's Press, 1991. Informative and readable book discussing eight "unconventional" groups, such as the Old Order Amish, Hasidim, and Mormons.

Nisbet, Robert A. *The Social Bond*. New York: Alfred A. Knopf, 1970. Written for the general reader, uses the notion of the social bond as its organizing idea. Nisbet's conception of the social bond is somewhat expansive, containing such core notions as authority, roles, and norms.

Ritzer, George. *Sociological Theory*. 5th ed. New York: McGraw-Hill, 1999. Explains theory without jargon. Includes photographs and biographical sketches of sociological theorists.

Skolnick, Arlene, and Jerome H. Skolnick, eds. *Family in Transition*. 10th ed. New York: Longman, 1999. Essays on changes taking place in families. Every article is easy to read and understand.

Dean Harper

Cross-References

Bureaucracies; Family: Functionalist Versus Conflict Theory Views; Socialization: Religion; Socialization: The Family; Socialization: The Mass Media; Workplace Socialization.

SOCIAL MOBILITY
Analysis and Overview

Type of sociology: Social stratification
Field of study: Social mobility

Social mobility refers to movement (or lack of movement) by individuals or groups from one social role or social status to another. Mobility is an important element of social interaction and an indicator of the strength of stratification and the potential for social change in society.

Principal terms

HORIZONTAL SOCIAL MOBILITY: movement across social ranks of approximately the same status

INTERGENERATIONAL MOBILITY: changes in social status from one generation to the next

INTRAGENERATIONAL MOBILITY: vertical mobility an individual experiences in his or her own lifetime

STATUS ATTAINMENT: individual's arrival at a socially defined position in a specific group, usually based on a socioeconomic category

STRUCTURAL MOBILITY: mobility that occurs because of changes in the economic or social system rather than through personal achievement

VERTICAL SOCIAL MOBILITY: movement upward or downward in the social hierarchy

Overview

Social mobility refers to the movement of people from one status category to another in society. Essentially, then, the study of mobility is the study of social behavior from the perspectives of both the composition and organization of social groups, and it generally emphasizes some sort of disruption. Social mobility is a complex field of study which may involve consideration of causes, rates, processes, functions, and dysfunctions. Many social scientists consider the study of mobility significant because it is suggestive of the quality of life in a social group and of the extent to which social democracy is present in society.

Social mobility is often defined as the movement of people through the social structure, but this rather vague definition can be subject to a variety of interpretations. For example, some sociologists believe that changes such as salary increases, owning a home after years of renting, improvement in living conditions, or even steady employment are evidence of upward movement through the social structure. Others, however, search for more significant shifts in class standing—for example, movement from lower to middle class or from lower-middle to upper-middle class. Such differences of approach are important because the researcher's definition of the basic concept of mobility will affect the methods of measurement the researcher uses, which will in turn produce results and conclusions that may vary dramatically from those based on different concepts.

Despite such possible differences, the study of social mobility involves two basic elements, which at first seem simple. One is "position"—that is, the present level of the individual or group under investigation. The second component, "motion," also appears uncomplicated. Most simply, "motion" is the direction and distance the subject travels. Yet it may be very difficult to be certain of the exact position a person or group occupies in society and even harder to monitor movement, or lack of it, through a complicated social structure.

In addition, sociologists are interested in the mechanisms by which understandings of status are communicated and the ways in which individuals accomplish social mobility. Social groups vary in terms of the ease with which people can move from one social status to another. Although no society is completely open or closed to mobility, social structures may be described in terms of relative openness or closedness. Studies have shown that, in general, industrialized, technologically advanced societies tend to be open, and preindustrial, agricultural societies closed, to mobility. An open society tends to permit movement through any levels of status achieved through one's own efforts; in a more closed system, status and position are assigned according to standards (such as parentage, sex, and age) which are beyond the individual's control.

To complicate matters further, social scientists often equate position with inequality or social stratification. In every society, individuals and groups perform many different functions, which generate many different sorts of rewards, such as power, wealth, and prestige. This situation leads to a hierarchical ranking of individuals, groups, and activities according to the power, wealth, or prestige they accumulate or signify. Again, from the researcher's point of view, it is difficult to measure prestige or power empirically. In addition, such rankings often involve different sorts of rewards, and it is not clear how one type of reward, such as wealth, may be translated into an exact amount of another, such as power. Also, individuals may occupy several roles or positions simultaneously, such as lawyer, politician, and teacher. Each position has its own rewards, and the rewards of all social roles must be accounted for in order to measure an individual's social position accurately.

Changes in social position are generally referred to as either "vertical" or "horizontal." Vertical mobility indicates individual or group movement either upward or downward in the social hierarchy, although downward mobility is rarely investigated. It would seem a matter of common sense that the conditions determining downward mobility are merely the opposites of those for upward movement. In actuality, however, the variables affecting downward mobility can be quite complex and are not simply the flip sides of upward movement.

Upward mobility may be affected or prevented by factors such as urbanization, industrialization, geographic mobility, mass communication, form of government, and traditional social mores. Upward mobility may take two basic forms: "contest" and "sponsored." Contest mobility refers to upward mobility that is the result of competition based on some sort of supposedly objective standards of merit, such as high test scores. In contrast, sponsored mobility is dependent on special, subjective relationships, as in the case of an individual whose upward mobility is the result of having a mentor in an organization or group.

Horizontal mobility involves movement from one social rank to another social position of equivalent status. In addition, changes in social position involving nonhierarchical social categories, such as religion, political affiliation, or age are often considered kinds of nonvertical mobility. Because of the number and complexity of potential variables, coupled with complications arising from issues of definition and measurement, understanding the patterns and significance of social mobility is a challenging task.

Applications

Most studies of mobility have focused on men's intragenerational mobility or on intergenerational mobility, comparing sons with fathers. An important work by Peter M. Blau and Otis Dudley Duncan, *The American Occupational Structure* (1967), developed a formal model for investigating the ways in which a father's occupational status does and does not influence the status and mobility of his sons. While recognizing that life is a complicated, ongoing process, Blau and Duncan attempted to discover and trace a sequence of life events and social variables with measurable traits which could be correlated with later outcomes. That sequence is known as the process of status attainment. Of central interest to Blau and Duncan were the specific ways in which fathers influenced their sons. Using simple correlations, they found that a father's education and occupation each had about an equal influence on sons' occupations; that sons' education (both dependent and independent of family background) had the most significant impact on eventual occupation; and that family background could play a role in occupational choice even after formal education was completed. A later repetition of Blau and Duncan's work by David Featherman and Robert Hauser, published as *Opportunity and Change* (1978), reported reasonably parallel findings. Featherman and Hauser did note significant differences, however, when race was added as a status attainment variable.

In part because of the American and Western European dominance of data gathering and research after World War II, there is extensive analysis of the mobility patterns of white males. Until relatively recently, there has been little information about, or interest in, the mobility experiences of women or people of color. Certainly the lack of available data may be traced to the fact that members of subcultural groups often focus their energies and attention on forms of achievement other than occupation, the traditional focus of mobility studies. In addition, disadvantaged and minority members of society are often the victims of acts of discrimination, both historical and contemporary, which act as barriers to their occupational and social mobility.

Researchers such as Reynolds Farley, interested in understanding the mobility patterns of minority groups, began to investigate changes over time and comparisons among different groups in the same society. In his *Blacks and Whites: Narrowing the Gap?* (1984), Farley defined inequality as differences in income, occupational prestige, and education. From this set of elements, he was able to illustrate a complex set of relationships. Focusing on the period between 1960 and 1980, he found that income disparities between blacks and whites had narrowed, that the two groups were moving toward equality of access in education, and that occupational differences had also declined, although occupational parity had by no means been achieved.

Mobility and status attainment researchers most often absorb sexual difference as a variable in whatever model they employ, applying the same methods and measurement categories to men and women. As a result, despite the different experiences men and women have in the labor market, their occupational and marital mobility patterns are, for the most part, the same. These findings should not be taken as evidence of gender mobility equality, however, because variables such as pay, educational status, and marriage can affect women's social mobility differently from the ways they affect men. For example, a review of data available for the period from 1962 to 1973 led Robert Hauser and David Featherman to conclude, in an article entitled "The Measurement of Occupation in Social Surveys" (1977), that while women's social "origins" may be the same as men's, the social "destinations" available to, or chosen by, women are often very different.

Discussion of mobility among different groups in society raises the issue of differences in attitudes toward social mobility in any social group. It has long been a central part of American ideology that everyone in society has a common definition of success and mobility and has the ability to rise in social status. The stories of Horatio Alger, a popular novelist of the nineteenth century, embody this American Dream: A poor boy, through "pluck and luck," becomes rich and successful beyond his wildest imaginings. Various studies, however, make clear that there are differing attitudes toward social mobility as well as various experiences of both upward and downward mobility within the geographical boundaries of the United States. A number of studies have found that social mobility indeed exists in the United States, but not to the extent that "rags-to-riches" stories would have one believe. Upward mobility usually involves movement of one or two steps up the social ladder. Therefore, moving from poverty to wealth, although it cannot be called impossible, is an extremely rare event in any society, including American society. Variables such as social class, race and ethnicity, aspiration level, the role of family, and the effects of downward mobility are all beginning to receive increased attention from scholars, including Judah Matras in his book *Social Inequality, Stratification, and Social Mobility* (1984). It may be that the assumption that mobility is a central social value whose increase, by any means, is to be universally desired, must be examined more critically. Questions of both the assets and liabilities of social mobility in the context of the larger social order and in terms of individual lives are increasingly at the center of research on mobility and status attainment.

Context

While most of the research and writing in the field of social mobility has occurred since World War II, even ancient social philosophers such as Plato and Aristotle considered social mobility an important element of efficiency and stability in the formation and maintenance of the state. In his *Republic* (c. 380 B.C.E.), Plato categorized individuals as being made of gold, silver, or bronze thread, and he argued that while a heredity of social status should be expected, the gold children of bronze parents needed to be recognized and advanced to their rightful places in society. Similarly, the bronze children of gold parents needed to be detected and not given access to power. (Prophecy foretold the destruction of the state if led by men of bronze.) In his work *Politics* (384-322 B.C.E.), Aristotle discussed the establishment of the social class system and the logic of the rule of the middle class, seen as a "mean" that could counterbalance the ambitions of the upper and lower classes.

The first modern treatment of social mobility was Pitirim Sorokin's classic *Social Mobility* (1927). His central argument was that there are inevitable, permanent, and global points of occupational, and therefore social, inequality. Like Karl Marx, Sorokin held that a belief in vertical mobility has a stabilizing effect in that it provides motivations to the lower orders which keep them from disrupting the prevailing system. High rates of social mobility act as a safety valve, releasing the pressures of a discontented lower class. While Sorokin argued that social mobility was inevitable, however, he was unwilling to suggest any sort of enduring linear progression or digression in its spread or intensity.

Right after World War II, mobility studies tended to focus on specific societies, communities, and populations. In large measure, this interest was generated by concern for "openness," a term used in this context to describe the fluidity of movement among social strata and seen as a measure of social inequality. A society was described as open, fair, or just depending on the rates of both intergenerational and intragenerational mobility. The International Sociological Association encouraged and supported comparative research on this topic in the early postwar period. Despite problems with many of these studies, especially in terms of incompatible data categories and structural variables, cross-cultural studies continue to make up a large percentage of work in the field.

The most significant works in the area of social mobility studies since Sorokin's theoretical breakthrough have perhaps been in the collection and analysis of data. Beginning in the late 1940's, for example, social mobility studies focused on social inequalities rather than on social stability. A major theme of this branch of research became the consequences of mobility for individuals and societies. For example, in *Political Man: The Social Bases of Politics* (1960), Seymour Lipset emphasized the destabilizing effects of too much mobility. His analysis was based on a view of social stratification, which acknowledged its multidimensional nature. For Lipset, society is a complex system of multiple, often mutually exclusive hierarchies based on status, class, and authority. An individual might be mobile on one dimension but not on another. For example, a person might attain a high occupational position yet encounter prejudice because of ethnicity or social origin. Similarly, although an upper-class family might suffer a reversal of its financial standing, it might still retain a high social position. Lipset concluded that these sorts of inconsistencies were dysfunctional and could provoke frustrations which might lead to interest in radical political and social changes.

Few social scientists have systematically investigated nonvertical social mobility; as a matter of fact, most research has focused on vertical, intergenerational occupational changes. Although a few studies have included consideration of the possible influences of differences in stratification structures and economic systems, few, if any, have investigated differences other than those considered occupational or economic.

Scholars of social mobility must address issues of exactly what is being measured and what precisely is being described in discussions of mobility. The important connections between mobility, social inequality, and individual attitudes and values present sociologists with a special challenge to include both quantitative and qualitative data in their analyses of social mobility's importance and meanings. Just as modern social mobility studies emphasize the idea that class structures and social categories are never static, so the study of mobility must be prepared to meet the challenges of a dynamic and diverse area of research.

Bibliography

Blau, Peter M., and Otis Dudley Duncan. *The American Occupational Structure*. New York: John Wiley & Sons, 1967. Comprehensive work on intergenerational mobility. Makes substantial contribution to methodological issues.

Farley, Reynolds. *Blacks and Whites: Narrowing the Gap?* Cambridge, Mass.: Harvard University Press, 1984. Examines the differences and similarities in social mobility between African American and European American men during the period from 1960 to 1980.

Featherman, David, and Robert Hauser. "The Measurement of Occupation in Social Surveys." In *The Process of Stratification: Trends and Analyses*. New York: Academic Press, 1977. Discusses sexual difference as a variable in stratification and mobility. The volume in which it appears includes several excellent articles on the subject of mobility in relation to social stratification.

_____. *Opportunity and Change*. New York: Academic Press, 1978. Well-written and well-researched examination of mobility, stratification, and occupational issues among various racial, ethnic, and socioeconomic groups in the United States.

Lipset, Seymour. *Political Man: The Social Bases of Politics*. Baltimore: Johns Hopkins University Press, 1981. Theoretical and empirical analysis of the relationship between social and political behaviors and structures.

Lipset, Seymour, and Reinhard Bendix. *Social Mobility in Industrial Society*. Berkeley: University of California Press, 1959. Still important source of theory and empirical information on social mobility in different societies.

McMurrer, Daniel P., and Isabel V. Sawhill. *Getting Ahead: Economic and Social Mobility in America*. Washington, D.C.: Urban Institute Press, 1998.

Matras, Judah. *Social Inequality, Stratification, and Mobility*. 2d ed. Englewood Cliffs, N.J.: Prentice-Hall, 1984. Basic summary of research and theory in the fields noted in the title.

Sorokin, Pitirim. *Social Mobility*. New York: Harper & Brothers, 1927. First systematic study, and still-classic work, in the field of social mobility theories and research.

Jackie R. Donath

Cross-References

Caste Systems; Culture of Poverty; Social Stratification: Analysis and Overview; Social Stratification: Functionalist Perspectives; Social Stratification: Marxist Perspectives.

SOCIAL STRATIFICATION
Analysis and Overview

Type of sociology: Social stratification
Fields of study: Basic concepts of social stratification; Components of social structure

Social stratification refers to a phenomenon that exists in all complex societies: the hierarchical ranking of groups of people according to such criteria as relative economic wealth, political power, and social honor.

Principal terms

BOURGEOISIE: term used by Karl Marx to define those who control a society's means of production

CLASS: group of people of similar social rank; largely defined in economic terms, but also often considering such factors as political power and lifestyle

INTERGENERATIONAL SOCIAL MOBILITY: social movement from one class to another that takes place over the course of generations

INTRAGENERATIONAL SOCIAL MOBILITY: social movement from one class to another that occurs within an individual's lifetime

POWER: ability of individuals or groups to attain desired objectives or to force others to do as they wish

PRESTIGE: reputation or social honor; generally used to define status

PROLETARIAT: term used by Karl Marx to define workers, those who survive by selling their labor to the bourgeoisie

PROPERTY: income, wealth, and other material resources

SOCIAL MOBILITY: movement of groups and individuals within and between social levels in a stratified society

STATUS: any defined or acknowledged position within a group or society

Overview

Social stratification is as old as human civilization. When humans moved from fishing or hunting and gathering societies to sedentary agricultural societies with a surplus economy, a variety of occupations developed that were essential to the proper functioning of that society. Inevitably, these occupations began to be ranked hierarchically, usually based on the amount of preparation and training needed or the importance of that occupation to a particular society.

So prevalent was social stratification in all societies that over the centuries its existence was seldom questioned. It was generally accepted as part of the "natural" order. Religion was used to support stratification, for example, with the head of state often being considered divinely sanctioned. In the eighteenth century, however, the American and French Revolutions, with their emphasis on human rights and their call for equality, changed the accepted way of thinking. Efforts were made both to understand the reasons for social inequality and to seek means of lessening its negative effects.

Since the second half of the nineteenth century, four broad sociological theories have been used to explain and interpret social stratification: the natural superiority theory, the functionalist theory, the Marxist class conflict theory, and the Weberian multiple-hierarchies theory.

The natural superiority theory, also known as social Darwinism, was a popular and widely accepted theory of social stratification in the late nineteenth and early twentieth centuries. Promoted by Herbert Spencer in England and William Graham Sumner in the United States, social Darwinism saw social organization as an environment. Certain individuals or groups had the requisite skills or attributes to compete and to rise in that environment; they would become the leaders and the economically fortunate. Others, not so endowed, would fail. The not-so-subtle implication of this idea was that the rich deserved to keep their great fortunes intact. The poor also deserved their lot, because it was the result of sloth, ignorance, or some other flaw; they deserved no pity. The social Darwinists believed that their theory was part of the law of nature. Spencer coined the widely quoted phrase "survival of the fittest."

Some of the ideas of the social Darwinists were contained in the functionalist theory of social stratification, promoted by Kingsley Davis and William E. Moore in the 1940's. Essentially, the functionalist theory maintains that a variety of skills are needed for the effective functioning of a modern industrialized society. Some of these skills require greater ability and longer, more costly training than others. It is argued that people would only undergo the training necessary for these more demanding occupations if they knew that they would be amply rewarded in money and respect. Social stratification, then, can be seen as an organizing force in society—a kind of ladder with closely adjacent rungs that individuals may climb or descend according to their ability.

If any one individual could be called the founder of the study of social classes, it would be Karl Marx, who saw the conflict between social classes as the driving force in history. For Marx, writing in the mid-nineteenth century, there were only two classes: the bourgeoisie, controlling wealth and the means of production, and the proletariat. The proletariat work for the bourgeoisie and are increasingly exploited and increasingly thrust into poverty; ultimately, according to Marx, they will take political action. Although often challenged and, arguably, partially discredited, Marx's work was that of a careful and brilliant scholar. In an increasingly polarized Western society, many of Marx's theories are being re-examined. Among his lasting contributions are the idea of social mobility and the concept of "class consciousness"—a subjective feeling without which, Marx maintained, individuals are powerless.

Even though the functionalist approach, with its basic idea that talent, persistence, and hard work ultimately will be rewarded, was popular (especially in the United States), its limitations soon become apparent. Rising in the stratification system of a complex, industrialized society requires more than those character traits. Many sociologists were drawn to the theories of the German sociologist Max Weber. Weber's approach was multihierarchical and dynamic. He viewed social stratification as resulting from the interaction of three factors: class, status, and power. To Weber, social class is largely based on property. Social status, on the other hand, is mainly determined by occupation and how that occupation is socially evaluated. Power—the capacity to get others to act in accordance with one's wishes even when they prefer not to do so—was also considered by Weber. Other factors, such as being the right sex, attending elite schools, having wealthy, supportive parents, and belonging to the right religious and ethnic groups are also contributory factors to social stratification.

Weber's theory became the basis for the "objective method" of determining social stratification—that is, establishing a number of criteria for each of several strata. The subjective method is the other form of determining social stratification. In the subjective method, the composition of each stratum is determined either by the way individuals view themselves or by the way others view them. The limitation of this method is that individuals seldom view themselves objectively; moreover, people's evaluations of others would be valid only for a relatively small, stable community.

Any system of social stratification must be viewed in the context of whether it exists in an open or closed society. An open society is one in which individuals can move freely from one social stratum to another. A closed society is one in which there is no movement and children inherit the social status of their parents. The term "caste system" is usually applied to this kind of society. In practice, the completely open or closed society no longer exists. Societies only tend toward being one or the other, with a general (if often slow) movement toward open societies.

Applications

Functionalist theory has provided a widely cited and widely applied view of social stratification at least partly because of the work of functionalist theorists who have made it relatively easy to identify the status of individuals by their occupations. In 1946 the National Opinion Research Center asked a representative sample of American people to rank ninety different occupations. The ranking system, which was established according to prestige, training, and income ranged from the highest occupation, a U.S. Supreme Court Justice, to the lowest, a bootblack. Numbers one to thirty-six could be considered professions with considerable requisite training.

Although many sociologists have argued that the work of Karl Marx has been discredited, his ideas have been tremendously influential in sociological studies of class and stratification. Moreover, his ideas increasingly seem to be coming back to life. Marx envisioned the increased polarity of society into the "haves" and the "have-nots," with a group consciousness developing for each. Eventually, Marx held, the proletarians whose income has fallen below the subsistence level will rise in revolt. Sociologists are uncomfortably aware that in the United States and other industrialized countries there is an increased concentration of wealth in the hands of a few and increased poverty among the masses. In 1980, less than 2 percent of the population of the United States controlled 44 percent of the country's wealth and 62 percent of its corporate shares. With computer networking that enables wealthy individuals to work with others on a global basis and with the ability to transfer vast amounts of money electronically in a matter of seconds, the spread between the rich and the poor seems destined to grow. In 1972 Richard Parker wrote *The Myth of the Middle Class*. Twenty years later, Greg J. Duncan, Timothy M. Smeeding, and Willard Rogers echoed the ideas of these writers in an article entitled "The Incredible Shrinking Middle Class," which appeared in the May, 1992, *American Demographics*. A number of economists and sociologists reinterpreted and adapted Marxist theory in the late twentieth century.

A composite portrait of the U.S. class structure on the Weberian model was constructed by Dennis Gilbert and Joseph A. Kahl in *The American Class Structure: A New Synthesis* (1987). They list six social classes, ranging from the capitalist class (people with a very high income, prestige university degree, and an executive or professional occupation), which makes up 1 percent of the population, to the working poor and underclass (those with some high school or grade school education who are in service work or are laborers, unemployed, or surplus labor), which makes up 25 percent of the population.

An aspect of the Weberian multiple-hierarchies theory that interests many sociologists is the use of power in social stratification. In 1956 C. Wright Mills argued that the heads of government, the military, and business made up a "power elite." Later other sociologists concluded that less than one-half of one percent of the population makes up this "governing class." Power can be obtained through contributions to politicians and political parties or through control of the media; most often, however, it is family related. The family, in this view, may be seen as the greatest force in maintaining social stratification.

A belief in social mobility—the idea that through hard work and perseverance anyone can rise on the social scale—is a central part of the American ideology. Yet a number of studies have shown that social mobility is about the same for all industrialized countries. If and when movement does occur, it usually involves, at most, a few vertical steps; more often movement is horizontal—to another position on the same social stratum. The "rags-to-riches" story, although it does happen occasionally, is more myth than reality.

Possibly the greatest practical application of a concept based on studies of social stratification involves what are called "life chances." High social position translates into better schooling, housing, and medical facilities, which means that upper-class persons live longer, are in better health, and live in healthier surroundings than lower-class persons. Lower-class people live in poorer housing and are more likely to commit crimes and to be imprisoned; they are also more likely to be the victims of crime. One's position in the stratification system, then, can determine not only health or sickness but also life or death.

Context

Auguste Comte, often called the founder of sociology, was strongly influenced by the nineteenth century faith in science. Comte believed that the laws of the social sciences were as unchangeable as the laws of the physical sciences. This belief was shared by Karl Marx and Herbert Spencer. Marx believed that revolutions would inevitably result from class conflict. Comte and Spencer advocated a laissez-faire or "hands-off" attitude which would result in the formation of class and status in every society. The study of "social classes" became part of the academic discipline of sociology. The term "social stratification" did not come into general use until the 1940's.

The first social scientists to explore the system of ranking in modern communities in any depth were W. Lloyd Warner and Paul S. Lunt, in their *Yankee City* series (1942). Using a stable New England community as their model, they divided the social classes into six parts, two each for upper, middle, and lower. The upper two classes constituted 3 percent of the city's total population; the lower classes, 58 percent. Studies by Dennis Gilbert and Joseph A. Kahl in 1987 and by Daniel W. Rossides in 1990 found virtually identical percentages existing in similar class categorizations.

World War I and its aftermath—with its destruction of the traditional class structure in many European countries and the economic dislocation of millions—destroyed the concept of sociology as an exact science. Sociologists began to rely on empiricism based on experience or educated guesswork. They established ideals, or working models, rather than attempting to study human social phenomena exactly as a "hard science" would. After World War I, fascist regimes rose in Europe. Marx had noted that the bourgeoisie would use their control of the police and of governments to keep themselves in power. Indeed, such actions seemed to account for the rise of fascism in nations such as Germany, Italy, and Spain. What probably spared the United States from a similar upheaval during the Great Depression of the 1930's, when millions were unemployed and there was widespread malnutrition, even starvation, was the deeply ingrained American belief that theirs was an open society and that with perseverance and hard work, any person could rise and succeed in it.

World War II and its aftermath continued the dislocation of World War I. Now the dislocation was global, with the fall of the great colonial empires; India, for example (traditionally the most "closed" of societies), emerged as an independent state. The polarization between the wealthy and poor, however, continued and generally became even more pronounced. Riots by members of subgroups of the lower classes became more common. Some observers argued that these were a prelude to the revolutions that Marx had predicted. The old assumption that revolutions such as those that occurred in Russia, China, and Cuba only happen in agricultural, underdeveloped societies was challenged.

Today, industrialized countries are committed in varying degrees to lessening the most severe economic inequities among their citizens. This commitment manifests itself in two ways: "negatively," through taxation, transfer payments, and subsidies; and "positively," through providing greater opportunities for advancement by education and the outlawing of discrimination. Nevertheless, stratification will continue to exist, because while those in power—whether known as the upper class, the power elite, or another name—may make concessions to other groups, they will not willingly relinquish their power or control of society. If social stratification or structured inequality cannot be eliminated, however, at least some of the worst abuses can be corrected.

Bibliography

Bottomore, T. B., et al., eds. *Classes in Modern Society*. New York: Pantheon Books, 1966.
    Among the best short introductory works on social stratification. Written in a concise,

straightforward manner, it discusses its historical development, its application to industrial societies, and its impact on politics and culture.

Bryjak, George J., and Michael P. Soroka. *Sociology: Cultural Diversity in a Changing World.* 3d ed. Boston: Allyn & Bacon, 1997. Clear and comprehensible introductory sociology text with a good chapter on social stratification. Chapters end with well-written summaries. Profusely illustrated with numerous charts and graphs, the book also contains a glossary.

Dahrendorf, Ralf. *Class and Class Conflict in Industrial Society.* Stanford, Calif.: Stanford University Press, 1959. Treats social stratification within the context of a modern industrial society. Carefully researched and translated from the German, this work would be valuable to the reader interested in pursuing the study of social stratification in depth. The detailed bibliography is divided not only into subject areas but also by time periods.

Krauss, Irving. *Stratification, Class, and Conflict.* New York: Free Press, 1976. Broad study on all aspects of social stratification, including its historical development, its importance to group life, its relation to life chances such as good health and longevity, its effect on class behavior, and the unique aspects of American social stratification. Discusses the potential for class conflict using as examples the French Revolution, Civil War draft riots in the United States, and rise of the Populist movement.

Nis Petersen

Cross-References

Caste Systems; Class Consciousness and Class Conflict; Conflict Theory; Marxism; Racial and Ethnic Stratification; Social Groups; Social Stratification: Functionalist Perspectives; Social Stratification: Marxist Perspectives; Social Stratification: Weberian Perspectives.

SOCIAL STRATIFICATION
Functionalist Perspectives

Type of sociology: Social stratification
Field of study: Theoretical perspectives on stratification

The functionalist perspective on social stratification proposes that social stratification is inevitable in society and is therefore universal. Generally, functionalist scholars have argued that stratification is both necessary and desirable to ensure that difficult and important positions will be filled by individuals capable of fulfilling the duties associated with such positions.

Principal terms

ACHIEVED STATUS: refers to the assignment of individuals to positions in society based upon their achievements, such as education or the attainment of some skill

ASCRIBED STATUS: refers to the assignment of individuals to positions in society based on intrinsic characteristics, such as birth order, kin network, sex, or race

DIVISION OF LABOR: refers to the manner in which work is allocated in society, with increasing specialization of different tasks/occupations leading to a more complex division of labor

SOCIAL CLASS: category of group membership that is generally based on one's position in the economic system with respect to economic resources, income, occupational prestige, and educational attainment

SOCIAL PRESTIGE: esteem with which one is regarded in society

SOCIAL STRATIFICATION: hierarchical ranking system, often represented as a "ladder," in which there are differences in access to social resources; individuals at the top ranks have more access, while those at the bottom lack social resources; also called structured inequality

Overview

The study of social stratification developed from sociological concerns about social inequality and social classes. In his 1993 book *Inequality and Stratification*, Robert Rothman says that "the study of social class has been a central theme in sociology since its origins in the nineteenth century." According to Rothman, the most important contribution sociology makes to understanding social stratification is in presenting the view that stratification, or inequality, is patterned into societies. For Rothman, these patterns of inequality must be viewed in relation to values and beliefs, social institutions, laws, norms, and patterns of power. These together, he argues, support and maintain social stratification. Sociologists have studied social stratification to understand the extent of its occurrence and the consequences of institutionalized inequality for members of society. In the United States throughout the twentieth century, the leading sociological theory of social stratification has been functionalist.

Functionalist theory, in the United States most often associated with Talcott Parsons, is a theory that is most concerned with how societies maintain order. Generally, functionalist theorists have tended to stress stability, consensus, and integration in society. They view society as similar to the human body with its many organs. Like the body's organs, society's institutions must function properly to maintain the general stability of the entire social system. Parsons, perhaps more than other functionalist theorists, believed that this social order was based upon values shared by members of society.

Parsons differentiated societies as falling on a continuum between ascribed-status-based societies and achievement-based societies. Societies in which individuals were valued based on their family position, sex, race, or other traits of birth are viewed as falling at the traditional end of the continuum. On the other end is modern society, in which a system of rewards is used to aid in fulfilling a complex division of labor. Parsons argued that the more difficult positions that demanded considerable responsibility required a system of rewards to motivate individuals to take them. In his view, stratification—which is, by definition, social inequality—was both necessary and agreeable. Parsons believed that stratification was necessary to provide rewards for people who would take on the additional responsibility tied to difficult positions, and, in his view, stratification was desirable because it allowed the social system to function smoothly.

Parsons's articulation of a functionalist theory of social stratification was further developed by Kingsley Davis and Wilbert Moore in the 1945 landmark essay "Some Principles of Stratification," published in *American Sociological Review*. In their essay, Davis and Moore set forth a notion of social stratification that shared the basic premises elaborated by Talcott Parsons. They said that social stratification was universal (in varied forms), functional, and integral to fulfilling the division of labor.

For Davis and Moore, the reason social stratification, or structured inequality, is necessary lies in society's need to distribute individuals to vital social positions. Furthermore, society must motivate individuals to perform their duties once they have been recruited for positions. Davis and Moore argued that it was necessary and functional for society to have a varied set of rewards in relation to the varied levels of sacrifices required by some jobs. In other words, there are some jobs that require individuals to possess special talents or to develop special skills. These jobs may also require that the individual filling the position works with the utmost care. Therefore, Davis and Moore find it logical that societies have developed a system of rewards whereby those jobs requiring the greatest preparation and responsibility are rewarded more highly than are other positions. The social order has developed a differentiated system of rewards, which has led to social stratification.

Davis and Moore acknowledge that one way of rewarding people is to contribute more to their sustenance and comfort levels. Like Parsons, however, they focus most on social prestige, the rewards that contribute to one's self-respect. As the social order has developed, these rewards have been "built into" the position and have come to be viewed as rights and fringe benefits of the position. Rewards, however, do not necessarily have to be great, simply enough to ensure that individuals will fill the positions that are of great import to the functioning of society. Furthermore, there must be a hierarchy of rewards so that less-important positions are unable to compete with more important positions. Therefore, for positions that require considerable sacrifice and training, such as that of medical doctor, it is essential to reward individuals with a great amount of social prestige to attract them to the positions because training is so extensive and costly.

Davis and Moore were concerned about how to explain variations in social stratification among societies. They believed that variations in stratification systems ultimately developed because of differences in what they called "functional importance" of positions and in the "scarcity of personnel." In other words, a position of great functional importance to one type of society may not be important to a different type of society. For this reason, there may be few individuals to fill a position of great import to one society, while there may be no scarcity in another society because there is not even a requirement for that position. As Davis and Moore saw it, societies are divided into types depending on two sets of features: internal organization and external conditions. The important aspects of internal organization are whether they have a specialized division of labor; whether they are organized around family as their most important connections; sacred authority (in which there is little social mobility for people who are not religious leaders); and capitalism (in which technology and economic activity are most impor-tant). The external conditions that influence the form of social stratification are the level of development, because specialization is viewed as a sign of advancement; foreign relations, such as a state of war with other nations; and the size of the society, because smaller societies are assumed to have lower degrees of functional specialization.

In sum, both Parsons and Davis and Moore present a view of structured inequality as being necessary to maintain social order and therefore society's survival, and as being based on general agreement among members of society.

Applications

The functionalist theory of social stratification, influenced most by Parsons and Davis and Moore, has focused on explaining social stratification as a system of rewards resulting in differences in social prestige. Therefore, applications of the theory have generated studies of occupational prestige and income.

In his 1977 study *Occupational Prestige in Comparative Perspective*, Donald Treiman examined the issue of structured social inequality. Treiman examined various occupational prestige hierarchies, arguing in the manner of Davis and Moore and Talcott Parsons that stratification is inherent in complex modern societies. Treiman's study sought to clarify the determinants of prestige for various occupations and to determine whether this ordering operates universally (in all societies).

Using secondary data from a variety of societies, Treiman examined "occupational hierarchies of power, privilege, and prestige" by looking at differences in income, educa-tional level, and prestige. He found that prestige evaluations by students in all countries examined showed considerable similarity despite cultural differences. He also found that education and income are related to each other, as are education and prestige, and prestige and income. Those countries that were highly industrialized, however, had more in common with one another than they did with less-industrialized countries. Treiman also found that there were differences in stratification based on the economic system of the country; for example, the socialist nations in Eastern Europe did vary somewhat from the pattern of stratification found in capitalist societies. Furthermore, Treiman was unable to prove that the work that an individual does determines that individual's status in all societies. For some societies, it is not the work one does but the wealth, family membership, or ethnic identity that affects one's status.

Don B. Cullen and Shelley M. Novick's study "The Davis-Moore Theory of Stratification: A Further Examination and Extension," in the *American Journal of Sociology* 83, no. 6 (1979), also applies functionalist ideas about stratification to research. Cullen and Novick examined occupations to look at the amount of talent they required and the amount of "disagreeability," training, importance, and rewards through prestige and income that they entailed. They found that the amount of talent and training required for a position, and the importance of the position, did affect the levels of income and prestige accorded to that position. When jobs were physically demanding, there was a negative effect on prestige. Overall, Cullen and Novick believed that talent and training differences provide the best explanation of differences in rewards.

Generally, functionalist theories of social stratification have been assumed, as far as public policy is concerned, because they mirror and support the status quo. In other words, it is assumed that individuals at the upper end of the stratification system are there because the positions they hold merit higher rewards than do the positions of those at the bottom. In other words, the functionalist perspective on stratification has been complementary to the notion that American society is meritocratic, that people with the highest incomes and high social esteem have earned them. Furthermore, this line of reasoning may lead to the supposition that those with low incomes and low levels of esteem merit fewer social rewards because of the positions they hold.

In terms of social policy, critics have argued that social mobility is restricted by lack of access to training and education for people on the lower end of the stratification system. The governmental response has been varied, resulting at times in greater governmental support for students' educational expenses but contracting at other times, when students are expected to bear the sacrifice themselves. In the aftermath of the large social movements of the 1960's and 1970's, women and people of color have argued that some positions warrant higher rewards than they are currently given because they are demanding and are of great importance to society. Such premises guide the notion of comparable worth, for example, which seeks to provide higher rewards for jobs that have been feminized, or have been performed primarily by women. Comparable worth proponents argue that positions that women hold are rewarded at lower levels than are those that men hold simply because it is women who fill those positions.

Context

Functionalism is a major theoretical orientation in sociology, dating from the work of Émile Durkheim. In U.S. sociology, this perspective is most often represented by the work of

Talcott Parsons, who developed the contemporary functionalist perspective on social stratification. Indeed, functionalism has been the dominant perspective in American sociology throughout the twentieth century. Its major characteristics are a view of society as working to ensure its own survival; a view of social institutions as furthering the maintenance of social order; an emphasis on consensus, or agreement, undergirding the social order; and a belief in the universal applications of these notions. In keeping with these overriding concerns, then, the functionalist perspective on social stratification views this structured inequality as essential to the stability of society, necessary to the smooth functioning of society, based on consensus, and universal to all societies.

Although the functionalist notion of stratification introduced in the middle of the twentieth century was immediately accepted as the prevailing theory of stratification, it was not without its critics. Chief among these was Melvin Tumin, who argued that it was impossible to calculate the "functional importance" of any position in society objectively. According to Tumin, in his 1953 essay "Some Principles of Stratification: A Critical Analysis," "to judge that engineers in a factory are functionally more important to the factory than the unskilled workmen involves a notion regarding the dispensability of the unskilled workmen . . ." In other words, Tumin is saying that in any given line of production, every position is interdependent and is therefore of functional importance. Tumin also argues that, instead of encouraging the use of talent, a rigid system of stratification may suppress the discovery of new talent. This is particularly salient in the areas of training and education. Tumin states that wealth may determine access to training and education, thus depriving large portions of the population of the opportunity to attain those positions that reward training and education. Based on this thinking, Tumin asserted that stratification was dysfunctional to society. He further argued that it cannot be assumed that people actually make sacrifices to get greater amounts of training and education. Instead, he suggested that one might view the ability that some parents have to support their children through college and medical school as a resource that those parents have as a reward for their high positions in the system of stratification.

Other sociologists have debated the functionalist perspective on stratification. In particular, they have been concerned with the proposed inevitability of stratification and the use of consensus on occupational rankings to determine functional importance. For example, Abrahamson et al. argue in their 1976 book *Stratification and Mobility* that the notions guiding this theory are not clearly testable, objective notions. They cite Polish sociologist Wlodzimierz Wesolowski, who argued that the Davis-Moore notion of rewards presupposes that human nature is selfish and greedy, motivated by materialistic desires. Generally, the major debate against functionalist theories of stratification has come from the conflict theorists in sociology.

The conflict-theoretical perspective contrasts sharply with that of the functionalists. Conflict theorists view social inequality as emanating from conflict between social groups in society, in which the most powerful group can shape and impose an unequal system of rewards and punishments. Though they agree that social stratification is universal, they view it negatively, as a practice that inhibits the development of the talents of most of the population by giving unfair advantage to the upper levels of society. Furthermore, conflict theorists do not agree that structured inequality is either agreeable to most of society or inevitable in modern, specialized societies.

The conflict-functionalist debate on stratification was further expanded following the impact of the social movements of the 1960's and 1970's on U.S. sociology. In particular, it was argued by feminist sociologists and some racial minority sociologists that studies of stratification had to include more rigid examination of the roles played by race and gender—ascriptive characteristics—in placing individuals in positions. In fact, Rothman argues, in *Inequality and Stratification*, that "no development has been more salient than recognition that considerations of color and gender are central to a full appreciation of the composition and dynamics of class systems." It is the growing understanding that race, color, and gender have played a central role in determining access to training, education, and positions in society that is posing the greatest challenge to the traditional sociological theory of stratification—the functionalist perspective.

Bibliography

Abrahamson, Mark. "Stratification." In *Functionalism*. Englewood Cliffs, N.J.: Prentice-Hall, 1978. Clearly lays out functionalist theory of stratification. Discusses, briefly, the origins of American functionalism in the work of the French sociologist Émile Durkheim; then turns to a consideration of Talcott Parsons, Davis and Moore, and W. Lloyd Warner; and then discusses the critics of functionalism.

Abrahamson, Mark, Ephraim H. Mizruchi, and Carlton A. Hornung. *Stratification and Mobility*. New York: Macmillan, 1976. Overview of the functionalist theory of stratification and its critics in chapter 4, along with a comparison of functionalist theory and conflict theory. Geared more toward scholars than lay readers.

Bendix, Reinhard, and Seymour Martin Lipset, eds. *Class, Status, and Power*. 2d ed. New York: Free Press, 1966. Essays of major theorists on social stratification. In part 1, "Theories of Class Structure," the original essays by Davis and Moore and Tumin, with replies to each other, are included. The original essays are very clearly and succinctly written; even the nonsociologist can easily follow the arguments of Davis and Moore and the criticisms presented by Tumin.

Rothman, Robert A. *Inequality and Stratification: Class, Color, and Gender*. 3d ed. Upper Saddle River, N.J.: Prentice-Hall, 1999. Overview of class, race, and gender stratification in American society, with a presentation of sociological theories of stratification and other types of stratification. This highly readable text also presents a different side of stratification, including the consequences of one's placement in various positions on the social ladder.

Treiman, Donald J. *Occupational Prestige in Comparative Perspective*. New York: Academic Press, 1977. Quantitative study of the international application of functionalist theories of stratification. The analysis is statistical, but nonsociologists can follow his substantive discussion of the dilemmas in functionalist theory and his concluding arguments.

Sharon Elise

Cross-References

Conflict Theory; Education: Functionalist Perspectives; Family: Functionalist Versus Conflict Theory Views; Functionalism; Racial and Ethnic Stratification; Social Stratification: Analysis and Overview; Social Stratification: Marxist Perspectives; Social Stratification: Weberian Perspectives.

SOCIAL STRATIFICATION
Marxist Perspectives

Type of sociology: Social stratification
Field of study: Theoretical perspectives on stratification

Social stratification is the hierarchical arrangement of social groups. Marxist perspectives generally regard modern society as being divided primarily into two classes—the bourgeoisie and the proletariat—on the basis of property ownership or nonownership of property.

Principal terms

BOURGEOISIE: modern social class, also known as the capitalist class, which owns the means of production, employs wage-labor, and has profit as its source of income

CLASS: fundamental social group determined by its economic relationship to the means of production in terms of ownership and nonownership and in terms of producing or nonproducing

CLASS CONSCIOUSNESS: awareness of belonging to a definite socioeconomic class and a conscious sharing of the political interests of that class

CLASS STRUGGLE: historical conflict between the oppressors and the oppressed; in modern society, the antagonism existing between the bourgeoisie and the working class

EXPLOITATION: extraction of unpaid labor from the working class

MODE OF PRODUCTION: distinct structure of economic relations composed of the form of property ownership and the arrangement between the producing and nonproducing classes

PROLETARIAT: modern social class that is composed of the nonowning working class; the proletariat produces commodities and derives its income from wages that it has obtained in return for its labor

RELATIONS OF PRODUCTION: structure of economic relations or the way in which people are related to one another in the production process and in terms of property ownership

Overview

Although class theory and the idea of class struggle are associated with the nineteenth century German philosopher Karl Marx, these ideas did not originate with him. He admitted as much in a letter written in 1852: "no credit is due to me for discovering the existence of classes in modern society, nor yet the struggle between them." In fact, Marx never fully set forth a systematic theory of social classes. He did, however, appear to begin a manuscript on social classes that appears at the end of *Das Kapital* (1867; *Capital: A Critique of Political Economy*, 1886), where he stated, following classical political economy, that modern society is made up of three classes: wage-laborers, capitalists, and landowners. They are differentiated by their respective sources of income: wages, profit, and ground-rent.

Laborers live on wages, capitalists on profits, and landlords on rent. Marx goes on to say that class differentiation based on sources of revenue would result in an unnecessary multiplication of classes. At this point, the manuscript suddenly breaks off.

In *Der achtzehnte Brumaire des Louis Bonaparte* (1852; *The Eighteenth Brumaire of Louis Bonaparte*, 1852), Marx offers a provisional definition of class: "In so far as millions of families live under economic conditions of existence that separate their mode of life, their interests, and their culture from those of the other classes, and put them in hostile opposition to the latter, they form a class." Thus, economic conditions determine class formation. In addition, classes stand in antagonistic relations with one another.

Generally, Marx understood classes to be economically determined by the difference between the owners of the means of production and the nonowning direct producers. In his words: "it is always the direct relation between the owners of the conditions of production and the direct producers which reveals the innermost secret, the hidden foundation, of the entire social edifice" (*Das Kapital*).

Class differences, therefore, are determined by the mode of production. Marx and Friedrich Engels have divided history into five distinct epochs of production: primitive communism, Asiatic, ancient Greece and Rome, feudal society, and capitalism, or the bourgeois. Of these only the ancient, the feudal, and the bourgeois receive special treatment. Ancient society was based on slavery, feudal society on serfdom, and capitalism on wage-labor.

Each of these societies was divided into two major classes: the oppressors and the oppressed, or the exploiters and the exploited. In every case, the exploiters are made up of those who own the means of production but do not produce. The exploited are those who do not own the means of production but are the direct producers of social goods and services. Because the exploited do not own the means of production, they are forced, in order to live, to work for those who own and control the productive conditions of life. The exploiters live by means of the surplus produced by the exploited. As a result, the social mode of production also reproduces the social relations of production. Thus, the relationship between the exploiters and the exploited is constantly renewed and conserved.

The two fundamental economic classes in modern society, according to Marx, are the bourgeoisie and the proletariat. The bourgeoisie is the capitalist class—the class that owns the conditions of production. The proletariat is the nonowning class that sells its labor to the capitalist class for wages. The capital-labor relationship, therefore, is a wage relationship.

It should be pointed out that Marx never equated all workers with the proletariat. Marx made a distinction, typical of classical political economy, between productive labor and unproductive labor. Productive labor is labor purchased by wages and utilized in the production process to produce commodities the surplus value of which accedes to the capitalist a profit over and beyond the outlay in labor and means of production. Unproductive labor is service that is exchanged for a fee. This service does not yield a profit to the buyer but is consumed. For example, a laborer making pianos in a piano factory undertakes productive labor and is therefore a proletarian. A piano player who is employed to play music at a wedding, although receiving a fee, is not making profit for the employer and is therefore not a proletarian. It is important to remember that, from a Marxist perspective, the proletariat does not include all workers. It should also be understood that capitalist production includes intellectual and cultural production as well as material production. In the words of Hal Draper (1978), "There is a whole sphere of intellectual or mental production that is proletarian."

Capitalist social relations are marked by a distinctive contradiction: the contradiction between social production and private appropriation. The mass production of commodities is produced by masses of laborers working in cooperative forms, yet ownership of those commodities belongs to the capitalist class. This contradiction is the heart of the exploitative relationship.

Jon Elster, a Norwegian philosopher and Marx scholar, insists that class denotes a relationship of exploitation: "class . . . is the collective social expression of the fact of exploitation, the way in which exploitation is embodied in a social structure" (1985). Exploitation is the private appropriation of social labor. Thus, from a Marxist perspective, the ending of exploitation means abolishing the existence of social classes, and particularly, the capital-labor relationship.

This goal implies struggle, but the proletariat will not struggle until it attains a certain level of class consciousness. More than any other Marxist theoretician, György Lukács, a Hungarian Marxist philosopher, attributed crucial importance to the development of class consciousness. In his important work *Geschichte und Klassenbewusstsein* (1923; *History and Class Consciousness*, 1971), Lukács made a significant distinction between actual class consciousness and imputed class consciousness. By actual class consciousness, Lukács means what members of a definite class really think. By imputed class consciousness, Lukács recognizes the fact that while the working class may not actually think correctly about economic reality and political facts (that is, may not have class consciousness), the working class would have class consciousness if it had all the facts; it would then think in a revolutionary manner. Class consciousness refers to the conscious interests shared by members of a class by virtue of their class position. Class consciousness is absolutely indispensable for organization, mobilization, and political activity. The absence of class consciousness is referred to as false consciousness. Trade union activity is the best way to instill class consciousness and to get workers to participate in class struggle, but there is a debate in Marxism regarding whether class consciousness is a necessary feature of class definition or of class conflict.

In *Manifest du Kommunistischen Partei* (1848; *The Communist Manifesto*, 1850), Marx and Engels asserted the idea that class conflict was the driving force of history: "The history of all hitherto existing society is the history of class struggles." Class struggle is the essential relationship between oppressors and oppressed. In modern society, the struggle is the antagonistic relationship between the bourgeoisie and the proletariat. In the *Manifesto*, Marx and Engels claim that the modern epoch "has simplified the class antagonism: Society as a whole is more and more splitting up into two great hostile camps, into two great classes directly facing each other: Bourgeoisie and Proletariat."

The essential interests in this conflict are those involving exploitation and resistance to exploitation. The political interests of the bourgeoisie are to conserve the social relationships based on economic exploitation. The interests of the proletariat are to resist the exploitation of the bourgeoisie and to overthrow a society based on the division of classes. One must be careful to note that these interests are the interests imputed to these classes by virtue of their structural position and not actual conscious interest known to the members of the bourgeoisie and the proletariat.

The struggles between classes constitute one of the major causes of historical societal change. As Jon Elster puts it: "Classes should be defined by what people have to do, not by what they actually do."

Applications

Various questions that have been raised by Marxist social theory have to do with its explanatory power. To what extent does the theory of classes and class conflict help explain historical social changes? Does the Marxist theory of social classes correspond to the actual form of social stratification in modern society? Does the Marxist theory of social stratification apply to all epochs or only to modern capitalism? Are historical changes really explained by the theory of class struggle? Are the bourgeoisie and the proletariat the two major social classes in modern society? What about the middle classes? What about other social forces that account for historical change, such as nationalism, racism, imperialism, and the women's movement?

From 1844 until his death in 1883, Marx grappled with the political economy of capitalist society. He wanted to uncover the logic of capitalism, the motivating forces of modern society. To that extent, his class analysis is basically applicable only to modern capitalist society. The bourgeoisie and the proletariat are social products of the modern industrial era.

Perhaps the most oft-repeated criticism of Marxism is that which questions Marx's theory about the increasing widening in the lifestyles between the bourgeoisie and the proletariat. It is believed that Marx claimed that the working classes would become more impoverished as capitalism progressed. Not only has the gulf not widened, say the critics, but the working classes are better off than ever. Marx, however, was not speaking in absolute terms or in solely materialistic terms. He was speaking in relative and spiritual terms. That is, relative to its output, the return of the working class in the form of wages would decrease. In addition, the world of commodities created by capital does not allow for the full development of human beings as human beings. Instead workers become alienated.

Along similar lines, critics claim that Marx's theory cannot account for the rise of the middle classes. In *Das Kapital*, however, in the unfinished manuscript on social classes, Marx does recognize other strata besides the major social classes. In another work, Marx claims that bourgeois society tends to give rise to new middle classes. In a few places, Marx and Engels claimed that the intermediate strata between the bourgeoisie and the proletariat would disappear. According to Tom Bottomore, the growth of the new middle classes—office workers, technicians, and so forth—interposes between the bourgeoisie and the proletariat a whole range of status groups. Such a range, or continuum, according to Bottomore, based on factors other than property ownership, would deflate the theory of class conflict. Bottomore believes, however, that Marx's theory of classes is less falsifiable than are other theories of social stratification. For example, if one accepts the continuum theory of social stratification, then one has to account for the possibility of nonarbitrary division in the continuum between extremes. Jon Elster (1985) asks the interesting question "When does an individual own enough property to be considered no longer a worker but a capitalist?"

Property ownership in Marxist terms becomes a thorny issue. It is not so simple to divide society into property owners and the propertyless. Corporate property, profit sharing, and other such financial assets pose problems. Do stockholders own property or do they only have entitlements to shares of dividends? Is the source of power in the ownership of property or in the management of property? Although these questions are difficult to answer, it cannot be denied that Marx's fundamental principle is incontestable—the masses of people can only survive by selling their labor power on the market for wages. As long as this remains true, Marxist theory is applicable.

Context

As noted above, Marx did not invent the term "class" or the idea of class struggle. The Marxist idea of social stratification in class terms was rooted in classical political economy on the one hand and in the socialist literature of nineteenth century Europe on the other hand. "Class" and "class struggle" are explanatory terms.

As mentioned above, other historians have used the terms "class" and "class struggle." These terms were used in socialist literature as well as in classical political economy. Political economy centered on the question "What is the source of value?" In the medieval period, the Scholastics spoke of the just price; they believed that remuneration should be proportionate to outlay and effort. For the Mercantilists, value came to be identified with the customary price or the market price. The Physiocrats equated value with agricultural labor or the labor costs in agricultural production. Eventually, political economists began to identify value with production costs in manufacturing. In other words, labor was seen as the creator of social wealth. In their analyses of the economy, Adam Smith and David Ricardo divided society into three major classes: the capitalists, the landowners, and the laborers. Neither writer, however, elaborated on the exploitative relationship existing between the property-owning class and the propertyless working class. This was left to Marx.

Marx, as editor of the *Rheinische Zeitung* between 1842 and 1844, dealt with discussions, proceedings, and debates on such economic questions as wood theft, landed property, the conditions of the peasantry, and free trade and tariffs. It was not until his 1844 critical review of Georg Hegel's *Grundlinien der Philosophie des Rechts* (1821; *Philosophy of Right*, 1875), however, that Marx began to apply historical materialism to the study of society. In that work, Marx set forth the claim that legal relations and forms of state have their origin in the material conditions of life. At that time, Marx also became acquainted with Friedrich Engels, who had published his article "The Condition of the Working Class in England." Marx began using the term "class" in 1844. In his critique of Hegel, he wrote, "A class must be formed which has radical chains, a class in civil society which is not a class of civil society, a class which is the dissolution of all classes . . . the proletariat." In the *Ökonomische und philosophische Manuskripte* (1844; *Economic and Philosophic Manuscripts of 1844*, 1947), Marx began a criticism of classical political economy. While agreeing with the idea of classical political economy that society falls into two classes—the property-owners and the propertyless workers—Marx criticized classical political economy for failing to consider the direct relationship between the worker and production. In this relationship is found the core of capitalism—the antagonism between the capitalist class and the working class. In 1847, Marx asserted that the capital-labor relationship is the inner contradiction of capitalist society that will eventually culminate in the dissolution of that society.

Max Weber contrasted Marx's notion of classes with his own notion of *Stand*, or status group. *Stand* designates social rank and explains collective action in ways that class alone cannot. Collective action, according to Weber, must be accounted for in terms of the lifestyles and cultures of social groups. The latter not only determine the rise of ideas but also explain group behavior on the basis of honor, privileges, and distinctions attributed to social situations. For Weber, class is only an economic category and explains market behavior exclusively. Weber did not accept class as the sole explanatory force.

Bibliography

Bottomore, T. B., et al., eds. *Classes in Modern Society*. 2d ed. London: Routledge, 1992. Fine little study of social classes in modern industrial society. Inequality and social hierarchy are considered from a Marxist perspective.

_____. *A Dictionary of Marxist Thought*. 2d ed. Cambridge, Mass.: Blackwell Reference, 1991. Only work of its kind. Key terms and important figures in Marxism are dealt with expertly by the top scholars in the field.

Draper, Hal. *The Politics of Social Classes*. Vol. 2 in *Karl Marx's Theory of Revolution*. New York: Monthly Review Press, 1978. Studious and comprehensive look at Marx's theory of proletarian revolution.

Elster, Jon. *Making Sense of Marx*. Cambridge, England: Cambridge University Press, 1985. Critical examination of Marx's major ideas from the point of view of the analytical philosophy.

Levine, Rhonda F., ed. *Social Class and Stratification: Classic Statements and Theoretical Debates*. Lanham, Md.: Rowman and Littlefield, 1998.

Tucker, Robert C., ed. *The Marx-Engels Reader*. 2d ed. New York: W. W. Norton, 1978. Anthology of the writing of Marx and Engels. Includes letters, economic writings, political analyses, philosophical treatises, and the later writings of Engels.

Michael Candelaria

Cross-References

Conflict Theory; Marxism; Racial and Ethnic Stratification; Social Groups; Social Mobility: Analysis and Overview; Social Stratification: Functionalist Perspectives; Social Stratification: Weberian Perspectives.

SOCIAL STRATIFICATION
Weberian Perspectives

Type of sociology: Social stratification
Field of study: Theoretical perspectives on stratification

The pioneering German sociologist Max Weber showed how the many layers and ranks in capitalistic Western societies are defined by people's skills, credentials, market relationships, and property ownership—and by other determiners of stratification such as status and party. Weber rejected Karl Marx's view that the class conflicts inherent in capitalism were simplistic and could be resolved by socialism.

Principal terms

BOURGEOISIE: middle-class, property-owning social class
BUREAUCRACY: a goal-focused administrative system emphasizing specialized duties, fixed rules, hierarchy or rank, and chain of command
CAPITALISM: economic system featuring private or corporate ownership, investment free from state control, and a free-market system that controls prices, production, and distribution
ENTREPRENEUR: investor who undertakes a business venture
IDEAL TYPE: abstract case or situation; a hypothetical construct that makes it possible to generalize about real social experiences
RATIONALIZATION: in the Weberian sense, using formal procedures and rules (as in a bureaucracy) instead of informal, spontaneous patterns
SOCIAL MOBILITY: capacity to improve one's class standing
SOCIAL STRATUM: level of society based on class, race, or economic condition; stratification thus means division into layers or levels
VERSTEHEN: empathic (interpretive) understanding; Weber's main goal as a social analyst

Overview

Social "stratification" is an imperfect analogy because it suggests that the many layers of society—representing its identifiable groups—are like the stacked strata in geological formations. No one wants to be at the "bottom of the heap," yet some always are, because they lack power, money, property, respect, status, or marketable skills. Theorists study the makeup of society by identifying and defining the many social strata that exist and by explaining their origins, causes, features, and effects. The writings of the renowned German sociologist Max Weber (1864-1920) shed light on many aspects of social stratification.

Throughout history, societies have exhibited various systems of layered subdivision based on cultural values and economic organization. While historians and anthropologists focus on the past, sociologists examine modern Western societies, whose dominant economic patterns have been capitalistic. Weber's own interests ranged broadly over past and present, but his ideas have direct, ongoing implications for studies of modern social stratification.

Weber discussed all three major forms of social stratification: classes, castes, and estates. A class is defined in the *International Encyclopedia of Sociology* (1984) as "a form of social stratification in which allocation to, membership of, and relationships between classes are governed by economic considerations rather than law (as in *estates*) or religion and ritual pollution (as in *caste*)." Before the Renaissance, the established division into three estates (commoners, nobility, and clergy) officially described social organization in Europe. Social class, the most important factor in the stratification of modern free societies, was an aspect of some early societies—the Romans used the term to differentiate degrees of wealth—but its modern sense dates from the Industrial Revolution in the eighteenth century, when the capitalist system of social organization solidified in Western Europe. The prominence of the middle class and entrepreneurship are characteristic of capitalism.

As Wolfgang Mommsen (1989) points out, the sociological results of the advance of modern industrial capitalism are the focus of much of Weber's writing. Weber thoroughly described the complex ways in which capitalistic societies subdivide themselves into socioeconomic classes, combining the viewpoints of economist and sociologist in his analysis of stratification. Discussing what he called "rational bourgeois capitalism," Weber showed how people's economic behaviors determined their social ranking; "rational" is a complex and ambivalent modifier, suggesting "quantifiable," "calculating," "sensible," "systematic," and "opportunistic." Such aspects of the economic market as distribution and consumption of goods dominated Weber's theory of stratification: People can improve their social standings in a mobile society by having marketable goods and services, and by exploiting the existing system in order to market them profitably.

In *Wirtschaft und Gesellschaft* (1922; *Economy and Society*, 1968), Weber defines and analyzes three overlapping class categories: property classes, which are determined by property ownership; commercial (or acquisition) classes, which are determined by the marketability of services, goods, and skills; and social classes, which are characterized by social mobility and a sense of community (involving shared lifestyles and ideas about honor). Yet another of Weber's systems for categorizing class included four types: the working class; the petite bourgeoisie; specialists and intelligentsia (propertyless technicians, civil servants, and "white-collar" workers); and classes that are privileged because they have "property and education." The complexity of Weber's multiple classification systems is apparent.

Weber noted that members of classes do not always have a sense of class membership but do often act collectively in their own interests. Property ownership or the lack of it is, for Weber, the main determinant in class membership, but he notes that other determinants of social stratification include types of property that people own, the types of income they yield, and the types of services that individuals provide. Weber sees community power as being affected not only by class but also by status groups and parties. The former have prestige; the latter have memberships that may cut across economic, status, or class lines.

The origins of capitalism in Weber's view are closely tied to the "Protestant," or "work," ethic, an example of idealism that has practical implications. Capitalism itself, once in force, exerts social determinism, for people must adapt to the roles that the system creates: management, middle managers, and workers; producers and consumers; monopolists and outsiders; haves and have-nots; property owners and the landless.

Though hierarchical power structures have always existed in societies, the capitalistic bureaucracy is a distinctly modern feature of Western society that, Weber thought, would always limit ideal democracy. New elite groups would constantly be emerging in the modern bureaucratic systems according to which businesses and governments operate.

Applications

Merely by looking around, one can easily demonstrate Weber's basic belief that the multiple social categories in modern societies are defined by complex economic factors. Many of Weber's own examples of social stratification, however, come from historical situations and analyses of historical class conflicts. In those early prototypes, one can often see analogies with modern situations, whether or not Weber points them out specifically.

In his *General Economic History* (1966), Weber notes that the ancient Roman "knight-hood" was a social group operating, in effect, according to the principles of "modern rationalistic capitalism." The group analyzed market opportunities and responded to "mass demand," finding ways to meet "mass need." Group members detected various unmet needs of the state and then offered to meet them, for a price—by lending money, for example, to support government ventures. These knights were in conflict with the "official" Roman nobility.

Modern examples of "rationalistic capitalists" who can move quickly into new positions of high social rank include movie stars, rock stars, sports superstars, and television personalities, whose status comes from their ability to provide services that society values.

More generally, Weber shows how in earlier societies the traditional aristocracy— dominant patrician families—gradually lost power to the rising populace, the future middle class. This segment of the population included not only entrepreneurs and artisans but also knights with "status pride." Conflicts between the various bourgeois classes and the status classes inevitably emerged—and they continue to do so in modern times. Middle-class families, for example, may encourage their children to pursue lifestyles that are at odds with the values of the superstars whom the general culture idolizes. In countries such as Great Britain, clashes may occur between traditional aristocrats (who may not have money) and the newly rich (who lack traditional status).

In modern societies, families with both wealth and "family charisma" (such as the Rockefellers and Kennedys in America) enjoy class advantages that grow from more than just the family's economic status. The idea of "charisma" is one of Weber's contributions to sociology and to the modern vocabulary describing social influence. The power of the Kennedy family, particularly, can be attributed partly to the "charismatic" appeal of John Kennedy. Similarly, the "charisma" of superstars such as Elvis or the Beatles or Madonna is an important aspect of their socioeconomic power and cultural prestige.

As a sociologist of religion, Weber studied societies such as India in which the caste system operates. Weber specifically compared the ancient Indian system to the newer one in the American South (of the period c. 1910-1920), with its "white" and "black" coach cars and waiting rooms. American attempts at social integration since Weber's death have effectively eliminated the rigid element of caste, but many class differentiations remain to divide peoples of various colors, statuses, and economic conditions—supporting Weber's doubt that a fully democratic or "classless" society can ever emerge. Still, as Weber notes, the marketability of one's skills becomes a main determiner of social standing, so those born into families without property or status can "rise" if they use the capitalistic framework shrewdly to cultivate skills that are in demand. The emergence of a "black middle class" in the United States since World War II illustrates this pattern.

Weber's analysis of Judaism provides a different historical example of social stratification. Jews lived in caste-free societies but were ritually separated from all other classes. In the stratified context in which Jewishness first coalesced, Weber detected various social groups— desert Bedouins, city-dwelling patricians, artisans, merchants, and so on. Important in the uniquely emerging self-concept of the Jews was the idea of *berith*, an "oath-bound league." Since the Jews' pact was essentially with God, Weber believed that they enjoyed the stability that religious orders have traditionally exhibited—as opposed to the more volatile political alliances that have tended to come and go throughout history. In Weber's analysis, the early pattern of exile and the development of an intellectual tradition further contributed to the peculiar social history of the Jews. The shift of Jews into their "rational capitalistic" roles as the moneylenders of Europe was a later development in their cultural odyssey.

Julien Freund, in *The Sociology of Max Weber* (1968), explains Weber's notion that any socioeconomic group can be closed (like that of the Jews) or open. Historically, among the closed groups were the guilds, which functioned as monopolies. Within the groups, various levels (apprentices and masters, for example) established social stratification. Social strata such as "peasants, nobles, traders, liberal professions," and religious fraternities have traditionally had specific economic functions. Modern groups that are still relatively closed include those of physicians, lawyers, college teachers, members of Congress, and street gang members. It is possible, however, to enter into any of these groups by "rationally" working toward that end.

Trying to exemplify what the term "middle class" (or bourgeoisie) means in the Weberian sense is difficult. The group can be defined by separating out the "positively privileged property classes" (which live from income derived from their property), on the top end, and "negatively privileged" classes (including debtors, the poor, outcasts), on the bottom. People left "in the middle" are those who own various kinds of property or have marketable abilities from which they draw their livelihoods. The American middle class comprises many subcategories. Weber shows that, although a main factor in determining one's social class is the market value of what one does or owns, various status factors move beyond pure economics. Thus, priests, ministers, and college professors—who belong to the economic middle class because they are paid for marketable services—tend to have status that transcends economic class.

Context

Among Weber's important general concepts, according to Martin Albrow (1990), are the principles that people's actions in society can be understood best by looking at their motives, and that people are always self-responsible, are influenced by ideas, and are constrained by dominant patterns of social organization—which establish both opportunities and limits. These almost self-evident principles belie the complex ways in which Weber explored their implications.

After an early university career in economics, Weber was for two decades a private writer and scholar—following a mental breakdown in 1897. In his last several years, he resumed public life as a university professor of sociology at Vienna (1918) and Munich (1919), writing numerous pieces on a vast array of interconnected subjects—economics, history, law, philosophy, religion, and sociology. Most of his unfinished works were published posthumously. His major writings include *Die Protestantische Ethik und der Geist des Kapitalismus* (1904; *The Protestant Ethic and the Spirit of Capitalism*, 1930) and *Wirtschaft und Gesellschaft* (1922; *Economy and Society*, 1968). As Donald G. MacRae (1974) emphasizes, certain unique features of Weber's sociology—including his concern with bureaucracy—can be explained by examining the sociopolitical features of German society before and after 1900. Harvard professor Talcott Parsons's *The Structure of Social Action* (1937) helped to spread Weber's ideas and fame outside Germany.

Weber's historical and comparative studies of expansive institutional patterns are unequaled and remain influential. His subtle writings tend to use self-defined terminologies, however, and are hard to summarize. Hans H. Gerth and C. Wright Mills, in *From Max Weber: Essays in Sociology* (1946), observe that Weber's German sentences are built like Gothic castles. Disagreements about the meaning, accuracy, and value of Weber's ideas abound, and all generalizations about his views risk inaccuracy, especially because he was himself skeptical about the capacity of sociology to get at the truth.

Weber believed that "real" truth lay only in the actions of single individuals, that "social reality" did not really exist. He believed, however, that the use of "ideal types" could help scholars approximate social reality. This important proposal helped to establish the general investigative methodology that modern sociologists use. Weber also helped sociologists to clarify the position of their discipline (an "inexact" science) relative to the natural sciences, in which laboratory experimentation can verify or refute findings. As the "father of interpretive sociology," he saw the paradox in sociology that one must be objective in studying facts but must also exhibit sympathetic understanding (*Verstehen*). Thus, he helped to bridge the gap between positivists—who stressed the objective, scientific aspects of sociology—and more humanistic, subjective, or ingeniously creative scholars.

Weber's views are often compared to those of two other important sociological theorists, the French sociologist Émile Durkheim (1858-1917)—who followed the positivist views of Auguste Comte—and the German social thinker Karl Marx (1818-1883). Weber differs with Marx, but their differences are often oversimplified.

While Marx focused on class conflict and the inevitable triumph of the proletariat (or worker) over the bourgeois (the middle class or management level), Weber correctly envisioned the continued march of capitalism, with its stratification patterns based mostly on economic status. By 1893, Weber predicted that capitalism, as a modern revolutionary force, would destroy traditional social structures, but his attitude toward its advance was ambivalent. He disagreed with Marx's main conclusions but shared his concern over the alienation and unethical exploitation of the worker in the capitalistic system. Weber's writings sometimes view social causality under capitalism as being uncontrollable and inevitable—a perspective with which Karl Marx might have agreed.

By 1990, the collapse of socialism as a system of socioeconomic organization in the old Soviet Union and its satellites had renewed an interest in Weber's analysis of social stratification as a function of market economics. Capitalism and bureaucracy, as Weber predicted, had not disappeared, but rather had gained almost universal dominance. Thus, like others, Alan Sica argues in *Weber, Irrationality, and Social Order* (1988) that Weber's ideas continue to be relevant.

Bibliography

Albrow, Martin. *Max Weber's Construction of Social Theory*. New York: St. Martin's Press, 1990. Readable book on Weber's ideas, life, works, and times.

Käsler, Dirk. *Max Weber: An Introduction to His Life and Work*. Translated by Philippa Hurd. Chicago: University of Chicago Press, 1988. Wide-ranging, insightful book about Weber's contributions to the methodology of sociology.

Levine, Rhonda F., ed. *Social Class and Stratification: Classic Statements and Theoretical Debates*. Lanham, Md.: Rowman and Littlefield, 1998.

MacRae, Donald G. *Max Weber*. New York: Viking Press, 1974. Short book in the Modern Masters series that tries to cut through the complexities to get at the heart of Weberian sociology. It is generally useful but does not discuss class stratification directly.

Mommsen, Wolfgang J. *The Political and Social Theory of Max Weber: Collected Essays*. Chicago: University of Chicago Press, 1989. Includes pertinent essays on Weber's "dialogue" with Marx; bureaucracy and bureaucratization; and Weber's modern relevancy.

Poggi, Gianfranco. *Calvinism and the Capitalist Spirit: Max Weber's Protestant Ethic*. Amherst: University of Massachusetts Press, 1983. Tries to summarize the ideas of Weber's two-part essay *The Protestant Ethic and the Spirit of Capitalism*, arguing that Weber's ideas are not diametrically opposed to those of Marx.

Weber, Max. *Basic Concepts in Sociology*. Translated and introduced by H. P. Secher. 5th ed. New York: Citadel Press, 1968. Discusses topics with implications for social stratification, including "legitimate authority," "aggregate" and "communal" social relationships, "open" and "closed" relationships, "corporate groups" ("political" and "religious"), and "power and domination."

_____. *General Economic History*. Translated by Frank H. Knight. New York: Collier Books, 1966. Weber's historical overview analyzes class conflicts at various stages of history, the rise of modern capitalism, and modern social groupings based on economic functions.

_____. *The Protestant Ethic and the Spirit of Capitalism*. Translated by Talcott Parsons, with a foreword by R. H. Tawney. New York: Charles Scribner's Sons, 1958. Classic interpretive work about modern society and the idealistic forces that shaped its patterns of economic and social organization is central in the Weber canon and is often included in college curricula. Weber found close connections between Calvinistic religion (with its "work ethic") and economic progress in Western societies.

_____. *The Theory of Social and Economic Organization*. Edited and introduced by Talcott Parsons. Translated by A. M. Henderson and Talcott Parsons. New York: Oxford University Press, 1947. Long introduction helps to clarify this important primary text, whose last chapter ("Social Stratification and Class Structure") is particularly pertinent.

Wrong, Dennis, ed. *Max Weber*. Englewood Cliffs, N.J.: Prentice-Hall, 1970. Volume in the Makers of Modern Social Science series. Most relevant are the essays on capitalism (and its connections to Protestant ideology) and bureaucracy.

Roy Neil Graves

Cross-References

Capitalism; Class Consciousness and Class Conflict; Conflict Theory; Marxism; Social Stratification: Analysis and Overview; Social Stratification: Functionalist Perspectives; Social Stratification: Marxist Perspectives.

SOCIALIZATION
Religion

Type of sociology: Socialization and social interaction
Fields of study: Agents of socialization; Religion

Religious socialization is the process through which people learn to engage more deeply in the verbalizations, actions, and institutions of a religion which provides them with a sense of meaning and belonging. While the process of religious socialization is similar to socialization into other groups, what one recognizes as a religion will determine one's understanding of religious socialization.

Principal terms

CIVIL RELIGION: recognition of the values of one's culture or nation as the ultimate values of one's life

CONVERSION: acceptance of a religion as one's own

ROLE: what one does and says to be part of a group, and what a group needs one to say and do to ensure the group's survival

SECULARIZATION: process whereby religion loses its legitimizing role in society

SOCIALIZATION: process through which one learns the culture of one's society or group and thereby becomes a full participant in it; adopting the roles necessary to be a member of a group

Overview

The concept of religious socialization is complicated by what one understands to be the meaning of the word "religion" and is best approached, from a sociological point of view, by reference to a different concept: that of the "religious group." The discussion in this "Overview" section will therefore define the latter term before considering the relationship of religion to religious socialization in the "Applications" and "Context" sections that follow.

Every religious group has a way of speaking about that which is important to it; sociologists refer to this as "verbalization." Verbalizations are found in stories handed down from generation to generation, significant books, songs, and creedal formulas. What is common to these verbalizations is that they use words to express the religious reality. Every group also has a way of doing that which is important to it, and sociologists refer to this as "action." Action has two major subdivisions: moral or ethical behavior, and rituals. For example, every religious group has a way of ritualizing birth, marriage, and death. Every religious group conducts regular gatherings to mark special occasions and times of year. Finally, every group has a way of assuring that the words and actions are systematized and that the group itself is organized, a process known as "institutionalization." The institutional element is the organizational structure or skeleton that assures that the words and actions have a coherent form or pattern from day to day and from generation to generation.

Religious socialization, then, is the process through which people learn to engage more deeply in the verbalizations, actions, and institution of a religion. Anyone who becomes a member of a religious group learns how to say the religious words, perform the religious actions, and acknowledge the accepted pattern for religious life sanctioned by its institution. The recognition and description of the actual socialization process will depend on which religious group one is attempting to describe. The socialization process of Baptists, for example, is different from that of Roman Catholics because the two institutions have different concepts of membership: Baptists believe in adult baptisms; Catholics, in infant baptism. Hence, one becomes a Baptist through a deep experience of Jesus as Lord and Savior (recognized in the ceremony of adult baptism), whereas one becomes a Catholic when faith itself becomes part of one's life through infant baptism. A description of the socialization of the Baptist will see the born-again experience as a significant marker of one's entry into the group; Catholics' socialization process is more gradual, with conversion usually described as a lifelong process. The socialization process is well under way by the time one is baptized as an adult in the Baptist church; in the Catholic Church it usually begins with one's infant baptism.

If one puts aside membership considerations, one can describe religious socialization in terms of group development theory. For this description to be accurate, one must take for granted that the person undergoing religious socialization has been born into a family environment in which religion forms an important part. Most people are socialized into a religion through the religion of their parents. Some reject the religion of their parents and become part of another religious group, but in both cases the socialization process will follow roughly the same pattern. Early in life (or at the beginning of one's religious socialization, if one rejects the family's religion and becomes religiously socialized later in life), one learns how to act or behave in the religious manner; for example, in church one learns when to stand, sing, be quiet, or respond to the religious leader. One learns the words of a prayer uttered before meals. One learns the rituals and behaviors performed on significant festive days. Socialization into the family, therefore, often includes socialization into the religion of that family.

One next learns how to feel about what one does. Parents, friends, teachers, religious leaders, and others teach how it feels to say, "I am a sinner," "Love thy neighbor," or "Praise God." Prayer before meals incorporates the words and the feelings of thanks and gratitude. Feelings become associated with behavior.

In addition to doing and feeling, socialization involves thinking. Religious socialization gradually instills the ideas and concepts associated with what one does and feels. One begins to arrange these ideas and abstractions in certain common ways. "God," for example, becomes more than a word or sound that one utters, developing first into a feeling and then into an idea—one that can be discussed, questioned, argued about, and clarified. In the process of thinking and clarifying, one begins to recognize that one's religion defines certain ideas as correct ideas, certain behavior as correct behavior. One becomes socialized into the norms of the group, accepting as normal the ideas and behaviors that have been sanctioned by the religious group.

Some individuals continue their religious socialization by taking leadership positions within the religious group. These positions will require them to be able to adjust the group to changing conditions. They will become accustomed to recognizing the behavior, emotions, ideas, and norms that are sanctioned and projecting new ways for these to occur. In order to deal with life's changes, they come to understand various ways that religion may be verbalized, enacted, and institutionalized. A successful leader is one who enables the religious group to adjust its socialization process to changing times—for example, to stresses and changing conditions in the society in which it is situated—and thus to ensure the survival of the religious group.

Conversion, the process of accepting a religion to be one's own, can take place either in the context of the family or in the context of another group; one can be converted to the religion of one's parents or to another religion. Generally, conversion is a religious socialization experience that is associated with the individual who is older and is making choices consciously and actively, rather than passively accepting the status quo; conversion is therefore more often associated with a change, either in one's attitude about one's existing religion (that is, a reaffirmation or renewal of one's faith) or to a different religion. More often than not, one discusses "conversion" as the latter experience, but in its broadest sense, the conversion experience has played an increasingly important role in the latter half of the twentieth century as individuals have sought new, or renewed, sources of values to direct their lives.

Sociologists have advanced different theories of the reason people undergo religious conversion. Although structural sociologists (who consider people's choices as a by-product of social forces arising from social organization) are not often interested in the individual's reasons for conversion, they do identify some ways in which society's structure, specifically religious organization, contributes to this process. Some studies have supported the theory that disruptions in the individual's life (stresses such as marital problems, loss of a loved one, or being fired from one's job) tend to precede the conversion experience. Social connections with members of the new religious group can create another social force toward the conversion. Similarly, the severing of ties with or membership in a former religious group (or the lack of any such ties in the first place) creates another force toward conversion. Finally, family values expressed by parents during the potential convert's childhood (such as the importance of service to community or the need for a spiritual dimension to one's life) may lead individuals to convert to a religion that meets these needs, reiterating the importance of family in the religious socialization process. Situations in which the conversion process involves departure from the cultural mainstream to enter a cult is another interest of structural sociologists.

Unlike structural sociologists, action theorists are more concerned with the individual's search for moral meaning as a force in the religious socialization process. Action theorists see religious conversion primarily as a product of the individual's need to cope with life's problems or to find spiritual meaning in life, rather than as a product of social forces imposed from without. Likewise, the creation of religious meaning is often the result of the individual's own initiative, a conscious decision to live life in service of a code of values.

Applications

The real-world application of religious socialization depends on one's definition of religion. Religion is difficult to define, especially because most believe that they know what it is but have a difficult time pinning it down in words. North American culture, for example, has roots in Christian religion. Its principal features are God, the Bible, the Ten Commandments, attending church on Sunday, and experiencing God. Many sociologists unwittingly accept this cultural (Christian) definition of religion in their work. For them, religious socialization is a process in which one comes to a gradual realization of God and of what God has told human beings to say, do, and expect. Those who do not believe in God cannot be a member of a religion; they would be said to follow a philosophy or a "way of life."

Even many sociologists who do not believe in God accept these cultural presuppositions descriptive of what a religion is: God, a sacred book, commandments, prayer, and religious experience. If people have these, then they are seen to be religious; if they do not, they are secular (nonreligious). This definition of religion is culture dependent.

Many sociologists of religion do not accept such a narrow definition of religion. They look at all the religions of the world and claim that what is common to all of them is an involvement with, and recognition of, the supernatural. The supernatural, from this perspective, is that which is beyond and not subject to what human senses and ordinary knowledge reveal. Religious socialization, then, is an acknowledgment of the roles that one should play in the face of this supernatural reality. Certainly, this view of religion recognizes many of the religions that existed before the sixteenth century; however, if one accepts this definition of religion, many styles of life that have been adopted in opposition to supernaturalism would be dismissed as philosophies and ways of life. Consequently, some theorists find a need for a broader definition of religion.

Such a definition has been posited: A religion is a group of people who share an ultimate point of view. This view enables them to make sense of personal and universal existence. Religious socialization, in this context, is the process by which we share with others the common conviction of ultimacy. As long as we share verbalizations, actions, and institutions that provide us with a sense of wholeness and a way of understanding our existence, we may be said to be participating in a religion. Another way of articulating this definition of religion is that all people hold a point of view—a position from which they see and act in this world. This point of view has a physical component (people take up space), a social component (they live within a group of other people), an emotional component (they feel life in a way that is unique, different from others), and an intellectual component (they think slightly differently from others). When this point of view is their only way of understanding and dealing with life—when it becomes the ultimate viewpoint—then it is their religion. From this perspective, everyone has a point of view and therefore everyone is religious.

This definition of religion enables sociologists to understand a pluralistic world in which there are many competitors for ultimacy which seek people's total dedication. Such a definition also allows new religions to be incorporated into sociological models and compared with older religions. At the same time, it acknowledges that various competitors for people's limited energies seek to convert them to a particular way of life and are constantly engaged in the process of attempted socialization and conversion.

In the past, the role of religion was to legitimize the truths, morals, and institutions of a society. The religions that did so, such as Christianity, no longer perform this function to the degree they once did. The question could be asked, granted the foregoing broad definition of religion, "What does legitimize our laws, literature, and institutions?" That which legitimizes our culture may be seen as a civil religion. All people enter into a civil religion at birth and are socialized into it. A society's schooling, work, sports, politics, and media all play a part in the process of socialization into civil religion. An example of civil religion is nationalism—when one's nation becomes one's ultimate value.

To know people's religion and the socialization process whereby they enter more deeply into that religion is to know who they are and what motivates their thoughts and actions. Much sociological research investigates whether people are religious, using norms derived from the first and second definition of religion. Little sociological research exists which attempts to discover those deeper concerns, words, and actions suggested by the third, broad definition of religion.

Context

Sociologists, and most social scientists, find it difficult to incorporate the absolute nature of religion into their disciplines. Religions seek truth through faith, through address to a supernatural, nonempirical authority, whereas social scientists seek answers in the empirical world. If one defines religion in the sense of either a traditional institutionalized religion (Judaism, Christianity, Islam) or a supernatural one (as a significant number of sociologists do), then one might conclude that religion is having less and less influence in the modern world. Those sociologists who accept this view claim that today's North American society is a secular one in which religion has lost its legitimizing role and thus its influence over society. If, on the other hand, one extends the definition of religion to that broadest definition identified earlier—an ultimate point of view shared by a group of people—then the status of religion and religious socialization is much different and will be approached differently by sociologists. The future directions of research in the sociology of religion and religious socialization will therefore largely depend on the refinement of sociology's definition of religion.

Bibliography

Bellah, Robert N. *The Broken Covenant: American Civil Religion in a Time of Trial.* New York: Seabury Press, 1975. Foundational book that began a decade-long discussion about religion in the United States.

Berger, Peter, and Brigitte Berger. *Sociology: A Biographical Approach.* New York: Basic Books, 1972. Chapter 17, "Values and Ultimate Meanings," is an excellent review of socialization from the perspective of the broad definition of religion. This chapter describes how one is socialized into religions that offer ultimate answers to the meaning of life but do not necessarily appeal to the supernatural.

Johnstone, Ronald L. *Religion in Society: A Sociology of Religion.* 5th ed. Upper Saddle River, N.J.: Prentice-Hall, 1997. Chapter 3, "Becoming Religious," treats religious socialization from the supernaturalist point of view.

Kohlberg, Lawrence, Charles Levine, and Alexandra Hewer. *Moral Stages: A Current Formulation and a Response to Critics.* Basel, Switzerland: Karger, 1983. Claims that moral development happens outside religious development. His stages of moral development challenge those theories that claim that religion, in the traditional institutional and philosophical senses, is necessary for a moral society.

Luckmann, Thomas. *The Invisible Religion: The Problem of Religion in Modern Society.* New York: Macmillan, 1967. Description of what kind of new religion is developing to replace the supernaturalist religions.

Stokes, Kenneth, ed. *Faith Development in the Adult Life Cycle.* New York: W. H. Sadlier, 1982. Based on Stokes's work as head of a project that uses the methodologies of social science to investigate how people enter more deeply into religious life.

Wuthnow, Robert. *The Restructuring of American Religion: Society and Faith Since World War II.* Princeton, N.J.: Princeton University Press, 1988. Description of the socialization process outside the traditional religious institutions.

Nathan R. Kollar

Cross-References

Civil Religion and Politics; Religion; Religion: Functionalist Analyses; Religion: Marxist and Conflict Theory Views; Secularization in Western Society; Socialization: The Family; Socialization: The Mass Media.

SOCIALIZATION
The Family

Type of sociology: Socialization and social interaction
Field of study: Agents of socialization

Socialization is a continual learning process through which an individual becomes acquainted with the social customs of a group of people. In the family, socialization is accomplished through the application of a combination of learning methods and parenting styles.

Principal terms

CULTURE: total lifestyle that a group of people hold in common, including intangible qualities such as values and standards and tangible products such as art and technology

LEARNING THEORY: suggested explanation of how people learn

PARENTING STYLE: one's approach to rearing children; based on the amount of affection and control exhibited by the parent

SOCIALIZATION AGENT: source of socialization; the persons or means that instruct or impart information, either formally or informally

SUBCULTURE: portion of a broader culture that is set apart by certain unique characteristics

Overview

Socialization is a dual process in that it involves a teacher (or agent of socialization) and a learner, the person undergoing the socialization process. One person, group, or institution imparts information through training or education, and another person learns and internalizes the information. Socialization is the continuing process through which an individual becomes acquainted with the social customs of a group of people and accepts the group's attitudes and behavior. It is through socialization that children learn to participate in the various roles of their culture and subculture so that they can become full-fledged members of their society as adults.

The socialization process typically encompasses learning and adopting all aspects of group life that a person needs to know in order to establish interrelationships and associations with individuals and organizations. What one needs to know varies from group to group. Yet, according to human development specialists Carol K. Sigelman and David R. Shaffer, there appear to be three goals of socialization that cross cultural boundaries: survival, economic success, and self-actualization. In order to be able to attain these three goals, an individual is involved in a continuous process of learning values, standards, attitudes, language, skills, opinions, beliefs, roles, behaviors, goals, customs, expected behaviors, obligations, and responsibilities. Absorbing all these aspects of life shapes the individual and defines the range of the person's present and future thoughts and actions.

The family is almost always the first place that an individual encounters the socialization process, and the family and parent(s) are widely recognized as the primary agents of socialization. Although socialization is a lifelong endeavor, childhood is a time of concentrated socialization. It is during childhood that primary socialization takes place. This consists of basic indoctrination into a value system, language, and concept of the world. In addition to primary socialization, anticipatory socialization in childhood occurs. Anticipatory socialization is training for future roles. An example would be taking music lessons as a child in anticipation of being involved in a school marching band.

Since socialization is a continuing process, a third kind of socialization, referred to as developmental socialization, occurs as the person grows and has new experiences, learns new skills, and comes in contact with people that think and act differently. Gerald R. Leslie and Sheila K. Korman, in *The Family in Social Context* (1985), suggest that because learning how to be a part of the group is so dramatic and noticeable in children, there is a tendency to think that such learning ceases after adolescence. Adults and the elderly continue to learn, however, and are active participants in socialization. There may be times in one's life when it is necessary to relearn how to fit into a particular group or to learn how to fit into a new group. Examples include joining the military, marrying into a family of a different culture, changing religions, and coming to terms with a disability. Learning to adapt to a new environment, group, and lifestyle is referred to as resocialization.

To accomplish primary socialization, a child's parents use differing parenting styles. Socialization methods used by family members and other adults for primary, anticipatory, or developmental socialization (or for resocialization) can be examined through various learning theories. Social learning theory, which views learning as occurring through observation, modeling, and imitation, is certainly applicable to socialization.

Yet socialization through observation and imitation is only a partial explanation of how children acquire information about fitting into the adult world. At times, more specific and direct training happens; this may occur through either classical or instrumental conditioning. Through classical conditioning, individuals come to understand how events in their lives are related. Technically, classical conditioning refers to a neutral stimulus becoming associated with a stimulus that already produces a response. For example, a small child's trip to the doctor's office, itself a neutral event, may be accompanied by the painful experience of an inoculation. Particularly after this happens more than once, the child may come to fear going to the doctor. On the other hand, a child could come to associate going to the doctor with a toy given at the end of the visit and might then look forward to the visit.

In instrumental or operant conditioning, either a weakening or strengthening of behavior may occur because of positive or negative reinforcement. All behavior is reinforced, either purposefully or unintentionally. For the purposes of socialization, a parent may use rewards to produce a desired trait in a child. A parent may award stars to be placed on a child's personal hygiene chart for tooth-brushing behavior, for example. In this example, the parents are hoping that the reward of the stars will help develop a habit or strengthen a behavior in the child. Unintentional reinforcement also occurs during the socialization process. A busy parent may only half listen to a child's conversation, for example, thus conveying a message that children's thoughts and feelings are unimportant.

Applications

Socialization of children by adults, a major responsibility of the family, is accomplished with varying degrees of effectiveness. According to family specialist William J. Goode, effective socialization is facilitated by six major elements that may characterize the parent-child relationship: warmth, nurturance, and affection toward the child; the child's identification with the person doing the socializing; parental authority; consistency; freedom; and communication.

Warmth, nurturance, and affection are necessary from the moment the child is born. According to James Garbarino, infants will attach to their primary caregivers regardless of the level of nurturance and caring exhibited by the adult. Therefore, the kind of attachment that develops warrants attention. Sigelman and Shaffer report that secure attachments formed during infancy may lead to future positive interactional abilities and intellectual growth. Secure attachments are facilitated when a parent understands and responds to the baby's personal signals and when a parent sincerely likes and enjoys interacting with the child. Child development specialist Urie Bronfenbrenner believes that development—including cognitive, emotional, moral, and social—is more completely realized when the child experiences a relationship with one or more adults who have a lifelong and total commitment to the child.

The mother and the father can share equally in this secure relationship through nurturing. Research reported by Hilary M. Lips and by Sigelman and Shaffer demonstrates that fathers are comfortable and competent in the role of nurturing and providing warmth and affection. Thus, quality infant-parent relationships are not necessarily tied to the mother. Mothers and fathers do tend to spend their time with the infant differently. Fathers are more likely to play with the child, while mothers typically spend a larger portion of their time in primary care duties such as feeding. While the time spent by mother and father may be characterized differently, both are equally important in the socialization of the child.

Parenting style is associated with the quality of nurturance provided to the child, and it subsequently affects the quality of socialization. Sigelman and Shaffer integrate the available information on parenting styles into a model with a freedom/restriction dimension and a warmth, nurturance, and affection dimension. In the 1960's, psychologist Diana Baumrind developed a characterization of three main types of parenting styles: authoritarian, authoritative, and permissive. Sigelman and Shaffer used Baumrind's typology in describing their freedom/restriction dimension.

Authoritarian parenting is characterized by arbitrary, rigid rules and regulations; parents expect absolute obedience, and punishments are applied when the child is not doing as the parent wishes. An "I said so" attitude prevails. Children may interpret authoritarian homes as lacking warmth and affection. Authority and control are of utmost importance, and personal freedom is curtailed.

In an authoritative parenting style, authority is central but is accompanied by reasons and explanations. Limits are provided, yet warmth, affection, and attention to individual differences and development are provided. There is flexibility and consideration of each person's needs when making decisions. Children are included in decisions when possible, and freedom with responsibility is encouraged.

A third style, permissive parenting, is the absence of rules except for those involving personal safety. Children are allowed to go their separate ways, and individual freedom is highly valued. While love and affection may be there, they may not be communicated. Making one's own decisions is prized.

These parenting styles can be viewed as a continuum, with authoritarian and permissive at the extreme ends and authoritative in the middle. Warmth, nurturance, and affection appear in varying amounts in each style. Since all families and parents are unique, individual parenting styles will be found all along the continuum.

The second factor related to effective socialization is identification with the person doing the socializing. The child first identifies with the parent(s) and siblings in the family. According to Garbarino, a child forms a sense of self-awareness around the age of two. Self-identification is in large part facilitated through observational learning, modeling, and imitation. Parenting style, however, is also related to identification formation in children. Authoritarian parents may rely more on rewards and punishments to reinforce identity-forming behaviors. Garbarino suggests that children from authoritarian homes therefore may not consider certain options related to self-awareness.

Flexible and positive homes (homes whose style falls within or near the authoritative parenting style) produce children or young people who successfully formulate a definition of self. This may be related to findings that identity formation is facilitated by an atmosphere of warmth and emotion. Furthermore, as child development specialists Judith A. Schickedanz, David I. Schickedanz, Karen Hansen, and Peggy D. Forsyth report, children view parents who help them solve problems as desirable role models. The permissive parenting style is more likely to depend completely on observational learning and imitation. Parents with a permissive approach to child rearing believe that many of the things considered to be aspects of socialization—teaching and learning attitudes, values, morality, and so on—should be the child's own decision.

Parental authority is the third factor in the socialization process; the application and character of that authority appear to be crucial. Authority that is characterized by negativism may lead to incomplete identity formation. Again, the authoritative parenting style, empha-sizing authority balanced with reason and consideration of others, produces the most positive results. What appears to be the crucial factor regarding application of authority is that of perceived total parental acceptance of the child.

Consistency is the fourth factor Goode noted as facilitating effective socialization; consistency is important in two ways. First, when imitation is the primary form of learning, it is important that parents are consistent in their lifestyle and in what they expect of children's behavior presently and in the future. Children imitate what they see more than what they are told.

Consistency is crucial in providing guidance. Generally this entails treating a behavior with the same level of attention each time it occurs. Immediate reinforcement is important for changing a behavior; however, partial reinforcement (acknowledging certain actions at unpredictable times or introducing the element of surprise) also tends to encourage change. Sigelman and Shaffer recommend continuous reinforcement (consistency) for changing a behavior and partial reinforcement for maintaining the change.

A fifth quality fostering socialization is freedom. The amount of freedom given a child is associated with parenting style, and the most desirable characteristics or end products of socialization are directly linked to the authoritative approach. The authoritarian style represents the least freedom, and permissive parenting represents the most. Authoritative parenting typifies a balance of limits and freedom.

Finally, effective socialization is facilitated through positive communication. Positive communication skills include explanations, supportive statements and actions, demonstrations of empathy, and clear statements of instructions or problems. Again, the authoritative parenting style emerges as the one most likely to employ positive communication skills.

Context

Socialization of the young is one of the central functions of the family, but it is not the only one. The family unit has additional functions and responsibilities, both for society and for individual family members. These responsibilities or functions are generally agreed to include procreation and regulation of sexual activity, maintenance of health and safety, economic provision and responsibility, and affection and emotional support.

In all cultures, families engage in the socialization of the young. While socialization may be a function of all cultures, however, it is not implemented the same way in all. The desired results may also be different. Psychologists David White and Anne Woollett report that the goals of socialization in Western families may include independence, autonomy, and even high achievement. On the other hand, in some cultures the qualities of obedience, dependence, and passivity are more highly valued.

Studying socialization is not the domain of sociology alone. In *Human Socialization* (1969), Elton B. McNeil suggests that all the social sciences are interested in socialization; only the specific focus is different. Human ecologists/home economists might be interested in the interrelationship of the parent and child, the psychologist in the internal experience of the person, the historian in how socialization is affected by place in history, and an economist in the effects of poverty on socialization. The sociologist might emphasize the impact of individual socialization on society, and an anthropologist could examine the differences in socialization by cultures.

While the family is considered the most important socialization agent for the child, sociologists David B. Brinkerhoff and Lynn K. White suggest that with the increased use of day care and early childhood education centers, some of the responsibility for early socialization has been transferred from the home. A parent can exercise some control by choosing a day care facility carefully. Child care expert Janet Gonzalez-Mena reports that as long as the family can find a day care center that adheres to the same values and behavior expectations of the parent(s), there is relatively high satisfaction with the child care. When the day care staff is insensitive to the cultural differences within its own clientele, however, there is a chance for misinterpretation, miscommunication, and role confusion for the child.

The family also affects socialization—primary, anticipatory, and developmental—and resocialization by applying minimal or maximum control over external socialization agents in the child's life. During primary socialization, when the parent or parents are still making the bulk of decisions for the child concerning television viewing, reading, choice of religion, table conversation, friendships made, and so on, the control of the socialization process is greater. This control is displaced as the child matures and is able to make his or her own decisions. Parents typically feel that effective socialization has taken place when the late adolescent or young adult is able to take his or her place in society.

Bibliography

Bronfenbrenner, Urie. "The Parent/Child Relationship and Our Changing Society." In *Parents, Children, and Change*, edited by L. Eugene Arnold. Lexington, Mass.: Lexington Books, 1985. Combines sources from anthropology, psychiatry, folklore, medicine, and theology on how the family can expect to be affected by technological, social, economic, and biological advances.

Garbarino, James. *Children and Families in the Social Environment*. 2d ed. New York: Aldine de Gruyter, 1992. Interdisciplinary essays concerning family and child development issues and how they relate to society as a whole. Systems theory is the basis for Garbarino's interpretation.

Gonzalez-Mena, Janet. *Multicultural Issues in Infant Care*. Mountain View, Calif.: Mayfield, 1993. Practical information on how to minimize insensitivity to multicultural differences in early childhood programs, including day care and nursery school settings.

Goode, William J. *The Family*. 2d ed. Englewood Cliffs, N.J.: Prentice-Hall, 1982. Comprehensive look at the family as a social group. Research and historical data complement the chapters.

Leslie, Gerald R., and Sheila K. Korman. *The Family in the Social Context*. 7th ed. New York: Oxford University Press, 1985. Comprehensive look at the family covering cross-cultural, historical, and contemporary family issues. It is research-based but includes useful information on family theory.

Lips, Hilary M. *Sex and Gender: An Introduction*. 3d ed. Mountain View, Calif.: Mayfield, 1997. Research into the similarities and differences between men and women in a wide variety of personal and societal situations. Every attempt has been made to cross culture boundaries.

Schickedanz, Judith A., David I. Schickedanz, Karen Hansen, and Peggy D. Forsyth. *Understanding Children*. Rev. ed. Mountain View, Calif.: Mayfield, 1992. Introductory college text on child development. The child from infant to adolescent is discussed with research information and applications provided.

Sigelman, Carol K., and David R. Shaffer. *Life-Span Human Development*. Pacific Grove, Calif.: Brooks/Cole, 1991. Topical approach to all ages is employed in this introductory human development college text. Practical applications of research and illustrations are included.

White, David, and Anne Woollett. *Families: A Context for Development*. London: Falmer

Press, 1992. Written for beginning students but will also be interesting to those who work professionally with the family.

Diane Teel Miller

Cross-References

Cultural Norms and Sanctions; Family: Functionalist Versus Conflict Theory Views; Looking-Glass Self; Socialization: Religion; Socialization: The Mass Media.

SOCIALIZATION
The Mass Media

Type of sociology: Socialization and social interaction
Field of study: Agents of socialization

Mass media socialization refers to the manner in which mass media institutions such as television, film, magazines, radio, and newspapers contribute to the individual's socialization in terms of behaviors, attitudes, role expectations, value structures, and belief systems.

Principal terms

CULTIVATION HYPOTHESIS: study of the extent to which the mass media, and particularly television, cultivate distorted perceptions of social reality

MAINSTREAMING: process in which an individual, through extensive exposure to mass media, is moved from the margins of society to its center in terms of values and beliefs

MEDIA EFFECTS TRADITION: history of systematic inquiry by sociologists and mass media researchers into the effects of the mass media on such things as socialization, voting behavior, and attitudes toward violence

MODELING: observation of symbolic behaviors by an individual which results in the acquisition of these behaviors

SOCIALIZATION: continuing process in which people learn both the rules and norms of a society and how to interact with and be participants in that society

Overview

Socialization, the process in which the individual is integrated as a functioning member of society, is carried out by social institutions such as the school, the church, and the family. Although these forces, among others, are central to an individual's explicit socialization, the mass media are often the implicit teachers of societal norms, expectations, values, and beliefs. The mass media socialize people not only through the lessons they teach but also by providing topics of conversation and common experiences that they can share with others, thereby creating the mediated background against which socialization takes place.

Although most sociologists agree that socialization—particularly media socialization—occurs constantly throughout people's lives, research indicates that the mass media are an especially significant social force in the lives of children and adolescents. This is because the media provide young people with "scripts" for living that explain the types of behavior that are acceptable and appropriate in various situations, create expectations about the kinds of consequences that are likely to follow from certain behaviors, and define the numerous contingencies that can operate in given situations. Researchers argue that television, in particular, influences social behavior by shaping the expectations and norms that children hold regarding various behavioral situations. Perhaps more significant, however, is the claim of many psychologists that children's perceptions of social reality itself are largely dependent on socially mediated information, the most predominant sources of which are the mass media.

Although debate still exists about the extent of media impact as a socializing agent, it is generally accepted that mass media exert the most influence either when reinforcing existing attitudes and expectations about normative behaviors and beliefs developed originally through direct experience and/or interpersonal influence, or when providing normative information about situations which was not previously available to the individual. For example, one 1972 study found that children from rural and suburban areas claimed that they were more likely to use television for information about how to behave with African Americans than were children from city environments who relied upon direct experiences instead. The mass media, in other words, either reaffirm what people already "know" or fill in the gaps in our socialization process. It is important to note, however, that when the messages sent by the mass media contradict information either derived from direct experience or from significant interpersonal sources, the effects of these messages, although significantly reduced, are not completely eliminated.

The role modeling of observed symbolic behavior is one way in which individuals develop a repertoire of interpersonal behaviors. A theoretical model that explains behavioral acquisition through observation of symbolic behavior is Albert Bandura's social learning theory. According to social learning theory, the individual learns new behaviors not only by performing those behaviors (rehearsal) but also by observing others perform them (modeling). In fact, the repetitive trial-and-error method of learning is often unnecessary or impractical in the acquisition of skills when it is possible to observe symbolic behavior.

Many researchers agree that the mass media are a powerful source for social learning through observation of symbolic behavior. Television and film, for example, expose viewers to many "backstage" behaviors, allowing them to experience the private emotions and motivation of role occupants to whom they might not normally be exposed. These portrayals provide "unique opportunities to increase understanding of others' perspectives and the ability to predict how others may behave in similar real-life situations." Studies indicate, in fact, that viewers may make use of information gained from television characters when faced with situations that are similar to those experienced by those characters.

There are a number of factors that reinforce the likelihood that children and adolescents will model mass media behaviors. Bandura and other researchers have found, for example, that if the media role model is rewarded for a portrayed behavior, the child's performance of the behavior increases. If, however, the role model is punished for performing the behavior, the child's subsequent performance will decrease. In addition, the more realistic the portrayal, the greater the perceived similarity between the child and the media role model, the greater the similarity between the media performance situation and the child's performance situation, the more frequently and consistently the behavior is portrayed, then the more likely the child is to model the behavior and view it as appropriate. For example, when parents watch television with children and remark on television's portrayals of violence as inappropriate or unrealistic, the attitudinal and behavior influence of those portrayals are reduced.

While Bandura's work explains the mass media's effect on behavioral acquisition in children, another important mass media researcher, George Gerbner (1986), focuses on how the mass media, and television in particular, socialize people by cultivating certain beliefs and values. Even though television cultivates a distorted perception of social reality, Gerbner argues, the more television one watches, the more likely one is to espouse these values and beliefs. This is particularly true, Gerbner explains, in heavy television viewers' perception of the world as a "mean and scary" place. This is primarily a result of the amount of violence that is shown on American television.

Gerbner's most relevant finding regarding the socialization process, however, has to do with what he calls television's mainstreaming effect. According to Gerbner, heavy television viewers become "mainstreamed" in that they develop common outlooks or viewpoints about the world that bring them into the mainstream of American society. Thus, television socializes, for better or for worse, a more homogeneous, or "middle-of-the-road," population.

Applications

Researchers have explored a number of different issues and topics surrounding mass media socialization, some of the more prominent of which have been the effects of media portrayals on such things as gender socialization, stereotyping, expectations of family life, and perceptions of and predisposition toward violence.

Gender socialization is one area in which the mass media have had a demonstrated influence. It has been argued that television, in particular, provides children and adolescents with a vast array of same-sex models to learn from and emulate. Some researchers, for example, "maintain that once children recognize that their gender identity is stable and invariant, they will begin to imitate the activities and behaviors exhibited by same-sex models on television" (Gerbner et al., 1986) and that boys are more likely than girls to identify with same-sex characters. According to Gerbner, this phenomenon has been demonstrated in the finding that "children's gender role perceptions and expectations generally conform to the stereotypes of television." In addition, some research suggests that children who are heavy television viewers are more likely to prefer sexually stereotypical toys and activities. Gender stereotypes are not true only for children; research indicates that the more individuals watch television, the more likely they are to express stereotypical attitudes regarding gender (Gerbner et al., 1986).

The impact of mass media on family socialization has been another area of study. Mass media research indicates, for example, that media families are used by viewers as models for their own behavior in families. A mid-1970's sociological analysis of marital and family roles in situation comedies, for example, concluded that television, as far back as the 1950's, was an "important vehicle for teaching nonmarried viewers about marital obligations and role expectations." According to George Gerbner, "the seductively realistic portrayal of family life in the media may be the basis for our most common and pervasive conceptions and beliefs about what is natural and what is right. This may be problematic in that researchers have claimed, among other things, that the mass media reinforces traditional and stereotypical division of labor in the family.

A particularly well-studied area is that of the effects of mass media portrayals of violence on perceptions of violence, attitudes toward violence, and predisposition toward aggressive and/or violent behavior. The central finding regarding children and media violence is that "children who see a great deal of violence on television are more likely than children who see less to engage in aggressive play, to accept force as a problem-solver, to fear becoming a victim of violence, and to believe that an exaggerated proportion of the society is involved in law enforcement. These conclusions remain true when held constant for IQ, social status, economic level, and other variables" (Comstock et al., 1978).

Although some of the socialization lessons that people learn from the media may be antisocial, such as perceptions of the appropriateness of aggressive behavior or stereotypical views of women's role in the family, the prosocial nature of mass media must not be overlooked. A significant amount of research concerned with the impact of mass media actually indicates that many mass mediated messages are predominantly prosocial. Although the mass media often provide images that make individuals feel inadequate, films and television shows often give audience members a chance to be "a fly on the wall" observing, for example, someone else's "family." Thus, the media often provide positive or prosocial models that validate communication behaviors. They offer examples of communication behaviors, roles, and issues that help audiences better understand their own communication patterns, perceptions, and beliefs.

Despite their particular focus, most researchers on the mass media's effect on society either generally conclude or speculate that the media "teach—however misleadingly— norms, status positions, and institutional functions" (Elkin and Handel, 1984). The mass media are certainly a powerful vehicle of socialization.

Context

As early as 1968, Herbert Mead argued that the mass media had taken over the parental role of raising America's youth. By the mid-1970's, some sociologists declared that television had become the primary socializing agent, superseding both church and parents. By 1980, Gerbner and his associates suggested that the mass media provide "touchstones by which we gauge our experiences." In 1987, Taylor asserted, "Few contemporary forms of storytelling offer territory as fertile as television for unearthing changing public ideas . . . TV speaks to our collective worries and to our yearning to improve, redeem, or repair our individual and collective lives."

Despite these declarations, after more than forty years of research on the effects of the mass media, particularly television, on society, researchers still disagree about the extent of the impact of such things as television violence, portrayals of pornography, and the link between the mass media's influence on attitudes and behavior. Early research into mass media effects, for example, argued that the mass media had only limited or minor impact on individual behaviors. This was the case, researchers claimed, because people usually selectively exposed themselves to messages that supported preexisting beliefs ("selective exposure"), rationalized messages that were incongruent with their beliefs ("cognitive dissonance theory"), or relied on interpersonal sources of information rather than media sources ("personal influence theory"). If the media had any influence, it was asserted, their influence was disseminated through opinion leaders rather than directly ("two-step flow").

These limited effects findings, however, were in direct contradiction with the 1960's findings of experimental psychologists such as Albert Bandura, who argued that media portrayals of violence and aggression had a profound impact on children's predisposition toward aggressive behavior. Later laboratory studies of violence in the 1960's and 1970's found support for Bandura's work, but a lack of nonexperimental data kept these findings from receiving wide acceptance until the late 1970's. Additionally, while some researchers argued that media violence caused aggression, others asserted that media violence did the opposite, acting as a catharsis, or release, for the individual's aggressive impulses.

Other researchers, such as Gerbner, avoided making claims about the behavioral impact of the mass media, preferring instead to focus, in the 1980's, on the mass media's effects on attitudes and beliefs. Even today, what might be considered Gerbner's modest claims regarding the mass media as a "mainstreaming" force of socialization are debated by sociologists and mass media researchers alike.

In summary, most analysis of mass media's role as an agent of socialization has come from sociology and mass communication in the form of experimental research, survey research, and content analysis of large quantities of data. This work has established baseline understandings of, for example, the predominance of certain roles, models, expectations, and interaction patterns in the media and in society. There is a growing interest, however, in research that qualitatively explores audiences' interpretations and use of media portrayals by placing those interpretations into situational, cultural, sociological, and ideological contexts.

Negotiation theory, based on the work of members of the British school of cultural studies (Stuart Hall, Charlotte Brunsdon, David Morley, John Fiske), has been a particularly dominant approach in the analysis of mass media's impact on attitudes and behaviors. Negotiation theory addresses the process by which individuals, as members of cultures, negotiate meaning in their interaction with the mass media and other cultural phenomena. Critics explore how individuals' own life experiences shape their responses to the visual, verbal, and acoustic signs and codes in discourse. Critics ultimately argue, with differing degrees of emphasis, that the individual's response to the mass media is neither completely idiosyncratic nor completely universal, neither completely free nor completely bound. In other words, both individual experiences and socio-ideologically significant messages (those that contextualize the media discourse in the contemporary condition and in the dominant, more enduring ideological forces in society at large) interact to shape meaning. The point of debate for various critics lies in describing the balance between structure and freedom in the discourse and in reconciling audience freedoms with audience constraints in meaning-making.

Bibliography
Asamen, Joy Keiko, and Gordon L. Berry, eds. *Research Paradigms, Television, and Social Behavior*. Thousand Oaks, Calif.: Sage Publications, 1998.

Bandura, Albert. *Social Learning Theory.* Englewood Cliffs, N.J.: Prentice-Hall, 1977. Bandura is the central figure in the development of social learning theory. This book describes his theoretical framework and summarizes the available research up to the mid-1970's.

Comstock, George, et al. *Television and Human Behavior.* New York: Columbia University Press, 1978. Significant review of most of the research up to 1977 on television and its link to human behavior. Covers such areas as the mass media's effect on political and psychological socialization as well as the potential prosocial and antisocial implications of mass media socialization.

Elkin, Frederick, and Gerald Handel. *The Child and Society: The Process of Socialization.* 5th ed. New York: Random House, 1989. Primer on the socialization process that focuses on children and adolescents. Includes a discussion of the mass media as a significant force in the socialization process.

Gerbner, George, et al. "Living with Television: The Dynamics of the Cultivation Process." In *Perspectives on Media Effects,* edited by Jennings Bryant and Dolf Zillman. Hillsdale, N.J.: Lawrence Erlbaum, 1986. Provides a clear explanation of the "cultivation hypothesis" and a thorough review of the findings of Gerbner and his associates regarding the effects of the mass media, particularly television, on attitudes and beliefs.

Morley, David. *The Nationwide Audience: Structure and Decoding.* London, England: British Film Institute, 1980. Discusses with attempts by Morley, a major figure in the British cultural studies tradition, to measure qualitatively British audiences' uses and interpretations of the mass media, particularly television. Good introduction to negotiation theory as a model of mass media socialization.

Pearl, D., L. Bouthilet, and J. Lazar, eds. *Television and Behavior: Ten Years of Scientific Progress and Implications for the Eighties.* Rockville, Md.: U.S. Department of Health and Human Services, Public Health Service, Alcohol, Drug Abuse, and Mental Health Administration, National Institute of Mental Health, 1982. Comprehensive anthology of social/scientific research on the effects of the media.

Perloff, Richard. "Social Effects of the Media." In *Mass Media: Process and Effects,* edited by Leo W. Jeffres. Prospect Heights, Ill.: Waveland Press, 1986. Readable summary of stereotypes fostered by the mass media and their effects on role modeling and the cultivation of attitudes and beliefs. Summarizes and critiques both Bandura's and Gerbner's work on media socialization. Also reviews research on the impact of the mass media on children's cognitive development and the research on the impact of media violence and pornography.

Susan Mackey-Kallis

Cross-References

Socialization: Religion; Socialization: The Family; Workplace Socialization.

SOCIOBIOLOGY AND THE NATURE-NURTURE DEBATE

Type of sociology: Origins and definitions of sociology
Field of study: Sociological perspectives and principles

Sociobiology refers to the application of the principles of evolutionary biology to the study of the social behavior of organisms, including humans. Sociobiologists often focus on the adaptive significance of social behavior and thus consider the contributions of an organism's environment (including social and cultural factors) and its biology (genes) to social behavior.

Principal terms

ADAPTATION: process in which a trait—either genetic or sociocultural—tends to increase the fitness of its possessors relative to the other members of the population; also, the functional interdependence of an organism (genes) and the environment

BEHAVIORAL PREDISPOSITION: genetically based tendency to behave according to, or to be socialized along, certain general sociocultural patterns

EVOLUTION: change over time of the proportion of a population's members who possess a certain trait or traits

FITNESS: measure of an individual's success in contributing genes to future generations relative to that of the other members of a population

INCLUSIVE FITNESS: sum of the fitness derived from one's own reproductive activities plus those of one's blood relatives (who possess and may contribute common genes)

NATURAL SELECTION: differential contribution of genes to the next generation by the members of a population on the basis of differential fertility and mortality

REPRODUCTIVE SUCCESS: one's relative success in producing offspring that survive to reproduce in the future generation

Overview

Rather than being a distinct discipline, sociobiology comprises the work of numerous scholars from such disciplines as sociology, anthropology, psychology, neurobiology, ethology, zoology, and primatology who incorporate the principles of evolutionary biology within the study of the social behavior of humans and other organisms. Although research that may be considered sociobiological has been conducted for some time, "sociobiology" and its application to human social behavior—human sociobiology—came into prominence with the 1975 publication of entomologist Edward O. Wilson's book *Sociobiology: The New Synthesis*. The "new synthesis" of human sociobiology, according to sociologist Joseph Lopreato, refers to the marriage of theories of sociocultural behavior and modern evolutionary theory.

The roots of sociobiological theory may be traced to nineteenth century naturalist Charles Darwin's theory of evolution by natural selection. Darwin was aware of economist Thomas Malthus's observation that the growth of populations tends to outpace the growth of the supply of the resources upon which the population is dependent. He argued that competition for scarce resources generally occurs and results in some members of a population being more successful than others in terms of survival and reproduction. He reasoned that the differential abilities of the members of a population to survive and reproduce reflect variations in the traits possessed by the members—that is, some members of a population have traits that are adaptive, given the environmental conditions. Darwin went on to argue that if traits that are adaptive in one generation are heritable and continue to yield a survival and reproduction advantage to their possessors in future generations, the proportion of the population possessing the adaptive traits will increase.

This process, the differential survival and reproduction among the members of a population on the basis of the possession of different and heritable (genetically influenced) traits, is known as natural selection. Numerous examples of evolution by natural selection pertaining to human physiology are evident, including the development of opposable thumbs, bipedalism, and large, complex brains. Following the logic of natural selection, these traits developed and became prominent within human populations because of advantages they conveyed to their bearers in the form of enhanced survival and reproduction. Sociobiologists contend, in essence, that because the human brain—the seat of an individual's cognitive and behavioral functioning—has developed across the millennia through evolution by natural selection, this process has shaped human behavioral traits as well.

In order to characterize the influence of natural selection on behavior, sociobiologists have derived a general principle, commonly referred to as the maximization principle. Lopreato has stated this principle as follows: "Organisms tend to behave so as to maximize their inclusive fitness." The maximization principle is the cornerstone of the sociobiological theory of human nature, human nature being the set of behavioral tendencies or predispositions that characterize the members of the human species. Maximizing one's inclusive fitness entails, in part, contributing more of one's genes to future generations than do other members of the population. The tendency to maximize one's inclusive fitness thus reflects the competitive aspects of natural selection. On the surface, it seems to paint a selfish portrait of human nature. Yet sociobiologists have found in the maximization principle a possible basis for cooperative behavior. One's inclusive fitness can be increased by contributing any copies of one's genes to future generations; therefore, behavior in accordance with the maximization principle may involve helping or cooperating with those who share common genes: one's blood kin. Since most siblings have about half of their genes in common, one could increase one's fitness by helping to increase the reproductive success of one's siblings. Given that throughout most of human existence human societies were structured largely around kin groups, the saliency of this aspect of the maximization principle to the evolution of human societies becomes evident. Following the logic of the maximization principle, sociobiologists have proposed models of human nature consisting, in part, of such behavioral predispositions as reciprocation, an explanatory urge, a need for recognition, and territoriality.

Sociobiologists contend that behavior is at least somewhat influenced by biology. In contrast, many sociologists contend that human behavior is largely determined by learning, the environment, and other external factors; these factors are collectively called "nurture." For example, gender researcher Jean Lipman-Blumen contends that children generally assume so-called normal gender-specific behaviors because they were taught or socialized to do so, not because they are biologically predisposed to some different behaviors.

How can researchers tell whether biology influences behavior? The clearest evidence would come from genetic research, but in many respects this field is still in its infancy. Nevertheless, some studies have suggested that genes influence at least some aspects of behavior; the mental disorder schizophrenia is one example. Another approach is to compare the behaviors of separately reared but genetically identical twins. Some of the best research here was conducted by psychologist Thomas Bouchard, who found many remarkable similarities between twins who shared a common nature but not a common nurture. Bouchard concluded that genes substantially contribute to such behaviors as religiosity, political orientation, and intelligence. In the light of such findings, Daniel Koshland, biologist and editor of the journal *Science*, has remarked that the nature-nurture debate is basically over. Sociobiologists appear to be at least partially justified in their claims of the influence of biology on behavior, but it bears noting that the extent and magnitude of this influence remains largely unspecified.

Applications

One of the major tasks undertaken by sociobiologists is to characterize the interplay of nature and nurture. To clarify the sociobiological enterprise and the interaction of nature and nurture, the class of phenomena known as cultural universals may be considered. A cultural universal is a cultural attribute that is found in virtually all societies. Anthropologist George Murdock, after examining a vast array of historical and ethnographic data, has identified dozens of cultural universals, including an incest taboo, kin groups, kinship nomenclature, status differentiation, and courtship rituals. Sociobiologists view such uniformity as evidence of a commonly held human nature. The widespread existence of these cultural traits, they argue, could not be wholly capricious. Wilson, for example, argues that "few of these unifying properties can be interpreted as the inevitable outcome of either advanced social life or high intelligence." Sociobiologists contend that these common cultural traits reflect deep-seated, biologically based behavior predispositions that have evolved within human neuroanatomy to reflect some of the basic directives of the maximization principle.

The universal phenomenon of the incest taboo may be taken as an example. The specific details of the taboo vary somewhat between and within cultures, but, in general, this term refers to an aversion to and culturally supported prohibitions against marrying or mating with someone who is a close blood relative. Social scientists have often wondered why such a trait would prevail across the diverse range of cultures. Some anthropologists have argued that the incest taboo developed as a means of avoiding intrafamilial conflicts that might arise if incestuous relationships were commonplace; thus it acts to sustain family integrity. Yet explaining the avoidance of incestuous relationships in terms of cultural factors alone seems inadequate in the light of sociologist Joseph Shepher's research indicating the persistence of incest avoidance in a social environment void of cultural prohibitions against incest.

Sociobiologists, in contrast, propose a deeper explanation for the incest taboo that could conceivably operate in conjunction with the one noted above. They reason in the following manner. Each person has twenty-three pairs of chromosomes on which their genes reside. About half of each pair are inherited from one's father, and the other half come from one's mother, so in a sense, a person has two copies of most genes. Among the millions of genes residing in the chromosomes of the average individual are about four that can produce lethal effects. Most people do not suffer the effects of the lethal genes because these genes are usually superseded by their nonlethal complements. Because closely related kin share a greater than average amount of their genes in common, however, there is a heightened risk that offspring resulting from their mating will inherit the same lethal genes from both parents and thus have a greatly reduced chance of surviving and reproducing. Therefore, incestuous mating practices would be likely to decrease one's fitness and would thus oppose the basic tendency suggested by the maximization principle. Sociobiologists suggest that an aversion to mating with one's close relatives may be a behavioral trait that became prevalent across the millennia by means of evolution by natural selection. Furthermore, sociobiologists suggest that the various cultural sanctions discouraging incest may reflect cultural evolution following a trajectory based on biological evolution.

The cultural universals pertaining to kin groups and kinship nomenclature may also be considered. It has been widely documented that a basic institution characterizing human societies is the kin group or family. Furthermore, some set of titles or names (such as aunt, cousin, mother, and brother) is used within these societies to specify the relationships among family members. A host of sociocultural factors have been suggested as explanations of these common occurrences. For example, it has been suggested that families exist because they perform a variety of functions such as being reproductive units, socializing and nurturing the young, and being units of economic production. Sociocultural explanations of the kinship nomenclature often focus on the possible benefits accruing from such a classi-fication system. Incest avoidance, for example, would be aided by clear identification of family members.

Such accounts for the universal existence of kin groups and kinship nomenclature are often incorporated into sociobiological explanations of these phenomena, but sociobiolo-gists search for a deeper level of explanation. They view families as adaptive mechanisms; that is, through providing their participants with resources, nurturance, socialization, and the like, a family can enhance its participants' survival and reproduction.

The universal phenomenon of kinship nomenclature is probably closely related to the concept of inclusive fitness. Kin have a greater than average portion of their genes in common, and sociobiologists suggest that the possession of common genes facilitates cooperation. The extent of this genetic relatedness varies between kin. On the basis of basic Mendelian genetics, for example, the coefficient of relatedness between a parent and child or between two siblings is about 0.50. The coefficient for grandparent-grandchild is 0.25, and that for cousins is 0.13. Therefore, if one were to behave in accordance with the maximization principle, one would be more likely to cooperate with those to whom one was more closely related. Kinship nomenclature, in short, may provide a readily accessible representation of the genetic similarity between family members and hence may facilitate behavior in accordance with the maximization principle.

Context

The relevance of evolution to sociology has long been acknowledged by such prominent social theorists as Karl Marx, Vilfredo Pareto, Talcott Parsons, and George Homans, but its popularity among sociologists has varied over the years. The noted historian Carl Degler carefully chronicled the varying levels of acceptance of evolutionism among American social scientists and concluded that much of the waxing and waning has been attributable to shifts in ideology. Sociologist Joseph Lopreato offers an excellent example of this point. He notes that many of the social Darwinists of the late nineteenth and early twentieth centuries were immersed in a swell of capitalist ideology that characterized the United States at that time. He contends that many of these social Darwinists were more indebted to economist Adam Smith than to Charles Darwin.

Sociology was characterized by a different, liberal wave of ideology at the time of the publication of *Sociobiology: The New Synthesis*. Despite many sociobiologists' explicit recognition of the importance of both biological and sociocultural factors to human social behavior, some sociologists viewed sociobiologists as their opponents in the old nature-nurture debate. Any notions that humans' evolutionary past and biology contributed to human behavior in the present were generally discounted, explicitly or implicitly. Many sociologists considered humans and their behavior to be exclusively the products of environmental influences, social interactions, the sociocultural system, and the like. Degler argues that sociologists' dismissal of nature was attributable largely to a desire for humans to be completely malleable (thus facilitating a resolution to the social turmoil of that era) rather than to any discovery of facts that indicated the irrelevance of biology to human social behavior. Indeed, the assertion by sociobiologists that genes influence at least some aspects of human behavior earned them accusations of being social Darwinists and extreme ideological conservatives. Furthermore, it may not be too amiss to note that some sociologists viewed sociobiology as an attempt by biologists such as Wilson to overtake the domain of their discipline.

Sociobiology has gained more support among sociologists since the 1970's. Although many sociologists would still take issue with Koshland's declaration of the end of the nature-nurture debate, others have found persuasive the research upon which Koshland's position is based. Sociobiology's increasing acceptance is probably attributable to a number of other factors as well, not the least of which are the careful and fruitful sociobiological endeavors undertaken by such noted social scientists as Alice Rossi, Melvin Konner, Jane Lancaster, and Joseph Lopreato. Also, numerous professional journals and organizations have been formed to advance and publish interesting, high-quality research in the field. Given these facts and the tremendous progress being made toward the precise specification of the contributions of genes to behavior, it seems likely that sociobiology will continue to gain prominence within sociology in the years to come.

Bibliography

Alexander, Richard D. *The Biology of Moral Systems*. Hawthorne, N.Y.: Aldine de Gruyter, 1987. Adopts sociobiological perspective to discuss the development and future of moral systems among human populations. Discusses such wide-ranging topics as altruism, the rights of children and parents, and the arms race.

Barash, David P. *Sociobiology and Behavior*. 2d ed. New York: Elsevier, 1977. Well-written, accessible introduction to complex aspects of the nature-nurture debate, including elements of population biology, genetics, reproductive strategies, and ecology.

Dawkins, Richard. *The Selfish Gene*. New York: Oxford University Press, 1976. Lucid discussions of DNA, genetic inheritance, population biology, and the implications of the basic principles of these topics to human nature, the growth of the human population, and mate selection. Written for a popular audience, but influential in academic circles as well.

Degler, Carl N. *In Search of Human Nature: The Decline and Revival of Darwinism in American Social Thought*. New York: Oxford University Press, 1991. Thoughtful history of the nature-nurture debate within American social science. Especially interesting are the numerous insights into the influences of general social events, movements, and attitudes on relative emphasis of nature and nurture in the work of prominent social scientists.

Lopreato, Joseph. *Human Nature and Biocultural Evolution*. Boston: Allen & Unwin, 1984. Ambitious attempt to incorporate modern evolutionary biology into sociological theory. Lopreato, a sociologist, is quite appreciative of the importance of culture and quite knowledgeable about evolutionary biology; these traits are evident in the richness of the model of human nature contained in this book.

Lumsden, Charles, and Edward O. Wilson. *Promethean Fire: Reflections on the Origin of Mind*. Cambridge, Mass.: Harvard University Press, 1983. Offers a theory of gene-culture coevolution written for a popular audience. It is based on a highly technical book by the same authors entitled *Genes, Mind, and Culture: The Coevolutionary Process* (1981). Provides an interesting view of the interdependent evolution of the human brain, mind, and culture.

Richardson, Keith. *Developmental Psychology: How Nature and Nurture Interact*. Mahwah, N.J.: Lawrence Erlbaum Associates, 1999.

Wilson, Edmund Osborne. *Sociobiology: The New Synthesis*. 25th ed. Cambridge, Mass.: Belknap Press of Harvard University Press, 2000.

Wilson, Edward O. *On Human Nature*. Cambridge, Mass.: Harvard University Press, 1978. Although controversial and somewhat dated, this excellent book was the recipient of a Pulitzer Prize and much acclaim in the scientific community. Wilson integrates modern evolutionary theory, data from a variety of animal species, and numerous cross-cultural observations in this exploration of the foundation of human nature.

Arlen D. Carey

Cross-References

Cultural Norms and Sanctions; Gender Inequality: Analysis and Overview; Gender Inequality: Biological Determinist Views; Social Groups; Socialization: The Family.

SOCIOLOGY DEFINED

Type of sociology: Origins and definitions of sociology
Field of study: Sociological perspectives and principles

Sociology involves the study and understanding of human interaction. As people live their lives in relation to others—for example, in a family or at school—how they perceive themselves and others and how they act is a consequence of the types of interactions and expectations that occur in a given setting. Sociology analyzes how various group structures are organized, how they work, and what meaning individuals bring to and get from the groups in which they live.

Principal terms

NORMS: standards of conduct that exist within a particular sociological group or social system

ROLES: behavioral expectations related to positions (statuses) held by individuals in any particular group; identified by related clusters of behavioral norms

SANCTIONS: rewards or punishments that shape and reinforce norms and roles

SOCIAL SYSTEM: institutions of large subgroups that exist within a culture or society and which help to govern behavior

SOCIOLOGICAL GROUP: two or more individuals who are part of a defined membership and who meet regularly with purpose

STRATIFICATION: unequal distribution, within a particular culture or social system, of power, privilege, and economic resources and opportunities

Overview

Social scientists seek to understand why people behave as they do. For the sociologist, study centers on people as they interact with one another. This definition is tremendously broad, but it must be, because sociologists study a wide range of groups and human interactions. Macrosociology encompasses the study of large groups, for example, such as entire societies; microsociology, conversely, examines very small groups. Sociology may be broken down into a number of fields. Among them are the study of major social institutions (such as the family, education, religion, and medicine); social structure and the inequalities that result from various types of social stratification; the processes of social change; prejudice, discrimination, and race relations; deviance and crime; and gender roles and inequality.

In addition, it is important to realize that a number of different theoretical frameworks have evolved since sociology came into its own in the nineteenth century. These large-scale theories have strongly influenced, even determined, the ways sociologists view people and their societies. Functionalism emphasizes the need for societies to run relatively smoothly in order to meet the needs of its members. Conflict theory, on the other hand, stresses the underlying competition and struggle between those in power and society's subordinate groups. A third major approach, interactionism, studies small-group interaction and emphasizes the meanings that various types of behavior carry.

Sociologists employ a variety of research techniques in their work. One of the principal ways sociologists gather information about people is simply through observing what their subjects are doing. They also conduct interviews, use questionnaires and surveys, and study demographic information. After a sociologist has gathered enough information for it to be representative of the group under study, analysis is conducted. When conducting an analysis, sociologists try to discern patterns in the information gathered. Either patterns of attitude or patterns of behavior might be the focus of interest. Sociologists then make careful generalizations about the likelihood of these patterns occurring in other, similar settings.

Examining two of the basic concepts sociologists use in their study of human interaction can provide further insight into the sociological approach. The first of these is the relationship between norms and rules; the second is the concept of roles. One of the most basic areas of sociological analysis involves norms. Norms refer to the standards of behavior that are expected and accepted within a particular group. To understand the full implications of how this concept works, it is helpful to compare norms with rules. Whereas norms tell what the standard of conduct actually is in any group, rules delineate what conduct ought to be. The intent of a rule is that the behavior it is addressing will become the standard of conduct—a norm. Simply stating a rule, however, does not guarantee that it will become an actuality or a norm. For example, an office may have a rule that its employees must arrive at 8:00 A.M. Observation or interview, however, may reveal that employees do not adhere to the rule but instead arrive by 8:30 A.M. In this case, the norm is arrival by 8:30, even though the rule is different. Many rules do become norms, but many do not.

Norms within groups can emerge naturally, or they may be shaped or imposed by a group leader. In his study of deviance, sociologist Howard Becker explored how a group's norms and perceptions of deviance are imposed on others. In Becker's classic book *Outsiders: Studies in the Sociology of Deviance* (1963), he provides an especially insightful discussion of "moral entrepreneurs"—people who create and enforce rules. Becker uses this discussion to support his thesis that deviance is the product of enterprise, and that rule making and application are essential; otherwise deviance would not exist.

A second area of analysis involves the roles or positions that people assume in groups. Roles are defined by expected behavior associated with a particular position. Everyone in the group has virtually the same, or shared, expectations for each role. Sociologist Erving Goffman, in his book *Encounters: Two Studies in the Sociology of Interaction* (1961), refers to the relationships among roles as "reciprocal ties" that delineate the rights and responsibilities of the various positions within the group. Even though each individual brings his or her own interpretation to the role, conformity to shared expectations results in smooth operation within the group. Although not all behavior is role-related, much of it is, and considerable sociological investigation and analysis have centered on particular roles and how those are interpreted in different groups, cultures, or times. Whether studying small groups such as families or schools or large groups such as entire societies, sociologists work extensively with the concepts of norms and roles.

The self-fulfilling prophecy, a theorem proposed by sociologist W. I. Thomas and discussed by Robert K. Merton in his classic work *Social Theory and Social Structure* (1949), illustrates the complex relationships between roles and norms while identifying their application. Of Thomas's theorem, which states that if people define situations as real, then they are real in their consequences, Merton wrote:

> The first part of the theorem provides an unceasing reminder that men respond not only to the objective features of a situation, but also, and at times primarily, to the meaning this situation has for them. And once they have assigned some meaning to the situation, their consequent behavior and some of the consequences of that behavior are determined by the ascribed meaning.

Thus, the perceived meaning of a situation affects role definitions, which affect interactions. These, in turn, are subject to become norms for those engaged in the situation. Merton carefully points out that, in this the original definition of the situation is *false*, yet the new behaviors that are evoked cause the originally false conceptions to become true. Merton believed that this theorem is present in the everyday lives of all people and that understanding it could assist in explaining the dynamics of daily interaction, including racial and ethnic conflict.

Applications

Sociological study and analysis has been applied to almost every area of human endeavor. Frequently, sociological study results in increasing people's awareness of patterns of behavior which might otherwise go unnoticed. Sociological findings have also been consulted and applied by government as it tries to understand and to redress grievances and inequities that exist in society. In fact, societal institutions have sometimes adjusted their practices and policies to achieve more equitable treatment of individuals. One major social institution that has been strongly affected by sociological studies is education.

In the early nineteenth century, education emerged as one of the most important institutions for the American public. Viewed as a means for white males of any class to achieve political, social, and economic equity, schools began to define a new role for themselves. This role expanded after the landmark Supreme Court decision in 1954 of *Brown v. Board of Education*, in which segregation was held to be unconstitutional. This decision, bolstered by Title VI of the 1964 Civil Rights Act, forced schools to desegregate.

Desegregation had implications for admission, curriculum, and career placement of African Americans. Probably the best-known study of desegregation is the Coleman Report, conducted by researcher James Coleman in the mid-1960's. The purpose of the study was to evaluate, ten years after the *Brown v. Board of Education* decision, the education of minority students compared with that of white students. To highlight a few of Coleman's findings, he discovered that all minority students except Asian Americans scored lower on tests at each level; that the socioeconomic makeup of the school and the home backgrounds of students in the school had the most significant impact on academic achievement; and that white students had more access to college preparatory curricula.

Nearly twenty years later, sociologist Jeanne Ballantine, in her book *The Sociology of Education* (1983), presented evidence of continued discrimination against African Americans and students of other racial or ethnic origins. She explored the practice of schools of placing students into different curriculum tracks, tracks which ultimately led to professional or manual occupations in adulthood. Ballantine found that 53 percent of the students who were qualified to be placed in the upper, college-preparatory, tracks were in the lower track. Race and/or socioeconomic background appeared to be the deciding factor. The discrimination which tracking demonstrated and perpetuated continued into the 1990's. Evidence of its detriment was so overwhelming that all fifty state governors agreed to abolish the practice as they enacted educational reform.

Other than racial minorities, women represent the most prominent group that has struggled for equity in education and in the workplace. Sociologists have long been interested in how social and economic inequalities have perpetuated social stratification involving women, but it has only been since the 1980's that sociologists have extensively examined the relationship between education and gender-based socioeconomic stratification.

In her article "Where Are the Female Einsteins? The Gender Stratification of Math and Science" (included in Jeanne Ballantine's 1985 book *Schools and Society*), sociologist Donna Kaminsky contends that social, cultural, and educational factors combine to steer women away from taking mathematics and science courses in school. First, many young women still view being a wife, mother, and/or homemaker as the primary female role. Young women also view science and math careers as stereotypically isolated, impersonal, and unwomanly. Finally, young women are led to perceive a lack of future usefulness in taking courses in math, science, or computer technology.

In another example of the effect of schooling on life opportunities, sociologists Elsie Moore and A. Wade Smith examine both race and gender in their article "Sex and Race Differences in Mathematics Aptitude: Effects of Schooling" (in the second edition of Ballantine's *Schools and Society*, 1989). They found significant differences between males and females and between blacks and whites regarding arithmetic reasoning and mathematic knowledge scores on aptitude tests. This differentiation precludes pursuit of career opportunities in the sciences and math.

Context

Sociology, as a discipline of study, is said to have been founded by Claude-Henri de Rouvroy (comte de Saint-Simon) and Auguste Comte in the early 1800's. Initial study in the discipline looked at the stages of development of entire societies. Since then, sociology has evolved to include the examination of interaction in smaller groups, some of which are as small as two persons (such groups are referred to as dyads). As with all social and physical sciences, sociology uses theories to organize and explain the world in which humans live. Theories can be considered thought systems that are supported by ideas, propositions, and assumptions that researchers have about the world. Concepts, or ideas, are used to create connecting frameworks for various assumptions and propositions. Sociological theories are concerned with explaining the structure, organization, function, and interaction of groups, institutions, and social systems.

Two broad theoretical frameworks that dominated much of twentieth century sociology are functionalism and conflict theory. More recent approaches have also evolved, however, most notably interpretive theory and critical theory. In an effort to clarify the distinctions among all these theories, some sociologists have divided them into two perspectives: transmission theory, which includes functionalism and conflict theory, and transformation theory, which includes interpretive theory and critical theory. In her book *Women Teaching for Change* (1988), Kathleen Weiler describes the distinction between these two theoretical perspectives as reproduction versus production. In other words, people and social systems act either to reproduce existing societal conditions and structures or work to produce or create the society in which they live.

Transmission theory (including functionalism and conflict theory) examines how social structures are copied, or reproduced, from generation to generation, regardless of the influences of different groups in society. Max Weber, Talcott Parsons, and Émile Durkheim were foremost in developing and using functional theory to analyze societies. Key questions include how institutions are organized, who has decision-making power, and who is responsible for performing the work. Functional analysis focuses on such areas as the transmission of cultural norms and values and the distribution of goods and services. A major premise of functionalist theory is that each of the components must be healthy and in good working order or the entire system is put in jeopardy. Also central to functional theory is the idea that an institution or social system works best when it is in a state of balance or equilibrium. It assumes a state of consensus among its members and views conflict as disruptive to the required and desirable balance. Some sociological theorists criticize functional theory for these reasons.

Karl Marx, Georg Simmel, and Ralf Dahrendorf were the principal theorists in the development of conflict theory. Their work examined how different groups in society are in conflict with one another over power and privilege. Most simply, this theory contends that those groups who have money and positions of opportunity and power want to maintain things the way they are. Those groups who do not have these privileges are seen as being in constant conflict with those that do. In his central works, Marx provided a comprehensive and provoking examination of capitalism in modern industrial English society and heavily criticized this structure for exploiting the poor masses in order to increase the wealth and power of a few. Marx and other conflict theorists viewed economic organization and its purposeful unequal distribution of property and resources as the major source of societal conflict.

In contrast to social transmission theories, social transformation theories focus on how societies or institutions might be transformed or produced by individuals who take an active role in creating the world in which they live. The two dominant social transformation theories—interpretive theory and critical theory—are rooted in phenomenology, which analyzes social systems in terms of how meaning is constructed by participants within the group. Interpretive theory emphasizes the study of small groups, and sociologists obtain information for their analysis through observation, interviews, and descriptions provided by participants. These techniques, referred to as ethnomethodology, were adapted from anthropological modes of inquiry. Research within interpretive theory has been heavily influenced by the work of Herbert Blumer, author of *Symbolic Interactionism: Perspective and Method* (1969); Blumer was instrumental in using objectivity and qualitative research to study the symbolic meanings of interaction.

Like interpretive theory, critical theory is rooted in phenomenology and ethnomethodology. Critical theory, however, combines both macro- and microanalyses of social systems and includes the influence of sociopolitical forces. Critical theory has been widely applied to the study of education and is historically rooted in the work of social theorists who worked at the Institute for Social Research in Frankfurt, Germany. Those of the Frankfurt school, along with Italian Marxist Antonio Gramsci and the Brazilian educator Paulo Freire, have been instrumental in developing current critical analyses. Critical theory examines schools both within a historic context and in the light of the sociopolitical ideologies that dominate society.

Bibliography

Becker, Howard, ed. *The Other Side: Perspectives on Deviance.* New York: Free Press, 1964. Organized into three sections, this edited work looks at deviance with regard to its place in society and in personal interactions, and in terms of its role and structure. The reader will come away with an understanding of the nature and complexity of deviance, one of the central issues of sociological inquiry.

Callinicos, Alex. *Social Theory: A Historical Introduction.* New York: New York University Press, 1999.

Goffman, Erving. *Encounters: Two Studies in the Sociology of Interaction.* Indianapolis: Bobbs-Merrill, 1961. Two classic essays. One takes fun seriously and analyzes the dynamics and importance of games. The second is equally relevant and interesting, as Goffman examines roles—what they are, how they work, and how to understand them.

Hadden, Richard W. *Sociological Theory: An Introduction to the Classical Tradition.* Peterborough, Ontario: Broadview Press, 1997.

Lyman, Stanford M. *The Black American in Sociological Thought.* New York: Putnam, 1972. Representative of the merit and importance of sociology as a tool of inquiry and analysis, Lyman's work provides an excellent presentation of race relations theory and racial evolution. The text and its analyses are more relevant than ever to understanding the modern multicultural world.

Merton, Robert K. *Social Theory and Social Structure.* Rev. ed. New York: Free Press, 1968. Difficult in its treatment of theories, but readable and classic work. Gives readers a historical context while making major contributions to the field as he discusses theoretical sociology, structure, the sociology of knowledge, and the sociology of science.

Steiner, Gilbert. *The Futility of Family Policy.* Washington, D.C.: Brookings Institution, 1981. Although norms and legislation regarding families continue to change, Steiner's book provides a clear and comprehensive understanding of how policy is created around issues. Provides an essential foundation for understanding issues, events, and political responses.

Denise Kaye Davis

Cross-References

Conflict Theory; Functionalism; History of Sociology; Knowledge; Microsociology; Sociobiology and the Nature-Nurture Debate.

STATUSES AND ROLES

Type of sociology: Social structure
Field of study: Components of social structure

The related concepts of status and role are central to all studies of social organization and stratification. Stated most simply, status refers to an individual's position in a social structure, whereas role refers to the behavior that is expected of someone who occupies a given status.

Principal terms

FORMAL SOCIAL ORGANIZATION: behavioral organization of those individuals occupying particular paired statuses such as doctor and patient

ROLE ANTICIPATION: perception and prediction of how most individuals who are occupying a social position will behave

ROLE EXPECTATION: belief about how any individual who is occupying a particular status ought to behave

ROLE PERFORMANCE: actual behavior of most individuals who occupy a particular status

SOCIAL GROUP: set of individuals who interact in patterned ways, who share a culture that includes role expectations of how group members ought to behave, and who create a "boundary" by identifying with one another

STATUS: any particular position in a social structure

Overview

The way sociologists use the word "status" differs from the way the word is commonly used. Most people use it to mean "prestige" (as in the phrase "status symbol"). To sociologists, however, a status is any particular position that an individual holds in a social structure. The term, therefore, may refer to a wide range of positions and situations. Examples of statuses include such categorizations as student, mother, parent, child, friend, waiter, corporation president, farmer, husband, wife, male, female, physician, and patient. A role is the collection of behaviors, attitudes, privileges, and obligations that society associates with a particular status and expects of someone with that status. For example, someone with the status of "friend" is generally expected to be helpful, loyal, and considerate toward those who consider that person a friend.

Sociologists distinguish between ascribed status and achieved status. Ascribed status is a status with which one is born. A person, for example, is born either male or female, is born into a particular ethnic group, and may be born of rich or poor parents. Another type of ascribed status is contingent upon one's place in the life cycle (the statuses of child, adolescent, and so on). Achieved status, on the other hand, refers to a status that one acquires through effort or choice (such as becoming a college graduate or a parent or working in a certain occupation). These two classifications are closely related, however, because in any existing society, one's ascribed status affects the life chances one has to attain certain achieved statuses.

The statuses that people occupy and the related roles that they play are inextricably tied to the concept of social structure or organization. A structure is anything that consists of distinct or distinguishable parts that have a relationship to the other parts. Such relationships determine many of the aspects of the overall structure. A status cannot exist in isolation; it can only exist within the overall framework of a social organization. In other words, relationships among statuses in society are required for the idea of "status" to make sense.

The word "organization" can be used interchangeably with "structure"; organization connotes a pattern, system, or structure—something that is put together in some systematic way. Whatever is organized functions to accomplish certain things in a relatively effective way. Sociologists consider several forms of organizations or structures; two of these are informal and formal organizations. Statuses and roles are primarily important in formal organizations. Informal organization refers to the organized behavior that is characteristic of a specific set of individuals. In an informal structure, the parts are seen as individuals, and social ranking and individuals' behaviors are unique to the particular set of individuals involved. Formal organization, on the other hand, refers to the organized behavior that exists among categories of individuals—those who occupy particular statuses. Formal organization does not mean explicit or codified organization; rather, it directs attention to the underlying common forms of behavior.

A role, the organized behavior that is associated with a status, contains three distinguishable components: role expectation, role performance, and role anticipation. A role expectation is a statement of how an individual—any individual—who occupies a status ought to behave. It is a rule of conduct. In its emphasis on how one "should" behave, it is also a moral statement. Thus, for example, teachers should grade students objectively, and doctors should not take advantage of their patients. Some role expectations may be written down as policies or regulations; others exist only in peoples' minds. The fact that role expectations exist does not mean that status occupants are completely constrained in their behavior. Some expectations specify a range of appropriate behavior. In some aspects of interactions, no significant expectations exist. Further, expectations vary in their moral force. Some are strongly held, others much less so.

Thus, it is expected that a teacher should teach, but the definition of "teaching" is rather vague. If a teacher told her class jokes or conversed with her students about motion pictures for class after class, then she would not be conforming to what most people would define as acceptable teaching practices. On the other hand, lecturing and discussing assigned reading both fall within the range of acceptable conduct.

Role performance, then, refers to the actual behavior of those who occupy a particular status. In invoking this notion, the sociologist claims that all or most of those who occupy a particular status tend to act in roughly similar ways. These roughly similar ways constitute role performance. Thus, most college professors meet their classes at the allotted times, give assignments, evaluate student achievement, treat students without favoritism, and so on.

At the same time, there is some "slippage" in the conduct of status occupants; that is, actual behavior may deviate to some degree from the shared expectations. Thus, many college students perceive that their professors devote too much time to their own research and not enough time to teaching; many professors believe that a sizable number of their students are only interested in being graduated and are not interested in the subjects they are studying. These beliefs or perceptions are role anticipations. A role anticipation is a prediction or perception of how those or most of those who occupy a particular status will behave. Included in the concept of role anticipation is a recognition of the fact of minor degrees of deviation—of the sense that few individuals totally live up to their obligations. These minor deviations become tolerated or accepted but are also frequently noted.

All human interactions occur between individuals who are each occupying some status; therefore, each person brings to the interaction an idea of what is to be expected from it. The only time an individual can be free of a status (and therefore of role expectations) is when he or she is alone. Many statuses are typically paired with another status. For example, one can only occupy the status of teacher when interacting with someone who is occupying the status of student. A teacher may interact with a student's parent, but then a somewhat different (although related) pair of statuses is involved: teacher-of-student and parent-of-student. Thus, many statuses can only coexist with a single other status or, at most, a few other statuses.

Applications

Status and role are theoretical concepts, invoked and defined to help interpret social behavior and to provide an understanding of social life. They do not constitute a social theory to be tested. They are not specific ideas to be applied only in particular contexts. Rather, they appear—implicitly if not explicitly—in a broad range of studies. Although the terms may not always be used, in nearly every investigation or analysis descriptions of behavior emerge, some of which are in effect descriptions of formal organization, roles, and statuses.

A few examples will illustrate this point. In a study published in 1956 as *Union Democracy*, researchers Seymour Martin Lipset, Martin Trow, and James Coleman studied the International Typographers Union (ITU). They wondered what factors were involved in making the ITU one of the few truly democratic labor unions. They noted that, among other things, the ITU had a custom of having its union president serve only one term. This custom was found to be sustained by a strong role expectation. Another illustration can be found in *American Odyssey* (1984), a study by Michel S. Laguerre of Haitians in New York City. Laguerre found that many Haitians, when ill, go to physicians (typically, to Haitian doctors). At the same time, however, they also seek folk healers. This practice is supported by expectations transmitted from generation to generation. Even some well-educated and Westernized Haitians respond to such traditional expectations.

A third illustration concerns Charles L. Bosk's study of surgical residents, *Forgive and Remember* (1979). He discusses what he calls "normative errors." These occur when residents deviate from the role expectations held of them by the senior medical staff. The major expectation is that the residents will follow an implicit rule that states: "No surprises." The senor staff members want to be informed of any significant data about, and changes in, their patients who are being cared for by the residents. A resident who fails to inform an attending physician of an adverse medical development in one of the attending physician's patients is severely reprimanded. Bosk distinguishes normative errors from what he calls "quasi-normative errors," which, for example, would be deviations from the expectations held by a specific surgeon. Thus, normative errors are related to formal organization, while quasi-normative errors emerge from the informal organization in the hospital.

Although every social interaction occurs between individuals who are occupying some status, the status occupants have some freedom. To a greater or lesser degree, they can make decisions and act on those decisions. For example, an individual who is a lawyer is not constrained in the choice of which automobile to buy. He may say to himself: "As a lawyer, I need to make a good impression, so I should trade my automobile in for a new one every two or three years." In saying this he is responding to what he sees as an expectation—perhaps only self-created, but an expectation nevertheless. At the same time, however, there are other lawyers who will not think this way and who will make decisions free of any self-imposed ideas of what a lawyer "should" do.

Occupying a status over a sustained period of time can have a pronounced psychological effect on an individual. He or she comes to develop a particular worldview—a sense of self, particular attitudes, values, and beliefs—which may result from experiences in occupying the status. None of these may be explicit role expectations associated with a particular status. Nevertheless, they may become like expectations in that individuals interact with others who occupy the same status; in so doing, they come to acquire shared views and beliefs, all of which are consonant with the demands placed on those in that status.

Context

The *Oxford English Dictionary* states that the first known use of the word "status," which comes from the Latin word meaning "to stand," was in 1693. The first use of "role" was in 1606, and it came from the French word meaning "the part played by an actor." An early body of work that provided a setting for the emergence of the concepts of status and role was research focusing on norms, folkways, and mores. These phenomena, discussed in *Human Society* (1952) by Kingsley Davis and in *Folkways* (1906) by William Graham Sumner, can be seen as role expectations associated with the status of citizen of a society.

The contemporary usage of status and role are thought to have come from Ralph Linton's use of the terms in *The Study of Man* (1936). To Linton, status is a collection of rights and duties; role is the "dynamic aspect of status." It is what an individual does when occupying a status. As others have done since, Linton distinguishes between ascribed statuses and achieved statuses.

A more recent body of related work concerns the examination of interaction from a dramaturgical perspective—attempting to analyze interactions as instances of particular types of drama in which, for example, if the interaction is like a tragedy presented on stage, the real-life interacting individuals are playing roles that have tragic features. Erving Goffman discusses this concept in *The Presentation of Self in Everyday Life* (1959).

Other contexts for these ideas are found in various elaborations on the notions of status and role. There is role conflict, for example, which is the situation of an individual facing two or more conflicting expectations (such as the physician with a patient who demands a particular medication, which the physician believes is inappropriate and ineffective). Role strain is a situation in which the demands are excessive (as for the resident in medicine who finds that he or she is expected to work twenty hours without a break). A status set is the set of statuses through which a particular individual moves. A role set consists of the various other statuses that are tied to one of the statuses of an individual (the role set of a lawyer would include client, judge, fellow lawyer, parole officer, and so on). Role segmentation is the resolving of role conflict by allotting each set of expectations to a situation different from that of any other set. Role sequence is an individual's "movement" over time from playing a role one way to playing a role another way. Role gradations represent the movement of an individual through a sequence of statuses for which the associated roles vary only a little from one status to the next. Status inconsistency is the situation in which the rank of one status of an individual is greatly different from the rank of another of his or her statuses (for example, the bricklayer who has a Ph.D.).

Bibliography

Bosk, Charles L. *Forgive and Remember*. Chicago: University of Chicago Press, 1979. Well-written study of how surgical residents are trained in surgery—learning both the techniques of surgery and the appropriate ways of interacting with their superiors. Covers issues related to statuses and roles in a hospital setting.

Goffman, Erving. *The Presentation of Self in Everyday Life*. 1959. Reprint. Woodstock, N.Y.: Overlook Press, 1973. Influential discussion of performances, which conveys the dramaturgical perspective on role-playing.

Linton, Ralph. *The Study of Man*. New York: Appleton-Century, 1936. Book by a distinguished anthropologist was used by students both in sociology and anthropology. A central chapter concerns status and role.

Lipset, Seymour Martin, Martin Trow, and James Coleman. *Union Democracy*. Glencoe, Ill.: Free Press, 1956. Classic study on how sociologists think and perform research. Offers thoughtful ideas and findings concerning role expectations.

Sumner, William Graham. *Folkways*. New York: New American Library, 1960. Early sociological study of customs and laws, originally published in 1906, presents much information relevant to the concepts of status and role. Still has much to offer readers who are interested in the nature of society.

Szmatka, Jacek, John Skvoretz, and Joseph Berger, eds. *Status, Network, and Structure: Theory Development in Group Processes*. Stanford, Calif.: Stanford University Press, 1997.

Dean Harper

Cross-References

Dramaturgy; Microsociology; Role Conflict and Role Strain; Social Groups; Social Mobility: Analysis and Overview.

STRUCTURAL-STRAIN THEORY OF DEVIANCE

Type of sociology: Deviance and social control
Fields of study: Social implications of deviance; Theories of deviance

The structural-strain theory of deviance is an explanation of the violation of social norms that emphasizes the psychological pressure caused by exclusion from legal means of achieving success. This theory emphasizes the destructive consequences of social and economic inequality. It provided the intellectual underpinnings of both the largest delinquency prevention program ever attempted and the War on Poverty in the 1960's.

Principal terms

ANOMIE: normlessness; a stressful psychological condition associated with rapid social or personal change in which the sufferer loses confidence in authority structures and their rules

CASTE SYSTEM: hierarchical social arrangement in which people are assigned the same status as their parents and have no possibility of changing status through personal achievement

CONFLICT SUBCULTURE: distinctive subgroup in lower-class neighborhoods whose members engage in nonutilitarian violence because neither legitimate nor illegitimate opportunities for success are readily available

CRIMINAL SUBCULTURE: distinctive subgroup in lower-class neighborhoods in which techniques of crime and values supporting criminal behavior are taught and opportunities to engage in crime are provided

DISORGANIZED NEIGHBORHOOD: lower-class residential area in which there are neither sufficient legitimate jobs nor sufficient jobs in criminal organizations to employ most residents who are able to work

MOBILIZATION FOR YOUTH: largest delinquency prevention program attempted to date; it was located in the Lower East Side of Manhattan in the 1960's and was organized around principles of structural-strain theory

RETREATIST SUBCULTURE: distinctive subgroup in lower-class neighborhoods whose members have given up trying to succeed and use drugs to escape from the pain of failure

Overview

The structural-strain theory of deviance emphasizes the relationship between inequality and violation of social norms. Poverty alone is not viewed as the cause of deviance. Rather, the cause is the frustration that many poor people experience when they compare their own condition to the condition of middle-class people.

The "structural" component of this theory emphasizes the stable, hierarchical nature of Western democratic societies. The large concentrations of poor people, the common pattern in which poverty continues in families from one generation to the next, and the failure of many hard-working poor people to escape from poverty contrast sharply with the ideology of democratic societies. In a democracy, all people supposedly have an equal chance to succeed, regardless of their parentage, and hard work is rewarded by financial success.

Strain theorists assume that nearly all members of American society, including poor people, share middle-class standards of success that emphasize, above all else, the acquisition of material wealth. When poor people accept "middle-class measuring rods" as valid criteria for their own accomplishments, they inevitably appear to be failures. That sense of failure causes poor people to experience distress beyond the practical difficulties of managing their lives on low incomes. The structural-strain theory of deviance explains the deviance of poor people as a response to the frustration they feel from their "failure" according to middle-class standards.

The eighteenth century French social philosopher Émile Durkheim provided the theoretical foundation for structural-strain theory. In *Le Suicide: Étude de sociologie* (1897; *Suicide: A Study in Sociology*, 1951), Durkheim explained a fundamental difference between humans and other animals: Humans have the unique capacity to imagine a better existence, regardless of their present condition. Since biology does not place a limit on human desires, the task of limiting those desires falls to society. In caste societies, people could be happy because they could achieve "success"; it was defined differently for members of each caste. They could not even attempt to achieve success by the standards of a higher caste. With the destruction of caste systems and the development of democratic societies, the socially imposed limits to people's aspirations were lifted. This freedom has produced a situation in which success can be achieved only relative to other people's achievements, because no absolute standard can be defined. One theorized result of this is a condition called anomie, in which social norms seem no longer to apply.

In his key article "Social Structure and Anomie" (1938), sociologist Robert K. Merton took Durkheim's concept and applied it to American society. He found that all people were encouraged to achieve monetary success but that many people lacked legitimate means to achieve that success. Merton saw deviance arising from the mismatch between culturally approved goals and institutionalized means to attain those goals. Merton described five possible personal adaptations to this mismatch.

First is conformity, living a conventional life involving acceptance of both culture goals and institutionalized means. Second is innovation, accepting the culture goals but substituting alternative (sometimes criminal) means of obtaining them. Third is ritualism, giving up on the culture goal of material success but continuing to live and work in conventional ways. Fourth is retreatism, rejecting both culture goals and institutionalized means, sometimes escaping into drugs or alcohol. Fifth is rebellion, renouncing conventional goals and means and substituting new goals and means.

Structural-strain theory has been applied most extensively to juvenile delinquency. Sociologist Albert K. Cohen, in *Delinquent Boys* (1955), reported on a delinquent subculture among working-class males. He found that members of this subculture embraced middle-class standards of work and success. Their socialization, however, left them without the skills necessary to compete successfully with members of the middle class. Their decreased ability to succeed produced strain, so many of them joined with other people who experienced the same strain to form a delinquent subculture. Within this subculture, delinquent activities were characteristically "non-utilitarian, malicious, and negativistic." Cohen hypothesized that "reaction formation"—a forceful rejection of middle-class values to hold off their appeal—was behind the destructive nature of lower-class delinquency.

The most politically influential application of strain theory to delinquency was offered by sociologists Richard A. Cloward and Lloyd E. Ohlin in their book *Delinquency and Opportunity* (1960). Their argument was similar to Cohen's. They found three subcultural adaptations to the strain produced by blocking opportunities. The first was that the criminal subculture existed in neighborhoods that had criminal organizations. Within those organizations children learned how to be delinquent and were given opportunities to succeed through crime. The second was that the conflict subculture existed in "disorganized" neighborhoods, where there were neither legitimate nor illegitimate opportunities. Under such conditions boys formed fighting gangs whose major interest was in staking out and defending their "turf." A boy could achieve success in this subculture by being a brave and skillful fighter. Finally, these disorganized neighborhoods also spawned a retreatist subculture composed of youths who turned to drugs and alcohol as a way of dealing with their failure in both legal and illegal activities.

Applications

Among sociologists, structural-strain theory has been of interest primarily to those concerned with the relationship between poverty and delinquency. Sociologists investigating other forms of deviance have largely ignored this theory.

By far the largest-scale application of structural-strain theory was in the Mobilization for Youth program, a delinquency prevention program on New York's Lower East Side in the 1960's. The unifying principles of Mobilization for Youth were contained in Cloward and Ohlin's book *Delinquency and Opportunity*. The explicit strategy of this program was to reduce delinquency by expanding legitimate opportunities in the following ways: by improving education through better teacher training and new preschool programs; by creating jobs through a new Youth Service Corps, a Youth Jobs Center, and better vocational training; by organizing lower-class neighborhoods through new neighborhood councils and a Lower East Side Neighborhood Association; by providing services to youths, such as by assigning detached workers to gangs and establishing an Adventure Corps and a Coffee Shop Hangout; and, finally, by providing counseling to families through new Neighborhood Service Centers.

President John F. Kennedy, having adopted "the New Frontier" as his campaign slogan, sought ways to deal with social problems such as delinquency. He appointed the President's Committee on Juvenile Delinquency and Youth Crime in May, 1961. The leadership of the committee worked with the Ford Foundation, for whom Cloward and Ohlin worked as consultants. This collaboration produced the Juvenile Delinquency and Youth Offenders Act of 1961, which provided $10 million a year for three years for technical assistance to state and local agencies. The idea was that local agencies would develop delinquency prevention programs that would stress expanding opportunities through direct community action and by coordinating the efforts of government agencies.

In May, 1962, Mobilization for Youth was funded for three years by a $12.5 million grant from the Ford Foundation, the City of New York, and the federal government. The model of community action provided by Mobilization for Youth was adopted by an even larger effort shortly thereafter. In October, 1963, the Kennedy administration declared a War on Poverty, which was to involve $500 million of federal funds in its first year. President Kennedy was assassinated the following month, but the new president, Lyndon Johnson, expanded the War on Poverty and appointed the senior staff of the President's Committee on Juvenile Delinquency and Youth Crime to lead it.

Billions of federal dollars were spent on expanding legitimate opportunities for delinquents and the poor between 1965 and 1970. Mobilization for Youth alone received more than $30 million in government and private foundation grants. Many years later, the administration and consequences of these antipoverty and delinquency prevention programs remain controversial.

Mobilization for Youth stressed community-level organization, bypassing city officials, who traditionally controlled access to federal funds spent within their cities. They commonly used these funds at least partially to reward political supporters. City officials accused Mobilization for Youth officials of having "subversive" (in other words, communist) leanings and of stealing program funds. Though there was some evidence of mismanagement of funds, such attacks on the programs were largely politically motivated.

Assessing the impact of Mobilization for Youth on delinquency prevention proved difficult. The program operated in a geographical area where about twenty thousand people lived. This area, composed mostly of apartment houses, had high tenant turnover, so the "subjects" were exposed to the "treatment" for widely varying periods. Juvenile arrests did decrease during the project period, but arrests in adjoining areas increased, suggesting the likelihood of a displacement effect (some juveniles residing in the project area may have gone out of their neighborhood to commit their offenses).

The War on Poverty created a set of large new programs for poor people: Head Start, a preschool cultural enrichment program; the Job Corps, a job training program; Volunteers in Service to America (VISTA), a domestic Peace Corps; Neighborhood Legal Services, a program that provided free legal assistance; and the Community Action Program, a program to bring together community members to solve their own problems. Some of these programs, while providing useful direct services to poor people, adopted adversarial strategies that soon antagonized powerful political interests. For example, lawyers employed by Neighborhood Legal Services sometimes sued the government on behalf of poor clients. The Community Action Program organized protests to inform political leaders of the "demands" of the poor: better jobs, housing, education, and social services. Confronted with increasingly threatening activities by these federally funded programs, both local officials and Congress withdrew support.

Though they functioned for only a brief period, the War on Poverty and Mobilization for

Youth produced some enduring benefits unrelated to the focus and impact on delinquency prevention. The proportion of poor people in the United States was reduced for a time through antipoverty programs. Ethnic minority group leaders were identified and trained in community organizing. These leaders subsequently organized members of their own groups into enduring and powerful political forces. Government-sponsored preschool programs for poor children became a permanent fixture in American education.

Context

The historical background of the development of structural-strain theory helps explain why the theory emerged and evolved. Durkheim wrote *Suicide* at the end of the nineteenth century, after the world had seen 150 years of great social upheaval, including the end of absolute monarchy, elimination of most caste societies, reduction in the power of organized religion, success of several national revolutions, and emergence of the world's first democracies. Durkheim shared with many other people a concern for the future of humankind. His fear of the implications of the end of traditional authorities and his search for new sources of authority seem perfectly understandable.

The theme of structural strain was adopted by Merton in the 1930's, during the Great Depression. The widespread intense suffering caused by poverty provided the backdrop for the evolution of this theory, which emphasized the importance of economic deprivation. Without any explicit reference to structural-strain theory, but with a concern for the revolutionary potential of a huge group of disenchanted, unemployed citizens, the federal government introduced a variety of social reforms designed to protect people from the worst effects of poverty, disability, and unemployment.

Structural-strain theory was revived by Richard Cloward and Lloyd Ohlin around 1960, at the beginning of a period of growing restlessness among the United States ethnic minorities and poor. Again, the emphasis of structural-strain theory on social and economic inequality fit in well with the social conditions and liberal philosophical movement of the time.

On a superficial level, structural-strain theory appears to offer an accurate explanation for deviance: The inmates and patients of the institutions and programs established to manage, punish, and treat social deviants are overwhelmingly poor. It would be easy to conclude, therefore, that either poverty itself or the "strain" associated with poverty causes people to become deviant. Evidence gathered by sociologists since the 1960's, however, seriously challenges the assumed causal links between poverty, strain, and deviance. For example, a major assumption of structural-strain theory is that deviance is a phenomenon found largely in the lower class. Yet self-report studies have demonstrated conclusively that deviance exists in all social classes. Though serious violent crimes are committed overwhelmingly by members of the lower class, studies of white-collar crime routinely conclude that high-status offenders defraud the public of far more money than low-status offenders steal. Structural-strain theory is ill-suited to explain the serious, widespread deviance among people who have already attained material success.

Similarly, structural-strain theory assumes a high level of frustration among lower-class people who are unable to attain success by middle-class standards. In studying the relationship between aspirations and delinquency, sociologist Travis Hirschi (*Causes of Delinquency*, 1969), found *lower* rates of delinquency among lower-class youths who had high occupational aspirations. This finding challenges the assumption that delinquency is produced by frustrated ambitions.

The psychological strain that supposedly results from frustrated ambitions has seldom been studied directly. The few studies of strain among juveniles have found that it is related to relationships with parents and success in school but only weakly related to social class.

The popularity of structural-strain theory is largely a product of its philosophical attractiveness and intuitive logic. The available evidence suggests that it is not an accurate model of the cause of deviant behavior. Nevertheless, reducing poverty is a worthy goal in its own right. It would also almost certainly produce a diminution in serious, violent crimes, which are committed largely by poor people. The available evidence, however, does not lead to a prediction that reducing poverty alone would reduce other forms of deviance.

Bibliography

Agnew, Robert. "A Revised Strain Theory of Delinquency." *Social Forces* 64 (September, 1985): 151-167. One of the few studies involving directly measuring psychological strain. Agnew found, in a national sample of tenth-grade boys, that strain was unrelated to social class, undermining a central assumption of structural-strain theory.

Cloward, Richard A., and Lloyd E. Ohlin. *Delinquency and Opportunity: A Theory of Delinquent Gangs.* New York: Free Press, 1960. Important book describing the social arrangements that produce deviance. Introduced the idea that people choose deviant or conforming roles based on their perception of their relative positions in both legitimate and illegitimate opportunity structures.

Cohen, Albert K. *Delinquent Boys: The Culture of the Gang.* New York: Free Press, 1955. Examines the condition of lower-class boys who accept middle-class values of material success but lack the skills and resources to compete in the middle-class world. The strain they experience, Cohen argued, caused them to engage in destructive forms of delinquency as a way to demonstrate their rejection of middle-class materialism.

Durkheim, Émile. *Suicide: A Study in Sociology.* Edited by George Simpson. Translated by John A. Spaulding and George Simpson. New York: Free Press, 1966. First published in 1897, this is the first and, arguably, most interesting, work on strain theory; it tackles important and enduring questions about the human condition. A true classic of sociological theory and method. Not easy to read, but worth the effort.

Lemann, Nicholas. "The Unfinished War." *Atlantic Monthly* 262 (December, 1988): 37-56. A journalistic account of the War on Poverty based on interviews with the political leaders who guided it. Reveals that Attorney General Robert Kennedy was far more interested in the Cloward and Ohlin theory and Mobilization for Youth than was President John Kennedy. Describes in detail the complex politics and personal relationships surrounding this important federal initiative.

Merton, Robert K. "Social Structure and Anomie." *American Sociological Review* 3 (October, 1938): 672-682. This is the most frequently cited work in all sociology. Merton applies Émile Durkheim's concept of *anomie* to American society, spelling out the consequences of the extreme cultural emphasis on financial success, in the context of limited legitimate opportunities to achieve that success.

Pontell, Henry N., ed. *Social Deviance: Readings in Theory and Research.* Upper Saddle River, N.J.: Prentice-Hall, 1999.

Joseph E. Jacoby

Cross-References

Anomie and Deviance; Cultural Norms and Sanctions; Cultural Transmission Theory of Deviance; Deviance: Analysis and Overview; Labeling and Deviance.

SUBCULTURES AND COUNTERCULTURES

Type of sociology: Culture
Field of study: Cultural variation and change

Subcultures are groups of people who have cultural characteristics that differ in some significant way from the dominant culture. Countercultures, besides being different in their ways, are also consciously in opposition to the widely accepted norms and values of the dominant culture. Subcultures and countercultures are examples of ways in which cultural diversity exists in a single society.

Principal terms

BELIEFS: shared ideas about the meaning of life and other significant issues

COMMUNE: group of people who live together for the purpose of attaining some ideological goal

COUNTERCULTURE: group that is consciously in opposition to the norms and values of the dominant culture

CULTURE: beliefs, values, behavior, and material objects shared by a group; a system of normative guidelines

GROUP: small number of people who interact over time and establish patterns of interaction, identity, and norms governing behavior

NORMS: rules and expectations by which a society guides the behavior of its members

SOCIAL MOVEMENTS: collective efforts to resist or bring about social change

SOCIETY: grouping of people who share a culture and social structure

SUBCULTURES: variations in values, beliefs, norms, and behavior of societal subgroups

VALUES: central beliefs that provide a standard by which norms are judged

Overview

Subcultures and countercultures are aberrations of mainstream culture. Social scientists disagree on the exact definition of these concepts. Most social scientists would admit that the majority of groups considered to be either subcultures or countercultures could possibly fall into either category. For example, sociologist Donald Kraybill refers to the Amish as both a counterculture and subculture, whereas William Kephart and William Zellner consider the Amish a subculture. Sociologist J. Milton Yinger postulates that subcultures cannot be subsumed under the concept counterculture, but he is undecided whether countercultures can be subsets of subcultures.

Subcultures are shared systems of norms, values, and behaviors that distinguish some individuals and groups from others in the dominant culture. Neither membership in a particular group nor behavior alone is sufficient to define a subculture. The most important elements in defining a subculture are the degree to which norms, values, and behaviors are shared and the nature of the relationships between those who share these norms, values, and behaviors and those who do not. Subcultures can be identified by a variety of factors, including language, ethnicity, race, religion, region, social class, lifestyle, age, and occupation. Examples of subcultures therefore include juvenile gangs, homosexuals, Mormons, Hasidic Jews, Hispanics, and the Amish.

Countercultures are also shared systems of norms, values, and behaviors that distinguish some individuals and groups from others in the dominant culture. The significant difference between subcultures and countercultures is that countercultures are much more critical of society and the social order. The normative characteristics of members of subcultures are the product of socialization and interaction within the subculture rather than the result of conflict with the larger society. Countercultures are not rooted in small, tightly knit homogeneous groups such as ethnic groups, and they are much more affected by social forces. Subcultures evolve slowly, whereas countercultures are emergent phenomena that are much more susceptible to changes in the mainstream culture and that react based on the thrust of those changes.

According to Yinger, countercultural norms and values sharply contradict those of mainstream culture. Countercultures are generally opposed to the power structure (organization) of a society as well as to social relationships and behaviors that support and empower the dominant values of the society. Their norms and values tend to be known only by other group members, and their behavior is nonconformist. Some counterculturists drop out of society, while others remain hoping to bring about change in the social order.

Countercultures can be identified by their epistemologies (theories of knowledge and truth), ethics (theories of moral values and goodness), and aesthetics (theories of the nature and expression of beauty). Yinger suggests that countercultures can adopt a variety of forms including mixtures of prophetic activism (criticizing the status quo in order to transform it), communal or utopian withdrawal (an ascetic, isolated lifestyle based on a code of new values different from those of the mainstream culture), and mystical insight (search for spiritual insight and new consciousness-raising experiences).

In his book *Alienation and Charisma: A Study of Contemporary American Communes* (1980), sociologist Benjamin Zablocki constructs a typology (classification) of eight commune ideologies (Eastern, Christian, psychological, rehabilitational, cooperative, alternative family, countercultural, and political) that incorporates and broadens the discussion and application of Yinger's three varieties of countercultures. The one most pertinent to this discussion is the seventh commune type, countercultural.

According to Zablocki, countercultural communes are primarily concerned with bringing about change in society by first raising one's consciousness. Counterculturists view social or direct action as futile and unproductive. A typical counterculturist is concerned with an individualistic search for meaning in life. Political communes are more oriented toward direct action to bring about change in the social order even if it takes a revolution to accomplish that task. Political activists envision large-scale social change at the societal level rather than change at the individual level as sought by counterculturists.

In his book *Countercultural Communes: A Sociological Perspective* (1983), sociologist Gilbert Zicklin indicates that the communal movement of the 1960's and 1970's had its roots in a social movement that began in the late 1950's and early 1960's. This social movement became known as the countercultural movement of the 1960's. Young people turned to rural and urban communes as places of shelter and renewal. The majority of communalists were not trying to transform society and the social order but were attempting to find a meaningful system of belief.

According to Zicklin, the countercultural movement of the 1960's and early 1970's was based on four major themes: the new naturalism (focused primarily on getting back to nature), the spiritual quest (uncovering the fundamental meanings and purposes of life), the expressive mode (becoming less competitive, aggressive, emotionally restricted, and conformist), and a renewed American society (a political dimension supporting optimism, peace, equality, and freedom). Although these four themes were present throughout the 1960's and early 1970's, they were not woven into a unified, coherent system of belief. The counterculture movement of the 1960's and early 1970's included a mixture of agendas and outcomes.

Yinger postulates that social, cultural, and personality factors create the context in which countercultures emerge. For example, common structural and interactional sources of countercultures include: economic factors, demographic factors, relative deprivation (when people feel unfairly treated in comparison with others), and isolation.

Applications

The study of subcultures and countercultures can contribute to an understanding of social order and social change. Yinger believes that the task for social scientists is to measure the range of variation of culture, power, and reciprocity that exists in these groups. The knowledge and understanding gained can provide insight into the functioning of mainstream society and culture. People who are members of subcultures and countercultures usually believe that the social order of the larger society has failed them in some way. They believe that they have been cheated, exploited, neglected, or abandoned, or that the system is inadequate and lacking key values. They therefore seek alternative meaning systems and lifestyles. Countercultures, in particular, are barometers that point to weaknesses and inadequacies in mainstream culture.

Scholars have gleaned a number of significant insights from studying the Amish. Most social scientists would agree that the Old Order Amish are a subculture and that they have dealt with the issues of social order and social change in unique and relatively successful ways. In his book *The Riddle of Amish Culture* (1989), sociologist Donald Kraybill identifies the following five defensive tactics used by the Amish to resist modernity and encroachment by the dominant society: symbolization of core values, centralized leadership, social sanctions, comprehensive socialization, and controlled interaction with outsiders. These tactics are characteristic not only of the Amish but also of most subcultures. Adoption of these tactics contributes to the subculture's ability to maintain tradition and negotiate with the processes of modernity that challenge the social order of the group.

The paramount value guiding Amish culture is the concept of *Gelassenheit*, a German word meaning submission, humility, obedience, and simplicity. *Gelassenheit* works to control the destructive tendencies of the aggressive individualism that is the hallmark of the modern value system and the dominant American culture. The Amish have not allowed modernity and aggressive individualism to control their decision-making process. They have survived and multiplied because of their uncanny ability to use boundary maintenance (maintaining physical, social, and behavioral boundaries that set groups off from their environment) to their advantage. The Amish realize that boundaries are important for maintaining social organization and preserving their way of life. When necessary, therefore, they move boundaries (or, as Kraybill describes them, "fences") rather than discard them. The majority of the "riddles" of Amish life are actually practical solutions, or boundary-movings, used by the Amish to retain their distinctive traditional identity.

For example, the Amish of Lancaster County, Pennsylvania, can use modern hay balers and gasoline engines on farm equipment as long as the equipment itself is pulled by horses. This compromise has smoothed the conflict between modernity and tradition; it was reached so that modern harvesters, combines, and other self-propelled equipment would not challenge the productivity and economic viability of the Amish farm. This compromise kept the horse in the field, a strong traditional symbol for the Amish, and it allowed the family to maintain its farm while accepting limited amounts of technology. Controlled and limited social change in small doses has enhanced Amish survival and their ability to control and maintain social order.

An example of a counterculture is the countercultural movement of the 1960's and early 1970's. Predominantly, but not universally, this movement was a middle-class youth phenomenon. Zablocki has skillfully captured, in his study of 120 communes, the essence of this widely diverse counterculture. Although the communal movement was only a part of the overall countercultural phenomenon, it was the most visible and radical component of the movement. The movement's strong focus on social change and its assault on the social order shocked mainstream society. Communes are recurring historical phenomena that respond to perceived weaknesses in a society's meaning systems and point to problems concerning social order and social change.

Zablocki's most general overall finding about communes and their struggle to create new societies was that, in their search for consensus, they created intense interpersonal networks. If these personal relationships were not nurtured through charismatic renewal, the commune would become unstable and fail. (Charisma here refers to personal magnetism or charm that arouses popular devotion and enthusiasm.) When comparing communes, Zablocki found that the greater the number of love relationships experienced within the commune, the higher the probability that the commune would be unstable. Comparing individuals within the same commune, he noted that those who were involved in many relationships tended to be more committed to the commune.

Another major finding concerns the association between charismatic authority and the search for consensus. Those members who invest themselves in the group (are highly committed to the group) are most amenable to charismatic authority. Zablocki concludes that there is an urgent need for more study on the influence of charismatic authority and its role in the question of social order. Two tragic occurrences involving countercultural communes with charismatic leaders highlight this need. Members of the People's Temple, a group located in Guyana and led by Jim Jones, committed mass suicide in 1978. In 1993, the Branch Davidians in Waco, Texas, a group led by David Koresh, purportedly committed suicide rather than surrender to law enforcement agencies after a deadly shoot-out.

Context

Social scientists have always been interested in subcultures and countercultures. Yet since sociology is a relatively new field—the first department of sociology was not established in the United States until 1892 at the University of Chicago—the formal sociological study of subcultures is fairly recent.

Increased immigration as well as the urbanization of the American population in the late nineteenth and early twentieth centuries spawned the development and recognition of subcultures. Much of the early sociological study of subcultures was conducted by sociologists at the University of Chicago. Working throughout the city, they studied juvenile gangs and ethnic communities. This tradition continues today.

In the early 1960's, J. Milton Yinger proposed that there is a clear difference between subcultures and what he identified as "contracultures." Contracultures, he said, are subsets of subcultures. Most social scientists and commentators preferred to use the term "countercultures." Many people found this concept appealing because of the ongoing social development and sentiment tied to the student movement of the early 1960's. One of these thinkers was Theodore Roszak, who popularized the term and the concept in his book *The Making of a Counter Culture* (1969).

In his presidential address to the American Sociological Association in 1977, Yinger asserted that the fundamental reason for studying countercultures is to gain insight into the social order of mainstream culture as well as of the countercultures. The most important lessons that can be learned from the study of countercultures is what they say about the human condition. Countercultures, according to Yinger, are "calls for help in stressful times," and any society must be responsive to the messages and actions that emanate from its subcultures and countercultures.

Bibliography

Berger, Bennett M. *The Survival of a Counterculture: Ideological Work and Everyday Life Among Rural Communards*. Berkeley: University of California Press, 1981. Describes beliefs and practices of a commune known as "the Ranch" in rural California. Much of the book is devoted to the author's reflections on the research he conducted at the Ranch.

Hostetler, John A. *Amish Society*. 3d ed. Baltimore: Johns Hopkins University Press, 1980. Perhaps the most important volume written about the Amish. Its scope is comprehensive; its purpose is to communicate a knowledge of Amish life. See also Hostetler's *Hutterite Society* (Press, 1977) and Donald Kraybill's *The Riddle of Amish Culture* (1989).

Kanter, Rosabeth Moss. *Commitment and Community: Communes and Utopias in Socio-*

logical Perspective. Cambridge, Mass.: Harvard University Press, 1972. Important and creative investigation of the ideas and values underlying utopian communities and communal living. This book is known for its discussion of Kanter's theory of commitment.

Kephart, William M., and William M. Zellner. *Extraordinary Groups: An Examination of Unconventional Life-Styles*. 6th ed. New York: St. Martin's Press, 1998. Well-written study of a variety of subcultures, such as the Old Order Amish, Oneida Community, Shakers, and Hasidim, from a sociological perspective.

Poll, Solomon. *The Hasidic Community of Williamsburg*. New York: Schocken Books, 1969. Interesting and readable study of a traditional religious sect of Judaism. Discusses the implicit and explicit characteristics of this particular subculture.

Rochford, E. Burke, Jr. *Hare Krishna in America*. New Brunswick, N.J.: Rutgers University Press, 1985. Burke spent six years (1975-1981) studying the Hare Krishna. He observed and participated in nine Krishna communities around the country, but the majority of the research was done in Los Angeles. Extensive notes and a good bibliography.

Roszak, Theodore. *The Making of a Counter Culture*. Garden City, N.Y.: Doubleday, 1969. Examines some of the leading influences on the youth counterculture that questioned the conventional scientific worldview and foundation of technocracy (a government or social system controlled by scientists and technicians).

Yinger, J. Milton. *Countercultures: The Promise and the Peril of a World Turned Upside Down*. New York: Free Press, 1982. Focuses on the role countercultures play in regard to social change. Yinger relies on an interdisciplinary approach to study countercultures. Excellent introduction to countercultures.

Zablocki, Benjamin. *Alienation and Charisma: A Study of Contemporary American Communes*. New York: Free Press, 1980. Definitive study of sixty urban and sixty rural American communes during the period between 1965 and 1978. Studies how consensus is gained or lost among groups striving for similar ideological goals.

William L. Smith

Cross-References

Churches, Denominations, and Sects; Cultural Norms and Sanctions; Social Change: Sources of Change; Values and Value Systems.

SUICIDE

Type of sociology: Deviance and social control
Field of study: Forms of deviance

Suicide refers to death that results from a person purposely attempting to end his or her life. No social, cultural, or religious group is immune from the risk of suicide. Each year in the United States more than twenty-eight thousand persons commit suicide. Knowledge of the factors associated with increased suicide risk can be used in the design of interventions formulated to prevent suicide.

Principal terms

ALTRUISTIC SUICIDE: suicide that is related to a high degree of social regulation; suicides that are prescribed by cultural norms and suicides committed so that others may live

ANOMIC SUICIDE: suicide attributed to a breakdown in social regulation or a loss of a sense of belonging

DEMOGRAPHIC CHARACTERISTICS: vital and social characteristics such as age, gender, marital status, ethnicity, income, and location of residence

EGOISTIC SUICIDE: suicide related to a lack of integration of the individual into society

INCIDENCE RATE: number of new cases of a disease or behavior, typically expressed in cases per 100,000 population, occurring in a one-year period

INDIRECT SELF-DESTRUCTIVE BEHAVIORS: behaviors not typically classified as suicidal that are self-injurious, self-defeating, or self-destructive or that place a person's safety at risk

SOCIAL STRUCTURE: framework that includes both the shared values of a society and the degree to which people act in accord with social values

STATUS INTEGRATION: measure of role conflicts, incompatible status assignments, and demands based on status

Overview

Suicide is a self-initiated, intentional act directed toward, and resulting in, the ending of a person's life. While there may be an aspect of chance in the circumstances that result in the suicidal death, the events set in motion are a reflection of either psychotic thought processes or an intentional and conscious effort on the part of the suicidal individual to terminate his or her life.

It is not always easy to differentiate between suicide and indirect self-destructive behaviors. Persons who refuse to follow life-sustaining medical advice, persons who drive carelessly while under the influence of mind-altering substances, and individuals who knowingly ingest toxic substances such as tobacco products may be engaging in behaviors that will prove lethal; however, it would be a rare instance for their behavior to be classified officially as suicide. Even disregarding the preceding complications, suicide statistics are grossly underreported because of a reluctance of medical examiners, coroners, magistrates, or other responsible parties to classify questionable accidents (hunting, home, or automobile) or even fairly obvious events (in the absence of a suicide note) as suicide. This tendency to underreport is further exaggerated in countries or cultures where there is extreme outrage or adverse sanctions against people who commit suicide or against their surviving family members. While the preceding factors mitigate the validity of suicide statistics, they do not negate their value for prediction and sociological analysis.

Suicide occurs in all countries and among all peoples. Suicide has been variously treated as an abomination, a sin, a crime, an act of supreme sacrifice, or a cultural requirement. Although suicide occurs throughout the world, rates are higher in developed countries than in less-developed nations. Generally, persons who are more tied to traditional values and have supporting social ties are less prone to suicide than individuals who are isolated from or are not part of a sociocultural network. Worldwide, it is estimated that more than 400,000 persons end their lives by suicide each year. While suicide is a major problem in the United States (with 28,620 officially documented suicides in 1985), the suicide rate of the United States is notably lower than that of many developed countries. According to the World Health Organization, many countries have suicide rates that are more than double that of the United States (Hungary, Denmark, Finland, and Austria among them), and many others have rates that, while not double, are substantially higher (Japan, Sweden, Germany, France, and others). Of particular concern in the United States was the rapid rise in suicide rates of adolescents and young adults between the 1950's and the 1980's. During this period there was a near tripling of the youth suicide rates. In 1988, official suicide statistics reported that 2,059 teens (ages fifteen to nineteen) and 243 children (through age fourteen) committed suicide. As of 1990, suicide was the second leading cause of death of adolescents and the third leading cause of death among young adults between the ages of twenty and twenty-four.

In nearly all societies, suicide has long been considered an unnatural, even abominable, practice. Saint Augustine, a fifth-century Christian theologian, referred to suicide as a "detestable and damnable wickedness." In the 1662 edition of the dictionary *A New World of Words*, lexicographer Edward Phillips wrote the following: "One barbarous word I shall produce, which is suicide . . . it is derived from 'a sow' . . . since it is a swinish part for a man to kill himself." Judaism and Christianity both condemn suicide. The Roman Catholic Church continues to view suicide as a mortal sin and refuses burial in consecrated ground to persons who commit suicide. Islam damns the person who commits suicide, with an exception being offered for the suicide that is in direct pursuit of the causes of a holy war.

Through the eighteenth century in England, it was not uncommon for the "crime of suicide" to result in burying the body after midnight at a crossroad with a stake driven through the heart and a stone placed over the face. Suicide continued to be listed as a felony and attempted suicide as a misdemeanor in England until 1961. While suicide was never as universally or harshly condemned as a crime in the United States, many states have laws that designate aiding suicide as a crime, and several states still have laws that make attempted suicide a crime.

During times of war or religious conflict, certain suicides may be viewed as acts of supreme sacrifice. The soldier who covers a live grenade with his body so that his comrades will not be injured by the explosion or the driver who dies as his truck filled with explosives crashes the gate of a U.S. Marine barracks as part of an Islamic Jihad, for example, are held in the highest of esteem by their respective social groups. Under certain circumstances suicide can even be deemed a cultural requirement. In Japan, until the early twentieth century, the penalty for failure or shaming one's family could entail an obligation to commit *hara-kiri*. *Hara-kiri*, which the Japanese more often refer to as *seppuku*, required the disgraced individual to open his abdomen via a long, deep cut that exposed his intestines; this was followed by decapitation with a single blow from an aide's samurai sword. In India, the illegal Hindu rite of *Suttee* continues to be practiced in remote villages. *Suttee* is the voluntary self-immolation of a widow following her husband's death.

Applications

A major problem that complicates the prediction of risk and the development of interventions is that suicide has a low incidence rate. The incidence rate for suicide for the general population of the United States in 1990 was approximately 12 per 100,000. This means that in order to predict suicide accurately, a method that can separate the 9,999 people who will not commit suicide from the one who will must be devised. If one based suicide predictions on demographic characteristics, one would find that an overwhelmingly large number of people who are not at risk would be identified as being at risk. For example, it is known that in the United States, white males over the age of sixty-five are at relatively high suicide risk—there was an incidence of approximately 50 per 100,000 in 1988. If an intervention designed to lower suicide risk in this group were to be initiated, 9,995 people who would not have committed suicide would have to go through the program in order for the five who are at risk to be reached. Depending on how time-consuming, costly, and invasive an intervention is, it may not be appropriate to initiate, given the low probability that it will actually reach the individuals who are at risk for completing suicide.

While low incidence rates complicate prediction, they do not negate the fact that an appreciation for the cultural, social, demographic, environmental, experiential, behavioral, biological, and psychological factors can aid persons interested in suicide prediction and prevention. Suicide is greatly affected by culture. Not only do different national groups have different suicide rates, but also persons who share certain cultural practices manifest similarities in methods and distribution of suicides. For example, in the United States young adult males are most likely to commit suicide by firearms, and they are three times more likely to complete suicide as young adult females are. In Japan and India and among the Chinese of Singapore, the suicide rates for young adult males and females are approximately equal, and both groups are more likely to commit suicide by hanging or overdose than by firearms.

A variety of social factors affect suicide risk. In the preceding example of young adult suicides, it is quite likely that the low social status of women influences the rates of female suicide in Asia. Social status has also been associated with *shinju* (the double suicide of lovers) in Japan. In *shinju*, the lovers of different social statuses whose marriage would not be approved may choose double suicide as an option. Other social factors that have been shown to have an association with suicide include economic dislocation, loss of social cohesion, a constricted social support network, poor status integration, social disorganization, subculture memberships, and social deviance.

In examining the association between various social demographic factors and suicide risk, it must be kept in mind that relationships that hold for one national or cultural group may not hold for another. A few examples of social demographic factors associated with suicide risk in the United States include findings that males are more likely to commit suicide than females across all age groups; divorced men are three times more likely to commit suicide than married men; and whites are twice as likely to commit suicide as blacks. For white males suicide increases with age, whereas for black males suicide peaks in young adulthood. Some American Indian groups have suicide rates that are five times the national average.

Environmental factors associated with increased suicide risk include temporal associations, availability of method, and milieu. Regarding temporal associations, suicides peak in the spring, are highest on Mondays, and do not increase on holidays. (There is no association between lunar phases and suicide, and data fail to show a consistent relationship to weather changes.) Availability of method has been consistently associated with increased risk. For example, police officers both have increased risk compared with the general population and are more likely to use a handgun to end their lives. Milieu can also be associated with increased risk. For example, youths who are held in adult jails are at notably higher risk for suicide than are youths held in juvenile detention facilities.

Experiential, behavioral, biological, and psychological influences are also associated with suicide risk. Experiential factors associated with increased suicide include having a family member who committed suicide, a history of childhood physical or sexual abuse, widowhood, and being under stress. Behavioral factors associated with increased suicide include previous suicide attempts, drug or alcohol abuse, withdrawal from social relationships, and impulsivity. There have been a number of hereditary, dietary, neurotransmitter, hormonal, and other physiological factors purported to be related to suicide risk; however, because of failures to replicate findings or flaws in research design, it is not possible to confirm that these biological factors influence suicide risk. Still, certain biological conditions such as terminal disease, substantial recent weight loss, and dementia have a known relationship with suicide risk. Psychological factors associated with increased suicide risk include any of several psychological disorders, feelings of helplessness and hopelessness, an inability to experience pleasure, loneliness, and a preoccupation with death.

Context

In the late nineteenth century, Émile Durkheim, a French sociologist, published a groundbreaking work entitled *Le Suicide: Étude de sociologie* (1897; *Suicide: A Study in Sociology*, 1951). Durkheim's work is of more than mere antiquarian interest. Many current theories of suicide prediction are simply re-examinations and reinterpretations of the processes and correlates that Durkheim initially identified. Whether the more recent theories based on

Durkheim's work have validity that transcends the original is not yet proved.

Durkheim identified three primary types of suicide: egoistic suicide, altruistic suicide, and anomic suicide. Egoistic suicide, he wrote, stems from a lack of integration of the individual into society—from an excess of individualism. In support of the concept of egoistic suicide, Durkheim noted that there was a relatively high reported rate among Protestants compared with Catholics; that the suicide rate was lower among families with greater density; and that suicide rates declined during times of war and other national crises. Altruistic suicide was seen in many ways to be the opposite of egoistic suicide. Altruistic suicide was described as related to a high degree of social regulation. While some authors discuss Durkheim's work as segregating altruistic suicides into fatalistic and altruistic types, Durkheim identified three types of altruistic suicide: obligatory altruistic suicide, optional altruistic suicide, and acute altruistic suicide. Durkheim discussed suicides that are pre-scribed by, or not opposed by, cultural norms as well as suicides committed so that others may live as prototypical of altruistic suicide. Anomic suicide was attributed to a breakdown in social regulation. Increases in suicides during times of economic crisis and the differential effect of divorce on suicide rates for men and women were discussed in regard to anomic suicide.

In 1930 Maurice Halbwachs, a student of Durkheim's, expanded on Durkheim's findings. A notable contribution of Halbwachs was the support he provided for the concept that sociological and psychopathological explanations of suicide should be treated as comple-mentary. Sociologists Andrew Henry and James Short, Jr., in their 1954 book *Suicide and Homicide* provided a theory concerning suicide that combined sociological and psychologi-cal thinking. While their theory was provocative and stimulated considerable follow-up research, their statistical analyses were often inappropriate and improperly applied, thus making their conclusions speculative and of unknown validity.

In their 1964 book *Status Integration and Suicide*, sociologists Jack Gibbs and Walter Martin argue that suicide is inversely related to status integration. Their theory shares some commonalties with Durkheim's theory but reduces suicide to a single type. Given their tendency to redefine status categories, critics have argued, it is difficult to ascertain whether Gibbs and Martin use the theory to make predictions or whether categories are created in a manner that allows the theory to fit the idea. More recent sociological writings include labeling, critical mass, subculture, social deviance, opportunity, and role conflict theories of suicide. David Lester, in his 1989 book *Suicide from a Sociological Perspective*, provides a description of each of the theories listed except labeling theory.

Bibliography

Durkheim, Émile. *Suicide: A Study in Sociology*. Edited by George Simpson. Translated by John A. Spaulding and George Simpson. New York: Free Press, 1966. Based on a 1951 translation by John Spaulding and George Simpson of Durkheim's 1897 classic study. Shows how suicide can be explained through sociological events and processes. Expli-cation of egoistic, anomic, and altruistic suicide serves as a foundation upon which many current sociological theories of suicide continue to be based.

Farberow, Norman L., ed. *The Many Faces of Suicide: Indirect Self-Destructive Behavior.* New York: McGraw-Hill, 1980. Covers classification, causes, and meaning of indirect self-destructive behaviors. Noncompliance with medical treatment, substance abuse, hyperobesity, self-mutilation, prostitution, and a variety of other acts that can lead to self-injury or death are included.

Gibbs, Jack P., and Walter T. Martin. *Status Integration and Suicide.* Eugene: University of Oregon Books, 1964. Status integration, operationalized as proportional to the percentage of individuals in a status or role grouping, is hypothesized to vary inversely with suicide rates. Significant update of Durkheim's hypotheses.

Lester, David. *Suicide from a Sociological Perspective.* Springfield, Ill.: Charles C Thomas, 1989. Brief and readable review of the major sociological theories concerning suicide.

_____. *Why People Kill Themselves: A 1990's Summary of Research Findings on Suicidal Behavior.* 3d ed. Springfield, Ill.: Charles C Thomas, 1992. Comprehensive summary of information concerning biological, sociological, and psychological factors, based on material available in 1990. The fact that it is an integrated text rather than edited readings is a positive feature.

Taylor, Steve. *Durkheim and the Study of Suicide.* New York: St. Martin's Press, 1982. Four of the most positive aspects of this book are the consideration given to what the author refers to as microsocial forces, the integration of explanatory mechanisms that relate suicide to risk-taking behavior, the critique of official suicide rates, and an explication of problems associated with proving suicide.

Werth, James L., Jr., ed. *Contemporary Perspectives on Rational Suicide.* Philadelphia: Brunner/Mazel, 1999.

Bruce E. Bailey

Cross-References

Anomie and Deviance; Deviance: Analysis and Overview; Deviance: Functions and Dysfunctions; Role Conflict and Role Strain; Structural-Strain Theory of Deviance.

SURVEYS

Type of sociology: Sociological research
Fields of study: Basic concepts; Data collection and analysis

The survey is the most frequently used research technique in sociology. Surveys are used to examine behavior which cannot be directly observed and represent a valuable research method for gaining insights into important sociological issues.

Principal terms

CLOSED-ENDED QUESTIONS: questions that require survey subjects to respond by selecting one of several answers provided by the researcher

DEMOGRAPHICS: information that describes certain characteristics of research subjects; for example, age, gender, marital status, and education level

NONRESPONSE BIAS: effect that may occur when a significant proportion of a research sample does not return surveys; this nonresponse results in inaccurate survey results if the nonresponders differ from those who responded

OPEN-ENDED QUESTIONS: questions that permit survey subjects to respond in their own words

PARTIALLY OPEN-ENDED QUESTIONS: questions that both provide fixed answers that the subject can select and allow subjects the option of responding in their own words

SAMPLE: group of people chosen to represent a larger population; researchers usually attempt to choose a random sample

Overview

Surveys are used to ask people about their behavior, attitudes, beliefs, and intentions. Several steps must be considered in designing a survey. First, the topic of the survey must be clearly defined. Perhaps the biggest pitfall is that researchers sometimes try to do too much with a single survey. Surveys should be kept relatively brief. That is, they should have enough breadth to assess the behavior of interest thoroughly but not be so extensive that they lose focus and confuse the participant.

The type of information to be gathered in a survey depends on the survey's purpose. Typically, information on age, marital status, occupation, income, and education is collected; such information is known as demographics. Demographics are often used as predictor variables. That is, demographic information can be used to determine whether certain subject characteristics predict responses to other questions in the survey. For example, in a survey examining moral attitudes, it might be found that older people show more conservative responses than younger people or that males differ systematically from females.

Questions must be designed to examine the behavior of interest. For example, if the behavior of interest involves attitudes about marriage, questions will be specifically designed to measure these attitudes. There are several types of questions that can be included in a survey. Two of the more popular types are the open-ended item and closed-ended item. With an open-ended question, subjects are permitted to provide an answer in their own words. Although this type of question elicits information that is more complete and accurate, it is also possible that the subject may misunderstand the question and consequently fail to provide key information. Another problem with the open-ended question is that responses are difficult to summarize. That is, subjective decisions are required regarding how to classify and interpret open-ended responses, so there is a significant risk of incorrect classification.

A closed-ended or restricted item asks people to respond by selecting an answer from a fixed set of alternatives. D. A. Dillman, in his book *Mail and Telephone Surveys: The Total Design Method* (1978), distinguishes among three types of restricted items: closed-ended with ordered alternatives, closed-ended with unordered alternatives, and partially open-ended. The first type provides logically ordered alternatives. For example, respondents could be asked how many times they have been married, and the survey would provide the following alternatives: never, once, twice, more than twice. When alternatives do not lend themselves to this format, closed-ended questions with unordered alternatives are used. To illustrate, people could be asked which brand of soda they liked best, and the survey could list the following alternatives: Pepsi, Coke, Seven-Up. Note that when employing restricted items, rating scales are often used. Rating scales allow subjects to provide a graded response to a question. For example, if a question asked, "How well do you think the president is dealing with the economy?" the survey could provide graded responses ranging from "very poorly" to "very well." Rating scales can be constructed in several ways. Kenneth Bordens and Bruce Abbott, in their book *Research Design and Methods: A Process Approach* (1991), provide an excellent discussion of scale construction.

In making a decision on item format, a trade-off between restricted and open-ended formats must be considered. Restricted items permit control over response range. Hence, responses are easier to analyze than responses to open-ended questions. The drawback is that the information obtained is not as rich as that obtained with open-ended questions. For example, if an appropriate alternative response is not provided, the subject may select an inaccurate response. For this reason, the two types of questions are sometimes combined to produce a partially open-ended question. The strategy is to provide fixed alternatives along with an "other" category. Subjects have the opportunity to respond in their own words if alternatives are inappropriate.

Once item format is selected, the questions must be written. First and foremost, they must be kept simple. If a word being considered has more than seven letters, a simpler word should be selected if at all possible. Second, questions should be framed so that they ask only one thing. Third, questions should be precise. Fourth, they should not contain any biased or possibly objectionable wording; it is very important that no opinion be communicated from researcher to subject. Finally, the order in which questions are presented is important. It is suggested that socially important questions come first, that related questions should be presented together, that sensitive questions should come after less sensitive questions, and that specific questions should come before more general questions.

Once developed, the survey must be administered. The administration of a survey can be done by mail, telephone, personal interviews, or group administration. Each approach has special advantages and disadvantages. For example, when using the mail, the biggest concern is nonresponse bias. That is, subjects who do not complete the survey may differ in some important way from those who do. With interviews, whether using the telephone or a face-to-face format, the skills of the interviewer are very important. Finally, with group administration, people may not respond accurately if they believe that someone is watching them.

Applications

If appropriately constructed and administered, surveys can provide valuable insights into behavior, attitudes, and beliefs. If surveys are done incorrectly, however, results can be worse than useless; they may be misleading and potentially harmful. To illustrate, some issues involved with developing a survey to assess high school students' attitudes toward higher education will be examined.

First, the area of interest must be defined: What is meant by "attitudes toward higher education"? For example, the focus could be on whether high school students believe that college will lead to increased self-fulfillment, opportunities for social interactions, understanding of the world, or income in adulthood. Conversely, the survey may be directed at exploring whether high school students believe they have adequate access to higher education or whether they have been prepared adequately for success in college. One or all of these attitudinal domains could be examined, but a decision defining the domain must be made. The domain of whether students believe they have been adequately prepared for college might be selected as the focus of the survey. After such a decision is made, the domain of interest must be further explored to determine exactly which questions should be asked.

Once the area of interest has been defined, one must decide upon the appropriate demographic information to obtain. The best approach is to examine the literature on the selected topic and identify relevant demographics. Regarding the present example, certainly subjects would be asked about their age, gender, income, occupation of parents, marital status, and whether they have any children of their own. It may well be found, for example, that the occupation of the students' parents permits prediction regarding perception of higher education. Next, a decision must be made about the item format. Recall that closed-ended questions are less ambiguous to interpret than open-ended questions but may not produce all the information desired. To settle this dilemma, a partially open-ended response format could be selected. In this way, subjective interpretation can be kept to a minimum without losing the richness and precision of the open-ended question.

With a decision about item format made, the development of the actual questions can begin. First, questions must be simply worded. For example, a researcher might want to ask, "Do you think your high school experience has prepared you for matriculation at the university level?" (The following alternatives could then be provided: Strongly Agree, Agree, Strongly Disagree, Other.) The question, although a good one, is far too complex for most high school students. One can obtain the same information with a more simply worded question: "Do you feel high school has prepared you to succeed in college?" By using simpler terms, it is more likely that answers will be accurate. Another aspect to consider is precision. Questions should be precise but not overly precise. The question, "What should be done in high school to better prepare students for success in college?" is too vague; subjects could say nearly anything in response. The examiner might instead ask, "What changes in high school English classes should be made to prepare students better for success in college?" This question, however, is too precise. It asks subjects to tell exactly how the curriculum should be changed, and this may not be what is desired. Finally, the examiner could ask, "Do you feel you would be more likely to succeed in college if you were given more training in how to write?" This question asks subjects to respond to a specific issue but does not overly restrict their answers.

In writing the questions, great effort must be used to ensure they are unbiased. For example, if the examiners' opinion is that high school does not prepare students well for college, they might be tempted to ask, "Do you feel that high school is a joke?" This question conveys the researchers' attitude and may therefore bias responses. Objectionable or implicitly judgmental questions should also be avoided. For example, the examiner may ask, "How many times a week did you skip high school classes?" This question puts the subject on the spot. Instead it could be asked, "Which of the following best describes how often you missed classes in high school each week?" This question does not force the issue yet permits the subject to provide fairly accurate information. Care must also be used not to ask for too much information in a question or to ask two questions with one item. Regarding the first point, it would not be appropriate to ask students to rank the fifty most important issues that should be addressed to increase preparation for college. This is too much to ask. Nor does the examiner want to ask, "To be better prepared for college, do you think you should get more training in mathematics or English?" Items should ask only one question at a time, especially when using restricted items.

Once developed, questions must be properly arranged. It is unwise to place demographic information at the beginning, as this signals that the survey is going to be boring. Instead, more specific questions should be placed at the beginning. For example, a good first question might be, "Do you feel that high school prepares males for college better than females?" Such a question is likely to catch respondents' interest and get them immediately involved with the survey. One should start with specific questions and then move to more general questions; one should also cluster related questions together. A survey that is too long leads to boredom and fatigue, which in turn leads to careless responding.

With the survey finally developed, a decision regarding administration must be made. Given the susceptibility of high school students to peer pressure, it would be unwise to use the group administrative procedure. With a mailed questionnaire, it is likely that only students with an interest in going to college would respond. This same problem may influence telephone surveys as well. The best approach here, assuming that the administrator has the necessary skills and time, is the face-to-face interview. In this way students could respond to the questions freely, and the accuracy of the answers obtained would be maximized.

Context

According to Alex Thio, in his textbook *Sociology* (1992), the survey is the most frequently used research technique in sociology. Unstructured surveys seem to have been around since the beginning of written history. That is, public opinion regarding various social issues has always been solicited. Structured surveys began to be employed in Europe in the latter part of the nineteenth century. The German sociologist Max Weber, for example, used surveys to attempt to understand how people interpreted their own thoughts and feelings.

Surveys began to be used in the United States around 1900. Early American sociologists used surveys in attempts to understand problems such as crime, broken homes, and racial unrest. Shortly thereafter, surveys began to be used for predictive purposes. Early attempts were far less structured and less accurate than are contemporary efforts. Consequently, they often produced distorted or simply incorrect information. One often-cited example was the prediction made by a magazine called the *Literary Digest* as to the outcome of the 1936 presidential campaign between Franklin D. Roosevelt and Alfred M. Landon. The magazine drew its sample from automobile registration lists and telephone books. In 1936, those people with automobiles and telephones tended to be well-to-do and Republican. The survey showed that Landon would win by a landslide; the results of the election, however, were just the opposite. The magazine's survey was wrong because its designers used a poor sampling strategy.

Following such dramatic errors, investigators began to realize the importance of appropriate survey construction, administration, and sampling. For survey results to produce valuable information, it must be ensured that neither the questions nor the administrative procedure lead the responses of subjects and that the subjects sampled are representative of the population of interest. Surveys are now one of the better ways to gather information about unobservable variables of interest. Because people's attitudes, beliefs, and feelings about a wide spectrum of issues cannot be directly observed, the survey represents an avenue by which insights into such issues can be gained.

A central problem with surveys, however, is that no matter how well designed and administered they are or how carefully the sample is selected, scientists cannot draw causal inference through their use. In other words, they cannot conclude, based upon the results of a survey, that a particular belief or attitude causes a person to behave in a particular fashion. The reason for this is that no independent variable is employed in survey research, as it is in experimental research. In other words, in a survey, a situation is never directly manipulated so that researchers can observe how the change affects behavior. Research in which such systematic manipulation takes place is called a controlled experiment and is considered to be the cornerstone of science. Because sociology seeks to understand human attitudes and behavior, however, there is a wide range of important issues that can never be studied through controlled experimentation. For example, sociologists could never force married couples to get a divorce to understand how broken homes affect adult and child adjustment. Hence, the survey represents an excellent compromise method of gathering such important information.

Bibliography

Bordens, Kenneth S., and Bruce B. Abbott. *Research Design and Methods: A Process Approach.* 4th ed. Mountain View, Calif.: Mayfield, 1999. Contains excellent chapter on the construction and administration of surveys as well as techniques for appropriate sampling. Very comprehensible; appropriate for both high school and college students.

Dillman, D. A. *Mail and Telephone Surveys: The Total Design Method.* New York: John Wiley & Sons, 1978. Comprehensive treatment of the most important issues in survey research and represents a classic in the field. Information related to item construction and to administrative techniques pertaining to mail and telephone surveys is emphasized. Suited for high school and college students.

_____. *Mail and Internet Surveys: The Total Design Method.* New York: John Wiley, 2000.

Kanuk, L., and C. Berenson. "Mail Surveys and Response Rates: A Literature Review." *Journal of Marketing Research* 12 (November, 1975): 440-453. This paper reviews the literature on how to maximize return rates while minimizing response bias. Incentives for improving response rates are discussed. Best suited for college students or readers with some background in research methods.

Moser, C. A., and G. Kalton. *Survey Methods in Social Investigation.* 2d ed. New York: Basic Books, 1972. Particularly useful for the inexperienced researcher. A thorough discussion of how to ask appropriate research questions and how to refine them so the survey can be kept both manageable and meaningful is presented. Appropriate for both high school and college students.

Singer, Eleanor, et al. "Effect of Interviewer Characteristics and Expectations on Response." *Public Opinion Quarterly* 47 (Spring, 1983): 68-83. This paper discusses how the behaviors of an interviewer can affect responses obtained. Very valuable for anyone considering using the interview approach to survey administration, whether face-to-face or via telephone. It is well written and is appropriate for both high school and college students.

Alan J. Beauchamp

Cross-References

Hypotheses and Hypothesis Testing; Quantitative Research; Samples and Sampling Techniques; Sociology Defined; Surveys.

SYMBOLIC INTERACTION

Type of sociology: Socialization and social interaction
Field of study: Interactionist approach to social interaction

Symbolic interactionism is the perspective that mind and self are not innate parts of the human body but are created in the social process of interaction among people in intimate, personal communication with one another. Linguistic communication is seen as a central aspect of symbolic interaction; it constitutes the process that makes human society possible.

Principal terms

GENERALIZED OTHER: social groups or organized communities which give people their unity or disunity of self

MIND: process which manifests itself whenever an individual is interacting with himself or herself by using significant symbols

ROLE: behavior evidenced by an individual and sanctioned by others

ROLE-MAKING: process wherein a person's activity is constructed to fit the definition of a given situation while remaining consonant with the person's own role

ROLE-TAKING: process wherein a person imaginatively occupies the role of another, looking at self and situation from that position in order to engage in role-making

SELF: person's representation of himself or herself as an object in the world of experience

SIGNIFICANT OTHER: anyone who has or has had an important influence on a person's thoughts about self and the world

SIGNIFICANT SYMBOL: gesture that has a shared, common meaning

SITUATION: organization of perceptions in which people assemble objects, meanings, and others and act toward them in a coherent, organized manner

SYMBOLS: arbitrary signs of objects or concepts that can stand in place of the objects or concepts themselves

Overview

The symbolic interactionist perspective in social psychology is usually traced to the works of social philosopher George Herbert Mead. Much of Mead's influence on symbolic interactionists came through his students at the University of Chicago, who organized and published his lectures and notes in *Mind, Self, and Society* (1934) after his death in 1931. One of these students, Herbert Blumer, is responsible for originating the term "symbolic interactionism" to describe this perspective.

In their book *Symbolic Interaction: A Reader in Social Psychology* (3d ed., 1978), social psychologists Jerome Manis and Bernard Meltzer describe seven basic propositions that summarize the main features of modern symbolic interactionism. The first proposition, and the central idea in symbolic interactionism, is that distinctively human behavior and interaction are carried on through the medium of symbols and their meanings. Human beings do not typically respond directly to stimuli; instead, they assign meanings to the stimuli and act on the basis of these meanings. The meanings of the stimuli are socially derived through interaction with others rather than being inherent in the stimuli themselves or idiosyncratically assigned by the individual. Meanings exist in people, not in objects, and when meaning has been constructed, people act toward the object or event based on the meaning that has been ascribed. For example, the U.S. flag does not have intrinsic meaning; it consists of cloth and dye. Americans attribute meaning to the flag, and when that occurs, they may hold it in reverence or use it symbolically to show disapproval.

The second aspect of symbolic interactionism is that human beings become capable of distinctively human conduct only through association with other human beings. By "distinctively human conduct," Mead and his colleagues meant the ability to imagine how other people feel in given situations, the ability to use symbols, and the ability to behave toward oneself as toward others. This last ability is essential in creating the concept of "self." The roles of the generalized and significant others is especially important. This proposition expands the previously existing view of socialization from the individual's social learning of culture, statuses, and roles, to the symbolic interactionist conception of socialization as comprising humanization, enculturation, and personality formation. Human interaction becomes of paramount importance because it makes possible the acquisition of human nature, thinking, self-direction, and all other attributes that distinguish the behavior of humans from that of other forms of life.

Third, human society consists of people in interaction; therefore, the features of society are maintained and changed by the actions of individuals. Symbolic interactionists recognize that the organization of any society is a framework within which social action takes place, not a set of complete determinants of the action. Social roles and social classes set conditions for human behavior and interaction, but they do not cause or fully determine the behavior and interaction.

This idea sets the stage for the fourth proposition, which is that human beings are active in shaping their own behavior. This view is in direct opposition to the view of behaviorists, who believe that humans passively react to the dictates of specific internal and external stimuli or impersonal forces. Symbolic interactionists believe that humans have the ability to select and interpret stimuli and the ability to interact with themselves by thinking; therefore, humans are capable of forming new meanings and new lines of action. Symbolic interactionists do not believe that humans transcend all influences, but they do believe that humans can modify these influences and in so doing create and change their own behavior.

The fifth proposition is that consciousness, or thinking, involves interaction with oneself. Symbolic interactionists believe that when one thinks, one necessarily carries on an internal conversation. This conversation involves two components of the self: the "I," that part of the individual that is impulsive, spontaneous, and unsocialized by society, and the "Me," which is the social self. The Me is that object which arises in interaction and the one which the individual communicates toward, directs, judges, identifies, and analyzes in interaction with others. This proposition is crucial to understanding symbolic interactionism, for it is only through the use of socially derived symbols in intrapersonal activity that the individual can perform such uniquely human functions as abstract and reflective thinking. These kinds of thinking allow the individual to designate objects and events remote in time and space, to create imaginary phenomena and other abstractions, and thereby to learn without having direct experience of the things to be learned.

The sixth proposition states that human beings construct their behavior in the course of its execution. Symbolic interactionists believe that the individual is not necessarily a product of past events and experience, although he or she is influenced by them.

The seventh proposition states the chief methodological implication of symbolic interactionism. This proposition states that an understanding of human conduct requires study of the individual's covert behavior as well as overt behavior. Symbolic interactionists believe that human beings act on the basis of their interpretations or meanings; therefore, it becomes essential to understand the individual's meanings in order to understand and explain their conduct. Consequently, the use of procedures allowing sympathetic introspection is part of the methodology of most symbolic interactionists.

In summary, symbolic interactionism focuses on interaction rather than personality or social structure, definition rather than response, the present rather than the past, and the human as an active rather than passive participant in the world.

Applications

The concept of symbolic interaction can be applied to any human experience and can describe and explain everyday situations as well as complex social problems. Because symbolic interactionists believe that human beings are not easily manipulated, altered, or predictable, the goal in using this perspective is to understand human complexity, not to suggest how to predict behavior or change people. Among many other uses, the perspective is regularly applied in sociology to understanding social deviance and the problem of racism and racial conflict.

In his book *Violent Criminal Acts and Actors: A Symbolic Interactionist Study* (1980), sociologist Lonnie Athens investigated violent offenders to find out why some people choose violence in their life situations. His subjects described in detail what happened in situations where they committed violent acts and what they were thinking. The data show that violent actors construct violent plans of action before they commit violent criminal acts and that they take the role of a violent generalized other that approves of this type of action in this situation. View of self, type of generalized other, and length of violent career are all factors that contribute to the definition of the situation as one calling for violence. Actions by the other are interpreted; in turn, they influence whether the actor maintains a violent definition or alters the definition.

Violence is not the only kind of deviance that has been examined using this perspective. In *Sexual Stigma* (1975), sociologist Kenneth Plummer examines sexual deviance from a symbolic interactionist perspective and concludes that sexuality is a social construction learned in interaction with others. Therefore, sexual practices that are defined by certain societies as deviant, such as homosexuality, are deviant only because of the prevailing definition, and the reasons an individual chooses a particular sexual orientation rather than another are contained in a process of definitions and interactions. People learn to be sexual; therefore, the question of why some individuals are led to certain kinds of sexual experiences and not others requires an understanding of their interaction with significant others. Like all other human action, sexuality must be understood as consisting of a stream of action involving decisions influenced by interaction with others and with self.

Sociologist Joel M. Charon presents a symbolic interactionist explanation of racial conflict in his book *Symbolic Interactionism: An Introduction, an Interpretation, an Integration* (1992). According to Charon, people who interact with one another form society. They take one another into account, they communicate, role-take, and cooperate. They share an understanding of reality, and they develop a set of rules to live by. The development of society through cooperative symbolic interaction will, by its very nature, cut off interaction with those outside that interaction. This is the basis for racial problems in society. When interaction creates separate societies, as it has in the United States, each will develop its own culture, and individuals will be governed by different sets of rules and will share a different perspective. Without continuous interaction between the societies, members of each will fail to communicate and to understand the other, and role-taking between them will be minimized. If one of the separate societies has more political power than the other, its members will be able to define the other as having a culture that is unacceptable and even threatening to the dominant society. Through interaction, people in the dominant society develop a perspective that is useful for their understanding of reality. Included in this perspective is their definition of those in the other society and the reasons for their differences, as well as a justification for the inequality that exists between the dominant society and the other society. Through this definition of those who are different (as heathens, infidels, savages, slaves, or enemies), one society develops a justification for taking land from, enslaving, discriminating against, or segregating the other society.

Where interaction is segregated, and all people are therefore unable to develop a shared culture, the others will continue to be seen as different; these differences will be exaggerated and condemned. To the extent that people see their own culture as right and true, others who are different will be perceived and defined as threats. This perception of the other makes destructive actions against them appear justifiable. Destructive action against others also seems justifiable if they can be made into objects instead of people. When people do not regularly interact, communicate, and cooperate with others, it is easy to see others as objects instead of people. This viewpoint not only encourages destructive action but also works against efforts to help the other. Finally, without interaction, which includes communication, role-taking, and recognizing the mutual identities of actors who are necessary for cooperative action, no shared culture is likely to develop, and the conflict is likely to continue. In the symbolic interactionist view, social problems such as racism and racial conflict can be understood through focusing on interaction, cooperation, communication, culture, and definition. When interaction is cut off between societies, perspectives cannot be easily shared, the acts of each cannot be understood by the other, problem solving becomes impossible, and emotion and habitual response replace cooperative symbolic interaction between the groups.

Context

Symbolic interactionism is a distinctively American sociological perspective that arose in the early part of the twentieth century and whose roots lie in the philosophy of pragmatism. This philosophical tradition, identified with such scholars as Charles Peirce, William James, John Dewey, and George Herbert Mead, the principal founder of symbolic interactionism, takes the view that living things attempt to make practical adjustments to their environment, actively intervening in order to create reality. Two other theories that influenced the formation of symbolic interactionism are Charles Darwin's theory of evolution and psychologist John Watson's theory of behaviorism.

Darwin was influential on Mead in his emphasis on an evolutionary, dynamic universe rather than a static one, which set the stage for conceptualizing humans as dynamic, changing actors always in the process of being socialized. Watson's theory of behaviorism influenced Mead in a negative way. Watson was a student of Mead's who rejected pragmatism in favor of behaviorism, which ignores all aspects of thought and behavior except those which can be observed directly. Mead reacted vigorously to this theory, believing that without an understanding of mind, symbols, and self, human behavior cannot be understood for what it is. Mead believed that as scientists observe overt action they must always consider what is occurring in terms of definition, interpretation, and meaning.

Symbolic interactionism is considered the largest and most influential field in modern American sociology, with a separate society and several journals dedicated to it. It adds to the understanding of the sociology of knowledge, describes the social nature of reality, and explains the power available to those who control symbols, perspectives, and definitions. As sociologist Joel M. Charon points out, symbolic interactionism can be applied to understanding other sociological theories such as the "collective consciousness" in Émile Durkheim's works, the "class consciousness" and "false consciousness" in Karl Marx's, and the religious perspectives in Max Weber's. Symbolic interactionism has also been instrumental in the development of two related theoretical approaches: dramaturgy and ethnomethodology. Dramaturgy, as developed by sociologist Erving Goffman, is based on the premise that when human beings interact, each desires to manage the impressions the other receives of him or her. Ethnomethodology is concerned with the methods people use to produce meaning.

In the 1980's, symbolic interactionism experienced a resurgence within the field of sociology as sociologists used the concept of symbolic interaction in their analysis of socialization, culture, society, and social structure. Several other disciplines, including communication studies and philosophy, realized that the perspective could have valuable applications; this trend is expected to continue in the future, because the nature of reality, the meaning of self, the emergence and importance of society, the nature of symbols, and the importance of human communication are all topics that symbolic interactionists share with these disciplines.

Bibliography

Blumer, Herbert. *Symbolic Interactionism: Perspective and Method.* Englewood Cliffs, N.J.: Prentice-Hall, 1969. A student of Mead's at the University of Chicago, Blumer is largely responsible for continuing the symbolic interactionist tradition. This book integrates Mead's ideas with those of John Dewey, William James, Charles Peirce, William Thomas, and Charles Horton Cooley.

Charon, Joel M. *Symbolic Interactionism: An Introduction, an Interpretation, an Integration.* 4th ed. Englewood Cliffs, N.J.: Prentice-Hall, 1992. Presents a clear, organized, and interesting introduction to symbolic interactionism. The last chapter is particularly useful because it presents specific examples of applications as well as examples of representative studies using symbolic interactionism.

Deegan, Mary, and Michael Hill, eds. *Women and Symbolic Interaction.* Boston: Allen & Unwin, 1987. Articles describing how social customs, institutions, and patterns of interaction create gender differences. The editors take a strong feminist perspective as they try to show the potential of symbolic interaction to link the everyday, public actions of people with the hidden rules of social life.

Denzin, Norman. *Symbolic Interactionism and Cultural Studies.* Cambridge, Mass.: Blackwell, 1992. Offers historical overview of symbolic interactionism, complete with several useful charts, and then examines the perspective as it relates to poststructural and postmodern theory. Although the ideas offered are valuable and thought-provoking, the prose is dense and difficult to read; it may not be easily accessible to an audience which does not have an understanding of deconstructionist theory.

Fernandez, Ronald. *The I, the Me, and You.* New York: Praeger, 1977. Lively, thorough book covering socialization, human development, personality, roles, dramaturgy, reference groups, and collective behavior from the perspective of symbolic interactionism.

Hewitt, John. *Self and Society: A Symbolic Interactionist Social Psychology.* 8th ed. Boston: Allyn & Bacon, 2000. Provides an excellent discussion of the basic tenets and concepts of symbolic interactionism. Although there is no glossary, the terms are defined clearly in the text, and the writing is easy to understand. The last chapter is particularly valuable because it discusses the value of symbolic interactionism and the use of participation and observation as a specific methodology.

Manis, Jerome, and Bernard Meltzer, eds. *Symbolic Interaction: A Reader in Social Psychology.* 3d ed. Boston: Allyn & Bacon, 1978. Still one of the best and most readable books about symbolic interactionism. Its coverage is thorough and far-reaching, encompassing theory and methods, research implications and applications, and appraisals of symbolic interactionism by various sociologists.

Mead, George Herbert. *Mind, Self, and Society.* Chicago: University of Chicago Press, 1934. After Mead's death in 1931, his students gathered their notes from his lectures, together with material from his unpublished manuscripts, and published them in this book. The result is a surprisingly well-organized and readable treatment of Mead's ideas on social behaviorism, the mind, the self, and society. Includes an extensive bibliography of Mead's writings.

Karen Anding Fontenot

Cross-References

Dramaturgy; Ethnomethodology; Looking-Glass Self; Microsociology; Significant and Generalized Others.

TECHNOLOGY AND SOCIAL CHANGE

Type of sociology: Social change
Fields of study: Sources of social change; Theories of social change

Social change refers to the transformation of culture and social institutions over time, as reflected in the living patterns of individuals. Technology refers to the application of cultural knowledge to tasks of living in the environment. As technological advances occur, changes in culture naturally occur. The study of the relationship between technology and the changes it brings about is crucial as sociologists seek to understand today's increasingly technological society.

Principal terms

CHANGE AGENT: something that provides a bridge between the source of an item to be diffused and the potential recipients

CULTURAL LAG: term coined by William Ogburn to describe the situation that occurs when a technological invention, device, or process is developed but the social setting cannot keep pace with changes and thus lags behind

CULTURE: beliefs, norms, values, language, behavior, and material objects shared by a particular set of people

CYBERNETICS: study of complex, self-regulating, probabilistic systems, both human and technological

DIFFUSION OF INNOVATION: process whereby innovative ideas and traits are communicated and presented to people not previously familiar with them

INVENTION: novel design that has meaning and a useful function

MATERIAL CULTURE: tangible products of human society

NONMATERIAL CULTURE: intangible creations of society, such as ideas and beliefs

SOCIETY: group of people who interact with one another within a limited territory and who share a culture

Overview

Norbert Weiner, an expert on cybernetics, made a startling pronouncement in 1954: "We are the slaves of our technical improvement. . . . We have modified an environment so radically that we must now modify ourselves in order to exist in this new environment." Others, however, such as Robert Nisbet, a historical sociologist, have argued that "even the most massive pieces of technology can in themselves exert no influence upon human behavior except insofar as they are caught up in sets of human purposes." Social change is brought about by many forces; technology is only one of them. Theorists have dealt with the issue of social change from the time of the ancient Greeks. Many causes have been postulated for change, including geographic and climate factors, the development of certain types of material culture, and the existence of some "essence" of humankind that makes change inevitable.

Technological changes that have had an impact on social change include sources of power, such as nuclear energy; cybernetics and automation (as in the "computer revolution"); changes in transportation including space travel; and the growth of the mass media as forms of communication. Technological advances in the field of medicine, such as birth control and extension of life expectancy, also influence social change, as do other medical issues such as organ transplants, artificial body parts, and genetic manipulation. The mechanisms whereby technology influences social change are of interest to some sociologists; others are interested in the "chicken or egg" question regarding whether social change brings about technological change or vice versa.

A major concern in the area of technology and social change is society's ability or inability to place controls on technology. In other words, is technological change inevitable, or should society exercise controls to ensure that unwanted changes do not "just happen"? William F. Ogburn's idea of "cultural lag" is perhaps one of the most important concepts influencing this facet of the discussion regarding technology and social change. Ogburn posited that material culture changes by a process which is different in pace from changes in nonmaterial culture. The larger the technical knowledge of a society, the greater the possibility of new combinations and innovations. Thus, material culture tends to grow exponentially. Because society cannot develop methods of controlling and utilizing new technology before the technology is accepted and used, there exists a "cultural lag" in creating controls and altering social relationships related to the new conditions brought about by the new technology. Many examples of this phenomenon have occurred in recent history.

Everett Rogers, in *Social Change in Rural Society* (1960), did much groundbreaking work on the issue of adoption of new technologies and the accompanying social changes that might occur. Rogers pointed out that for an innovation to be adopted, it must have relative advantage over whatever it is going to replace (a mechanized potato peeler, for example, should be easier and faster to use than a knife and one's hand). It should have compatibility with the existing values and experiences of the adopters, be fairly simple, and be able to be tried on a limited basis. It should also be easy for people to observe the innovation in use and communicate about it. Rogers also pointed out that, in a group of individuals, there are usually about 2.5 percent who are very willing to try an innovation (they are called "innovators"). Another 13.5 percent are fairly willing to try something new and can be called "early adopters." About 34 percent adopt just before the normative "average" person would adopt a new idea; another 34 percent adopt just after this average person; and finally, some 16 percent ("laggards") tend to resist any change. Early adopters tend to be the most influential in terms of helping others adopt a technological change. They also tend to have relatively high incomes and high social status, and they tend to be younger and more educated than the average person.

Neil J. Smelser, in his history of social change, *Social Change in the Industrial Revolu-*

Super highways, trains, airplanes, and other forms of high-speed mass transportation have had an incalculable impact on modern social change. *(PhotoDisc)*

tion: An Application of Theory to the British Cotton Industry (1959), laid out a pattern of stages for social change vis-à-vis technology which has provided a paradigm for examining social change. These stages, based on his study of the Industrial Revolution, include "dissatisfaction," described as a general feeling that "all is not as it should be." A stage of "manifest unrest" follows, in which people make (in Smelser's terms) "unjustified" and "unrealistic" movements against the current situation; most of these activities are misdirected (when one takes a historical view of them). A third stage involves the search for and assessment of solutions. In this stage there are many innovations and "trial balloons" in a frantic search for improvements that will solve the unrest. The next stage involves formalization of patterns. Testing of various solutions occurs, and some with potential benefit are instituted. Surviving patterns are not always the "best," but rather appear to be those which can achieve public acceptance. Next comes the stage of legitimization and institutionalization. In this stage, innovations become accepted and become a part of "day-to-day" activities.

Applications

The relationship between technology and social change can perhaps best be illustrated through examples from modern industrial society; among those that readily come to mind are changes related to medical technology, computer technology, and the technology of mass communications. Medical technology, for example, has far-reaching impacts on social issues. Among the issues with relevance to social change are definitions of life and death;

how to provide equal access to life-giving technologies to all individuals rather than to an elite few; controlling the costs of medical care; the costs of increasing the life span, with the attendant issues of housing and medical care of the aged; and population problems caused by such medically influenced changes as decreases in infant mortality. The list could continue, making it very obvious that efforts to improve medical technology are not changes which occur in a vacuum; they affect humans in all spheres of their lives.

In addition to the changes mentioned above, advances in medical technology have caused other social changes that might go unnoticed unless attention was called to them. For example, increased medical knowledge has caused increased medical specialization. This has changed the type of training that medical students receive, creating a nation of specialist physicians and a move away from the general practitioner, which was the historic social mechanism for the delivery of medical care. Specialization also has increased the cost of medical care, as specialists can charge more for their services. In addition, specialists tend to congregate in urban centers, creating hospitals which seek to obtain a reputation for medical excellence in a certain field. All these social changes contribute to changes in the accessibility of medical care for the average individual and to changes in how persons obtain routine care.

The computer revolution has changed and is changing the way individuals communicate, do business, and spend their work and leisure time. The rapid changes in computer technology from the mainframe era to the present has affected most people in the United States in the workplace, the school, and, for many, the home. For some people, the computer has become an extension of themselves, allowing electronic communication with the world, as well as a device with which to work, play, and learn. Computerized databases in banks, lending agencies, insurance companies, and law enforcement have profound implications in the area of individual privacy. One's medical records, records of conviction, telephone calls, credit history, and much more are stored permanently in various banks of computer memory, accessible to those who can tap into them.

Telephone networks and computerized access numbers allow many transactions to be made without physical exchange of currency, leading to a day when individuals may not need to carry coins or paper money at all in order to purchase goods and services. Automation of routine assembly, guided by computerized systems, has altered the routine of the factory worker markedly. Secretarial and managerial staff alike also find the computer changing the way they handle work. In fact, there is hardly anyone in the work world whose job descriptions have not changed because of the computer revolution.

The technology of mass communication has changed so rapidly that it is possible for a person born in the early twentieth century to have lived through an age in which there were hardly any telephones to an era of telephones, fax machines, picture phones, fiberoptics, and satellite dishes. Television has brought the world (at least the world pictured by television cameras) into many homes. Interactive television devices, televised shopping networks, and other alterations have made television much more than it was at its beginning.

Given the ability of television to transmit culture to the masses, the widespread adoption of this invention creates a primary example of technology as an influence on social change.

There are those who approve of television's mass distribution of culture and others who strongly oppose its potential. Those opposing such mass distribution point out that, since few broadcasting companies exist, the net effect is to maintain an ideological hegemony and legitimize the status quo. These critics warn that mass-mediated culture emphasizes quantity over quality, encourages mediocrity, causes a loss of individuality, reduces creativity, and creates a public addiction. Those supporting mass culture via television say that it gives people what they want, increases potential access to cultural riches, may encourage creativity, and opens new technological horizons.

Some observers (Alvin Toffler, for one) see technology bringing about a reversal of the trend toward mass culture distributed by television. His book *The Third Wave* (1980) foresaw a "de-massifying of the media." Major network television stations are threatened in viewership by such "individualized" media delivery systems as cable and satellite television, video games, rented videotapes, and computer information services. As Toffler pointed out, "All these different developments have one thing in common: they slice the mass television public into segments, and each slice not only increases our cultural diversity, it cuts deeply into the power of the networks that have until now so completely dominated our imagery."

Transportation is another area in which rapid technological changes have occurred. Changes have shrunk the world so that a traveler can go around the world in a few days instead of a few years. Changes in transportation appear to change people's sense of time and to thereby affect many related issues of how they do business and even plan leisure travel. Speedier transportation implies the accessibility of perishable products from other geographical areas, making (at least for those with the funds to purchase them) fruits and vegetables always "in season." In addition, a day in the tropical sunshine is rarely more than half a day away from any traveler tiring of winter's cold.

Jacques Ellul, one of the most prolific and frequently quoted writers on technological change, set forth four propositions (in *The Technological Bluff*, 1990) which relate to applications of technology and their effects on social change: "First, all technical progress has its price. Second, at each stage, it raises more and greater problems than it solves. Third, its harmful effects are inseparable from its beneficial effects. Fourth, it has a great number of unforeseen effects." In examining any of the technological applications mentioned above, the veracity of these propositions can be seen.

Context

Early sociologists, including Auguste Compte, dealt with the issue of social change as they attempted to explain the growth and evolution of societies with a large-scale conception of the history of social change. Compte saw societies progressing from superstition through a metaphysical stage, in which all things are explained via abstract conceptions and principles, to a positivistic society in which explanations would be "truly scientific." Herbert Spencer laid out a formula for progressive evolutionary change in his works in the late nineteenth century. Most of the individuals trying to produce one evolutionary model of social change eventually were replaced by sociologists who dealt with more small-scale aspects of social change.

William F. Ogburn was one of the most influential sociologists working in the area of technology and social change in the early twentieth century. His concept of cultural lag, previously discussed, has influenced work in social change from the 1920's to the present. Ogburn and S. C. Gilfillan (Gilfillan published *The Sociology of Invention* in 1935) held the view that social change arises as a result of technological innovations and that, if the time is ripe, the appropriate technological invention will arise. In other words, technological ideas combine and recombine to form new inventions, which cause social change when material culture has accumulated sufficiently to make this happen.

Numerous scholars (sociologists, anthropologists, and others) point to specific technological changes which they feel have been the major force in terms of social change. These scholars include historian Louis Mumford, who cites the clock as a key machine of the modern age. In the 1950's, Fred Cottrell proposed that technological advances in the area of energy were the prime movers in terms of social change. Other scholars who have studied technology as a major force in social change include S. McKee Rosen and Laura Rosen (*Technological and Social Change*, 1941), Meyer Nimkoff (*Technology and the Changing Family*, 1955), and Gerhard Lenski and Jean Lenski. Such popular works as Toffler's *Future Shock* (1970) and *The Third Wave* have highlighted the effects of mass communications, the "knowledge explosion," and the computer revolution on individuals and societies. These books have also pointed out the social effects of increasingly rapid change experienced by those living in current decades.

Critical theorists point out that any "technological revolution" affects the haves and have-nots in society inequitably. The tensions and conflicts generated between these groups also lead to social change, which is sometimes gradual, sometimes revolutionary. Access to the benefits of technology is not equally available to all, thus leading to other sources of social change and unrest.

Bibliography

Ellul, Jacques. *The Technological Bluff.* Translated by Geoffrey W. Bromiley. Grand Rapids, Mich.: Eerdmans, 1990. Somewhat more optimistic than his earlier book, this details the events of the thirty years since Ellul wrote *The Technological Society*, pointing out his correct predictions and raising issues regarding social change vis-à-vis technology.

_____. *The Technological Society.* Translated by John Wilkinson. New York: Alfred A. Knopf, 1964. Somewhat pessimistic work, warning of the problems of subordinating science to technology and interpolating the potential risks and dangers of such a scenario.

Haferkamp, Hans, and Neil J. Smelser, eds. *Social Change and Modernity.* Berkeley: University of California Press, 1992. Essays by influential individuals such as Alain Touraine and Neil Smelser. Especially relevant to this topic are sections on information technology, external and internal factors in theories of social change, and critical appraisals of theories of social change as technology is involved.

Kline, Ronald R. *Consumers in the Country: Technology and Social Change in Rural America.* Baltimore: Johns Hopkins University Press, 2000.

Ogburn, William F. *Social Change with Respect to Culture and Original Nature.* New York:

B. W. Huebsch, 1922. Classic work outlining Ogburn's theory and the concept of cultural lag.

Ryan, Bryce F. *Social and Cultural Change*. New York: Ronald Press, 1969. Readable text on social change. The chapter "Technological Change in Contemporary Society" is most useful to this particular topic; however, the chapters on theories of causation, innovation, and diffusion are also extremely helpful.

Scott, William G., Terence R. Mitchell, and Philip H. Birnbarum. "Technology and Organization Structure." In *Organizational Theory: A Structural and Behavioral Analysis*. Homewood, Ill.: Richard D. Irwin, 1981. Excellent view of technology and social change, discussing how technology affects management, the worker, and all aspects of the business world. Readable and illustrated with many charts and diagrams.

M. C. Ware

Cross-References

Culture: Material and Expressive Culture; Industrial and Postindustrial Economies; Industrial Sociology; Social Change: Sources of Change.

URBANIZATION

Type of sociology: Urban and rural life
Field of study: Sources of social change

Urbanization is the complex process by which large numbers of people form, settle in, work in, and live in cities. Although urbanization occurred in ancient and preindustrial times, it is most dramatically associated with the development of industrial and postindustrial societies, in both of which it has acted as an important agency of social change.

Principal terms

CITY: relatively large, densely populated, and diverse human settlement

INVASION-SUCCESSION: replacement of one group by a different group when the first group moves to a different area

MEGALOPOLIS: complex of overlapping metropolises that form a continuous sprawl, as is the case with the extended urban area from Washington, D.C., to Boston, Massachusetts

METROPOLIS: large urban area containing a central city and adjacent communities that are in many ways linked to it, such as that of Los Angeles

URBAN AREA: generally, a densely populated area; officially, any place with a population above 2,500, according to the U.S. Bureau of the Census

URBAN DIFFERENTIATION: process whereby cities develop distinct business districts, industrial areas, cultural centers, recreational areas, and residential sectors

URBANISM: refers to the lifestyles characterizing city dwellers, usually in contradistinction to the lifestyles of rural folk

Overview

Through prehistory as well as throughout most of historical times, human existence has been spent in small groups of nomads, hunter-gatherers, or agriculturalists. The precise beginnings of urban settlements are unknown, although legends, myths, archaeological evidence, and inferences drawn from the known origins of cities that have developed in recorded time have minimized some obscurities. Roughly ten thousand years ago, during the Neolithic period, villages of between two hundred and four hundred residents appeared, indicating that food production and associated technologies, along with increases in population and the specializations of labor, had made relatively permanent settlements feasible. For perhaps another five thousand years, this was as close to "urban" life as humans came.

About five thousand years ago (c. 3000 B.C.E.), what have since been defined as pre-industrial cities had developed along some of the world's major river valleys: the Nile in Egypt, the Tigris-Euphrates in the Middle East, the Yellow River in China, and the Indus in Pakistan. Elsewhere, preindustrial cities emerged within Inca and Mayan civilizations in South and Central America, as well as among the peoples of ancient Greek and Roman civilizations. These cities, often more appropriately identified as city-states, generally had populations of between five thousand and ten thousand, though in rare instances (such as pre-Christian Rome or Constantinople), the population may have reached several hundred thousand.

In many ways, these preindustrial cities differed markedly from later industrial and postindustrial societies. To begin with, they seldom dominated the overwhelmingly rural cultures surrounding them. Indeed, quite the contrary was true. Consequently, in regard to family and kinship networks, urban dwellers continued to live in social contexts that remained much like those of their rural brethren. In addition, the cosmopolitanism of later cities was lacking. Despite their mergers of residential and commercial quarters—a result of traders and artisans working at home—preindustrial cities were highly segregated. They confined different trades and crafts to distinct quarters of the city, frequently even walling them off from one another. Still further separations of the urban populations—along religious, ethnic, occupational, class, and caste lines—curtailed social mobility.

Obvious limitations checked the expansion of preindustrial cities. Agricultural techniques, for one thing, remained inadequate for the support of large, nonagricultural populations. One study, for example, indicates that the labor of seventy-five farmers was required in the pre-Christian era to sustain one urban dweller. Reliance on human muscle power or that of animals, moreover, restricted the carriage of foodstuffs and other supplies—especially those needed for heavy construction—from countryside to city. Furthermore, endemic and epidemic diseases, fostered by poor sanitation, sustained high death rates, which went unmeliorated by early medicines and medical practices. Not least, the functions of preindustrial cities tended to be circumscribed. One authority notes that until the sixteenth century, urban centers tended to be court cities, cathedral cities, markets, ports, fortresses, or simply country towns that satisfied the demands of their immediate rural hinterlands and of highly stratified societies.

Sociologists and other social scientists attribute urban development before and since the appearance of preindustrial cities to the interactions of four major factors: the size of total population; control over the natural environment; technological advances; and changes in social organization.

A significant coalescence of these factors, under way in the late eighteenth century and accelerated during the nineteenth century by the Industrial Revolution, produced the industrial city, typified by boomtowns such as England's Manchester and Birmingham. A beneficiary of more efficient commercial agriculture and its surplus capital, the industrial city's rapid development was facilitated by many factors. Certainly the utilization of coal and steam power was essential, but growth of the industrial city also relied heavily on new modes of transportation and communications, the use of new materials, and new production and managerial techniques. Improved diets, sanitary conditions, and medical knowledge contributed to a population explosion that sustained increases in the size of industrial cities. At the end of the nineteenth century, Great Britain, France, the Low Countries, Germany, and, preeminently, the United States were dotted with industrial cities. By 1850, England had become the world's first urban nation, with more than half of its population living in cities.

Comparatively, industrial cities were larger and more numerous than their preindustrial counterparts. For example, by the opening of the nineteenth century, London's population had exceeded one million. New York's topped that mark by 1865, to be followed before 1925 by Tokyo, Paris, Berlin, Chicago, Buenos Aires, Osaka, Philadelphia, and eighteen others with populations ranging between 1.2 million and 7.8 million. Within their respective countries such cities evolved integrated urban networks, and major centers like New York, London, Paris, Tokyo, and Shanghai, in addition, were linked by international networks of diplomacy, trade, and ideas.

Industrial cities were also more heterogeneous in their functions and compositions than were their predecessors. Besides vast complements of skilled artisans, white-collar workers, businessmen, and managers, they included many cosmopolites: artists, journalists, professionals, and intellectuals. Because industrial cities culturally and physically dominated the rural hinterland, tending to drain the countryside of its best talents, they were filled with immigrants—those from rural areas and the farms and cities of other countries. The scale on which they incorporated various ethnic groups, socioeconomic classes, religions, customs, and political beliefs was unprecedented in world history. They were characterized, too, by their dynamism. Their denizens constantly altered their schemes of land use, devised new forms of governance, changed neighborhoods through invasion-succession, expanded into suburbs even as they grew internally, and (as some sociologists have insisted) altered human behavior by producing distinctive urban types who pursued uniquely urban ways of life.

Almost within a generation of industrial cities spilling over their original bounds to become metropolises, many of them between the 1960's and the 1990's further evolved into megalopolises. Both metropolitan and megalopolitan growth had become a hallmark not only within the world's "advanced" or highly developed nations but also with the developing nations of Asia, Africa, and Latin America. There, after the mid-twentieth century, the growth of cities and the rates of urbanization have been more rapid and dramatic than were those of their counterparts in the first industrialized countries.

Applications

Entire societies within relatively brief spans of time—between 1850 and the close of the twentieth century—have been completely transformed by urbanization. This is explained in part because urbanization, the increased size and density of urban populations, has been both a cause and a consequence of economic modernization, and with the way in which humans secure their livings. Urban populations have generated the increases in productivity, the intensive divisions of labor and specializations, and the complex forms of economic activity that have yielded the unprecedented high standards of living that characterize modern life. To state it another way, urbanization, for all of the problems common to it, has been synonymous with expanding individual and organizational opportunity.

American experiences with urbanization have much in common with the experiences of other countries that were also early leaders in industrialization and in subsequent economic development. In 1800, the new United States conformed almost totally to a world that was overwhelmingly nonurban. Of the world's estimated population of 900 million in 1800, only about 1.7 percent lived in cities of 100,000 or more; only 2.4 percent lived in cities of 20,000 or more; and 3 percent lived in urban places of 5,000 or more: In sum, only 7.1 percent of the world's people were urban. While the United States' total population growth and urban concentration soon after 1800 were to far exceed estimates of world rates, the first U.S. census, in 1790, indicated that 95 percent of the population lived in rural places of fewer than 2,500 persons. The first census counted a mere twenty-four urban places, only two of which—Boston and New York— had populations greater than 25,000.

Thereafter, between 1800 and 1950, there were notable increases in both world population and urbanization. World population, for example, soared by more than 2.5 times, while the number of people living in places of 5,000 and over rose 26 times; those living in places of more than 20,000 increased 23 times; and those living in cities of 100,000 or more grew 20 times. By 1950, one-third of the world's population resided in urban communities of more than 5,000 people. In the meantime, by 1925 half of the U.S. population, which had grown from the 3.5 million of the 1790's census to 105 million, had become urban. By the close of the 1950's, the United States counted 5,400 urban places in which more than 70 percent of its population lived. These two trends continued. According to the census of 1990, 77.1 percent of the United States' 248.2 million people lived in the nation's 283 metropolitan areas, which accounted for about one-third of the world's 1,046 metropolitan areas.

These momentous demographic manifestations of urbanization have generated profound changes in social life that have also drawn the attention of sociologists—especially since twentieth century technologies (such as electricity and the automobile) have obliterated previous restraints on urban growth, and, as Lewis Mumford observed, allowed urban places to burst their bounds and sprawl into megalopolitan dimensions.

Accordingly, urban sociologists have proposed a number of theories about cities as physical constructs, about whether they tend, in functional terms, to grow in concentric zones, or sectors, or tend to expand from several, functionally distinctive nuclei. Urban sociologists have likewise examined effects on human behavior of the greatly increased interpersonal contacts that seemed to distinguish the daily lives of urbanites from the lives of rural dwellers. Because, in American cities in particular, these contacts include interactions among a wide variety of socioeconomic, religious, ethnic, and racial groups, urban specialists have explored the processes of "Americanization."

They have asked, too, whether urban heterogeneity has nurtured a comfortable cosmopolitanism, has strengthened the integrity of specialized groups, or, on the contrary, has eroded normative standards of conduct and increased individual disorientation and isolation—that is, whether heterogeneity has contributed to anomie. In these connections, they have studied the interdependence of personal and group relations, as well as the shift of personal relationships away from status toward utilitarian, impersonal, contractual relations.

Not least, urban sociologists have sought to explain changes in social structures that have been attributable to urbanization. They want to know how the extended family and kinship networks gave way to the nuclear family; how urban social institutions came to be "enacted" by legislative or administrative fiat rather than created spontaneously; how urban bureaucracies and other rational-legal organizations became all-pervasive. They also seek to discover how urbanization altered social stratification and to understand the roles of the middle classes in redefining traditional schemes of social stratification. Generally, therefore, urban sociologists have found inexhaustible materials in the social changes that accompanied the creation and expansion of the mass societies that urbanization created.

Context

As an area of intellectual inquiry and a scholarly discipline, sociology has evolved simultaneously with industrial and postindustrial urbanization. The growth and proliferation of cities, and their effects upon and dominance over modern cultures, consequently engaged the interests of pioneer sociologists right from the early years of their profession. Representative of these figures were Europeans, such as Max Weber, Georg Simmel, and Oswald Spengler (the so-called German school), along with Émile Durkheim, Ferdinand Tönnies, Numa-Denis Fustel de Coulanges, and Henri Pirenne. Not all of these figures could be classified only as sociologists, of course, and none was interested solely in studying cities.

Some of their works were purely theoretical, while others, if geographically and historically wide-ranging, were more specific in focus. Weber, for example, not only theorized about humanity's collective urban experiences but also closely studied medieval cities of the Low Countries as well as those of Renaissance Italy. In general, however, these nascent urban sociologists tended to apply historical techniques to analyses of their subjects. Generally, too, they perceived industrial urbanization as a disruptive, even corrupting, process, harmful both to society-at-large and to individual personalities. Accordingly, they tended to be pessimistic, or at least dubious, about its outcomes.

On a selective basis the influences of these Europeans, particularly those of Weber and Simmel, contributed to the development of America's Chicago school of urban sociology. During the early 1900's, Chicago, not New York, was widely regarded as the quintessential "American" city. Economically it dominated the country's heartland, and demographically it lay close to the nation's center of population. It likewise enjoyed vital colonies of poets, novelists, journalists, and the beginnings of a brilliant academic community at the University of Chicago.

Whereas America's earliest observers of urban life had been inclined to moralize about the character and impact of cities, the Chicago school of urban theorists concentrated on developing a viable ecological framework for their observations. Three men, in particular, were responsible initially for the school's national—soon international—reputation: Robert E. Park, Ernest W. Burgess, and Louis Wirth. Park and Burgess wrote and edited *The City*, a collection of insightful essays, in 1925, and subsequently all three men published numerous works dealing variously with urban spatial patterns, concentric-zone theory, cities and civilization, urbanism as a way of life, Chicago's urban immigrants and ghettos, community life and social policy, collective behavior, urban news and opinion, and measurements of urbanization. Like their European counterparts, Chicago's pioneer urban sociologists published most of their works between 1900 and 1950. All of them viewed the city, not as a mirror of the whole society (and its problems), but as a distinctive entity, as an independent variable, in which major social changes were being generated and in which new ways of life were being evolved.

By the mid-1920's, the Chicago school had helped found modern American urban studies as a distinct branch of sociology precisely at the time when demographics indicated that the United States had become a predominantly urban nation. Its inquiries, of course, were augmented by related ones conducted elsewhere. Prominent among such studies, for example, were those of Helen M. Lynd and Robert S. Lynd, Pitirim Sorokin, Otis Dudley Duncan, Horace Miner, Philip Hauser, Gideon Sjoberg, Beverly Duncan, Albert J. Reiss, Jr., E. Franklin Frazier, and Donald Bogue, along with contributions by other social scientists such as anthropologist Robert Redfield and historians Lewis Mumford, Charles Glabb, and Oscar Handlin. Building on the theories and empiricism of these works, urban sociologists during the last half of the twentieth century continued producing insightful studies of great diversity, as indicated by the publications of Theodore Roszak, Oscar Lewis, Raymond Williams, Claude Fischer, Scott Greer, William Whyte, Herbert J. Gans, S. N. Eisenstadt, and Richard Sennett.

Bibliography

Boskoff, Alvin. *The Sociology of Urban Regions*. New York: Appleton-Century-Crofts, 1962. Clear, standard introduction to the subject. Coverage ranges from analyses of human communities, demographics, and urban ecology to social organization and urban planning. Many useful tables, graphs, charts, and illustrations.

Hatt, Paul K., and Albert J. Reiss, Jr. *Cities and Society*. 2d ed. Glencoe, Ill.: Free Press, 1968. Major scholarly essays on important aspects of theoretical and empirical urban sociology. Well organized and splendidly referenced. Needs updating but remains the best work of its kind.

Hauser, Philip M., and Leo F. Schnore, eds. *The Study of Urbanization*. New York: John Wiley & Sons, 1965. First-rate essays by distinguished urban sociologists, historians, anthropologists, and demographers. Hauser's introduction is outstanding.

Jones, Gavin W., and Pravin Visaria, eds. *Urbanization in Large Developing Countries: China, Indonesia, Brazil, and India*. New York: Oxford University Press, 1997.

Schwab, William A. *The Sociology of Cities*. Englewood Cliffs, N.J.: Prentice-Hall, 1992.

Sennett, Richard, comp. *Classic Essays on the Culture of Cities*. New York: Appleton-Century-Crofts, 1969. Edited by a major urban scholar, this collection lives up to its name. The ten essays, by seven distinguished sociologists, an anthropologist, and Sennett, are thought-provoking. Sennett's fine introductory essay briefly reviews the development of urban sociology.

Sirjamaki, John. *The Sociology of Cities*. New York: Random House, 1964. Useful work for lay readers. Approach is historical, and concentration is on American cities. The book is written from the perspective of the national community and the social-cultural changes it has wrought on cities.

Smith, Michael P. *The City and Social Theory*. New York: St. Martin's Press, 1979. Diagnostic and prescriptive essays by Wirth, Sigmund Freud, Simmel, Roszak, and Sennett have been chosen for critical analysis by Smith because they share the view that modern urban culture is repressive, and Smith seeks to refute them. Clearly written, convincingly argued.

Weber, Max. *The City*. Translated and edited by Don Martindale and Gertrud Neuwirth. Glencoe, Ill.: Free Press, 1958. A classic, like so much of Weber's work. Indispensable reading, and better yet it is exciting, insightful, and provocative. Few notes or other aids.

Clifton K. Yearley

Cross-References

Demographic Factors and Social Change; Demography; Immigration and Emigration; Industrial and Postindustrial Economies; Industrial Sociology.

VALIDITY AND RELIABILITY IN MEASUREMENT

Type of sociology: Sociological research
Field of study: Basic concepts

Research in the social sciences involves studying behavior. Accurately recording what subjects are doing is difficult, and research is always in danger of being influenced by the expectations of the researcher. The concepts of validity and reliability are employed to ensure the soundness and consistency of measurement techniques. Validity refers to whether research actually measures what it was intended to measure; reliability refers to whether the research produces consistent results.

Principal terms

ASSESSMENT: estimation or measurement of some quality or event; an evaluation or judgment about a performance, behavior, or skill

CONSTRUCT: abstract attribute or group of related ideas that cannot be observed but that is associated with observable behavior (loyalty cannot be observed, but acts of loyalty can)

CORRELATION: statistical concept that measures how frequently two events co-occur, thereby suggesting either a relationship or a lack of relationship between the events

CRITERION: standard to which something is compared or upon which a judgment is made

ERROR: with respect to assessment, reliability, and validity, error refers to variation in scores generated by the measurement device when measuring the same thing more than once

RELIABILITY: consistency or stability in scores generated by some method of measurement

VALIDITY: extent to which an assessment device actually measures what it claims to measure

Overview

Science depends on accurate and systematic measurement. Because researchers must demonstrate that they are recording events accurately, scientific instruments are tested regularly for accuracy. Obviously, instruments that do not give true readings are not useful. Though dependence on instrumentation is necessary for all science, demonstrating reliability and validity in the social sciences is often more difficult than it is in the natural sciences. In the natural sciences, for example, official standards for items such as weight, temperature, or chemical purity are available for testing instruments. Social scientists do not usually have this luxury. Measuring such things as attitudes or intelligence is very difficult, because there are no universally accepted "official standards." Verifying behavioral records or surveys and determining what standard to compare data to are therefore problematic.

The credibility of field studies, naturalistic observations, and archival research (collectively known as qualitative research) depends on clear and convincing evidence that recording techniques are acceptable. Thus, investigators must demonstrate that behavioral measures are reliable and valid. Reliability and validity refer to data collection. That is, they refer to whether data recording devices are reliable and valid and to whether surveys, tests, or observational systems really address what the investigator is studying.

Reliability refers to consistency—whether the measuring device generates the same data repeatedly if measuring the same thing. If the behavior has not changed, then neither should the data. Variability means that an error has occurred, and the researcher cannot then be sure if the behavior truly occurred. There are four main types of reliability: internal consistency, test-retest, equivalent forms, and interjudge.

Internal consistency refers to the degree of agreement between various items on the measurement device. If assessing aggression among children on a playground, one could record many types of behavior. There could be acts of physical violence, vocal outbursts, angry gestures, and facial expressions. One would record many types of each and then check to see if certain behaviors correlate with others. For example, certain facial expressions might always accompany certain acts of violence. If the data show no relationships between the measures, one might wonder if one's observers are recording real behavior—in other words, whether the observers and devices are reliable.

Taking a measurement more than once is common to both the test-retest and the equivalent form types of reliability. A test-retest procedure is one in which the same device is used two or more times, as when one weighs oneself each morning on the bathroom scale. If one goes from a spring scale (as most bathroom scales are) to a balance scale (as in most doctors' offices), however, one is using an equivalent form. In either case, one expects the data to agree; the weight should be the same each time.

When measuring aggression in children, one would expect the amount to remain relatively constant if no new children are added, none leaves, and there are no new reasons for the children to get along more or less amicably. If one uses the same recording system for many days, one is employing test-retest. If, instead, one uses different definitions of aggression each day, one is using equivalent forms. Finally, recording techniques often require judgment. Observers studying aggression have to judge intent. Two boys wrestling on the ground may be playing without harmful intent. Interjudge reliability compares data collected from different observers to see if they agree about the behavior.

Though reliability is necessary, it is not sufficient. Data records may agree without being accurate. If the bathroom scale is broken, for example, one may get the same incorrect weight each time. Likewise, taking records on different days and using different techniques or observers does not guarantee that the data are really about the topic of interest. A testing device may be reliable without being valid.

The validity of a measurement device addresses whether it measures what it claims to measure. Validity is in question if a researcher intending to measure aggression actually measures frustration. Even if investigators can demonstrate reliability (because the data are stable), they are not assured that aggression is being addressed. There are six major categories of validity: criterion (with two subtypes, concurrent and predictive), content, construct, internal, ecological (also called external validity), and face validity.

A criterion is a standard used for comparison purposes. Criterion validity is comparing the data to some established or desired criterion. The standard for predictive validity is the occurrence of a future event. For example, the Scholastic Aptitude Test (SAT) is supposed to predict how students will perform in college. Though there are individual exceptions, the test performs reasonably well as a group predictor. Usually, students with high scores perform better in college than those with poor performances do. Since the test does predict future events, it is generally valid. (There has been considerable controversy, however, about whether the SAT is equally valid for males and females and for those of Asian, African, European, Hispanic, and American Indian ancestry.)

Another criterion is concurrent validity. Here, the investigator compares the data to a current, accepted standard. The criterion is whether one's data agree with the other indicators. Considering SAT scores, one might expect agreement with high school grades: Do the students with the best grades get the highest scores? If so, this concurrent criterion suggests that the SAT is valid.

A second major type of validity is content validity—whether the test measures a sufficient breadth of its intended topic. If researchers are measuring aggression, are they recording enough of the different types? If only physical violence is noted, the sample does not include a sufficient variety of aggressive acts. The researchers need to include verbal and gestural behaviors as well.

Construct validity is a difficult topic. Much of the behavioral research concerns phenomena that have no objective existence. That is, they are not things; they are ideas, abstract attributes. Yet they are related to observable events. Gravity is a good example of a construct. One cannot see gravity, but one can see its effects. Color and shape are other examples. Though squareness and blueness can be seen, they are attributes of objects and not objects themselves. In sociology, such concepts as racism, culture, and social structures are not things; though their effects are observable, they cannot be seen directly. Construct validity is concerned with the essence of a concept. Data collected must be demonstrated to correlate with other behaviors believed to be involved with the construct one is studying.

Internal validity is usually used in experimental research, and it refers to experimental design: Does the research methodology address the construct in question, or are there errors in design that make conclusions from the study impossible? Ecological validity addresses the generalizability of results (often called external validity). Experimental conditions may be so controlled that an experiment's results have no relevance to the "real world." If a study is performed in a natural setting, conditions may be so contrived that the investigator can learn nothing about normal behavior. If so, the results will be invalid for any other circumstances.

A final type is called face validity, which is often the first one employed. One simply looks at the data collection method and judges its apparent usefulness: Does it look like it will do the intended job? Investigators with considerable experience can generally make a good guess about the validity of a measuring device simply by examining it.

Although, as stated before, a measurement device can be reliable without being valid, it cannot be valid without being reliable. Since validity concerns measuring what is intended, if the device does this correctly, it will necessarily generate agreement when performed again.

Applications

Though the concepts of reliability and validity are necessary for scientific advances, they are also relevant to our everyday life in innumerable ways. Every day, decisions are made that are based on judgments concerning the validity and reliability of information. From an employer's decision regarding whom to hire to a physician's analysis of the results of a laboratory test, decisions must be made, often with very little information.

Personnel managers, for example, must determine the best prospective employees for their company from a combination of written applications and personal interviews. They have to decide what information (such as education, work experience, or letters of recommendation) best predicts who will be the most productive and trustworthy employee and must decide which factor should carry the most weight. Similarly, physicians must decide what diagnostic tests to perform, college boards must decide whether grades or test scores are better predictors of college success, and attorneys need to know which potential jurists are most likely to sympathize with their clients. In each of these cases, a decision must be made. The method of making the decision is often subjected to tests of reliability and validity.

The various types of reliability and validity can be explored through the example of how teachers create tests to check their students' acquisition of knowledge. In this example, an English teacher has assigned his class two plays by Shakespeare. The teacher will wish to evaluate how well the class understood the plays. Generally, this means that the class will take a test from which the teacher will determine a grade for each student. It is presumed that this grade will "mean something"—that it will be measuring, reasonably accurately, something truly relevant to the course content. Issues of reliability and validity are important to this procedure.

A reliable test should yield consistent results. If the teacher asks multiple choice questions about the characters in the plays and, in addition, asks students matching questions and fill-in-the-blank questions about the same characters, one would expect the students' performance on each of these sections of the test to agree. This is internal reliability. If a student takes the same test twice (without studying between times) and gets similar scores, test-retest reliability has been demonstrated. If a student takes a different test covering the same material and gets a similar grade, equivalent forms of reliability have been shown.

If the teacher scores the test more than once, students should get the same grade each time. This might not be true, however, if someone else were to grade the test. This type of checking of reliability is especially helpful regarding essay examinations, for which grading is more subjective than a multiple choice (or other "short answer") type of test. If a new grader's scores agree with those given by the first grader, then interjudge reliability has been demonstrated.

So far, the issue of what the grade means has not been addressed. Reliability refers only to consistency. A test that does not address the Shakespeare plays that were read may produce similar grades. Whether the test measures knowledge of the plays' content is a validity issue. Schools may occasionally compare class performance on in-class tests to performance on standardized tests purchased from a testing service. When this is done, the administration is checking concurrent validity, and the criterion is the standardized test. The other type of criterion validity is predictive validity. To determine this type, the teacher must wait for some future event. Perhaps, for example, the students are required to take a second English class in which other Shakespeare readings are assigned. One might expect students' performance in both classes to agree. If the first accurately predicts the second, then the criterion has been met. The test should also reflect the content of the assignments. If two plays are assigned and the test covers only one (or covers plays not assigned), the test is invalid because it does not possess content validity.

Construct validity is difficult to demonstrate. Does the test really demonstrate knowledge of the topic assigned? One would expect students who do well in related areas also to do well when studying Shakespeare. They could be expected to recognize key issues from the assigned readings if they appear in other places, even other media. If they truly understand the plays, they should be able to discuss them intelligently, write about them, and use that knowledge elsewhere. Construct validity refers to these matters.

Internal validity is a practical concern. If the grading sheet is not correct, then the grades will not reflect performance. Also important are whether the teacher calculated the grade correctly and whether the students can (and do) cheat on the test. Ecological validity refers to generalizability. Does performance in this class tell anything about the student's abilities? Students should be able to use the knowledge they have gained outside this particular class. If the test and the class are so narrowly focused that the students do not recognize the plays' characters or topics outside the class, one would question the validity of the test and the usefulness of the class.

Finally, face validity can be tested. Does the test look like it is a valid measure of the plays? It might appear to be either too easy or too difficult. Could a student who did not do the readings pass? Is the test impossible even for diligent students? An experienced teacher can usually tell these things simply by looking at the test.

Context

John J. Macionis, in his text *Sociology* (4th ed., 1993), says that sociology "may be defined as the scientific study of human society." To study human society, researchers must be able to determine general patterns of behavior while observing individual people. Whether by observation or experimentation, through standardized tests, surveys, or unobtrusive measures, researchers are hoping to discover something about the individual subjects. Through their behavior, investigators hope to form general conclusions about the group(s) to which the subjects belong. If the techniques for collecting data are not trustworthy and do not address the attributes that the researchers are studying, efforts are wasted. Issues of reliability and validity of assessment devices are among the most important in any research venture.

The most important criterion that must be met in order for any study to qualify as a scientific endeavor is systematic observation. Different fields of science use different approaches to reach this end; astronomy depends on observation, chemistry on laboratory experiments, some subfields of psychology and sociology on testing or surveys, and so on. Yet all require that their methods generate consistent results and that the results actually reflect the existence and occurrence of the attributes of interest. The attributes of interest for the behavioral sciences are often invisible; they include attitudes, beliefs, emotions, or intellectual capacities. Since these cannot be observed directly, the data collection devices are especially subject to error. Demonstrating acceptable levels of reliability and validity is critical.

Bibliography

Jackson, Douglas Northrop, and Samuel Messick, eds. *Problems in Human Assessment.* New York: McGraw-Hill, 1967. The chapter "Standards for Educational and Psychological Tests and Manuals" in this work is intended for professionals in the field of behavioral research. Thus, it is rather advanced, but it is also a classic. Presents and defines virtually all concepts relevant to educational psychological testing, including reliability and validity.

McCain, Garvin, and Erwin M. Segal. *The Game of Science.* 5th ed. Pacific Grove, Calif.: Brooks/Cole, 1988. Immensely popular book for beginning students and readers interested in scientific research in any field. Addresses concepts of reliability and validity in the context of a larger, general discussion of all scientifically relevant concepts.

Murphy, Kevin R., and Charles O. Davidshofer. *Psychological Testing: Principles and Applications.* 4th ed. Upper Saddle River, N.J.: Prentice-Hall, 1998. Reliability and validity as applied to psychological testing are discussed in chapters 5 through 8. These chapters are clearly written and may be read independently of the rest of the text. Written for somewhat advanced readers.

Pyke, Sandra W., and Neil McK. Agnew. *The Science Game: An Introduction to Research in the Social Sciences.* 5th ed. Englewood Cliffs, N.J.: Prentice-Hall, 1991. Written for lay readers, but at a relatively advanced level. Presents the principles of behavioral research well and includes chapters on validity and qualitative methods.

Rosnow, Ralph L., and Robert Rosenthal. *Beginning Behavioral Research: A Conceptual Primer.* New York: Macmillan, 1993. Text for introductory college courses in research design. Very easy to understand, but its best feature is that it collects all the relevant concepts, types, and subtypes of reliability and validity in one chapter.

Salvador Macias III

Cross-References

Hypotheses and Hypothesis Testing; Quantitative Research; Samples and Sampling Techniques; Sociology Defined; Surveys.

Values and Value Systems

Type of sociology: Culture
Field of study: Components of culture

Because values are a key determinant of behavior, an understanding of a group's values makes it easier to understand the behavior of its members.

Principal terms

CULTURAL RELATIVISM: view that a culture is to be judged by its own standards
ETHNOCENTRISM: attitude that one's own culture is best and that other cultures are to be judged by its standards
NORMS: patterns of behavior that are generally followed in particular situations
VALUE SYSTEM: set of values held by an individual or shared by a group
VALUES: general ideas of what is desirable

Overview

Values and norms are different but closely related. Values are general ideas about what is desirable, but such general ideas do not specify how one should act in particular situations; norms do that. Societies that value cleanliness, for example, may have different norms about how often one should bathe. As a value, however, cleanliness provides reason to have some norm about bathing. Because values are general ideas, they can lead to conflicting norms. For example, the value of fairness might lead to the norm "hire the best-qualified candidate" or to the norm "hire the candidate from the group that has suffered from discrimination in the past." Such situations might arise from having different ideas about the nature of the value at stake. In some cases, the norms of a society do not reflect its professed values. When American society claimed that segregated schools would be equal, it professed the value of equality and proceeded to uphold the practice of inequality.

In general, values are expressed in norms and norms reflect values. The norm "one does not chew one's food with one's mouth open" reflects the value placed on social refinement, and the norm "one does not murder human beings" reflects the value placed on human life. Knowing a culture's values provides some insight into how its members are likely to behave. When members of a society share the same values, the values let them know what to expect from one another. As a source of consensus, the values help to hold the society together. Values and norms are an important part of a culture's identity. Transmitting values is essential for transmitting the culture to the next generation.

Children learn values from their parents, family members, peers, and teachers. One function of schools is to transmit values. Beginning every school day by pledging allegiance to the flag of the United States tends to instill patriotism in students. Schools also aim to teach the values of self-discipline, hard work, and social adaptability. Churches teach the importance of religious faith and a caring regard for others.

A society's literature can provide insight into its values. The Hebrew Bible gives primacy to obedience to God. The *Iliad* and the *Odyssey* strongly suggest that personal glory was a major value for Homeric Greeks. Fifth century B.C.E. Athens's relish for rational discussion is embodied in the dialogues of Plato. Aeneas, the hero of the Roman epic *The Aeneid*, reflects in his behavior the values of piety and patriotism. His devotion to the gods and to Rome's greater glory prompt him to leave the woman he loves and to sacrifice his own happiness. Rama, in the Indian epic the *Ramayana*, exemplifies the virtues of a model ruler, husband, son, and brother. Architecture can reveal values as well. Classical architecture expresses the value of rational order, sober simplicity, and due proportion; medieval Gothic cathedrals express the importance of communion with the divine; and sleek twentieth century business towers embody the value of efficiency.

Sociologists can seek out values in a variety of ways. First, they can simply ask people what values they hold. Second, they can systematically study choices that people make in experimental or nonexperimental situations. For example, during an interview, they might ask, "If you could only save one person from drowning, would you save the Queen or your mother?" They might also detect values by seeing what kind of behavior tends to be encouraged and rewarded, since such behavior is valued behavior.

A society's value system is the set of values that the majority of its members tend to favor. Those who reject major elements of the predominant system constitute a counterculture. For example, nonreligious people in a very religious society make up a counterculture. Detecting a society's value system involves determining what its values are and how they are related to one another. Some values may be interdependent, such as democracy, freedom, and equality. Others may be hierarchically ordered; for example, tradition may be considered more important than individual freedom.

In *American Society: A Sociological Interpretation* (1970), sociologist Robin Williams, Jr., set out to detect important American values. He asked himself various questions: "How widespread is this value?" "How long has it been a value?" "How strongly is it held?" "Which groups within the society accept the value, and which groups do not accept it?" Guided by such questions, he cataloged such traditional American values as the following:

Achievement and success in one's occupation are key American values. Hard work and strenuous activity, as related to success, are also valued. Efficiency and practicality are valued as effective means for accomplishing tasks. Science is valued because it makes it possible to control nature, thereby leading to material comfort—that is, adequate food, shelter, and medical care. Material comfort is another key American value. Americans value a moral approach to living. They have a humanitarian regard for others, whether near or far, and try to help the victims of natural disasters. They value an equality of rights and opportunities. They consider freedom—the ability to live as they like—a major advantage of the American political system. They also value responsible, autonomous individuals and democracy, because it is a form of government that respects individual dignity.

Not surprisingly, in culturally diverse American society, Williams discovered conflicts between values. For example, the emphasis placed on nationalism, patriotism, and conformity may at times conflict with individual freedom. Traditionally, some Americans have

Popular film comedian Charles Chaplin was one of many film stars who appealed to the patriotic values of Americans to encourage them to purchase Liberty Bonds during World War I. *(National Archives)*

made racial or group membership the basis of worth or privilege. Placing such a value on group membership conflicts with the values of individual worth and equality.

In such cases, whereas some members of society are confused about which value to uphold, many others are not. A systematic denial of equal rights and opportunities to African Americans led to the civil rights campaign of the 1960's. As a result, the U.S. Congress passed laws against segregation and discrimination. Subsequently, equality has become more important than racial membership. In 1944, 55 percent of American whites opposed equal employment opportunities for African Americans. In 1972, however, only 3 percent of whites opposed this kind of equality.

Applications

In *New Rules: Searching for Self-Fulfillment in a World Turned Upside Down* (1981), survey researcher Daniel Yankelovich claims that the twentieth century has seen a variety of shifts in American values. For example, the importance of marriage for women has decreased. In 1957, 80 percent of those surveyed regarded women who did not marry as "sick," "neurotic," or "immoral." In 1978, however, only 25 percent held this view.

The value of traditional gender roles has also shifted. In 1938, 75 percent disapproved of a married woman who worked outside of the home if her husband could support her. By 1978, however, only 26 percent disapproved. The percentage of those believing that child care duties should be shared by both parents increased from 33 percent in 1970 to 56 percent in 1980. Those willing to vote for a woman for president increased from 31 percent in 1937 to 77 percent in 1980. In addition, there have been important shifts in attitudes toward work. In 1970, 34 percent of those surveyed regarded work as the center of their lives. This figure decreased to 13 percent in 1978. Those agreeing that "hard work always pays off" decreased from 58 percent in 1969 to 43 percent in 1976.

Attitudes have also shifted regarding the relative importance of being financially well-off and having a meaningful philosophy of living. In 1988, nearly 75 percent of the college freshmen surveyed regarded financial well-being as very important, up from 44 percent in 1967. Only 50 percent of the 1988 freshmen, however, made "developing a meaningful philosophy of living" a major goal, down from 83 percent of the 1967 freshmen.

In some countries, shifts in values have been caused by political propaganda or the use of force. In *Pyramids of Sacrifice* (1976), sociologist Peter Berger details the techniques used by the communist Chinese regime to undermine traditional Chinese peasant values, such as family, ancestor worship, and private land ownership. The government sent out teams of government officials whose goal was to persuade the peasants of the wisdom of government policies. The first teams executed those they considered "antirevolutionary." That made open disagreement with the teams less likely in the future. The teams preached the primacy of obedience to the party. Lyrics of propaganda songs extolled Chairman Mao as dearer to the people than their own families. Ancestor worship was declared an opiate of the masses, and private land ownership was decried as a potential source of capitalism. Open disagreement with the teams could result in execution, prison, the loss of privileges, or reeducation through manual labor. These policies, which were consistently applied, led to extremely uniform expressions of support for government policies and the values they embodied.

When the values of two different cultures come into conflict, one culture may try to impose its ways on the other. For example, British missionaries in Kenya pressured the Gikuyu tribe to abolish its practice of female circumcision, calling the custom barbarous. The missionaries and the European politicians who supported their cause were charged with ethnocentrism, which is a tendency to judge other cultures in terms of one's own culture and to assume that the ways of one's own culture are best. Besides leading to attempts to force others to be like oneself, this bias in favor of one's own culture can undermine attempts to study other societies objectively.

Hence, sociologists advocate cultural relativism regarding the study of other societies. According to this idea, other cultures should be judged on their own terms. Their practices that conflict with the practices of one's own culture are not necessarily wrong. These practices cannot be properly understood or evaluated without reference to their cultural context.

In *Facing Mount Kenya* (1965), Jomo Kenyatta explains female circumcision in the context of Gikuyu culture. Uncircumcised females are ineligible for full membership in the tribe. The Gikuyu regard clitoridectomy as a culminating part of the rite of passage from girlhood to womanhood. The circumcision ceremony creates a unity between the girl and her community, both living and dead. In fact, the ceremony symbolizes this unity. It also signifies that the girl has gone through an initiation that teaches her the social and moral customs of the tribe. It has taught her to face pain and to bear it with dignity. Gikuyu who continued this custom in the face of British opposition valued loyalty to tribal traditions over avoidance of pain and conformity to British demands. A cultural relativist approach to clitoridectomy demystifies this custom by focusing on the role it plays in Gikuyu culture and not on whether it is morally right.

Some sociologists have taken variations in cultural practices as a basis for drawing conclusions about the ontological status of values. In *Folkways* (1960), sociologist William Graham Sumner notes that a custom might be regarded as good in one society and bad in another. On this basis, he concludes that good and bad are solely matters of societal opinion. In *The Elements of Moral Philosophy* (1986), philosopher James Rachels criticizes this reasoning. He states that different tribes might have different beliefs about the shape of the earth, but points out that this does not mean that the shape of the earth is solely a matter of societal opinion.

One may say that values, unlike shapes, are subjective, but this should not merely be assumed. It may be difficult to determine what is actually desirable, but that does not mean that being desirable is nothing more than being thought desirable. Another problem with the conclusion drawn by Sumner is that if being desirable amounts to being thought desirable, societies cannot make mistakes about what is desirable. Yet such mistakes do seem possible. For example, a society might value aggressiveness as a means to happiness, yet aggressiveness may not bring happiness. It seems that societies do make moral mistakes, and this much is presupposed by the ideas of moral reform and moral progress. In studying other cultures, it seems justifiable to suspend judgment about whether their practices are good or bad, but it does not seem justifiable to claim that good and bad are solely matters of societal opinion.

Context

For most of the first half of the twentieth century, sociologists tended not to study values. Believing that social scientists, like natural scientists, should concern themselves with empirically observable matters, sociologists noted that desirability was not an empirically observable quality. Thus, they regarded values as unsuitable for scientific study.

By mid-century, however, sociologists had begun studying values. They focused their attention not on whether a particular thing was really desirable but on whether people *regarded* it as desirable. This much was empirically detectable. After determining what a group believed to be valuable, sociologists could consider how these beliefs functioned in the group's social system. Sociologists described and explained cultural values, in many cases tracing them to an ideological source. Then they used the beliefs to predict and explain social behavior. Generally, such studies were descriptive and explanatory, without being evaluative.

Accepting the scientific legitimacy of such studies, many sociologists still maintained that for sociology to be a social science, it must be value free. They took value freedom to be an essential part of the scientific attitude. Yet what does it mean to say that "sociology must be value free"?

If it means "sociologists *as* sociologists must not make value judgments," it seems false because methods of sociology such as cost-benefit analysis and risk-benefit analysis involve ranking or valuing of alternatives. Sociologists may use these methods when they work as policy analysts for the government. They also make value judgments when they choose their research projects. If "sociology must be value free" means instead "the results of sociological research must not be determined by personal preferences," it also seems false because the results of sociological research are determined by a personal preference for science over superstition, knowledge over ignorance, and rationality over intuition. Finally, if value freedom in sociology means that "for social research to be scientific, its results must not be caused by researchers' believing just what they want to believe," it is plausible because scientific thinking is not mere wishful thinking. In science, theories are tested by evidence, not by hopes.

Though there is a sense in which sociology must be value free, there are other ways that values are involved in sociology. Professional standards of conduct for sociologists are based on values. Faithful reports of one's findings are based on a concern for truth, and a respect for individual persons and their dignity is behind the concerns raised about experiments that invade privacy or betray confidentiality. The values of individual sociologists also guide them in their choice of research topics. Do they work on problems of solely theoretical interest or on problems whose solution may be of social benefit?

With the development and use of nuclear weapons, some sociologists began to believe that they should include value judgments in their sociological works. For example, in *The Causes of World War Three* (1958), sociologist C. Wright Mills charged world leaders with immorality. Other sociologists criticized Mills for preaching instead of analyzing, but he regarded it as part of his obligation to humanity to speak out against what he regarded as the moral insensibility of those in power. Many sociologists upheld ethical neutrality as a condition of social science and therefore condemned political advocacy within sociological writings.

Sociologist David Popenoe, in *Sociology* (1977), reports that more and more sociologists have become dissatisfied with this separation between politics and sociology. They reject the separation because they believe that it provides support for the political status quo. They see nothing wrong with sociological writings that make evaluative judgments of particular political ideologies. Many sociologists disagree with this approach, but as the twentieth century has progressed, increasing numbers of sociologists have written social critiques.

Bibliography

Berger, Peter L. *Pyramids of Sacrifice*. Garden City, N.Y.: Doubleday, 1976. Interesting book on political ethics of Third World development strategies.

Kenyatta, Jomo. *Facing Mount Kenya*. New York: Vintage Books, 1965. Kenyatta's classic work includes a chapter on Gikuyu initiation rites for boys and girls and European attempts to abolish this ancient practice.

Mills, C. Wright. *The Causes of World War Three*. New York: Simon & Schuster, 1958. Sociology outside the value-free tradition. Mills worried that the "crackpot realism" of the world's leaders would lead to another world war.

Popenoe, David. *Sociology*. 3d ed. Englewood Cliffs, N.J.: Prentice-Hall, 1977. Discussion of values is especially good.

Rachels, James. *The Elements of Moral Philosophy*. 3d ed. New York: McGraw-Hill, 1999. Written by a leading moral philosopher, this introductory ethics text is well written and well argued. The chapter on cultural relativism covers the strengths as well as the weaknesses of the approach.

Sumner, William Graham. *Folkways*. New York: New American Library, 1960. Originally published in 1906, this work initiated the important distinction between norms whose violation was not severely sanctioned (folkways) and norms whose violation was severely sanctioned (mores).

Williams, Robin M., Jr. *American Society: A Sociological Interpretation*. 3d ed. New York: Alfred A. Knopf, 1970. Long chapters on values in American society is a classic starting point for studies of American values.

Yankelovich, Daniel. *New Rules: Searching for Self-Fulfillment in a World Turned Upside Down*. New York: Random House, 1981. Yankelovich is a psychologist and a survey researcher. This valuable resource provides survey data on major twentieth century shifts in American values.

Gregory P. Rich

Cross-References

Cultural Norms and Sanctions; Cultural Transmission Theory of Deviance; Culture and Language; Religion: Functionalist Analyses; Subcultures and Countercultures.

WAR AND REVOLUTION

Type of sociology: Major social institutions
Field of study: Politics and the state

The study of international and internal conflict focuses on the clashes between various states, groups of states, or elements within states, which are intended to transform or preserve the international or domestic political, social, economic, and/or cultural status quo.

Principal terms

BIPOLAR INTERNATIONAL CONFIGURATION: international system in which two powers outclass all other powers in terms of strength and importance

IDEOLOGY: coherent system of values, beliefs, and concepts that attempts to explain social, economic, political, and/or cultural reality, change, and goals

MULTIPOLAR INTERNATIONAL CONFIGURATION: international system composed of three or more powers that are roughly equal in strength and importance

NATIONAL INTERESTS: general goals that states pursue over a prolonged period of time

POLITICAL OBJECTIVES: specific goals whose attainment will help secure the state's national interests

Overview

In his celebrated book *Vom Kriege* (1832-1834; *On War*, 1873), the famous nineteenth century Prussian military theoretician Carl von Clausewitz defined war as "an act of force to compel our enemy to do our will." Clausewitz emphasized that wars are not merely acts of violence that are ends in themselves but are acts of violence that are designed to attain political objectives. Clausewitz further stated that the perceived value of the objectives of a war influences the degree of resolve of the belligerents and their willingness to make sacrifices in pursuing the war. Indeed, he observed, "Once the expenditure of effort exceeds the value of the political object, the object must be renounced and peace must follow." Thus, the perceived value of the objectives of the war, ranging from the total socioeconomic and political destruction of the enemy to more limited objectives, such as border adjustments, territorial exchanges, and so forth, influences the scope, intensity and duration of the war itself. Conversely, however, the longer the duration of the war and/or the greater its intensity and scope, the stronger the tendency among the belligerents to escalate their respective objectives and the less likely it is that the dispute will be resolved by compromise.

Clausewitz goes on to delineate three broad elements of enemy strength against which military power may be focused in war: the will of the enemy, the enemy country, and the enemy armed forces. He argued that, in the context of wars for unlimited objectives, the enemy's armed forces must be completely neutralized and the enemy's territory occupied. He noted, however, that even after this goal has been accomplished, the war may continue until the will of the enemy population has been completely broken. In short, wars fought for unlimited objectives usually require total victory over the enemy.

The total wars of the nineteenth and twentieth centuries are characterized by, among other things, the complete mobilization of the socioeconomic resources of the belligerents, intense popular identification with nationalistic and/or ideological beliefs, liberalization of the rules of engagement of the respective armed forces, significant effects of hostilities on both the urban and rural elements of the belligerents' populations, and massive civilian and military casualties caused by the large-scale application of the increasingly destructive firepower of modern weaponry.

Alternatively, however, if limited objectives are sought (limited war), then something less than total victory over the enemy may suffice. In limited wars, the capture of one or a group of specific geographic locations and/or the limited battlefield defeat of the enemy's armed forces may be sufficient to induce the enemy to abandon the struggle and yield to the victor's limited demands. Moreover, limited wars are often characterized by mutual restraints by the belligerents, including the degree to which the civilian population is affected by the war, the types of weapons utilized, the geographic definition of the war zone, and the definition of military targets within the war zone.

In short, the experience of the last three and a half centuries indicates that wars vary markedly in terms of their objectives, as well as in scope, intensity, and duration. Furthermore, hostilities have extended across the spectrum of conflict, ranging from guerrilla warfare pursued by small groups of soldiers who are often indistinguishable from the larger civilian population upon which the guerrillas are dependent for support, to conventional operations involving concentrated field armies utilizing a complete array of military weapons except nuclear, lethal chemical, or biological weapons, to hostilities involving all weapons systems, including weapons of mass destruction.

Since the emergence of the modern state system with the Peace of Westphalia in 1648, the character of wars has been influenced by a series of environmental factors. First, they have been influenced by the degree to which the belligerents subscribe to a common set of values and loyalties. During periods in which the leaders of the warring states subscribe to shared concepts upon which the existing political order is founded and, further, when these common loyalties are reinforced by cultural, family, and/or class bonds that transcend national boundaries, these ruling elites generally display a willingness to pursue clearly defined, limited political objectives that are susceptible to compromise and to keep the level of violence proportionate to the objectives sought. Alternatively, when the leaders of the warring powers, joined by the people of these states, do not subscribe to common values and perspectives concerning the desired character of the international order and are not united by personal bonds, but instead are sharply divided by nationalism and/or ideology, conflicts tend to assume an unlimited character in pursuit of unlimited objectives.

Second, the configuration of the international system has influenced the character of wars during the past three and a half centuries. In fluid, multipolar configurations in which the principal states are not rigidly aligned into permanent blocs but frequently realign into various coalitions as their respective interests demand, and, further, in which neutral powers play a significant role in contests between conflicting states, wars tend to remain limited in objectives, scope, intensity, and duration. Alternatively, when the multipolar international configuration rigidly solidifies into two rival coalitions, leaving little or no room for neutrals, or when the international configuration transforms from multipolar to bipolar, then wars tend to assume an unlimited character.

Third, the physical destructiveness of weaponry influences the character of warfare. In one respect, in situations in which the sheer destructiveness of the weapons quickly results in high casualties and enormous physical destruction to the respective belligerent societies, it often becomes very difficult for political leaders to prevent the escalation of wartime objectives, as well as the scope and intensity of the war itself. In this sense, military technology tends to promote war. From another perspective, however, the terrible power of the weapons of mass destruction of the mid- and late twentieth century has had a mutually stabilizing deterrent effect in those situations in which neither side has an incentive to use these weapons to obtain victory in war.

Clausewitz stressed that all types of wars are waged by the people, the government, and the armed forces, all acting in concert. The government determines the objectives of the war, the armed forces provide the means for waging the conflict, and the people provide the will to pursue the war until the political objectives are attained. Each element is indispensable to the success of the war effort.

Many of these observations concerning international conflict also apply to internal conflicts involving indigenous groups of individuals within a particular state. In these internal conflicts, those in rebellion seek to displace the authorities presently in control of the central government or to dismember the state by establishing independent, or at least autonomous, control over a portion of the country. In some cases, these internal conflicts merely involve elite factionalism in which the mass of the population is only marginally involved and do not result in any fundamental socioeconomic, political, or cultural change. Alternatively, other internal conflicts involve large-scale popular support and seek to transform radically the existing political, economic, social, and/or cultural character of the state and society by displacing the entire ruling elite and the established political order with another order controlled by and embracing the values and goals of the revolutionaries. In either case, the internal conflict may range across the conflict spectrum and involve the whole of the country or may be concentrated within a particular portion of the country, leaving the remainder of the country comparatively untouched by the hostilities.

Applications

Between 1648 and the French Revolution of 1789, the international system was configured along relatively fluid, multipolar lines. In addition, the states were governed by elites who subscribed to common values and were united by common sociocultural bonds. Moreover, military technology was comparatively primitive during this preindustrial period. Hence, warfare was limited in terms of the objectives sought by the belligerents, as well as in terms of the scope, intensity, and duration of the conflicts. Typically, these wars involved disputes over issues that normal diplomatic interaction had failed to resolve, such as territorial or colonial conflicts, dynastic succession, trade patterns, and so forth. The conflicts themselves were limited in that they were often characterized by comparatively bloodless maneuvers designed to compel the enemy to surrender, as opposed to battles yielding high casualties for both belligerents. Moreover, the wars were conducted in such a way as to minimize their impact on the civilian urban and rural populations.

The French Revolution at the end of the eighteenth century represented a major turning point in the evolution of both social change and warfare. As Crane Brinton pointed out in his important study *The Anatomy of Revolution* (1938), the French Revolution bore a number of similarities to the English Revolution during the seventeenth century, the American Revolution of the 1770's and 1780's, and the Russian Revolution, which began in 1917. In these cases, prior to the actual outbreak of the revolution, each society had experienced significant economic growth. The impetus to revolt came not from society's downtrodden members but from those individuals who had prospered from that growth but had recently come to believe that they were restricted from acquiring additional socioeconomic and political benefits. Moreover, each society exhibited significant class antagonisms, with intellectuals transferring their allegiance to the forces of the revolution. All four governmental systems had failed to meet new challenges effectively, and the old ruling elite had lost confidence in its legitimacy and capacity to govern. In each case, a particular event

The storming of the notorious Bastille prison in 1789 was a defining moment in the French Revolution. (*Library of Congress*)

or sequence of events triggered the actual revolution. In three of the four examples, financial pressures were central and, in the context of the crisis, the discontented organized and made revolutionary demands upon the ruling elite. Although the elite rejected these demands and attempted to use force to crush the rebellion, the instruments of coercion were applied ineptly and, indeed, elements of the military began to side with the revolutionaries. In the end, in each of the four revolutions, the revolutionaries took power. Immediately following the takeovers, however, in the cases of France, England, and Russia, the relative cohesion that had characterized the revolutionaries prior to the seizure of power broke down and extreme elements displaced the moderates. Eventually, the movement toward extremism culminated in France and Russia in reigns of terror. In the end, however, the moderates reemerged as the cycle of revolution came full circle. In short, for Brinton and other analysts, the French Revolution has served as a basis for comparison in studying revolutions.

The French Revolution was not significant only in the history of sociopolitical change; in fact, the revolution and the subsequent Napoleonic era fundamentally transformed the character of the international system and, largely as a result of that transformation, fundamentally altered the character of warfare. The overthrow of the French monarchy destroyed the common bonds and consensus concerning basic values that had united the ruling elites of the international system since 1648. Instead, the French revolutionary leaders, backed by the mass of the French people, were inspired by both nationalism and ideology to spread the revolution throughout Europe under French leadership. Consequently, the relatively fluid multipolar system of the previous period reconfigured into two confronting coalitions, one led by France and the other composed of France's enemies. As a result, the wars between these coalitions assumed an unlimited character that was much different from those of the wars of the preceding period. French society was fully mobilized, first in defense of the French Revolution and, subsequently, under Napoleon, to spread French hegemony throughout Europe. The wars were fought by armies larger than any that had been seen in Europe for centuries, and, unlike military commanders during the previous period, Napoleon focused his campaigns on the battlefield annihilation of the enemy field forces. In the broader sense, European society suffered more during the period between 1789 and 1815 than during any comparable period of time since the Thirty Years War (1618-1648).

Following the demise of Napoleon in 1815, the victors gathered at the Congress of Vienna to restore the international system to its pre-French Revolutionary character. The French monarchy was restored to power, thereby reestablishing the basis for consensus among the ruling elites concerning the values upon which the international system rested. Moreover, at least until the outset of the twentieth century, when the multipolar system ossified into two alliance systems, rigidly reinforced by the war plans of the major powers, the multipolar system established at the Congress of Vienna remained sufficiently fluid and flexible to serve as an ameliorating influence on the character of international conflict. Another factor that contributed to limiting the character of warfare during this period was that one side was rapidly able to assert battlefield superiority over the other, thereby ameliorating pressure to escalate the war as a result of high casualties and operational stalemate. Thus, notwithstanding the gradual reemergence of the forces of ideology and nationalism, and the dramatic increase in the availability and firepower of weapons as a result of the Industrial Revolution, the wars of the ninety-nine-year period between 1815 and 1914 remained limited in objectives, scope, intensity, and duration.

Indeed, the only example of total war between 1815 and 1914 was the American Civil War (1861-1865). During the course of this secessionist conflict, both the U.S. federal government and the Confederacy fully mobilized their socioeconomic resources. Eventually, however, the Confederates abandoned the cause of national independence and availed themselves of the generous peace terms offered by the federal government when they were no longer capable of sustaining concentrated field armies; the option of continuing the conflict via guerrilla warfare was rejected as being too costly. In retrospect, however, the American Civil War, more than the limited European wars of the nineteenth century, provided a glimpse of the infinitely more destructive wars that were to take place between 1914 and 1945.

By 1914, the characteristics of the international system were very conducive to total war for unlimited objectives. Thus, although World War I was a limited conflict focusing on the Balkan power balance, the conflict quickly escalated to a system-wide war, because of the dynamics of the alliance network and the war plans of the major powers. These factors, combined with the operational stalemate that rapidly developed on the western front and exacerbated by the tremendous casualties sustained by all the belligerents as a result of advances in military technology, led to a popular nationalistic response and a resultant further escalation of the war's objectives, scope, intensity, and duration. In the end, World War I led to the collapse of the Russian, German, Austro-Hungarian, and Ottoman Empires, casualties unequaled in any war for centuries, massive societal destruction, and revolution throughout many areas of Europe. Indeed, when the war finally ended in November, 1918, Europe emerged severely crippled.

During the interwar period, the nationalism that contributed to the unlimited character of World War I was intensified and exacerbated by the influence of ideology, as the principal powers divided into democratic, fascist, and communist blocs. Indeed, many historians view World Wars I and II as one continuous conflict. World War II, a composite conflict that engulfed the entire globe, brought total war for total objectives to heretofore unimagined dimensions of human death and suffering, and caused socioeconomic devastation.

Since 1945, the international power configuration has shifted from a bipolarity in which the United States and the Soviet Union dominated the immediate postwar system to a configuration that is increasingly characterized by political, military, economic, and cultural multipolarity. The lack of consensus regarding values and perceptions that has characterized the international system throughout the entire twentieth century and that sharply divided the two superpowers immediately following World War II, however, continues and, in some respects, has been further supplemented with the rise of new nationalist/ideological movements, such as militant Islam. Yet, throughout the second half of the twentieth century, the principal military powers of the international system have refrained from actively utilizing their unprecedentedly lethal weapons of mass destruction to resolve international conflicts. This has largely been the result of the nuclear deterrent balance, which has deprived the principal military powers of any incentive to use their weapons of mass destruction for anything other than to dissuade others from attacking them or challenging their vital interests.

Although the world community has thus been spared from an infinitely more devastating repetition of World War II, which destroyed Europe and much of East Asia, there have been a number of limited wars and revolutionary struggles throughout the post-World War II period. These have ranged from internal guerrilla wars born out of revolution to conventional wars, such as the Korean War, the 1967 and 1973 Arab-Israeli Wars, the Iran-Iraq War, and the Gulf War. Some wars have involved only regional powers, while others have involved powers from outside the region. All, however, have remained geographically localized and limited in character.

Context

After the states of the international system convulsed under the horrors of the two total wars of the twentieth century and stood on the brink of nuclear annihilation throughout the post-1945 period of superpower confrontation, sociopolitical analysts attempted to place the experiences of modern war and revolution into a broader context in order to understand better both these phenomena, as well as their future impact upon humankind.

Two principal perspectives have emerged concerning this issue. The "realist school" holds that, in the same way that individuals are prone to resort to violence to resolve disputes, states also periodically resort to warfare to resolve disputes when national interests clash and other means of conflict resolution fail. Hence, the realists argue that war is both an inevitable and a permanent feature of international relations. Consequently, all states should attempt to maximize their power individually and in coalitions with other states in order to defend their interests. Peace results when the balance of military power between the states and coalitions denies the members of the international system an incentive to resort to war to satisfy their ambitions.

Alternatively, the "idealist school" holds that, unlike animals, people have the capacity to resolve disputes rationally, without resorting to violence. Indeed, the idealists maintain that all people throughout the world seek common goals, including personal security for themselves and their families, reasonable prosperity, personal freedom, and so forth. If individuals keep in mind their common aspirations, they will compromise and reach a consensus in the resolution of personal disputes, rather than inflict harm upon themselves and others. Similarly, the idealists argue that when national interests conflict, the leaders of these states must keep in mind humankind's common aspirations and rationally approach the dispute in order to resolve the conflict peacefully, without resorting to violence or the threat of violence.

According to the idealist school, wars are the products of bungling, power-seeking, and/or greedy elites who lead their countries into war to satisfy their own ambitions against the greater interests of the people of their respective societies. Hence, the idealists believe that wars are avoidable. They maintain that democratically elected governments of states that are based on the principle of national self-determination of peoples and are united by the bonds of economic interdependence are humankind's best guarantee that conflicts, when they occur, will be resolved peacefully. They assert that governments that are truly representative of the interests of the people who elected them will never needlessly inflict the suffering of war and economic deprivation upon their own and other societies. Indeed, for the idealists, war is a legitimate instrument of policy only when it is used to preserve the principles of national self-determination of people, the democratic process, and respect for human rights against an outlaw regime or coalition that threatens the security of the peace-loving members of the international community.

In short, for the realist, war is simply a normal, if regrettable, part of the functioning of the international system, whereas the idealist views war as a failure of the international system to function properly. Hence, while both schools provide approaches for preserving peace, the assumptions underpinning the two schools are very different. Similarly, sociopolitical analysts disagree concerning the inevitability of violent revolution and internal war as a method of social change in future societies. As technology provides humankind with an increasingly destructive array of weaponry with which to pursue violent social change and military hostilities internally and on an international level, these questions will inevitably become increasingly urgent.

Bibliography

Brinton, Crane. *The Anatomy of Revolution*. Rev. and exp. ed. New York: Vintage Books, 1965. Well-written landmark study, originally published in 1938, highlights similarities in the English, American, French, and Russian Revolutions.

Changyi, Feng, and David S. Goodman, eds. *North China at War: The Social Ecology of Revolution, 1937-1945*. Lanham, Md.: Rowman and Littlefield, 2000.

Clausewitz, Carl von. *On War*. Edited and translated by Michael Howard and Peter Paret. Princeton, N.J.: Princeton University Press, 1984. First published in 1832, remains the point of departure for all discussions of warfare.

Johnson, Chalmers. *Revolutionary Change*. Boston: Little, Brown, 1966. Formulates a model for the analysis of revolutions. It is particularly useful when read in conjunction with Brinton's study.

Osgood, Robert E. *Limited War*. Chicago: University of Chicago Press, 1957. Excellent study carefully examining the phenomenon of limited war.

Osgood, Robert E., and Robert W. Tucker. *Force, Order, and Justice*. Baltimore: Johns Hopkins University Press, 1967. Examines the evolution of and rationale for the use of force in the international arena.

Wright, Quincy. *A Study of War*. Chicago: University of Chicago Press, 1942. Classic, two-volume work examining the history of warfare and providing a framework for the analysis of war.

Howard M. Hensel

Cross-References

Civil Religion and Politics; Class Consciousness and Class Conflict; Conflict Theory; Political Sociology; Social Change: Sources of Change.

WORKPLACE SOCIALIZATION

Type of sociology: Socialization and social interaction
Field of study: Agents of socialization

Workplace socialization encompasses two types of socialization. First, it refers to the ways in which a particular society uses a person's job to promote its values, norms, and desired behavior. Second, it refers to the mechanisms and processes used by work organizations to promote their own values, norms, and desired behavior. Generally speaking, workplace socialization is a means of social control.

Principal terms

NORMS: standards of behavior created and observed by a society or organization
RESOCIALIZATION: process of learning the norms, values, and behaviors of a new role
ROLE: behavior associated with a social or organizational position
SOCIALIZATION: lifelong process of learning norms, values, attitudes, and behaviors appropriate to one's role in society
VALUES: beliefs shared by members of a society (or organization) of what is good, bad, desirable, undesirable, proper, or improper

Overview

Socialization is a lifelong learning process in which an individual learns the values, norms, and roles of a particular society; a society's shared values, norms, beliefs, and symbols are collectively known as its culture. Societies use various social institutions to promote culture among their members. Institutions used for these purposes are called socialization agents. The workplace is one such agent. In it, a person learns the values and behaviors desired by the employer or that are necessary to perform a job effectively. Similarly, a person's occupation is sometimes used by society to transmit its generally accepted values, norms, and roles.

Sociologist Wilmer Moore has described four phases of workplace socialization. These are career choice, anticipatory socialization, conditioning and commitment, and continuous commitment. According to Moore, occupational socialization begins when a person decides (often early in life) to pursue a particular vocation or career. After a choice is made, he asserts, the person will purposely try to obtain the necessary training and education to obtain such a job.

After getting the job, the person will adjust his or her behavior and values to the pleasant and unpleasant aspects of the job with the help of superiors, peers, informal leaders, and perhaps organizational consultants. According to Moore, later in his or her career, the median person will have achieved a high degree of job satisfaction and will have internalized the norms, values, and role content of the job and will act accordingly. In short, the person will have become successfully socialized.

This socialization process, however, may find resistance from some individuals. For example, a male police recruit at the police academy may wish to wear long hair. It is an organizational (and societal) norm, however, that police officers should conform to certain codes of dress and appearance. Therefore, peer pressure, superior's orders, application of the police manual, and dismissal threats would make the recruit quit or have his hair cut.

Another aspect of workplace socialization is the external or social aspect. A person's job is frequently used by society to "complete" or enhance a person's socialization during adulthood. For example, in contemporary society people are often socialized in their jobs to avoid drugs and alcohol, to dress appropriately, not to engage in sexual harassment or corruption, and in general to avoid antisocial behavior. Employees who fail to change their conduct could be fired or face sanctions from management. Work organizations generally promote socially accepted values that are consonant with their own.

The workplace is also a resocialization agent. Frequently, organizations have structured processes to change employees' dysfunctional values or behavior. For example, as a requisite to keep a job, a person could be resocialized to avoid laziness and become a productive employee. In the case of jobs that require interaction with the public, people could be resocialized by means of training programs to overcome rudeness or impoliteness in their relationships with peers, superiors, and customers. Organizations use a number of methods to encourage accepted behavior and to limit unacceptable behavior among their employees. Economic bonuses, vacation plans, fringe benefits, career advancement, peer pressure, and other positive reinforcements are often used to promote accepted behavior among workers. On the other hand, organizations also have instruments to avoid undesired employee behavior. Peer pressure, disciplinary sanctions, and dismissals are among the methods used to avoid undesirable employee behavior.

Frederick W. Taylor's *Principles of Scientific Management* (1911, repr. 1982) provides a good example of managerial attempts to resocialize workers. Taylor, a businessman, engineer, and writer, believed that businesses were losing considerable money and effort because the managerial methods used in those days promoted "systematic soldiering," or laziness among workers (an undesired behavior). His managerial theory and method (named "Taylorism" or scientific management) were aimed at eliminating these undesired behavioral traits. This was accomplished by studying the ways in which the best workers in each trade performed their jobs (using stopwatch studies) and by training all workers in that trade to perform their job in the same way as the "best man." Workers would obtain economic bonuses for the improvement in their performance using these new methods.

Applications

The study of workplace socialization enables social scientists and students to identify the instruments and processes used by work organizations to mold employee behavior in ways consonant with social and organizational values and norms. Similarly, it provides managers, management consultants, and industrial psychologists with theories and instruments to affect employee behavior in order to increase their productivity and reduce organizational conflict.

For example, many American companies place considerable emphasis on the physical appearance of employees at work. They have, for example, adopted dress codes and grooming codes. By establishing such codes, organizations communicate to their employees the way they should dress and "look" at work. Studies have revealed that close to 70 percent of U.S. companies have dress codes. Although such codes may appear unconstitutional, the U.S. Supreme Court has generally validated dress and grooming codes if they are in accordance with "generally accepted community standards" and are evenhandedly applied. This exemplifies the fact that occupational socialization may serve to reinforce social values.

Similarly, since the early 1980's, as a corollary to former U.S. president Ronald Reagan's "war on drugs" policy, many companies in the United States have adopted rules and processes to eliminate illegal drug use among their employees. Many companies enacted codes against drug use and adopted programs for detection of drug use among their employees. Indeed, according to the Bureau of Labor Statistics, 67 percent of large companies in the United States have put in place some kind of drug-testing policy. In addition, many of these companies have also established programs to rehabilitate employees with drug abuse problems. The dual dimension of workplace socialization can be easily understood by using these policies as an example. On one hand, companies socialize their workers to stay away from drugs because it is considered antisocial behavior. On the other hand, companies adopt such policies in order to increase productivity and reduce work-related accidents and employee absenteeism.

There are many other occupational areas in which management, management consultants, and informal groups exert their socialization efforts. For example, new employees are strictly supervised and coached until they internalize many organizational norms and rituals. For example, employees are expected to comply with strict work schedules, often having to begin their work at 8:00 A.M. and leave at 5:00 P.M. They are also expected to be productive at work. Many jobs have production and quality standards. The new employee is trained and given an adjustment period to see if he or she can meet such established standards. If this does not happen, the employee could be fired.

Workers are also socialized by informal groups. For example, if a new employee is exceeding her production quota by many units, her peers may let her know that she should slow down a little. Similarly, informal groups could teach a new employee not to "blow the whistle" on fellow workers in certain circumstances. On the other hand, informal group socialization may also make a lazy employee more productive. For example, if an employee's unproductiveness in the assembly line is making all the employees in that unit appear unproductive, the person could be rejected from social activities of the group. Hence, the employee might increase productivity in order to be accepted by the social group.

Professional groups are also agents to occupational socialization. The American Bar Association (ABA), for example, regulates lawyer socialization in the United States. First an aspiring lawyer has to have a bachelor's degree, and then he or she must continue legal studies at an institution accredited by the ABA. After graduation, the person must pass a state bar exam. Then the behavior and practice of this professional attorney will be regulated by the state and national bars' codes of ethics. Similar situations exist in the medical, nursing, and educational fields.

Another practical application of workplace socialization and resocialization occurs in the management of organizational change. Workplace resocialization is necessary for organizational changes to occur smoothly. For example, in the 1980's, secretaries who were used to using typewriters needed to be resocialized in the use of word processors and computers in order to keep pace with advancements in their profession. The need for change involving resocialization occurs in many fields and for many reasons. Technology is responsible, directly or indirectly, for much resocialization. Physicians, for example, need to be more versed in human relations than they once were because many of their patients are now generally better informed by the media and want their physicians to give them detailed explanations of treatments and alternatives.

The relative importance accorded the study of workplace socialization has markedly increased since the 1960's. The concept has been widely discussed in sociology, psychology, management, and public administration journals under such rubrics as change management and management of organizational culture. Its practical applications have also been widely explored by management. Indeed, the importance of the training department, which is in charge of formal socialization and resocialization efforts in many firms, has increased significantly.

Context

It is almost impossible to determine the historical beginnings of workplace socialization. Some may argue that this phenomenon is as old as work itself. The greatest importance of workplace socialization, however, is its application to companies employing large numbers of workers, and these began with the factories of the Industrial Revolution of the eighteenth and nineteenth centuries. Inventions such as the steam engine and the spinning jenny as well as the use of coke (a more efficient derivate from coal) as a combustible revolutionized the ways in which goods were produced. They made it possible to produce more goods more efficiently.

In the historical period previous to the Industrial Revolution, goods were generally produced in a workshop by an artisan. The artisan, usually a man, was generally self-employed; he owned his own tools and determined his work schedule and tempo. Artisans were experts in a particular craft or trade (for example, shoemaking) and made their goods from the beginning to the end, keeping a close eye on their quality. The guild (an early version of today's unions) determined the cost of goods and consequently the artisan's earnings per unit.

After the Industrial Revolution, work was organized differently. Workers were specialized in the production of only one part of the end product—an approach called the division of labor. Generally, they were not business owners and worked for a wage. Work and workers were more strictly controlled. Management determined when the job would begin and end and set the workers' wages.

The writings and managerial practices of the eighteenth century writer and businessman Robert Owen show an unusual system of workplace socialization and control. In his factories, Owen established a "silent monitor" system, consisting of a small wooden figure with different colors on different sides that hung near each employee. The color that was displayed rated the employee's performance during the previous day and was aimed at making workers adjust their performance to the desired production rate.

Another perspective on workplace socialization was presented by German sociologist and philosopher Max Weber. In his book *Wirtschaft und Gesellschaft* (1922; *The Theory of Social and Economic Organization*, 1947), he explains the legal or bureaucratic form of social domination. From his explanation of this form of domination, it could be inferred that employees in modern organizations are controlled (and socialized) in an impersonal manner through the use of abstract norms and routinized procedures.

In the early 1900's, another interesting perspective on occupational socialization and resocialization was presented by Frederick W. Taylor. As stated before, this author popularized a managerial system (scientific management) that consisted of systematically studying the way in which the "best worker" of each trade performed and then training all employees in that trade in that "one best way."

A very different approach to workplace socialization was studied in the Hawthorne studies during the 1920's and 1930's. These studies revealed, for the first time, the existence of informal groups, norms, and leadership within work organizations. Thus, a very important aspect of workplace socialization consists of the values, norms, and behaviors transmitted and learned through informal groups.

Bibliography

Davis, Keith, and John W. Newstrom. *Human Behavior at Work: Organizational Behavior*. 7th ed. New York: McGraw-Hill, 1985. Presents valuable information related to the topic of workplace socialization. Of special interest are chapters on leadership and supervision, performance rewards systems, and the individual and the organization.

Hersey, Paul, and Kenneth Blanchard. *Management of Organization Behavior*. 5th ed. Englewood Cliffs, N.J.: Prentice-Hall, 1988. Although directed toward a managerial audience, provides students of the social sciences with a solid understanding of the theories and principles underlying workplace socialization. Topics such as the role of leadership and the management of change are of special interest.

Merton, Robert K. *Social Theory and Social Structure*. Rev. ed. New York: Free Press, 1968. Written by a famous sociologist, this book is important for the understanding of workplace socialization. Well written and extensive.

Roucek, Joseph S., ed. *Social Control*. 2d ed. Westport, Conn.: Greenwood Press, 1970. Collection of classic essays by Roucek and others on social control. Provides wide frame of reference to understand the phenomenon of workplace socialization: social control theory.

Schaefer, Richard T. *Sociology*. 6th ed. New York: McGraw-Hill, 1998. Introductory sociology textbook presenting well-documented chapter on socialization. Among the few sociology textbooks to discuss workplace socialization. Many graphs, photographs, and charts.

Schein, Edgar. *Organizational Culture and Leadership*. San Francisco: Jossey-Bass, 1985.

Explains process of the formation of the norms and values inherent to every organization. In addition, the process of diffusion of this "organizational culture" are fully explored. Finally, the process of cultural change in organizations is explored.

Taylor, Frederick W., and Frank B. Gilbreth. *Principles of Scientific Management*. 2d ed. Easton, Pa.: Hive, 1982. Originally published in 1911, provides good theoretical and philosophical explanation of Taylor's concept of scientific management. Highly recommended for those interested in workplace socialization.

Weber, Max. *The Theory of Social and Economic Organization*. Edited and introduced by Talcott Parsons. Translated by A. M. Henderson and Talcott Parsons. New York: Oxford University Press, 1947. Translation of the original 1922 German version. Emphasizes study of social domination. The influences of abstract norms in the process of molding human behavior in society and organizations arise from his explanation of the legal or bureaucratic form of social domination.

Hernán Vera Rodríguez

Cross-References

Industrial Sociology; Social Groups; Socialization: Religion; Socialization: The Family; Socialization: The Mass Media.

GLOSSARY

Acculturation: Process by which culturally distinct groups understand, adapt to, and influence one another.

Achieved status: Assignment of individuals to positions in society based upon their achievements, such as education or the attainment of some skill.

Acquaintance rape: Rape committed by someone who is known to the rape victim.

Affirmative action: Policy designed to redress past discrimination against minority groups by targeting them for recruitment into jobs and educational institutions.

Age cohort: Category of people born at about the same time who enter various stages of the life cycle together and experience historical events at the same approximate ages.

Ageism: Any ideology that justifies and rationalizes discrimination on the basis of age.

Alienation: Individual's feelings of estrangement from a situation, group, or culture.

Androgyny: Possession of both masculine and feminine social, emotional, or behavioral traits.

Anglo-conformity: Cultural mold that people of English ancestry established in the United States into which others had to fit.

Anomic suicide: Suicide attributed to a breakdown in social regulation or a loss of a sense of belonging.

Anomie: Social condition characterized by the breakdown of norms and values governing social interaction.

Apartheid: Type of segregation that developed in South Africa; separateness was the principle guiding contacts between whites, blacks, and "Coloureds."

Ascribed status: Assignment of individuals to positions in society based on intrinsic characteristics, such as birth order, kin network, sex, or race.

Ashkenazi: Diaspora Jews who migrated to the Franco-German area of Europe during the medieval period.

Assimilation: Process by which individuals take on the language, behavior, and values of another culture, as well as the process by which outsiders are incorporated into a society.

Attitude: Evaluation or opinion, regarding a person or thing, that affects one's thoughts, feelings, and behaviors.

Authoritarian personality: Syndrome of personality characteristics that predispose a person to hold extreme views and to act on them.

Authoritarianism: Form of rule in which one person or a small group of people has a monopoly of political power.

Authority: Power accepted as legitimate by the people over whom it is exercised.

Baby boom: Unusually large cohort of individuals who were born between 1945 and 1962.

Bargaining unit: Clearly defined group of employees whose shared common interests warrant their negotiation of labor-related issues as a group.

Behavior: How individuals overtly act in the presence of others; actions that are observable and measurable, including verbal expression.

Bias: Deviation of the expected value of a statistical estimate from the true value for some measured quantity.

Bilingualism: Fluency in two languages.

Biological determinism: Belief that most human behavior is a result of genetic "programming" rather than learning.

Bisexuality: Type of sexual orientation in which the sexual behaviors and feelings of a male or female are directed toward both males and females.

Bourgeoisie: Class of capitalists who own the means of production and distribution and who hire workers for wages or a salary.

Bureaucracy: Formal organization that emphasizes the rational and efficient pursuit of goals through a highly structured and hierarchical network of statuses and roles.

Capital: Money or wealth, including land, factories, and machinery, that has been invested in means of production.

Capitalism: Economic system based on private ownership of property and the means of production; the guiding principle is maximization of profit.

Carrying capacity: Population density of a given species that can be sustained indefinitely in an ecosystem.

Case study: Detailed study of a particular individual, group, organization, or situation; a combination of research techniques may be used to describe the "case."

Caste system: Hierarchical social arrangement in which people are assigned the same status as their parents and have no possibility of changing status through personal achievement.

Censorship: Procedure of suppressing or changing material or expression that the government or another group finds objectionable.

Chattel: Slave; the term emphasized the fact that the slave was property that could be used, moved, or sold at will by an owner.

Child abuse: Psychological, physical, or sexual maltreatment of a person under the age of eighteen in which that individual's welfare, health, or safety is endangered.

Child neglect: Failure on the part of adult caregivers to provide a child with adequate supervision, nourishment, shelter, education, medical treatment, or emotional and intellectual stimulation.

Citizenship: Membership accorded to individuals within a particular nation-state that guarantees certain rights and requires certain responsibilities.

City: Relatively large, densely populated, and diverse human settlement.

Civil rights: Legal rights that have been accorded to all citizens within a political state.

Class: Group of people of similar social rank; largely defined in economic terms, but also often considering such factors as political power and lifestyle.

Class consciousness: Awareness of belonging to a definite socioeconomic class and a conscious sharing of the political interests of that class.

Class struggle: Pervasive range of social conflict that emerges from the antagonistic relationship between social classes that exploit and the classes that are exploited.

Closed shop: Form of labor organization, which the Taft-Hartley Labor Relations Act of

1947 made illegal, that required employees of unionized firms to be union members before they were hired.

Coalition: Alliance among interest groups; may include committees or institutions of the government.

Cognition: Mental activities involved in the acquisition and retention of knowledge, such as thinking, remembering, understanding, perceiving, and learning.

Cognitive dissonance: Theory that individuals try to achieve internal harmony, such as consistency between attitudes and behavior.

Cohort: Group of people who simultaneously share some common social events, with year of birth being one possible social characteristic.

Collective bargaining: Process of a company and a union jointly negotiating wages or salaries, hours, and conditions of employment.

Collective behavior: Activity engaged in by a number of people who are oriented toward the same goal.

Colonialism: Geopolitical phenomenon in which one nation's state power is imposed upon foreign territories, typically for the political, economic, and/or military benefits of the colonizer.

Coloureds: Under South Africa's former apartheid system, the designation for South Africans of racially mixed backgrounds.

Coming out: Psychological process of acquiring and acknowledging a gay or lesbian identity—first to oneself, then to friends, family, and others.

Communicable diseases: Diseases capable of being transmitted from person to person; also known as infectious diseases.

Community: Any stable group, such as a neighborhood or professional association, sharing a geographical area, common traits, and a sense of belonging that shape it into a distinct social entity.

Comparable worth: Proposed solution to wage inequality between men and women that would require equal pay for work of equal value regardless of a job's title or classification.

Compensatory education: Educational programs and experiences designed to help overcome the economic disadvantages and the cultural dissimilarities students may bring to school.

Compositional theory: Theory that urbanites experience as many warm and direct interactions with family, friends, and neighbors as do people in small towns and rural environments.

Compulsory education: School attendance required by law for youths between certain specified ages.

Concentric zone theory: Theory that urban expansion takes the form of concentric circles, in each of which land use is devoted to specific types of activity.

Concept: Abstract idea that mentally categorizes a recurring aspect of concrete reality by identifying its key components and thereby defining it.

Conflict perspective: Theory that views conflict as being a ubiquitous force in shaping arrangements between social classes and competing groups in society.

Conformity: Behavior by members of a society or group that is compatible with the norms and values of that society or group.

Consanguine: Related by blood; having the same ancestry.

Conscientious objector: Status held by a person who, by virtue of his or her objection to war because of religious, moral, or political reasons, does not serve in the armed forces but instead performs alternative government service, serves time in jail, or becomes a fugitive.

Consensus: Unanimous or almost unanimous agreement, usually achieved through persuasion.

Content analysis: Unobtrusive research in which human communications, such as written materials, are used as data.

Content validity: Type of experimental validity determined by whether an experiment actually measures a property that it is intending to measure.

Control variable: Any variable other than the independent variable or the dependent variable that is controlled by the researcher to prevent it from becoming a confound.

Convergence: Process in which the structures of different industrial societies increasingly resemble one another.

Core: In world-system theory, Western European countries, the United States, and Japan, which have specialized in banking, finance, and highly skilled industrial production.

Corporate crime: Type of white-collar crime committed by a group of individuals or a corporation for corporate gain.

Corporation: "Juristic person," founded on the legal basis of limited liability; since the middle of the nineteenth century, the corporation has evolved into the dominant form of business within capitalist societies.

Correlation: Statistical concept that measures how frequently two events co-occur, thereby suggesting either a relationship or a lack of relationship between the events.

Counterculture: Group that is consciously in opposition to the norms and values of the dominant culture.

Credentialism: Tendency in modern societies to require particular academic credentials for entry into certain occupations even though the educational qualifications may have very little to do with the skills actually used in the job.

Crime: Behavior that violates laws prohibiting such behavior and may be punished; often poses a threat to personal well-being and safety.

Crime rate: Comparative tool for reporting crime; it allows population differences and different times to be compared when crime is measured.

Criminalization: Process of converting specific behaviors into criminal behaviors through the passing of criminal laws.

Criminology: Branch of sociology that scientifically studies the various aspects of crime.

Critical theory: School of thought developed in Frankfurt, Germany, during the 1920's that employed the early humanistic ideas of Karl Marx to criticize positivism and scientific Marxism.

Crowd: Temporary group of individuals who come together for some particular activity, such as Christmas shopping, a sporting event, a film, or a rock concert.

Cultural lag: Term coined by William Ogburn to describe the situation that occurs when a technological invention, device, or process is developed but the social setting cannot keep pace with changes and thus lags behind.

Cultural pluralism: System in which different ethnic and racial groups can coexist without losing their respective cultural traits.

Cultural relativism: View that a culture is to be judged by its own standards.

Culture: Beliefs, values, behavior, and material objects shared by a particular people.

Culture of poverty concept: Ideology that maintains that poverty is caused by the defective values and attitudes of those who are poor.

Data: Information collected or observed that is relevant to the research question under study.

Day care: Any type of arrangement that is used to provide care, supervision, or education for children under age six when parents are at work.

De facto segregation: Racial and other forms of social separation that result from informal social mechanisms of discrimination.

De jure segregation: Racial and other forms of social separation that are produced by formal, legal mechanisms.

Decriminalization: Changing the law to legalize something that was formerly illegal.

Deduction: Process of arriving at a specific conclusion or prediction by applying a premise (a general law, hypothesis, or assumption) to a particular case.

Definition of the situation: Individuals' definition of a social interaction by means of explicit or implicit agreement.

Deindustrialization: Closing of industrial facilities in one country or region as a result of the movement of capital to other countries or regions, or to nonindustrial investments.

Delinquency: Behaviors for which a juvenile can be formally sanctioned; collectively, these behaviors include status offenses and those behaviors prohibited under criminal law.

Democracy: Form of government based on the freely given consent of its members; it is characterized by majority rule, protection of the rights of all of its members, and effective control over the exercise of power.

Democratization: Process of moving from an authoritarian to a democratic system.

Demographics: Information that describes certain characteristics of research subjects; for example, age, gender, marital status, and education level.

Demography: Scientific study of human populations, with an emphasis on the age, sex, racial/ethnic, and socioeconomic structure of society and how the structure changes.

Denomination: Religious group that is often considered a subgroup of a particular religion; Anglicans, Baptists, and Catholics may be considered Christian denominations.

Dependency theory: Theory in which underdeveloped regions are considered "internal colonies" that are dependent on, or controlled by, modern industrial states.

Dependent variable: Observed, consequent, or outcome variable; this variable is the one on which the effects of the independent variable are observed.

Descriptive statistics: Branch of statistics that involves the use of numerical indices to summarize basic characteristics of a distribution of scores, without any attempt to attribute causation or to infer other amounts of data.

Desegregation: Elimination of laws or statutes restricting the rights of specific groups to housing and public facilities, especially schools.

Deterrence: Purpose of punishment according to which an offender is punished as an example to discourage other people from committing similar crimes or to discourage the offender from continuing to commit crimes.

Deviance: Action or behavior that is inconsistent with what a particular society defines as normal and acceptable.

Dialectical materialism: Marxian theory of change that regards knowledge and ideas as reflections of a society's material condition.

Dictatorship: Another term for authoritarianism, or a form of authoritarian government in which power is concentrated in the hands of a single person or a small group of rulers.

Differential association theory: View that criminal behavior is learned through social contacts.

Diffusion: Geographic spread of ideas, technologies, or products.

Discrimination: Denial of opportunities and rights to certain groups on the basis of some identifiable characteristic, such as race and ethnicity.

Displacement: Loss of employment caused by the disappearance of specific types of jobs; also, the phenomenon in which people are forced to move from their homes by urban renewal, gentrification, highway construction, and the like.

Distributive justice: Justice in the distribution of the "good things" in life, the most critical of which are class, status, and power.

Division of labor: Manner in which work is allocated in society, with increasing specialization of different tasks/occupations leading to a more complex division of labor.

Domestic abuse and violence: Mistreatment, injurious actions, or the abuse of power occurring in the home.

Dominant group: Group that exercises control over societal resources.

Dual labor market: Idea that the labor market is divided into two sectors, one characterized by higher-paying, more stable, and prestigious jobs, the other by less desirable, dead-end jobs.

Dysfunction: Negative consequence that may lead to disruption or breakdown of the social system.

Dysfunctional families: Families that fail to perform important social or psychological functions such as the nurturance and socialization of children.

Ecological fallacy: Error in logic that occurs when a researcher tries to apply a conclusion drawn from one level of analysis (such as social systems) to another level (such as individuals).

Ecology: Relationship between populations and their physical environments.

Economies of scale: Savings in production or marketing costs that are better exploited by large operations than by small ones, up to some ceiling, above which there are no more gains.

Education: Transmission of knowledge by either formal or informal means.

Egalitarianism: System emphasizing equal political, social, and economic rights for all persons.

Egoistic suicide: Suicide related to the victim's inability to become integrated into society.

Element: Basic unit of a population, such as an individual, household, segment, or social organization, for which information is sought.

Elites: Those groups in society that manage to control the largest amount of social or economic resources and obtain a privileged position in relation to other groups.

Emergent norms: Normative guidelines that direct and control the course of action during mob-induced riots, panics, or similar occurrences and that replace the norms and laws of the governing social order.

Emigration: Leaving one's native country in order to move to a new country.

Eminent domain: Right of the government to take private land for public use as long as the owners are compensated.

Empirical: Based on direct observation and measurement using the physical senses.

Endogamy: Practice or custom of marrying within a particular group to which one belongs.

Entitlement programs: Government payments or services to which individuals who meet certain criteria are "entitled."

Entrepreneur: Investor who undertakes a business venture.

Equal opportunity: Situation in which all members of society have an equal chance of achieving power, social status, and economic resources.

Equal Rights Amendment (ERA): Proposed as the twenty-seventh amendment to the U.S. Constitution, it stated that "equality of rights under the law shall not be denied or abridged by the United States or by any state on account of sex."

Error: With respect to assessment, reliability, and validity, error refers to variation in scores generated by the measurement device when measuring the same thing more than once.

Ethics: Rules and guidelines that regulate the research and work of professionals; ethics in the social sciences are primarily concerned with protecting the rights of the human subjects being studied.

Ethnic group: Group classified according to a perceived common ancestry or common cultural characteristics, such as language, religion, food habits, and folklore, and seen by themselves and others as distinctive.

Ethnic stratification: Structured social inequality on the basis of ethnicity.

Ethnocentrism: Tendency to judge other people's behavior and values on the basis of one's own culture, which is usually considered superior.

Ethnography: Detailed study of a particular society and its culture.

Eugenics: Study of genetics and selective breeding to alter and improve the composition of the human gene pool.

Evolution: Change through a sequence of stages.

Exogamy: Practice of marrying outside a particular group to which one belongs.

Exploitation: Unequal social relationship in which a dominant individual or group acquires a valued commodity from a subordinate individual or group.

Extended family: Household consisting of spouses, their children, and other relatives.

External validity: Quality that enables the generalizing of results from a limited sample of subjects to a larger population.

Extramarital sex: Sexual relations between a married person and someone other than his or her spouse.

Fad: Frivolous trait or activity that temporarily becomes popular within a peer group, only to disappear just as quickly.

False consciousness: Marxist term referring to beliefs held by the working class that run counter to, or do not further, their best interests.

Family: People related to one another on the basis of blood, marriage, or adoption and who constitute a social system.

Female-headed families: Single-parent families headed by women.

Feminism: Movement promoting social, political, and economic equality of men and women.

Feminization of poverty: Trend under which an increasing percentage of the poor are women, many of whom are supporting children.

Field notes: Written account of the social behavior observed by a field researcher while studying a culture.

Field research: Research in which an observer goes to a culture and either records observations of that culture or participates to some extent in the culture and makes observations based on that participation.

Formal organization: Large collection of people whose activities are specifically designed for the attainment of explicitly stated goals.

Functionalism: Theoretical perspective that proposes that society is composed of various social institutions that work together to maintain a stable social environment.

Functionalist perspective: Theory that focuses on the way the various parts of society work together to maintain stability and order in the social system as a whole.

Gemeinschaft society: Any society characterized by the predominance of face-to-face personal relationships—usually a reference to rural or small-town society.

Gender: Term that refers to the culturally defined (rather than biologically defined) attributes of each sex or to the meanings people give to the biological differences.

Gender roles: Specific patterns of behavior and expectations for each gender; learned through the socialization process.

Gender socialization: Differential child-rearing and other practices based on gender.

Gender stratification: System in which groups are ranked hierarchically by gender.

Generalized other: Stage in a child's development where he or she takes the role of numerous others in society in general.

Gentrification: Movement of affluent people into poor urban neighborhoods that they hope to upgrade, though in the process they often displace poorer residents.

Gerontology: Study of the biological, psychological, and sociological implications of aging.

Gesellschaft society: Any society characterized by limited, impersonal, and instrumentalist relationships among its people.

Ghetto: Urban ethnic enclave, originally designating Jewish quarters in European cities.

Glass ceiling: "Invisible" obstacles and impediments confronting minorities when they try to reach higher-level, high-paying jobs; the term has most frequently been used to describe discrimination against women.

Global village: Concept of the interconnectedness of human societies, under which social and environmental policies of one community may have far-reaching effects on distant communities.

Grounded theory: Theory that is generated and modified during field research; different from a conventional theory in that theory and data-gathering perpetually interact.

Group: Small number of people who interact over time and establish patterns of interaction and identity and norms governing behavior.

Hate crimes: Crimes of violence toward or degradation of others prompted by extreme prejudice against them, for reasons such as their race, gender, sexual orientation, or religion.

Hegemony: Preponderance of influence and power, especially when wielded by one state or country over others.

Heterosexuality: Type of sexual orientation in which an individual's sexual behavior and feelings are directed toward a person of the opposite sex.

Hidden curriculum: Set of unwritten rules of behavior taught in school to prepare children for academic success and for social relations outside school.

Hierarchy: Organizational system of graded positions, from high to low, that considers such factors as authority, prestige, and income.

High culture: Form of leisure pursuit often chosen by cultural elites.

Historical/comparative method: Unobtrusive research in which historical records and published materials are used as data; typically, more than one data source are analyzed.

Homeless: Those persons who lack the necessary resources and community ties to provide for their own shelter.

Homogamy: Tendency of individuals to marry people with similar social backgrounds.

Homophile: Literally "love of same," this term was employed by homosexual activists in the 1950's as a more positive one than "homosexual," which referred to sex acts.

Homophobia: Irrational fear of or aversion to people with a same-sex sexual orientation.

Homosexuality: Type of sexual orientation in which the sexual behavior and feelings of a male (gay) or female (lesbian) are directed toward a person of the same sex.

Horizontal social mobility: Movement across social ranks of approximately the same status.

Human capital: Talents, skills, and knowledge that may enhance a worker's value in the labor market.

Hypothesis: Statement predicting a relationship between variables; it is a theoretical statement that has been operationalized.

Ideal type: Logical, exaggerated model used as a methodological tool for the study of specific phenomena.

Ideology: System of beliefs used to justify an existing social arrangement.

Immigration: Movement of individuals from one country to another, with permanent resettlement usually in mind.

In-group: Group to which an individual belongs and feels loyalty.

Indentured servant: Immigrant who contracts to work for a certain period of time in exchange for passage.

Independent variable (IV): Variable that is manipulated in an experiment because it is thought to cause change in another (dependent) variable.

Induction: Process of arriving at a general law, premise, or hypothesis by discovering some similarity across a set of related facts.

Inequality: Disparity in status and opportunity among people and groups within a society.

Infant mortality rate: Rate of death among infants under one year of age.

Inference: Process of making an educated guess about something using either induction or deduction; alternatively, the outcome or conclusion resulting from that process.

Inferential statistics: Techniques used to make estimates about a population based on data collected regarding a sample (a part) of the population.

Informal organizations: Unofficial relations and practices found in all bureaucracies of formal organizations.

Informed consent: Subject's consent to participate in research, based on appropriate knowledge of that research.

Institutional discrimination: See *Institutional racism.*

Institutional racism: Way society's institutions operate so as systematically to favor some groups over others with regard to opportunities and resources; often such racism is unintentional, but the discrimination is nevertheless real.

Institutions: Stable social patterns and relationships that result from the values, norms, roles, and statuses that govern activities that fulfill the needs of the society; for example, economic institutions help to organize the production and distribution of goods and services.

Integration: Condition that exists when all people in a society live together freely, experience equality under the law, and have equal opportunities to secure society's rewards.

Intergenerational mobility: Vertical social mobility that is measured by comparing offspring with their parents; the comparison usually entails comparison of the occupational status of parents at a given age with the occupational status of their offspring at approximately the same age.

Internal colony: Community that is subjected to colonial control and is located within the national borders of the colonizer.

Interval scale: Scale of measurement in which equal differences between numbers correspond to equal differences in that which is being measured.

Intragenerational mobility: Vertical social mobility that is measured by observing the same person across time; studies usually entail comparing occupational status at an early stage with status at a later stage.

Jim Crow laws: Statutes that enforced racial segregation in the American South until the Civil Rights movement.

Juvenile delinquency: See *Delinquency.*

Kin group: Social unit in which individuals are related to one another by blood or marriage.

Labeling theory: States that once an individual's behavior has been classified, society will see and treat the individual with respect to that definition, which in turn will cause the individual to conform to the definition; for example, individuals labeled as schizophrenics will be treated by others as mentally ill and will act accordingly.

Labor market segmentation: Division of the employment field into discrete areas, each of which is open predominantly to certain workers on the basis of race, gender, or other characteristics.

Laissez-faire: Doctrine opposing government interference in industry and trade.

Latent function: Unrecognized or unintended consequence.

Laws: Norms that have been formally included in a written legal code.

Legitimation: Set of beliefs, values, and attitudes that attempt to explain and justify existing social conditions and inequalities.

Liberation theology: Theology that makes explicit connections between religious experience and struggles for social justice.

Life course: Biological progression and social sequence of expected behaviors that individuals assume from birth to childhood, middle age, old age, and death.

Looking-glass self: Sense of personal identity that is the image reflected by the "mirror" of other people; it includes both identity and self-esteem.

Low-intensity warfare: Conflicts that are limited in scope, particularly in terms of the weaponry involved; examples are terrorism, guerrilla warfare, and insurgencies.

Macro-level: Concern with large-scale patterns that characterize society as a whole.

Macrosociology: Level of sociological analysis that is concerned with large-scale social issues, institutions, and processes.

Majority group: Group in a society that is socially, economically, and politically dominant.

Manifest function: Intended or obvious consequences.

Manumission: Granting of freedom individually to slaves before formal emancipation.

Marginal man: Individual who stands between two distinct cultures or races but is not at home in either group.

Marriage: Union between two or more individuals that is usually meant to be permanent, is recognized legally or socially, and is aimed at founding a family.

Marxism: General term for the several schools of sociological thought deriving from Karl Marx, which share notions of social class and material production as pivotal social determinants.

Mass culture: Term initially used to characterize the culture of a modern mass society with its mass media; now often used to mean popular culture. See also *Popular culture.*

Master status: Status (such as father, farmer, or wife) with which an individual identifies most strongly.

Material culture: Tangible products of human society.

Matriarchy: Society ruled by or otherwise under the control of women.

Matrilineal descent: Transmission of authority, name, property, privilege, and obligations primarily through females; also called uterine descent.

Matrilocality: Often associated with primitive agricultural societies, matrilocality refers to family residence patterns revolving around matrilineal kinship groups, including women, their unmarried sons, daughters, and sons-in-law.

Mean: Measure of central tendency that is the sum of all the scores divided by the number of scores, sometimes referred to as the "average."

Measurement: Specific indicators of variables for the purpose of testing hypotheses, developing theory, and discovering the incidence of variables.

Median: Point in a distribution below which lie 50 percent of the scores and above which fall the remaining 50 percent.

Melting pot theory: Belief that individuals from various ethnic backgrounds eventually blend into one homogeneous American culture.

Meritocracy: Any society in which ability and effort are deemed more important than inherited privilege and status in the allocation of cultural, economic, political, and social position.

Micro-level: Concern with small-scale, or individual-level, patterns of social interaction within specific settings.

Microsociology: Level of sociological analysis concerned with small-scale group dynamics.

Migration: Movement from country to country or place to place.

Minority group: Any group that, on the basis of physical or cultural characteristics, receives fewer of society's rewards; a "minority" group can therefore be in the majority numerically.

Miscegenation: Racial intermarriage or cohabitation, including especially sexual intercourse and procreation between whites and either blacks or other people of color.

Misogyny: Devaluation or hatred of women.

Mode: Score in a distribution that occurs most frequently.

Mode of production: Combination of the social relations of production and its sources; capitalism is one example of a mode of production.

Modernization: Gradual change in the social, economic, and political institutions of a society as a result of increasing industrialization, urbanization, and literacy and education, as well as changes in traditional values and beliefs.

Monogamy: Marital relationship in which an individual has only one spouse at a time.

Monopoly capitalism: Type of capitalism in which major sectors of the economy are dominated by a few capitalists or by managers.

Moral entrepreneurs: Persons who attempt to define behavior as deviant; some have official power, but many do not.

Multicultural education: Educational approach that strives for inclusivity and fairness regarding the contributions of all cultures and races, and both genders, to society; it sometimes challenges the dominant culture's views.

Multinational corporation: Typically, a private corporation principally headquartered in one nation and having branch offices and significant economic activities in one or more other nations.

Nationalism: Ideological and political expression of social groupings that seek to advance the interests of their established, suppressed, or emerging nations.

Nativism: Favoring of native inhabitants over immigrants; the revival or perpetuation of indigenous culture, especially in opposition to acculturation.

Nominal scale: Measurement scale in which data are in the form of names, labels, or categories.

Nonresponse bias: Effect that may occur when a significant proportion of a research sample does not return surveys; this nonresponse results in inaccurate survey results if the nonresponders differ from those who responded.

Norm: Rule or expectation about appropriate behavior for a particular person in a particular situation.

Normal distribution: Continuous distribution of a random variable in which the mean, median, and mode are equal; sometimes called a "bell-shaped" curve.

Nuclear family: Unit consisting of a husband, a wife, and their children.

Observer biases: Beliefs or attitudes of a researcher that can alter the outcome of research by interfering with collection of accurate data or objective analysis of the data.

Occupational prestige: Shared value members of a society place on different jobs.

Occupational segregation: Separation of jobs by gender, race, or other criteria.

Occupational sex segregation: Concentration of women in particular positions in the labor force, usually low-paid, low-skilled jobs such as clerical and service work.

Oligarchy: Small group of people who control an organization or rule a society.

Oligopoly: Control over a market by only a few producers or sellers.

Open-ended questions: Questions that permit survey subjects to respond in their own words.

Open marriage: Form of consensual adultery in which both spouses openly engage in extramarital sexual experiences while putting the marriage itself first.

Operational definition: Specific description of a variable that will enable it to be measured; it outlines the precise steps or operations for other researchers to use in assessing the variable.

Oppression: Any unjust act or situation that prevents a person or group from full self-actualization or self-realization; oppression may be mental or physical.

Ordinal scale: Scale of measurement in which data are ordered by rank.

Organizations: Groups guided by specific goals, rules, and positions of leadership.

Organized crime: Collective criminal behavior that is structured in the manner of a legitimate business enterprise, commonly a partnership or a syndicate of interlocking partnerships.

Out-group: Group composed of people who are not members of one's in-group and are considered outsiders.

Outlier: Value that lies outside the normal range of responses for a particular variable.

Pandemic: Phenomenon of multinational or global proportions, such as a pandemic disease.

Paradigm: In the exemplary sense, a scientific achievement embodying experimental results and theoretical interpretations that serve as a model of how puzzles are to be solved; also the constellation of beliefs, values, methods, theories, and laws shared by members of a scientific community.

Parameter: Measure of a variable taken from a population.

Participant-observer method: Research technique first applied in anthropology but extended to sociology and political science at the University of Chicago in the 1920's whereby the student of an institution or group lives among the people being studied.

Paternalism: Practice by which governing individuals, businesses, or nations act in the manner of a father dealing with his children.

Patriarchy: Institutionalized system of male dominance that is expressed in everyday social practices and their corresponding social ideologies.

Patrilineal descent groups: Form of kinship structure in which family ties are organized with respect to males, making all children members of their father's descent group.

Patrilocality: Family residential pattern that revolves around the male who lives with his wife, his unmarried daughters, and his sons and their wives and children.

Peer group: People who are the same age and are roughly equal in authority.

Periphery: In world-system theory, the exploited former colonies of the core, which supply the core with cheap labor and raw materials.

Phenomenology: Approach that emphasizes the socially constructed nature of knowledge, especially knowledge of everyday life.

Physiognomy: Study of human facial features in the belief that personality and intelligence can be inferred from facial characteristics.

Pluralism: Theory that views power as being dispersed among competing groups in society; also, the maintenance of social equality and respect for the cultures and peoples of different ethnic groups living in the same society.

Pogrom: Systematic persecution and massacre, especially of Jews.

Political action committee (PAC): Political organization whose purpose is to further the goals of a particular special-interest group or political candidate, primarily through fund-raising.

Political economy: Framework linking material interests (economy) with the use of power (politics) to protect and enhance interests.

Political machine: Party organization made up of professional politicians whose primary goal is to win and maintain power; although political machines have existed at different levels of government, in many places, and at many times, historically the heyday of the political machine and the boss has been identified with the late nineteenth and early twentieth century U.S. city.

Polygamy: Marital relationship in which an individual has more than one spouse at a time; sometimes used to mean "polygyny," the form of polygamy in which a man has more than one wife.

Polygyny: See *Polygamy.*

Popular culture: Cultural forms enjoyed by the populace, including the leisure and recreational activities of typical segments of a society.

Population: Entire aggregate of individuals, items, scores, or observations from which random samples are drawn.

Population control: Refers to control over the size, growth, distribution, and characteristics of populations; most often used with respect to population growth.

Pornography: Written and visual materials of a sexual nature that are used for sexual arousal.

Positivism: View that sociology should model itself in method and theory after the physical sciences and that all knowledge can be hierarchically arranged.

Postindustrial society: Formerly industrial society noted for its manufactured goods that subsequently produces fewer goods than it provides services and information.

Poverty: Condition in which people find themselves lacking the means for providing basic material needs.

Poverty line: Income measure of poverty based on a federal formula that accounts for insufficiency in food, housing, clothing, medical care, and other items required to maintain a decent standard of living for families of varying sizes.

Power: Ability of a social actor (individual or group) to achieve its wishes against the opposition of other social actors.

Power elite: Term used by C. Wright Mills to identify those at the top of the power structure who formulate policy designed to perpetuate their own interests.

Praxis: Practice as distinguished from theory; in liberation theology, praxis is the practical application of church teachings and theology.

Predestination: John Calvin's Protestant doctrine that all individuals are born into (and must forever remain in) one of two groups, the Elect or the Damned.

Prejudice: Arbitrary beliefs or feelings about a certain ethnic, racial, or religious group and about the individuals belonging to that group.

Primary group: Small social group whose members interact frequently with one another on a face-to-face basis, have intimate knowledge of one another, and share emotional ties.

Primary sector: Part of the economy that offers high wages and job security, including industries that are unionized and engaged in monopoly production.

Productivity: Amount of goods produced, or services provided, in relation to the work hours used; fewer hours and more production equals higher productivity.

Profession: Vocational group whose practitioners need higher education and advanced training; a profession typically has clearly defined entrance requirements, certification of competence, and procedures for internal control.

Proletariat: Term used by Karl Marx to define workers, those who survive by selling their labor to the bourgeoisie.

Public opinion: Public's expression of its preferences on issues of public interest or policy.

Push/pull factors: Circumstances that force (push) individuals or groups out of their native country or attract (pull) them toward a particular destination.

Qualitative research: Research that relies heavily on direct observation and descriptive analysis of social interaction, principally to examine the underlying meanings and patterns of these phenomena.

Quantitative research: Numerical examination and interpretation of observations, relying heavily on statistical analysis to evaluate differences in the variability and central tendency of variables.

Race: Conventional way of referring to a population that has been socially defined as being physically different from another population; race is a social reality, but not a meaningful biological one.

Racial discrimination: Behavior, practices, or policies that result in harm, intended or not, to individuals on the basis of their race.

Racial prejudice: Dislike and fear of others based on real or perceived physical differences.

Racism: Ideology contending that actual or alleged differences among different racial groups assert the superiority of one racial group over another.

Random sampling: Method of sampling in which all items in the population have an equal probability of being selected.

Range: Highest score minus the lowest score of a distribution.

Rape: Sexual intercourse as a result of force or threats of force rather than consent; the legal definition varies from state to state.

Rational-legal authority: Legitimization of power by law, rules, and regulations rather than by tradition or personality.

Rationalization: In the Weberian sense, using formal procedures and rules (as in a bureaucracy) instead of informal, spontaneous patterns.

Recidivism: Commission of a criminal act by a person who has previously been convicted for criminal activity and served time.

Reference group: Group or category that people use to evaluate themselves and their behavior.

Reification: Process by which habitual patterns of behavior and categories of thought are apprehended by members of society as if being external to them and having a life of their own.

Relations of production: Structure of economic relations or the way in which people are related to one another in the production process.

Relative deprivation: Theoretical perspective on social movements that states that social movements occur when there is a gap between expectations and objective conditions experienced by members of society.

Relative poverty: Determinant of poverty based on the standards of living in a given society, rather than on some absolute level.

Reliability: Ability of an instrument to measure a variable or construct consistently over repeated measurements.

Religion: System of communally experienced human thoughts and beliefs about the assumed nature of reality involving some supernatural or transcendent nonhuman deity or principle.

Reproduction: Theoretical proposition that institutions within the capitalist social system reproduce class, gender, and racial inequities to benefit those in positions of power.

Research design: Plan followed by a researcher to structure data collection and analysis.

Research hypothesis: Specifically worded statement or prediction that can be verified or falsified through the collection of data; a tentative answer to a research question.

Resocialization: In the context of total institutions, the deliberate control of a social environment to alter a subject's personality radically.

Resource mobilization: Social movement theory that the success of a movement depends substantially on the ability to organize effectively to obtain necessary resources, such as money, mass media coverage, and the support of influential people and important groups or organizations.

Revolution: Transformation of political, economic, and/or social structures in which a dominant class loses power.

Riot: Relatively spontaneous form of collective behavior that is often characterized by violent and destructive attacks on people and property.

Rite: Ceremony, such as a christening, baptism, marriage, or burial, often recognizing a stage of life; a rite of passage (such as the Jewish bar mitzvah) is an initiation ceremony into adulthood.

Ritual: Prescribed formal behavior, often symbolic, fixed, and solemn, that follows a cultural tradition.

Role ambiguity: Unclear expectations concerning the normative performance of a social role.

Role conflict: Condition that occurs when two or more of a person's roles contain incompatible expectations.

Role strain: Condition that occurs when the expectations found within a single role are incompatible.

Role-taking: Seeing the world from the perspective of other individuals and groups, and directing one's own actions accordingly.

Roles: Behavioral expectations related to positions (statuses) held by individuals in any particular group; identified by related clusters of behavioral norms.

Romantic love: Form of affectional relationship based on interpersonal attraction, emotional attachment, and passion.

Rotating credit association: Method of raising cash, prevalent in some ethnic groups, that involves the continuous pooling and withdrawal of money.

Rumor: False information that moves by word of mouth or, occasionally, through the mass media.

Rural sociology: Systematic study of rural society and the knowledge obtained from that study; currently it is an international discipline.

Sacred: Social classification of phenomena that includes extraordinary and awe-inspiring events and processes distinct from the everyday, mundane aspects of social life.

Sample: Set of items, scores, or observations selected from a population. See also *Random sampling.*

Sampling frames: Actual list of sampling units from which the sample, or some stage of the sample, is selected.

Sampling unit: Element or a set of elements considered for selection in some stage of sampling.

Sanctions: Rewards and punishments for conforming to or violating norms.

Scapegoating: Practice of unfairly blaming a person or category of people for the troubles of others.

Scientific method: Method for acquiring knowledge that is characterized by systematic observation, experimentation, experimental control, and the ability to repeat the study.

Scientific revolution: Historical event during which a scientific community abandons a traditional paradigm in favor of a new one whose worldview, methods, and logical structure are incompatible with the paradigm it replaces.

Secondary sector: Portion of the economy in which wages are low, employment is erratic, and benefits are few, often involving nonunionized, competitive industries.

Sect: Group that has broken away from an existing religious body, usually to maintain its traditional roots.

Sector theory: Theory of urban growth that asserts that urban development proceeds outward from the central business district in wedge-shaped sectors, each containing a particular social class.

Secularization: Process whereby the influence of religious values and beliefs over various aspects of life is reduced.

Segregation: Act, process, or state of being set apart; for example, stringent separation between racial or ethnic groups.

Self-concept: Personal identity; the collection of ideas that one has about oneself and one's nature.

Self-esteem: Affective or emotional appraisal of value regarding the self.

Self-fulfilling prophecy: Situation that occurs when other people's expectations for a person lead him or her to act in ways that confirm those expectations.

Semiperiphery: In world-system theory, the intermediate societies between the core and the periphery.

Sepharidi: Diaspora Jews who migrated to the Andalusian-Spanish area of Europe during the medieval period.

Sex: Term that refers to the physical, biological differences between men and women.

Sex discrimination: Behavior, practices, or policies that, whether intended or not, result in harm to individuals on the basis of their sex, such as denying opportunities and rights to women or giving preferential treatment and privileges to men.

Sex-role stereotyping: Notions that only certain pursuits or behaviors are appropriate for each gender; not based on individual ability or motivation for those pursuits.

Sex roles: Social expectations and norms that are different for each gender.

Sex segregation: Separation of jobs on the basis of sex; sex segregation devalues women's work by paying them lower wages.

Sexism: Individuals' prejudicial attitudes and discriminatory behavior toward persons of a particular sex; institutional practices that subordinate persons of a particular sex.

Sexual abuse: Sexual contact with or exploitation of a nonconsenting individual, including exhibitionism, voyeurism, fondling, sodomy, and rape.

Sexual orientation: Direction of one's sexual feelings and behavior; the term is preferred to "sexual preference," which implies that a conscious choice has been made.

Significance test: Statistical test for determining whether the conclusion based on a sample holds true for the population from which the sample was drawn.

Significant other: Anyone who has or has had an important influence on a person's thoughts about self and the world.

Slave mode of production: Economic system in which slaves were the principal workforce and slavery was central to the overall economic structure.

Social change: Any alteration in the social behavior or institutions of a society that results in important long-term consequences.

Social class: Category of group membership that is generally based on one's position in the economic system with respect to economic resources, income, occupational prestige, and educational attainment and whose members usually share the same attitudes and values and an identifiable lifestyle.

Social cohesion: Forces that bind a society together, in ideological, social, and material aspects, to produce unity and harmony.

Social conflict: The struggle over values and resources between disparate social groups.

Social control: Use of formal and informal mechanisms by society to enforce dominant beliefs, values, and behavior.

Social demography: Scientific study of human populations, with an emphasis on the age, sex, racial/ethnic, and socioeconomic structure of society and how it changes, stressing the importance of the social determinants and consequences of fertility, mortality, and migration.

Social distance: Mode of measuring varying degrees of intimacy, understanding, and influence between individuals and groups in society.

Social ecology: Interactions between geographically separate human societies and between all human individuals or societies and their physical-chemical, biological, and cultural environments.

Social engineering: Process by which government or industry impinges upon a populace in order to achieve specific social ends, such as racial integration.

Social epidemiology: Scientific study of the occurrence and spread of disease, defects, or diseaselike conditions.

Social evolution: Regular change from one form of society to another, following general laws or principles; often associated with progress and with progression through a sequence of stages.

Social gerontology: Area within sociology that focuses on the study of aging and the elderly, with special emphasis on the social determinants and consequences of aging for the individual and society.

Social group: Set of individuals who interact in patterned ways, who share a culture that includes role expectations of how group members ought to behave, and who create a "boundary" by identifying with one another.

Social inequality: Unequal distribution of such things as wealth, income, occupational prestige, and educational attainment.

Social institutions: See *Institutions.*

Social integration: Extent to which the members of a society identify with that society, share its values, and accept its structure.

Social mobility: Movement of groups and individuals within and between social levels in a stratified society.

Social movements: Collective efforts to resist or bring about social change.

Social sciences: Behavioral sciences, including sociology, anthropology, political science, psychology, and economics; these sciences are differentiated from the "natural" or "physical" sciences in that the subject of study is the group or individual behavior of human beings.

Social strain theory: Explanation of the emergence of social movements using the idea that social tensions and/or disequilibrium stimulate the actions of a complaining group.

Social stratification: Structured, hierarchical ranking system with differences in access to social resources; individuals at the top ranks have more access, while those at the bottom lack social resources.

Social structure: Relatively stable patterns of social relationships organized around statuses and roles.

Social support: Instrumental, informational, and emotional support that a person receives from others.

Social theory: Explanatory framework proposed to shed light on some facet of social life.

Socialism: Economic system based on the public ownership of goods and of the means of producing them in a market controlled by the state.

Socialization: Process by which individuals learn the roles, norms, and values of the society to which they belong.

Socialization agent: Source of socialization; the persons or means that instruct or impart information, either formally or informally.

Society: Group of people who interact with one another within a limited territory and who share a culture.

Sociobiology: Study of the biological and evolutionary underpinnings of social behavior; controversial because its biological determinist assumptions sometimes have political implications, especially regarding gender and racial relations.

Socioeconomic status: Individual's socially defined position in society, determined by a combination of factors such as income, occupation, and education.

Sociometrics: Quantitative analysis of social parameters indicative of social change.

Sodomy: Overarching term for sexual deviation; its legal definition specifies anal intercourse or oral-genital contact, either consensual or coerced.

Spouse or partner battering: Physical, psychological, or sexual mistreatment that occurs in a relationship between married couples or among individuals in a sustaining partnership.

Standard deviation: Measure of variability that reflects the average amount of distance the scores of a distribution are from the mean.

State: Powerful institution that holds the legitimate monopoly on the use of force in society.

Statistic: Measure of a variable based on a sample of scores or observations.

Statistical inference: Inference made by applying some basic assumptions and/or laws of statistics to a set of observations.

Status: Socially defined positions occupied by an individual throughout the life course; examples include child, student, or parent.

Status attainment research: Study of whether or not social mobility takes place, including an evaluation of the factors that account for patterns of mobility.

Stereotype: Standardized mental picture held by members of a group that represents an oversimplified, critical, or prejudicial judgment about members of another group; stereotypes are often used to legitimize discrimination.

Stigma: Intense social disapproval and alienation that follow the assignment of a deviant status.

Stockholm syndrome: Condition in which hostages begin to identify or sympathize with their captors.

Strain theories of delinquency: Theories that explain the cause of delinquency by emphasizing the frustration experienced by youths who do not have access to legal methods to achieve success.

Stratification: See *Social stratification.*

Structural: Level of human reality that is directly attributable to the patterns of social organization and that is not reducible to the level of the individual.

Structural differentiation: Notion that as institutions increase in size in terms of the complexity of the functions that they perform, they necessarily form specialized subsystems with distinct responsibilities.

Structural-functionalist theory: Theory according to which society is held together by the sharing of ideals and values; holds that society is a system of interrelated parts.

Structural unemployment: Unemployment caused by a change in structure of the economy, with most workers not expecting eventual reemployment in the same location and industry.

Structured inequality: See *Social stratification.*

Subculture: Group of people who hold many of the values and norms of the larger culture but also certain beliefs, values, or norms that set them apart from that culture.

Subordinate groups: Society's "have-nots" who are disadvantaged compared with other groups.

Sudden infant death syndrome (SIDS): Cause ascribed to the sudden, inexplicable death of an infant of less than one year of age.

Symbol: Something that represents something else, particularly a material object that stands for something invisible or intangible.

Symbolic interactionism: Theoretical perspective analyzing day-to-day interactions among individuals; symbolic interaction theory holds that social life is dependent on an individual's ability to interpret social symbols correctly and to perceive correctly his or her own role in relation to the roles of others.

Taboo: Absolute ban against the performance of a particular behavior; stronger in its meaning than "rule" or "prohibition."

Taylorization: Process pioneered by Frederick W. Taylor of applying scientific management to the labor process.

Technology: Cumulative skills and knowledge applied in environmental adaptation, including such processes as food production.

Tertiary sector: Part of the economy engaged primarily in services, such as banking and retail sales.

Theoretical sampling: Technique in which data collection is controlled by the demands of an emerging theory rather than by an existing theoretical framework.

Third World: Contemporary term for the developing countries as defined through their engagement in the early and intermediate phases of industrialization.

Total institution: Form of social organization where the inmates are isolated from society and have every aspect of their lives controlled by staff, usually for the purpose of changing the personalities of the inmates.

Totalitarianism: Government that exercises nearly total control over individual citizens—a relatively recent and extreme form of authoritarianism.

Totemism: Belief in the power of a sacred plant, animal, or object that symbolizes a particular clan or social group.

Tracking: Putting students into certain curricula (such as technical, academic, or remedial) that control their later options in life.

Traditional authority: Authority based on customs and long-standing practice.

Underclass: Social class at the bottom of the social strata; the poorest of the poor, among whom poverty is an ongoing feature from generation to generation.

Uniform Crime Reports: Yearly compilation of crime based on a count of nine "index" crimes tabulated by local police forces and published by the Federal Bureau of Investigation.

Union shop: Shop in which membership in a union is mandatory for employees thirty days after employment or thirty days after the signing of the union shop's contract, whichever comes later.

Urban legends: Narrative stories that are hearsay and unverifiable and that deal with contemporary urban life.

Urbanization: Process of expansion of urban areas and culture through rural-urban population shifts.

Validity: Extent to which a measurement actually measures what it claims to measure.

Values: Beliefs shared by members of a society or organization of what is good, bad, desirable, undesirable, proper, or improper.

Variable: Trait that can vary in magnitude from case to case.

Verstehen: Empathic (interpretive) understanding; Max Weber's main goal as a social analyst.

Vertical social mobility: Movement upward or downward in the social hierarchy.

Volunteerism: Philosophy encouraging individuals to offer their services free of charge for a good cause.

Voucher: Certificate given to the parents of students indicating the amount of public money that the former may distribute to the schools attended by their children.

Welfare: General, informal term for government programs, particularly Aid to Families with Dependent Children, that provide payments and services to the poor.

White-collar crime: Crime committed by high-status individuals in the course of their occupations for personal gain.

White flight: Movement of white families from ethnic neighborhoods, and white students' abandonment of urban schools for private or suburban schools.

Workfare: General, informal term for welfare programs in which the acceptance of payments and services obliges the recipient to prepare for, seek, and accept employment.

Working poor: Those who lack the means for an adequate existence even though they are employed.

World system: According to Immanuel Wallerstein, the modern system of nations and their economies, which is dominated by wealthy capitalist economies.

Worldview: Way an individual or group perceives and conceptualizes the world.

Xenophobia: Irrational fear or hatred of foreigners or others with different appearances or customs.

Zionism: Movement to establish a Jewish state in Palestine.

Category List

INDEX

A

Abuse. *See* Child abuse; Domestic abuse and violence; Sexual abuse; Violent crime
Acculturation, 71-73, 580
Achieved status, 376, 450, 580
Acquaintance rape, 580
Advertising, 354
Aesthetics, 89
Affirmative action, 580
African Americans; and churches, 397; class structure, 31, 372, 377; and crime, 131, 137-138; and education, 163, 378, 498-499; employment, 25, 377-378; folk practices, 354; income levels, 168, 377; and language, 158; and poverty, 69, 102-103, 202; prejudice against, 339-340; stereotyping of, 341; urbanization of, 170
Age cohort, 580
Age/sex pyramid, 122-124
Ageism, 580
Aggressive behavior, gender and, 207
Alienation, 286, 288-289, 580
Allport, Gordon, 338, 343
Alpha errors, 34
Althusser, Louis, 291, 314, 317
American Sociological Association (ASA), 212
Amish people, 515-516, 518
Androgyny, 580
Anglo-conformity, 168, 580
Anomic suicide, 580
Anomie, 580
Anomie and deviance, 7-13
Anthropology, 145, 181-182, 211, 221, 309-310, 352, 354
Anticipatory socialization, 477
Anti-Defamation League, 366
Apartheid, 28, 30-31, 333, 580
ASA. *See* American Sociological Association
Asceticism, 381
Ascribed status, 375-376, 450, 580
Ashkenazi, 580

Asian Americans, 168
Assemblies of God, 42
Assimilation, 580
Athens, Lonnie, 535
Attitude, 580
Authoritarian personality, 580
Authoritarianism, 580
Authority, 580
Automation, 55-56

B

Baby boom, 580
Band, 223-224
Bandura, Albert, 484-485
Baptists, 41, 44, 390; numbers, 391; and socialization process, 471
Bargaining unit, 580
Baumrind, Diana, 478-479
Becker, Howard S., 263
Behavior, 580
Bellah, Robert, 414-415
Berger, Peter L., 257, 259, 383-384, 389-390, 562
Beta errors, 34
Bias, 581
Bierstedt, Robert, 270
Bilingualism, 581
Biological determinism, 581
Biological determinist views of gender inequality, 205-210
Bisexuality, 581
Black English, 157-158
Blau, Peter M., 440
Blauner, Robert, 167, 370
Blumer, Herbert, 302, 533
Boas, Franz, 99, 367
Bourdieu, Pierre, 155-156
Bourgeoisie, 457-458, 460, 581
Bowles, Samuel, 155
Braverman, Harry, 53-54
Brehm, Sharon S., 401
Brown v. Board of Education, 335, 498
Burakumin, 28, 30
Bureaucracies, 14-20, 463, 581
Bureaucratic personality, 14

C

O

Observation in research, 175-176
Observer biases, 592
Occupational prestige, 452-453, 592
Occupational segregation, 592
Occupational sex segregation, 592
Ogburn, William F., 540
Ohlin, Lloyd E., 9, 510
Oligarchy, 592
Oligopoly, 592
Omi, Michael, 370
Open-ended questions, 592
Open marriage, 592
Operational definition, 592
Opinion polls, 408-409
Oppression, 592
Ordinal scale, 592
Organizations, 592; disasters and, 60;
    formal and informal, 18; schools as,
    148
Organized crime, 592
Out-group, 593
Outlier, 593
Outsiders (Becker), 263

P

PAC. *See* Political action committee
Pandemic, 593
Paradigm, 593
Parameter, 593
Parenting styles, 478-479
Pareto, Vilfredo, 110, 314, 493
Parsons, Talcott, 62, 183; on class conflict,
    312; on doctor-patient relationship,
    294-295; on education, 161-162, 164;
    on evolution, 493; and functionalism,
    69, 81, 194-195, 199, 302, 393, 428,
    451, 500; on group norms, 300, 302;
    on social stratification, 451; and
    sociology, 183, 214, 306
Participant-observer method, 593
Partner battering, spouse or, 600
Passeron, Jean-Claude, 155-156
Paternalism, 593
Patient, role of, 294-296
Patois, 158
Patriarchy, 593
Patrilineal descent groups, 593

Patrilocality, 593
Peer group, 593
Periphery, 593
Peter principle, 14, 16
Phenomenology, 381, 593
Physiognomy, 593
Pirenne, Henri, 550
Plummer, Kenneth, 535
Pluralism, 593; political, 313-314; the
    power elite and, 328
Pogrom, 593
Political action committee (PAC), 593
Political economy, 593
Political machine, 593
Political science; and sociology, 3
Political sociology, 312-318
Polygamy, 594
Popular culture, 594. *See also* Mass culture
Population, 594; control, 594; pressure, 217
Pornography, 594
Positivism, 594
Postindustrial society, 594
Poulantzas, Nicos, 314
Poverty, 594; absolute, 319; analysis and
    overview, 319-325; culture of,
    101-106; relative, 319-320
Poverty line, 594
Poverty rates, 320-321
Poverty thresholds, 319
Power, 594
Power-conflict theories of racial and
    ethnic relations, 167-168
Power elite, 326-331, 447, 594
Power Elite, The (Mills), 326-327
Praxis, 594
Predestination, 594
Prejudice, 594; and stereotyping, 338-344
Prejudice and discrimination: Merton's
    paradigm, 332-337
Presbyterian church, 42-43
Primary group, 594
Primary sector, 594
Principles of Sociology (Spencer), 212
Productivity, 594
Profession, 594
Proletariat, 457-459, 594
Protestant ethic and capitalism, 345-350
*Protestant Ethic and the Spirit of
    Capitalism, The* (Weber), 346-350,
    385